BASICS OF
ELECTRICAL ENGINEERING

for

Diploma Engineers

DRDO, BHEL, DMRC, SSC, RRB &
Other Engineering (Diploma) Competitive Examinations

G K Publications (P) Ltd

CL MEDIA (P) LTD.

Edition : 2019

© PUBLISHER

No part of this book may be reproduced in a retrieval system or transmitted, in any form or by any means, electronics, mechanical, photocopying, recording, scanning and or without the written permission of the publisher.

ISBN : **978-93-89573-31-2**
Typeset by : *CL Media DTP Unit*

Administrative and Production Offices

Published by : **CL Media (P) Ltd.**

A-45, Mohan Cooperative Industrial Area, Near Mohan Estate Metro Station, New Delhi - 110044

Marketed by : **G.K. Publications (P) Ltd.**

A-45, Mohan Cooperative Industrial Area, Near Mohan Estate Metro Station, New Delhi - 110044

For product information :

Visit ***www.gkpublications.com*** or email to ***gkp@gkpublications.com***

Preface

In the recent years PSUs like BHEL, BEL, GAIL, IOCL, HPCL, ONGC and other Government Sectors like DMRC, DRDO, RRB, Staff Selection Commission are preferring to hire Junior Engineers and Technicians which has resulted in a large job opportunities for diploma holders. As these PSUs also offer job security and decent perks, many candidates are attracted towards it, gradually increasing the competition level.

Unlike other competitive examinations, preparing for vacancy based exams of these PSUs is not an easy task as each exam has its own pattern, syllabus and trend. Most of these exams like to throw surprises based on the vacancies, leaving students amazed during their exam preparation with very less time for preparation. However, you can certainly guarantee yourself a smooth journey if you start early and plan it well. As the technical section of these exams hold the maximum scoring scope; it is very important to pay enough attention to this section.

This series focuses on the technical section of various exams conducted by PSUs such as DRDO, BHEL and other Government Sectors like DMRC and Railways for the Diploma Engineers. These books help to prepare for all the exams at a single go which saves time instead of preparing separately for each PSU's exam. Every chapter contains a brief theory followed by large number of practice questions. There is another section that includes questions asked in previous PSU exams. As a suggestion, please make sure that you spend enough time in understanding the fundamentals and concepts before going to practice exercise and previous years' solved questions.

GKP has also launched an Android App to provide you an update on all upcoming vacancies in the technical segment and it also has a lot of added content to aid your preparation.

We hope this little effort of ours will be helpful in achieving your dreams. If you have any suggestions on improvement of this book, you can write to us at gkp@gkpublications.com.

All the Best!

Team GKP

Contents

Basic Electricals

ALTERNATING QUANTITY

In an electrical circuit direct current flows continuously in one direction only and if the applied voltage and circuit resistance are kept constant, the magnitude of current flowing through the circuit remains constant over time. However, when current flowing varies in magnitude and direction periodically, it is called *alternating current*. Thus an alternating quantity (either current or emf) is one which periodically passes through a definite cycle, each consisting of two half cylces, during one of which the current or emf around the circuit varies in one direction and during the other, in the opposite direction.

Equations of Alternating Voltage and Currents.

Alternators produce an emf which is for all practical purposes is sinusoidal. The equation for the emf generated versus time is given as

$$e = E_{max} \sin \omega t$$

where, e = instantaneous emf

E_{max} = maximum emf

ωt = angle through which the armature has turned from neutral.

Taking frequency as f hertz (cycles per second),

$$\omega = 2\pi f,$$

$$\therefore \qquad e = E_{max} \sin 2\pi ft$$

Waveform.

Shape of the curve of the voltage or current when plotted against time as base is called *waveform*. The waveform of induced emf in an alternator differs slightly from that of sine wave but for calculation purposes it is treated as such. The advantage of doing so is that calculations become simple.

Alternation and cycle.

When a periodic wave, such as sinusoidal wave, goes through one complete set of positive or negative values, it completes one alternation and when it goes through one complete set of positive and one complete set of negative values it is said to have completed one cycle.

Periodic time (T).

The time taken in seconds by an alternating quantity to complete one cycle is called *periodic time*.

Frequency (f).

The number of cycles completed per second by an alternating quantity is called *frequency*.

In SI system, frequency is expressed in hertz (pronounced as hurts).

Periodic time or time period is reciprocal of frequency.

i.e. $\qquad T = \dfrac{1}{f} \qquad$ or $\qquad f = \dfrac{1}{T}$

In a multipolar machine having P poles and running at a speed of N rpm, frequency of generated emf

$$f = \frac{PN}{120}$$

Amplitude.

The greatest value, positive or negative, which an alternating quantity attains during one cycle is called the amplitude of the alternating quantity.

AC AMPERE.

The value of an alternating current is not based on its average value but is based on its heating effect.

AC ampere is that current, which when passed through a given resistance for a given time, produces same heat as produced by flow of one ampere of direct current through the same resistance for the same time.

Instantaneous value.

Alternating current or voltage changes from instant to instant. The value of alternating current or voltage at any particular instant is called **instantaneous value**. Instantaneous value of an alternating quantity can be determined either from the curve or from an equation of the alternating quantity.

Maximum value.

The greatest value, positive or negative, which an alternating quantity attains during one complete cycle is called its **amplitude or maximum or peak crest value.**

Average or Mean Value.

The average or mean value of an alternating current is expressed by that steady current which transfers across any circuit the same charge as is transferred by that alternating current during the same time.

Since in the case of a symmetrical alternating current (i.e. one whose two half cycles are exactly similar whether sinusoidal or non sinusoidal) the average or mean value over a complete cycle is zero hence for such alternating quantities average or mean value means the value determined by taking the average of instantaneous values during one half cycle or one alternation only. However, for unsymmetrical alternating current (such as half-wave rectified current), the average value means the value determined by taking the mean of instantaneous values over the complete cycle.

The average values for perfect sinusoidal, half-wave rectified, full-wave rectified, rectangular and triangular wave alternating currents are 0.636, 0.318, 0.636, 1 and 0.5 times the maximum value respectively.   The average or mean value is only of use in connection with processes where the results depend on the current only, irrespective of the voltage, such as electro-plating or battery charging.

Rms or effective value.

It is that steady current or voltage which when flows or applied to a given resistance for a given time produces the same amount of heat as when the alternating current or voltage is flowing or applied to the same resistance for the same time.

The effective or virtual value of alternating current or voltage is equal to the square root of the mean of the squares of successive ordinates and that is why it is known as root-mean-square (rms) value.

The root mean square of effective values for perfect sinusoidal, half-wave rectified, full wave rectified, rectangular and triangular wave alternating currents are 0.707, 0.5, 0.707, 1 and 0.578 times the maximum value respectively.

Equation for the instantaneous values of emf is given as

$$e = E_{max} \sin \omega t = E_{max} \sin 2\pi ft$$

Hence

(i) maximum value of an alternating emf is given by the coefficient of the sine of the time angle.

(ii) frequency is given by coefficient of time t divided by 2π

i.e. $f = \dfrac{\text{Coefficient of time} t}{2\pi}$

Similarly we can also find the maximum value and frequency of the current from the equation of instantaneous values of current.

Form factor.

It, is defined as the ratio of effective value to the average or mean value of a periodic wave.

Mathematically,

$$\text{Form factor} = \dfrac{\text{effective value}}{\text{average value}}$$

The values of form factor for perfect sinusoidal, half-wave rectified, full-wave fectified, rectangular and triangular wave alternating currents are 1.11, 1.57, 1.11, 1 and 1.16 respectively.

Peak factor.

It is very essential in connection with determining the dielectric strength since dielectric stress developed in any insulating material is proportional to the maximum value of the voltage applied to it.

Peak or crest or amplitude factor of a periodic wave is defined as the ratio of maximum or peak to the effective or rms value of the wave.

i.e   Peak factor, $K_p = \dfrac{\text{maximum value}}{\text{effective value}}$

The values of peak or crest factor for perfect sinusoidal, half-wave rectified, full-wave rectified, rectangular and triangular wave alternating currents are $\sqrt{2}$, 2.0, $\sqrt{2}$, 1 and $\sqrt{3}$ respectively.

Phase and Phase angle.

Phase of an alternating current means fraction of the time period of that alternating current that has elapsed since the current last passed through the zero position of reference. The phase angle of any quantity means the angle the vector representing the quantity makes with the reference line (which is taken to be at zero degrees or radians).

Phase difference.

When two alternating quantities are considered simultaneously, the frequency being the same, they may not pass through a particular point at the same instant. One may pass through its maximum value at the instant when the other passes through the value other than its maximum one. These two quantities are said to have a phase difference. Phase difference is always given either in degrees or in radians.

The phase difference is measured by the angular distance between the points where the two curves cross the base or reference line in the same direction.

The quantity ahead in phase is said to lead the other quantity while the seond quantity is said to lag behind the first one.

If I_1 is taken as reference vector, then two currents can be expressed as

$$i_1 = I_{max} \sin \omega t, \quad \text{and} \quad i_2 = I_{2max} \sin (\omega t - \phi)$$

The two quantities are said to be in phase with each other if they pass through zero values at the same instant and rise in the same direction. But the two quantities passing through zero values at the same instant but rising in opposite directions, are said to be in phase opposition, i.e. phase difference is 180°. When the two alternating quantities has a phase difference of 90° or $\dfrac{\pi}{2}$ radians they are said to be in quadrature.

NETWORK ANALYSIS

Network analysis consists in finding the response (or output) when stimulus (or input) and the network components are given

Fig. Factors involved in network analysis

DIRECT METHOD.

Here the network is left in its original form and the currents and voltages in different elements of the network are determined using a standard method of analysis such as loop analysis or node analysis. In addition use is made of Kirchhoff's laws and different network theorems such as superposition theorem, compensation theorem, reciprocity theorem etc. Such a direct approach is generally used in case of relatively simple networks.

Kirchhoff's laws.

There are two laws given by Kirchhoff namely Kirchhoff's current law and Kirchhoff's voltage law.

(i) Kirchhoff's Current Law (KCL) : It states that in any electrical circuit, the algebraic sum of current meeting at a point (or node) is zero.

If we take the current component convergent (entering) at the node as positive and current component divergent (leaving) at the node as negative, then KCL implies that : *at any zunction (node) in electrical circuit, the sum of current components entering the junction equals the sum of the current components leaving the junction.*

This statement is true for any point because there can not be continued accumulation of charges or continued depletion of charges. Symbolically we may write,

$$\Sigma \pm j = 0$$

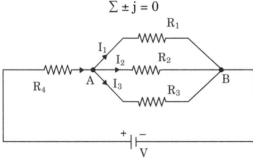

Above figure shows a simple electrical network with one energy source V. At node A, current I enters the node while currents I_1, I_2 and I_3 leave the node A.

Obviously then as per KCL,

$$I + (-I_1) + (-I_2) + (-I_3) = 0$$

or $\quad I = I_1 + I_2 + I_3$

In the circuit of figure, directions of current components. In a complicated network, we do not know the actual directions of all current components at any specific node. In that case, we arbitrarily assign directions to the current components and analyze the network to find the values of these current components. If the value of any current component comes out to be positive, then its actural direction is the same as the assigned direction. On the other hand, if any current component is found to be negative, then its actual direction. On the other hand, if any current component is found to be negative, then its actual direction is opposite to assigned direction.

(ii) Kirchhoff's Voltage Law (KVL) :

It states that : *the algebraic sum of potential rises (or potential drops) in any set of branches forming a closed circuit or loop is always zero.*

Symbolically we may write,

$$\Sigma \pm v = 0$$

The validity of kVL is quite obvious. Thus starting from any node, as we travel along a closed path and come back to the same node, the net voltage drop or the net voltage rise must be sero

Use of sign + or – : In the above equation, plus sign may be used for voltage rise and minus sign may be used for voltage drop (alternatively opposite notation may be used). Thus while we move along the closed path along the current in any branch, there results a voltage drop across the resisitor R and a – sign may be used as shown in Fig. (a). Thus voltage rise from A to B is (–jR) . On the other hand, if we travel opposite to the current in any branch, there results a voltage rise and + sign may be used as shown below in Fig. (b). Thus voltage rise from A to B is + jR.

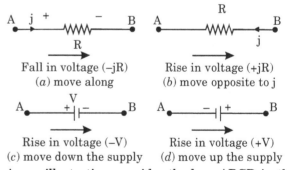

Fall in voltage (–jR)   Rise in voltage (+jR)
(a) move along   (b) move opposite to j

Rise in voltage (–V)   Rise in voltage (+V)
(c) move down the supply   (d) move up the supply

As an illustration, consider the loop ABCD in the network of figure and travel along ABCDA in this loop.

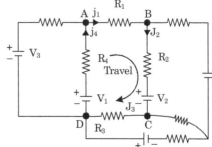

Then

$j_1 R_1$ is a voltage fall and hence negative

$j_2 R_2$ is a voltage fall and hence negative

$j_3 R_3$ is a voltage rise and hence positive

$j_4 R_4$ is a voltage fall and hence negaitve

V_2 is a voltage fall and hence negative

V_1 is a voltage rise and hence positive

Then application of kVL gives

$$- j R_1 - j_2 R_2 + j_3 R_3 - j_4 R_4 - V_2 + V_1 = 0$$

or $\quad V_1 - V_2 = j_1 R_1 + j_2 R_2 - j_3 R_3 + j_4 R_4$

Note : Kirchhoff's laws are applicable to both dc and ac circuits.

ELECTRO-MAGNETIC INDUCTION

The phenomenon whereby an emf and hence current is induced in any conductor which is cut across or is cut by a magnetic flux is called *electro-magnetic induction*.

Faraday's laws of Electro-magnetic induction.

Faraday's first law :

This law states that, when the flux linking with the coil or circuit changes an emf is induced in it or whenever the magnetic flux is cut by the conductor an emf is induced in the conductor.

Faraday's second law :

This law states that, magnitude of emf induced is directly proportional to the rate of change of flux linking the coil.

i.e $\qquad$ induced emf $\propto N \cdot \dfrac{d\phi}{dt}$

where $N \dfrac{d\phi}{dt}$ is product of number of turns and rate of change of linking flux and is called rate of change of flux linkage.

Lenz's law.

The law states that, direction of induced emf is such that the current produced by it sets up a magnetic field opposing the motion or change producing it.

$\therefore \qquad$ Induced emf, $e = - N \dfrac{d\phi}{dt}$

INDUCED EMF.

EMF can be induced by changing the linking flux in two ways:

1. **Dynamically induced EMF.**

   This is induced by moving a conductor in a uniform magnetic field and emf produced in this way is known as dynamically induced emf.

When a conductor of length l metres is moved in a magnetic field of strength B wb/m² with a velocity v m/s in a direction perpendicular to its own length and at an angle θ to the direciton of magnetic field, the induced emf will be given as

$$e = B \, l \, v \sin \theta \text{ volts}$$

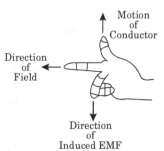

The direction of this induced emf is given by Fleming's right hand rule. If thumb, fore-finger and middle finger of right hand are held mutually perpendicular to each other, fore-finger pointing into the direction of the field and thumb in the direction of motion then middle finger will point in the direction of the inuced emf.

2. **Statically induced emf.**

Increasing or decreasing the magnitude of the current producing the linking flux. In this case there is no motion of the conductor or of coil relative to the field.

TYPE OF STATICALLY INDUCED EMF .

(i) Self induced EMF.

When the current flowing through the coil is changed, then flux linking with its own winding changes and due to the change in linking flux with the coil, an emf called self induced emf is induced.

Since according to Lenz's law, any induced emf acts to oppose the change that produces it, a self induced emf is always in such a direction as to oppose the change of current in the coil or circuit in which it is induced. This property of the coil or circuit due to which it opposes any change of the current in the coil or circuit, is called *self-inductance*.

Self induced emf in a solenoid of N turns, length l metres, area of cross-section a square metres and of relative permeability μ_r when the current flowing through the solenoid is changed is given as

Self induced emf, $e = - \dfrac{N^2 \mu_r \mu_o a}{l} \cdot \dfrac{di}{dt}$

The quantity $\dfrac{N^2 \mu_r \mu_o a}{l}$ is a constant for any given coil or circuit and is called *coefficient of self-inductance*. It is represented by symbol L and is measured in *henrys*.

$$\therefore \quad \text{self induced emf, } e = -L\frac{di}{dt}$$

where, $L = \dfrac{N^2 \mu_r \mu_o a}{l}$ henrys

(ii) Mutually induced EMF :

The phenomenon of generation of induced emf in a coil by changing the current in the neighbouring coil is called the *mutual induction* and emf so induced is called mutually induced emf.

The mutually induced emf in a solenoid B of N_2 turns, placed nearby another coil A of N_1 turns, length l metres, area of cross-section a square metres and of relative permeability μ_r when the current flowing through coil A is changed is given as

Mutually induced emf, $e_m = \dfrac{N_1 N_2 \mu_r \mu_o a}{l} \cdot \dfrac{di}{dt}$

assuming that whole of the flux produced due to flow of current in coil A is linking with coil B.

The quantity $\dfrac{N_1 N_2 \mu_r \mu_o a}{l}$ is called *coefficient of mutual induction of coil B with respect to coil A*. It is represented by symbol M and is measured in henrys.

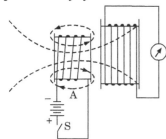

$$\therefore \quad \text{Mutually induced emf } e_m = -M\frac{di_1}{dt}$$

where, $M = \dfrac{N_1 N_2 \mu_r \mu_o a}{l}$ henrys.

COEFFICIENT OF COUPLING.

When two coils are placed near each other, all the flux produced by one coil does not link the other coil, only a certain portion (say K) of flux produced by one coil links with the other coil, K being less than unity. K is called *coefficient of coupling*.

The coefficient of coupling between two coils having self inductances L_1 and L_2 respectively and mutual inductance M is given as

$$K = \frac{M}{\sqrt{L_1 L_2}}$$

When coils are tightly coupled, *i.e.* when flux due to one coil links with the other coil completely, then coefficient of coupling, K is unity. If flux due to one coil does not link with the other coil at all, then value of coefficient of coupling is zero.

INDUCTANCES IN SERIES AND PARALLEL.

(i) Inductances in series.

When coils are connected in series such that their fluxes (or mmf) are additive i.e. in the same direction, then equivalent inductance of the combination is given as

$$L = L_1 + L_2 + 2M$$

where L_1 and L_2 = coefficients of self induction of coils A and B respectively

M = coefficient of mutual induction.

When coils are connected in series in such a way that their fluxes (or mmfs) are subtractive, *i.e.* in opposite directions, then equivalent inductance is given as

$$L = L_1 + L_2 - 2M$$

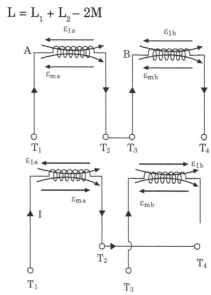

(ii) Inductances in parallel.

When two coils of self inductances L_1 and L_2 and mutual inductance M are connected in parallel, then equivalent inductance of the combination is given as

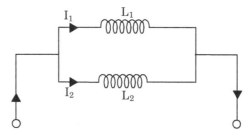

When mutual flux helps the individual flux, then

$$L = \frac{L_1 L_2 - M^2}{L_1 + L_2 - 2M}$$

When mutual flux opposes the individual flux, then

$$L = \frac{L_1 L_2 - M^2}{L_1 + L_2 + 2M}$$

EXERCISE – I

1. The most important advantages of using electrical energy in the form of ac is
   (a) the construction cost per kw of ac generator is lower than that of dc generator
   (b) conductor of smaller x-section is required in case of ac in comparison to dc for carrying the same current.
   (c) less insulation is required in case of ac.
   (d) transformation of voltage is possible in case of ac only.

2. The time period of periodic time T of an alternating quantity is the time taken in seconds to complete
   (a) one cycle   (b) one alternation
   (c) any of these   (d) none of these

3. Average value of an unsymmetrical alterating quantity is calculated over the
   (a) whole cycle
   (b) half cycle
   (c) unsymmetrical part of the waveform
   (d) none of these

4. The frequency of an alternating quantity is the number of
   (a) direction reversals in per second.
   (b) cycles completed per second.
   (c) cycles completed per minute.
   (d) all of these

5. When an electric current is passed through a bucket full of water, lot of bubbling is there. The electric current is
   (a) ac.   (b) dc
   (c) pulsating   (d) none of these.

6. A voltage source of emf E volts and internal resistance r ohms will supply, on short circuit, a current of
   (a) $\dfrac{E}{r}$ amperes   (b) zero
   (c) infinite   (d) E × r amperes

7. The internal voltage drop of a voltage source
   (a) is independent of load current supplied
   (b) depends upon internal resistance of the source
   (c) does not influence the terminal votlage
   (d) does effect the emf of the source

8. The insulation on a current carrying conductor is provided to prevent
   (a) current leakage   (b) shock
   (c) both (a) and (b)   (d) none of these

9. The algebraic sign of an IR drop primarily depends upon the
   (a) direction of flow of current
   (b) battery connections
   (c) magnitude of current flowing through it
   (d) value of resistance

10. The terminals across the source are .... if a current source is to be neglected.
    (a) open-circuited
    (b) short-circuited
    (c) replaced by a capacitor
    (d) replaced by a source resistance

11. An active element in a circuit is
    (a) Current source   (b) Resistance
    (c) Inductance   (d) Capacitance

12. A bilateral element is
    (a) Resistor   (b) Inductor
    (c) Capacitor   (d) all of these

13. The circuit having same properties in either direction is called
    (a) bilateral circuit   (b) unilateral circuit
    (c) irreversible circuit (d) reversible circuit

14. Kirchhoff's laws are valid for
    (a) linear circuits only
    (b) passive time invariant circuits
    (c) non-linear circuits only
    (d) both linear and non-linear circuits

15. Kirchhoff's laws are not applicable to circuits with
    (a) distributed parameters
    (b) lumped parameters
    (c) passive elements
    (d) non-linear resistances

16. Kirchhoff's current law is applicable only to
    (a) electric circuits
    (b) electronic circuits
    (c) junctions in a network
    (d) closed loops in a network

17. Kirchhoff's voltage law is concerned with
    (a) IR drops   (b) battery emfs
    (c) both (a) and (b)   (d) none of these

18. According to Kirchhoff's voltage law, the algebraic sum of all IR drops and emfs in any closed loop of a network is always
    (a) negative
    (b) positive
    (c) zero
    (d) determined by emfs of the batteries

19. Maxwell circulating current theorem
    (a) utilises Kirchhoff's voltage law
    (b) utilises Kirchhoff's current law
    (c) is a network reduction method
    (d) is confined to single loop circuits

20. According to Faraday's law of electro-magnetic induction an emf is induced in a conductor whenever it
    (a) lies in a magnetic field.
    (b) lies perpendicular to the magnetic field.
    (c) cuts the magnetic flux.
    (d) moves parallel to the direction of magnetic field.

21. EMF of a zinc-carbon cell is about
    (a) 1.2 V   (b) 1.5 V
    (c) 1.75 V   (d) 2.2 V

22. The emf of primary cell depends upon the
    (a) physical dimensions of a cell
    (b) nature of electrolyte
    (c) both (b) and (c)
    (d) none of these

23. When two batteries of unequal voltages are connected in parallel, the emf of the combination will be equal to the
    (a) emf of the large battery
    (b) emf of the small battery
    (c) average of the emfs of two batteries
    (d) none of these

24. "In all cases of electromagnetic induction, an induced voltage will cause a current to flow in a closed circuit in such a direction that the magnetic field which is caused by that current will oppose the change that produces the current", is the original statement of
    (a) Lenz's law.
    (b) Faraday's law of magnetic induction.
    (c) Fleming's law of induction.
    (d) Ampere's law.

25. A ring shaped coil with fixed number of turns of it carries a current of certain magnitude. If an iron core is threaded into the coil without any change in coil dimensions, the magnetic induction density will
    (a) increase   (b) reduce
    (c) remain unaffected   (d) unpredictable

26. The emf induced in a coil due to relative motion of a magnet is independent of
    (a) coil resistance
    (b) magnet not visible
    (c) number of coil turns.
    (d) pole strength of the magnet.

27. Principle of dynamically induced emf is used in a
    (a) choke   (b) transformer
    (c) generator   (d) thermo-couple

28. The direction of dynamically induced emf in a conductor can be determined by
    (a) Fleming's left hand rule.
    (b) Fleming's right hand rule.
    (c) Helix rule.
    (d) Cork screw rule.

29. Principle of statically induced emf is used in
    (a) transformer   (b) motor
    (c) generator   (d) battery

30. Magnitude of statically induced emf depends on the
    (a) coil resistance
    (b) flux magnitude
    (c) rate of change of flux
    (d) none of these

31. The property of a coil by which a counter emf is induced in it, when the current through the coil changes, is called
    (a) self inductance   (b) mutual inductance
    (c) capacitance   (d) none of these

32. Lower the self inductance of a coil
    (a) more will be the weber-turns.
    (b) more will be the emf induced.
    (c) lesser the flux produced by it.
    (d) smaller the delay in establishing steady current through it.

33. When a single turn coil rotates in a uniform magnetic field, at uniform speed the induced emf will be
    (a) alternating   (b) steady
    (c) pulsating   (d) none of these

34. The ratio of total flux (flux in the iron path) to useful flux (flux in the air gap) is called
(a) utilisation factor
(b) fringing factor
(c) leakage factor
(d) depreciation factor

35. The direction of mechanical force experienced on a current carrying conductor placed in a magnetic field is determined by
(a) Fleming's left hand rule.
(b) Fleming's right hand rule.
(c) Helix rule.
(d) Cork screw rule.

36. In Fleming's left hand rule thumb always represents direction of
(a) current flow   (b) induced emf
(c) magnetic field   (d) mechanical force

37. If a current carrying conductor is placed in a magnetic field, the mechanical force experienced on the conductor is determined by
(a) simple product   (b) dot product
(c) cross product   (d) any of these

38. The force experienced by a current carrying conductor lying parallel to a magnetic field is
(a) zero   (b) BIl
(c) $BIl\sin\theta$ (d) $BIl\cos\theta$

39. An electric field is parallel but opposite to a magnetic field. Electrons with some initial velocity enter the region of the fields at an angle θ along the direction of the electric field. The electron path will be
(a) straight   (b) helical
(c) circular   (d) elliptical

40. The field at any point on the axis of a current carrying coil will be
(a) perpendicular to the axis.
(b) parallel to the axis.
(c) at an angle of 45° with the axis.
(d) zero.

41. Unit of mmf is
(a) AT   (b) weber/ampere
(c) Henry   (d) AT/m

42. Property of a material which opposes the production of magnetic flux in it is called
(a) mmf   (b) reluctance
(c) permeance   (d) permittivity

43. An air gap is usually inserted in magnetic circuits to
(a) prevent saturation
(b) increase in mmf.
(c) increase in flux.
(d) increase in inductance.

44. The magnitude of force acting on a current carrying conductor placed in a magnetic field is independent of
(a) flux density.
(b) length of conductor.
(c) cross-sectional area of conductor.
(d) current flowing through the conductor.

45. At the centre of a current carrying single turn circular loop, magnetic field is
(a) $B = \dfrac{\mu l}{2R}$ (b) $\dfrac{\mu l}{.2\,\pi R}$
(c) $B = \dfrac{\mu l}{4\pi R^2}$ (d) none of these

46. The magnetic flux inside the exciting coil
(a) is the same as on its outer surface.
(b) is zero.
(c) is greater than that on its outside surface.
(d) is lower than that on the outside surface.

47. If the two conductors carry current in opposite directions there will be
(a) a force of attraction between the two conductors.
(b) a force of repulsion between the two conductors.
(c) no force between them.
(d) none of these

48. If a straight conductor of circular cross-section carries a current, then
(a) no force acts on the conductor at any point.
(b) an axial force acts on the conductor tending to increase its length.
(c) a radial force acts towards the axis tending to reduce its cross-section.
(d) a radial force acts away from the axis tending to increase its cross-section.

49. mmf of magnetic circuit is analogous to
(a) current   (b) emf
(c) resistance   (d) power

50. Unit of reluctance of magnetic circuit is
(a) AT/m   (b) webers/m
(c) AT/weber   (d) H/m.

51. Conductance is analogous to

(a) reluctance

(b) mmf

(c) permeance

(d) inductance

52. Permeability is reciprocal of

(a) reluctivity

(b) susceptibility

(c) permittivity

(d) conductivity

53. The magnetic reluctance of a magnetic circuit decreases with

(a) decrease in cross-sectional area.

(b) increase in cross-sectional area.

(c) increase in length of magnetic path.

(d) decrease in relative permeability of the magnetic material of the circuit.

54. If in an iron cored coil the iron core is removed so as to make the air-cored coil, the inductance of the coil will be

(a) more   (b) less

(c) the same   (d) none of these

EXERCISE – II

1. A solid cylindrical conductor of radius 'R' carrying a current 'I' has a uniform current density. The magnetic field intensity '$\overline{H}$' inside the conductor at the radial distance 'r' ($r < R$) is

(a) Zero

(b) $\dfrac{I}{2\pi r}$

(c) $\dfrac{Ir}{2\pi R^2}$

(d) $\dfrac{IR^2}{2\pi r^3}$ **(RRB 2012)**

2. By inserting a slab of dielectric material between the plates of a parallel plate capacitor, the energy stored in the capacitor has increased three times. The dielectric constant of the material is

(a) 9   (b) 3

(c) $\dfrac{1}{3}$ (d) $\dfrac{1}{9}$ **(RRB 2012)**

3. For a given dielectric, with increase in temperature, the ionic polarizability

(a) increases   (b) decreases

(c) remains same   (d) fluctuates

(RRB 2012)

4. The forbidden energy gap in silicon at 300 K is

(a) 1.41 eV   (b) 1.1 eV

(c) 0.785 eV   (d) 0.72 eV **(RRB 2012)**

5. The average drift velocity V_d of electrons in a metal is related to electric field E and collision time T as

(a) $V_d = \dfrac{Q_e ET}{m_e}$ (b) $V_d = m_e Q_e T$

(c) $V_d = \dfrac{m_e Q_e T}{2E}$ (d) $V_d = \dfrac{Q_e Et}{2m_e}$

(RRB 2012)

6. An electric circuit with 10 branches and 7 nodes will have

(a) 3 loop equations

(b) 4 loop equations

(c) 7 loop equations

(d) 10 loop equations   **(RRB 2012)**

7. For the circuit shown in the given figure, the current I is given by

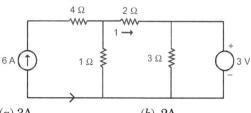

(a) 3A   (b) 2A

(c) 1A   (d) Zero

8. The response of a network is

$i(t) = kte^{-\alpha t}$ for $t \geq 0$

where α is real positive.

The value of 't' at which the $i(t)$ will become maximum, is

(a) α (b) 2α

(c) $\dfrac{1}{\alpha}$ (d) α^2 **(RRB 2012)**

9.

The current through 120 ohm resistor in the circuit shown in the above figure is

(a) 1 A   (b) 2 A

(c) 3 A   (d) 4 A   **(RRB 2012)**

10. An ac voltmeter using full-wave rectification and having a sinusoidal input has an ac sensitivity equal to
    (a) 1.414 times dc sensitivity
    (b) dc sensitivity
    (c) 0.90 times dc sensitivity
    (d) 0.707 times dc sensitivity   **(RRB 2012)**

11. The circuit generally used in digital instruments to convert sine waves into rectangular pulses is a
    (a) Saw tooth generator
    (b) Differential amplifier
    (c) Sample and hold circuit
    (d) Schmitt trigger   **(RRB 2012)**

12. What is the preferred type of CB to be installed in extra high voltage ac system?
    (a) Bulk oil type CB
    (b) Air Blast CB
    (c) Vacuum CB
    (d) Sulphur hexafluoride (SF_6) CB   **(RRB 2012)**

13. In a centre tap full wave rectifier, 100 V is the peak voltage between the centre tap and one end of the secondary. what is the maximum voltage across the reverse biased diode ?
    (a) 200 V   (b) 141 V
    (c) 100 V   (d) 86 V   **(RRB 2012)**

14. In a Hall effect experiment, a p-type semiconductor sample with hole concentration p_1 is used. The measured value of the Hall voltage is V_{H1}. If the p-type sample is now replaced by another p-type sample with hole concentration p_2 where $p_2 = 2p_1$, what is the new Hall voltage V_{H2} ?   **(RRB 2012)**
    (a) $2 V_{H1}$ (b) $4 V_{H1}$
    (c) $(1/2)V_{H1}$ (d) $(1/4)V_{H1}$

15. The reverse saturation current of a Si-based p-n junction diode increases 32 times due to a rise in ambient temperature. If the original temperature was 40° C, what is the final temperature?
    (a) 90° C   (b) 72° C
    (c) 45° C   (d) 50° C   **(RRB 2012)**

16. Copper losses in armature of dc generator amount to which of the following percentage of full load losses ?   **(RRB 2012)**
    (a) 5 to 10%   (b) 10 to 20%
    (c) 20 to 30%   (d) 30 to 40%

17. Ohm's law in point form in field theory can be expressed as   **(RRB 2012)**
    (a) $V = RI$ (b) $\bar{J} = \dfrac{\bar{E}}{\sigma}$
    (c) $\bar{J} = \sigma \bar{E}$ (d) $R = \dfrac{\rho l}{A}$

18. Which of the following equations is/are not Maxwell's equation(s)?
    1. $\nabla \cdot \bar{J} = -\dfrac{\delta lv}{\delta t}$
    2. $\nabla \cdot \bar{D} = lv$
    3. $\nabla \cdot \bar{E} = -\dfrac{\delta \bar{B}}{\delta t}$
    4. $\oint \bar{H}.d\bar{l} = \oint_s \left[\sigma \bar{E} + \varepsilon \dfrac{\delta \bar{E}}{\delta t} \right] \cdot d\bar{s}$ **(RRB 2012)**

    Select the correct answer using the codes given below:
    (a) 2 and 4   (b) 1 alone
    (c) 1 and 3   (d) 1 and 4

19. Which one of the following statements is not correct?   **(RRB 2012)**
    (a) Vacuum can act as a dielectric material
    (b) Piezoelectric, materials can act as transducers
    (c) Quartz crystal is a ferroelectric material
    (d) The dielectric constant of diectrics depends on the frequency of the applied field

20. Superposition theorem is hot applicable for
    (a) voltage calculation
    (b) bilateral elements
    (c) power calculations
    (d) passive elements   **(RRB 2012)**

21. Three currents i_1, i_2 and i_3 are approaching a node. If $i_1 = 10 \sin (400t + 60°)$ A , and $i_2 = 10 \sin (400t - 60)$ A, then i_3 is   **(RRB 2012)**
    (a) 0   (b) $10 (\sin 400t)$ A
    (c) $-10 (\sin 400t)$ A   (d) $-5\sqrt{3}$ $(3\sin 400t)$ A

22. In a network made up of linear resistors and ideal voltage sources, values of all resistors are doubled. Then the voltage across each resistor is
    (a) doubled
    (b) halved
    (c) decreases four times
    (d) not changed   **(RRB 2012)**

23. Which one of the following multi-range voltmeters has high and constant input impedance ?   **(RRB 2012)**
    (a) Permanent magnet moving coil voltmeter
    (b) Electronic voltmeter
    (c) Moving iron voltmeter
    (d) Dynamometer type voltmeter

24. Two identical RC coupled amplifiers, each having an upper cut-off frequency f_u, are cascaded with negligible loading. What is the upper cut-off frequency of the overall amplifier?

(a) $\dfrac{f_u}{\sqrt{\sqrt{2}-1}}$ (b) $f_u\sqrt{\sqrt{2}-1}$

(c) $f_u/2$ (d) $2f_u$ **(RRB 2012)**

25. What is the reverse recovery time of a diode when switched from forward bias V_F to reverse bias V_R? **(RRB 2012)**

(a) Time taken to remove the stored minority carriers

(b) Time taken by the diode voltage to attain zero value

(c) Time to remove stored minority carriers plus the time to bring the diode voltage to reverse bias V_R

(d) Time taken by the diode current to reverse

26. An emitter in a bipolar junction transistor is doped much more heavily than the base as it increase the

(a) emitter efficiency

(b) base transport factor

(c) forward current gain

(d) all of these **(RRB 2012)**

27. Kirchhoff's laws are valid for

(a) linear circuits only

(b) passive time invariant circuits

(c) non-linear circuits only

(d) both linear and non-linear circuits **(RRB)**

28. The magnitude of force acting on a current carrying conductor placed in a magnetic field is independent of **(RRB)**

(a) flux density.

(b) length of conductor.

(c) cross-sectional area of conductor.

(d) current flowing through the conductor.

29. A ring shaped coil with fixed number of turns of it carries a current of certain magnitude. If an iron core is threaded into the coil without any change in coil dimensions, the magnetic induction density will **(RRB)**

(a) increase (b) reduce

(c) remain unaffected (d) unpredictable

30. Principle of statically induced emf is used in

(a) transformer (b) motor

(c) generator (d) battery **(RRB)**

31. A bilateral element is **(RRB)**

(a) Resistor (b) Inductor

(c) Capacitor (d) all of these

32. Maxwell circulating current theorem **(RRB)**

(a) utilises Kirchhoff's voltage law

(b) utilises Kirchhoff's current law

(c) is a network reduction method

(d) is confined to single loop circuits

33. Unit of mmf is **(RRB)**

(a) AT (b) weber/ampere

(c) henry (d) AT/m

(c) is a network reduction method

(d) is confined to single loop circuits

34. Permeability is reciprocal of **(RRB)**

(a) reluctivity (b) susceptibility

(c) permittivity (d) conductivity

35. Lower the self inductance of a coil **(RRB)**

(a) more will be the weber-turns.

(b) more will be the emf induced.

(c) lesser the flux produced by it.

(d) smaller the delay in establishing steady current through it.

36. Assuming the diodes to be ideal in the figure, for the output to be clipped, the input voltage v_i must be outside the range **(RRB)**

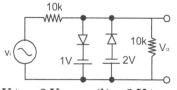

(a) -1 V to -2 V (b) -2 V to -4 V

(c) $+1$ V to -2 V (d) $+2$ V to -4 V

37. In a centre tap full wave rectifier, 100 V is the peak voltage between the centre tap and one end of the secondary. what is the maximum voltage across the reverse biased diode?

(a) 200 V (b) 141 V

(c) 100 V (d) 86 V **(RRB)**

38. Suppose that resistors R_1 and R_2 are connected in parallel to give an equivalent resistor R. If resistors R_1 and R_2 have tolerance of 1% each, the equivalent resistor R for resistors $R_1 = 300\ \Omega$ and $R_2 = 200\ \Omega$ will have tolerance of

(a) 0.5% (b) 1%

(c) 1.2% (d) 2% **(RRB)**

39. Kirchhoff's laws are not applicable to circuits with
(a) distributed parameters
(b) lumped parameters
(c) passive elements
(d) non-linear resistances   **(DMRC 2013)**

40. The force experienced by a current carrying conductor lying parallel to a magnetic field is   **(DMRC 2013)**
(a) zero   (b) B I l
(c) B I l sin θ   (d) B I l cos θ

41. If a straight conductor of circular cross-section carries a current, then   **(DMRC 2013)**
(a) no force acts on the conductor at any point.
(b) an axial force acts on the conductor tending to increase its length.
(c) a radial force acts towards the axis tending to reduce its cross-section.
(d) a radial force acts away from the axis tending to increase its cross-section.

42. The magnetic reluctance of a magnetic circuit decreases with   **(DMRC 2013)**
(a) decrease in cross-sectional area.
(b) increase in cross-sectional area.
(c) increase in length of magnetic path.
(d) decrease in relative permeability of the magnetic material of the circuit.

43. The direction of dynamically induced emf in a conductor can be determined by
(a) Fleming's left hand rule.
(b) Fleming's right hand rule.
(c) Helix rule.
(d) Cork screw rule.   **(DMRC 2013)**

44. Principle of statically induced emf is used in
(a) transformer   (b) motor
(c) generator   (d) battery **(DMRC 2013)**

45. Lower the self inductance of a coil **(DMRC 2013)**
(a) more will be the weber-turns.
(b) more will be the emf induced.
(c) lesser the flux produced by it.
(d) smaller the delay in establishing steady current through it.

46. Average value of an unsymmetrical alterating quantity is calculated over the   **(DMRC 2013)**
(a) whole cycle
(b) half cycle
(c) unsymmetrical part of the waveform
(d) none of these

47. A capacitor is made up of two concentric spherical shells. The radii of the inner and outer shells are R_1 and R_2 respectively and ϵ is the permittivity of the medium between the shells. The capacitance of the capacitor is given by

(a) $\dfrac{1}{4\pi\epsilon}\left(\dfrac{1}{R_1} - \dfrac{1}{R_2}\right)$

(b) $\dfrac{1}{4\pi\epsilon}\left(\dfrac{1}{R_1} + \dfrac{1}{R_2}\right)$

(c) $4\pi\epsilon\,\dfrac{R_1 R_2}{R_1 + R_2}$

(d) $4\pi\epsilon\,\dfrac{R_1 R_2}{R_1 - R_2}$ **(DMRC 2014)**

48. Two point charges ($Q_1 = Q$, $Q_2 = 2Q$) and an infinite grounded plane are shown in the figure. The forces F_1 and F_2, on Q_1 and Q_2, will be in the ratio

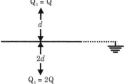

(a) 1 : 1   (b) 1 : 2
(c) 1 : 4   (d) 1 : 8   **(DMRC 2014)**

49. An infinite number of concentric circular loops carry a current 'I' each hut alternately in opposite directions. The radii of the loops are R, 2R, 4R.....in geometric progression. The magnetic flux density at the centre of the loops will be   **(DMRC 2014)**

(a) Zero   (b) $\dfrac{\mu_0 I}{3R}$

(c) $\dfrac{\mu_0 I}{4R}$ (d) $\dfrac{\mu_0 I}{6R}$

50. For a current element IdI situated at an arbitrary point, the magnetic vector potential A equals (R is the distance, of the observation point from the centre of the current clement)

          (DMRC 2014)
(a) $\mu IdI/(4\pi R)$ (b) $\mu IdI/(4\pi R^2)$
(c) $\mu IdI/(4\pi\sqrt{R})$ (d) $\mu IdI/(2\pi R)$

51. Tangential component of the electric field on a perfect conductor will be   **(DMRC 2014)**
(a) infinite
(b) zero
(c) same as the normal field component and 90° out of phase
(d) same as the normal component but 1800 out of phase

52. The force f per unit area on the surface of conductor, with surface charge density σ. in the presence of an electric field is (a_n is unit outward normal to the conductor surface) **(DMRC 2014)**

    (a) $\bar{f} = \dfrac{\sigma^2}{2\epsilon_0}\, \bar{a}_0$ (b) $\bar{f} = \dfrac{\sigma^2}{\epsilon_0}\, \bar{a}_0$

    (c) $\bar{f} = \epsilon_0\, \sigma^2\, \bar{a}_0$ (d) $\bar{f} = 0$

53. When a closed conducting loop 'C' is moving with a constant velocity 'V' through a non-uniform time-varying magnetic field 'B', the voltage induced in the loop is given by **(DMRC 2014)**

    (a) $e = -\int \dfrac{\partial \bar{B}}{\partial t} d\bar{s}$

    (b) $e = -\phi_c \left(\bar{V} \times \bar{B}\right).d\bar{I}$

    (c) $e = -\phi_c \left(\bar{B} \times \bar{V}\right) d\bar{s}$

    (d) $e = -\int \dfrac{\partial \bar{B}}{\partial t} d\bar{s} + \phi_c \left(\bar{V} - \bar{B}\right) d\bar{I}$

54. The dimensional equation of resistance is

    (a) $L^2 MT^{-2} I^{-2}$ **(DMRC 2014)**

    (b) $L^2 MT^{-2} I^{-2}$

    (c) $L^2 M^{-3} I^{-2}$

    (d) $L^2 MT^{-3} I^{-2}$

55. The resistance of a shunt for a precision grade ammeter can be best measured by

    (a) De Sauty bridge

    (b) Scherring bridge

    (c) Maxwell bridge

    (d) Kelvin double bridge   **(DMRC 2014)**

56. Which of the following is not a welding accessory?

    (SSC, CPWD 2008)

    (a) Cable   (b) Electrode holder

    (c) Hand screen   (d) Gloves

57. The scale of moving iron (M.I.) instrument is

    (SSC, CPWD 2008)

    (a) uniform   (b) cramped

    (c) linear   (d) All the above

58. Which of the following meters is an integrating type instrument?   **(SSC, CPWD 2008)**

    (a) Ammeter   (b) Voltmeter

    (c) Wattmeter   (d) Energy meter

59. A circuit component that opposes the change in circuit voltage is   **(SSC, CPWD 2008)**

    (a) resistance   (b) capacitance

    (c) inductance   (d) all the above

60. A series resonant circuit implies

    (SSC, CPWD 2008)

    (a) zero power factor and maximum current

    (b) unity power factor and maximum current

    (c) unity power factor and minimum current

    (d) zero power factor and minimum current

61. A current i = (10 + 10 sin$t$) amperes is passed through moving iron type ammeter. Its reading will be   **(SSC, CPWD 2008)**

    (a) zero   (b) 10A

    (c) $\sqrt{150}$A   (d) $\sqrt{2}$A

62. A DC ammeter has resistance of 0.1 Ω and current range is 0 – 100A. If the range is to be extended to 0 – 500A, then meter requires shunt resistance of   **(SSC, CPWD 2008)**

    (a) 0.010Ω   (b) 0.011Ω

    (c) 0.025Ω   (d) 1.0Ω

63. In which type of welding is a pool of molten metal used?   **(SSC, CPWD 2008)**

    (a) Electroslag   (b) Submerged arc

    (c) MIG   (d) TIG

64. Plan and butt welds may be used on materials upto approximately   **(SSC, CPWD 2008)**

    (a) 25 mm thick   (b) 40 mm thick

    (c) 50 mm thick   (d) 70 mm thick

65. In arc welding, arc is created between the electrode and work by   **(SSC, CPWD 2008)**

    (a) flow of current

    (b) voltage

    (c) material thickness

    (d) contact resistance

66. A PN junction is

    (a) a rectifier   (b) an amplifier

    (c) an insulator   (d) an oscillator

67. The value of V in the circuit shown in the given figure is   **(SSC, CPWD 2008)**

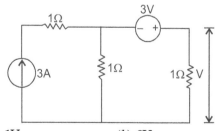

    (a) 1V   (b) 2V

    (c) 3V   (d) 4V

68. The value of current I flowing in the 1 Ω resistor in the circuit shown in the figure below will be

(SSC, CPWD 2009)

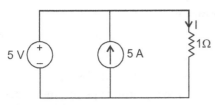

(a) 10A   (b) 6A

(c) 5A   (d) Zero

69. In the figure shown below, if we connect a source of 2-V, with internal resistance of 1Ω at AA' with positive terminal at A, then current through R is   (SSC, CPWD 2009)

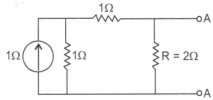

(a) 2A   (b) 1.66A

(c) 1A   (d) 0.625A

70. The curve representing Ohm's law is

(SSC, CPWD 2009)

(a) Linear   (b) Hyperbolic

(c) Parabolic   (d) Triangular

71. Specific resistance of a conductor depends upon

(SSC, CPWD 2009)

(a) Dimension of the conductor

(b) Composition of conductor material

(c) Resistance of the conductor

(d) Both (a) and (b)

72. Superposition theorem is essentially based on the concept of   (SSC, CPWD 2009)

(a) Reciprocity   (b) Linearity

(c) Duality   (d) Non-linearity

73. Which instrument has the lowest resistance?

(SSC, CPWD 2009)

(a) Ammeter   (b) Voltmeter

(c) Megger   (d) Frequency meter

74. The moving coil in a dynamometer wattmer is connected   (SSC, CPWD 2009)

(a) in series with the fixed coil

(b) across the supply

(c) in series with the load

(d) Any one of the above

75. In an R-L-C circuit susceptance is equal to

(SSC, CPWD 2009)

(a) $\dfrac{1}{X}$ (b) $\dfrac{1}{R}$

(c) $\dfrac{R}{Z^2}$ (d) $\dfrac{X}{Z^2}$

76. The current read by the ammeter A in the AC circuit shown in following figure is

(SSC, CPWD 2009)

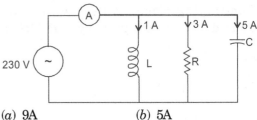

(a) 9A   (b) 5A

(c) 3A   (d) 1A

77. The voltage across the various elements are marked, as shown in the figure given below. The input voltage is   (SSC, CPWD 2009)

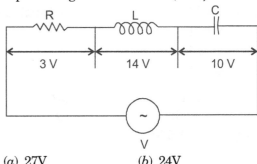

(a) 27V   (b) 24V

(c) 10V   (d) 5V

78. The value of voltage across the diode in figure given below is   (SSC, CPWD 2010)

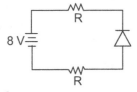

(a) Zero volt

(b) 4 V

(c) 8 V

(d) Depends upon the value of R

79. The temperature co-efficient of an intrinsic semiconductor is   (SSC, CPWD 2010)

(a) Zero   (b) Positive

(c) Negative   (d) Like that of metals

80. Which of the following is the best conductor of electricity ?   (SSC, CPWD 2012)

(a) Warm water   (b) Salt water

(c) Cold water   (d) Distilled water

81. SI unit of Electrical Energy is
(a) Watt-Second
(b) Joule
(c) KWh
(d) Volt-Ampere-Second **(SSC, CPWD 2012)**

82. The wave shape of current flowing through an inductor is **(SSC, CPWD 2012)**

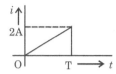

The wave shape of voltage drop (v) across the inductor is

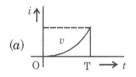 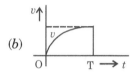

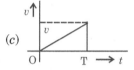 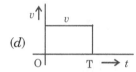

83. Two wires A and B of the same material but of different lengths L and 2L have the radius r and 2r respectively. The ratio of specific resistance will be **(SSC, CPWD 2012)**
(a) 1 : 4 (b) 1 : 8
(c) 1 : 1 (d) 1 : 2

84. In general, if a sine wave is fed into a Schmitt trigger, the output will be **(SSC, CPWD 2012)**
(a) a square wave
(b) a saw-tooth wave
(c) an amplified sine wave
(d) a triangular wave

85. In the given circuilt the function of the diode D is **(SSC, CPWD 2012)**

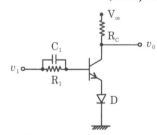

(a) To protect the base-emitte junction
(b) To hold the output voltage to a constant value
(c) To bias the transistor
(d) To clip the output voltage

86. FETs are **(SSC, CPWD 2012)**
(a) Either unipolar or bipolar
(b) None of these
(c) Unipolar devices
(d) Bipolar devices

87. In the circuit, forward resistance of the diode D is 2 Ω and its reverse resistance is infinitely high. **(SSC, CPWD 2012)**

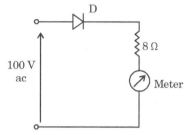

A list consists of meters (List - I) and another list shows the meter readings (List - II)

List – I	List – II
(i) PMMC	(a) 7.07 A
(ii) Hot wire	(b) 4.5 A
	(c) 10 A
	(d) 12.5 A

Which one of the options given here is correct to indicate the type of meter (List - I) and its reading (List - II) ?
(a) (i) → (a), (ii) → (c)
(b) (i) → (b), (ii) → (d)
(c) (i) → (a), (ii) → (b)
(d) (i) → (b), (ii) → (a)

88. A Ballistic galvanometer of constant equal to 1 micro-coulomb/degree gives a throw of 22.5°, when a capacitor discharges through the meter. If a battery of 15 V is used to recharge the capacitor, value of capacitance is **(SSC, CPWD 2012)**
(a) 22.5 μ F (b) 10 μ F
(c) 1.5 μ F (d) 15 μ F

89. A potentiometer is used to measure the voltage between two points of a dc circuit, which is found to be 1.2 V. This is also measured by a voltmeter, which is found to be 0.9 V. The resistance of the voltmeter is 60 kΩ. The input resistance between two points. **(SSC, CPWD 2012)**
(a) 60 kΩ (b) 20 kΩ
(c) 45 kΩ (d) 80 kΩ

90. During the measurement of a low resistance using a potentiometer, the following readings were obtained : **(SSC, CPWD 2012)**

Voltage drop across unknown

resistance = 0.531 Volt.

Voltage drop across a 0.1 Ohm standard resistance connected in series with the unknown = 1.083 Volt.

Value of the unknown resistor is

(a) 49.03 milliohm

(b) 108.3 milliohm

(c) 20.4 milliohm

(d) 53.1 milliohm

91. Which one of the following types of instruments does suffers from error due to magnetic hysteresis? **(SSC, CPWD 2012)**

(a) Induction type   (b) Electrodynamic

(c) Moving iron   (d) PMMC

92. Which one of the following does not employ a null method of measurement ? **(SSC, CPWD 2012)**

(a) Megger   (b) DC potentiometer

(c) Kelvin double bridge   (d) AC potentiometer

93. An electromagnetic torque is produced as an interaction between a flux and current. The angle between flux and current is 45°. If this angle is changed to 30°, flux increase by 100% and current reduces by 25%, then the torque **(SSC, CPWD 2012)**

(a) Increases to 183.7 % of the original

(b) Reduces to 81.6% of the original

(c) Reduces to 54.4% of the original

(d) Reduces to 66.7% of the original

94. Maximum temperature limit for class F insulation is **(SSC, CPWD 2012)**

(a) 130° C   (b) 120° C

(c) 105° C   (d) 155° C

95. AC series motors are built with as few turns as possible to reduce **(SSC, CPWD 2012)**

(a) Flux   (b) Reactance

(c) Iron losses   (d) Speed

96. Given two coupled inductors L_1 and L_2 having their mutual inductance M. The relationship among them must satisfy **(SSC, CPWD 2012)**

(a) $M > L_1 L_2$ (b) $M £ L_1 L_2$

(c) $M = L_1 L_2$ (d) $M > \dfrac{L_1 + L_2}{2}$

97. A coil with a certain number of turns has a specified time constant. If the number of turns is doubled, its times constant would

(a) Become four fold

(b) Get halved

(c) Remain unaffected

(d) Become doubled   **(SSC, CPWD 2012)**

98. The iron loss per unit frequency in a ferromagnetic core, when plotted against frequency, is a

(a) Straight line with positive slope

(b) Straight line with negative slope

(c) Parabola

(d) Constant   **(SSC, CPWD 2012)**

99. The mutual inductance between two closely coupled coils is 1 H. If the turns of one coil is decreased to half and those of the other is doubled, the new value of the mutual inductance would be **(SSC, CPWD 2012)**

(a) 1/4 H   (b) 1 H

(c) 2 H   (d) 1/2 H

100. Following graph shows the loss characteristic of a sheet of ferromagnetic material against varying frequency f. Pi is the iron loss at frequency f. Hysteresis and eddy current losses of the sheet at 100 Hz are **(SSC, CPWD 2012)**

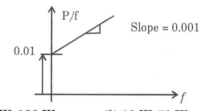

(a) 10 W, 100 W   (b) 10 W, 50 W

(c) 1 W, 5 W   (d) 1 W, 10 W

101. Hysteresis losses are present in iron core coil when **(SSC, CPWD 2012)**

(a) The current in the coil is alternating

(b) The current is unsymmetrical alternating only

(c) The current in the coil is d.c. only

(d) The current in the coil is sinusoidal only

102. Eddy current loss in ferromagnetic core is proportional to **(SSC, CPWD 2012)**

(a) square of frequency

(b) square root of frequency

(c) frequency

(d) reciprocal of frequency

103. The magnetic materials that are used to prepare permanent magnets should have

(a) Steeply rising magnetisation curve

(b) Small hysteresis loop

(c) High retentivity

(d) Low coercive force **(SSC, CPWD 2012)**

104. The voltage wave v = V_m sin (ωt − 15°) volts is applied across an ac circuit. If the current leads the voltage by 10° and the maximum value of current is I_m, then the equation of current is

(a) i = I_m sin (ωt + 5°) amps

(b) i = I_m sin (ωt − 25°) amps

(c) i = I_m sin (ωt + 25°) amps

(d) i = I_m sin (ωt − 5°) amps **(SSC, CPWD 2013)**

105. The average value of current (I_{av}) of a sinusoidal wave of peak value (I_m) is **(SSC, CPWD 2013)**

(a) $I_{av} = \dfrac{I_m}{2}$ (b) $I_{av} = \dfrac{\pi}{2}I_m$

(c) $I_{av} = \dfrac{2}{\pi}I_m$ (d) $I_{av} = \dfrac{I_m}{\sqrt{2}}$

106. The emf induced in a coil is given by

$$e = -N\,\dfrac{d\phi}{dt}$$

where e is the emf imduced, N is the number of turns and dϕ is the instantaneous flux linkage with the coil in time dt. **(SSC, CPWD 2013)**

The negative sign in the expression is due to

(a) Hans Christian Oersted

(b) Andre-Marie Ampere

(c) Michale Faraday

(d) Emil Lenz

107. The mutual inductance between two coils having self inductances 3 henry and 12 henry and coupling coefficient 0.85 is **(SSC, CPWD 2013)**

(a) 12.75 henry   (b) 5.1 henry

(c) 0.425 henry   (d) 1.7 henry

108. Two parallel conductors carrying current in opposite directions will exert on each other

(a) an attractive forces

(b) a repulsive force

(c) an axial force

(d) no force **(SSC, CPWD 2013)**

109. The unit of reluctance of magnetic circuit is

(SSC, CPWD 2013)

(a) AT/m   (b) Weber/m

(c) T/Weber   (d) Weber/AT

110. In indicating instruments the springs are mainly used to **(SSC, CPWD 2013)**

(a) conduct the current to the coils

(b) hold the pivot in position

(c) control the pointer movement

(d) reduce the vibration of the pointer

111. The total flux at the end of a long permanent bar magnet is 100×10^{-6} Wb. The end of this magnet is withdrawn through a 1000 turn coil in $\dfrac{1}{20}$ seconds. The induced e.m.f. in the coil is

(SSC, CPWD 2013)

(a) 20.0 V   (b) 2.0 V

(c) 0.2 V   (d) 0.02 V

112. For n-type semiconductor, the doping material is

(SSC, CPWD 2013)

(a) tetravalent   (b) pentavalent

(c) trivalent   (d) bivalent

113. A attenuator probe as shown, is connected to an amplifier of input capacitance 0.1 μF. Value of C that must be connected across 100 K to make the overall gain independent of frequency, is

(SSC, CPWD 2013)

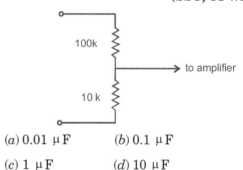

(a) 0.01 μF   (b) 0.1 μF

(c) 1 μF   (d) 10 μF

114. A wattmeter is marked 15 A/30 A, 300 V/600 V and its scale is marked up to 4500 watts. When the meter is connected for 30 A, 600 V, the point indicated 2000 watts. The actual power in the circuit is **(SSC, CPWD 2013)**

(a) 2000 watts   (b) 4000 watts

(c) 6000 watts   (d) 8000 watts

115. If the angular frequency of an alternating voltage is ω, then the angular frequency of instantaneous real power absorbed in an ac circuit is

(a) 2 ω (b) ω

(c) 3 ω (d) ω/2 **(SSC, CPWD 2013)**

116. If the transistor having $V_{CE} = 5$ V, $V_{BE} = 0.7$ has $\beta = 45$, value of R is   **(SSC, CPWD 2013)**

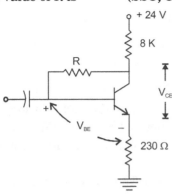

(a) 85.64 k   (b) 63.14 k

(c) 72.15 k   (d) 91.18 k

117. In the circuit, v is the input voltage applied across the capacitor of 2 F. Current through the capacitor is   **(SSC, CPWD 2013)**

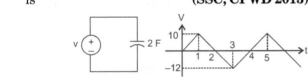

(a)

(b)

(c)

(d)

118. In a semiconductor, the resistivity

(a) depends on temperature

(b) depends on voltage

(c) depends on current through it

(d) None of the above   **(SSC, CPWD 2013)**

119. A geyser is operated from 230 V, 50 c/s mains. The frequency of instantaneous power consumed by the geyser is   **(SSC, CPWD 2013)**

(a) 25 c/s   (b) 50 c/s

(c) 100 c/s   (d) 150 c/s

120. Ampere-second is the unit of

(a) emf   (b) power

(c) electric charge (d) energy **(SSC, CPWD 2013)**

121. A solenoid of inductance 250 mH and resistance 10 Ω is connected to a battery. The time taken for the magnetic energy to reach $\frac{1}{4}$ th of its maximum value is   **(SSC, CPWD 2013)**

(a) $\log_e (2)$ (b) $10^{-3} \log_e (2)$

(c) $25 \log_e (2)$ (d) $\frac{1}{40} \log_e (2)$

122. The peak value of the output voltage of a half-wave rectifier is 100 V. The r.m.s value of the half-wave rectifier output voltage will be

(a) 100 V   (b) 50 V

(c) 70.7 V   (d) 35.35 V **(SSC, CPWD 2013)**

123. The given circuit represents a   **(SSC, CPWD 2013)**

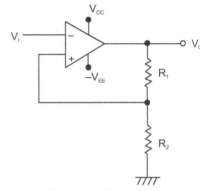

(a) monostable multivibrator

(b) astable multivibrator

(c) Schmitt trigger

(d) bistable multivibrator

124. The input resistance of a FET is of the order of   **(SSC, CPWD 2013)**

(a) 100 Ω (b) 10 kΩ

(c) 1 mΩ (d) 100 MΩ

125. In a series R-L circuit supplied from a sinusoidal voltage source, voltage across R and L are 3 V and 4 V respectively. The supply voltage is then   **(SSC, CPWD 2013)**

(a) 7 V   (b) 1 V

(c) 3.5 V   (d) 5 V

126. If the insulation resistance of 2 m long sample of a cable is 10 MΩ, then a 8 m long sample of the same will have an insulation resistance of   **(SSC, CPWD 2013)**

(a) 40 MΩ (b) 2.5 MΩ

(c) 2 MΩ (d) 5.5 MΩ

127. An inductor is supplied from a sinusoidal voltage source. The magnetic field energy in the inductor changes from peak value to minimum value in 10 msec. The supply frequency is

(SSC, CPWD 2013)

(a) 50 Hz   (b) 25 Hz

(c) 1 kHz   (d) 100 Hz

128. Two 2000 Ω, 2 watt resistors are connected in parallel. Their combined resistance value and wattage rating are **(SSC, CPWD 2013)**

(a) 1000 Ω, 2 watt

(b) 1000 Ω, 4 watt

(c) 2000 Ω, 4 watt

(d) 2000 Ω, 2 watt

129. We have three resistances each of value 1 Ω, 2 Ω and 3 Ω. If all the three resistances are to be connected in a circuit, how many different values of equivalent resistance are possible?

(SSC, CPWD 2013)

(a) Five   (b) Six

(c) Seven   (d) Eight

130. Three 3 μF capacitors are in series. A 6 μF capacitor is in parallel with this series arrangement. The equivalent capacitance of this combination is **(SSC, CPWD 2013)**

(a) 7 μF   (b) 15 μF

(c) 3.6 μF   (d) 1 μF

131. The voltage across R, L and C are 3 V, 14 V and 10 V respectively as in the figure. If the voltage source is sinusoidal, then the input voltage (r.m.s.) is **(SSC, CPWD 2013)**

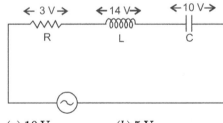

(a) 10 V   (b) 5 V

(c) 2.5 V   (d) 15 V

132. In 1-phase series RL circuit fed by voltage source, the resistance and reactance values are 4 ohm each. In this circuit **(SSC, CPWD 2013)**

(a) the current leads the voltage by 45°

(b) the current lags the voltage by 45°

(c) the current lags the voltage by 60°

(d) None of the above

133. Superposition theorem requires as many circuits to be solved as there are **(SSC, CPWD 2013)**

(a) nodes

(b) sources

(c) loops

(d) None of the above

134. The high-voltage and low-voltage winding resistances of a distribution transformer of 100 KVA, 1100/220 volts, 50 Hz are 0.1 Ω and 0.004 Ω respectively. The equivalent resistances referred to high-voltage side and low-voltage side are respectively **(SSC, CPWD 2013)**

(a) 2.504 Ω and 0.2 Ω

(b) 0.2 Ω and 0.008 Ω

(c) 0.10016 Ω and 2.504 Ω

(d) 0.008 Ω and 0.10016 Ω

135. A tank circuit consists of **(SSC, CPWD 2013)**

(a) an inductor and a capacitor connected in series

(b) an inductor and a capacitor connected in parallel

(c) a pure inductance and a pure capacitance connected in series

(d) a pure inductance and a pure capacitance connected in parallel

136. The instantaneous power of 1-phase series circuit supplying R-L load from a sinusoidal voltage source has in each cycle **(SSC, CPWD 2013)**

(a) negative twice, zero four times

(b) zero twice, negative once

(c) negative four times, zero twice

(d) negative twice, zero once

137. In a series R-L-C circuit the 'Q-factor' is given by

(SSC, CPWD 2013)

(a) $Q = \dfrac{1}{R}\sqrt{\dfrac{L}{C}}$ (b) $Q = R\sqrt{\dfrac{L}{C}}$

(c) $Q = \dfrac{1}{R}\sqrt{\dfrac{C}{L}}$ (d) $Q = R\sqrt{\dfrac{C}{L}}$

138. In an ac circuit, $V = (200 + j\,40)$ V and $I = (30 - j\,10)$ A. The active and reactive power of the circuit are respectively **(SSC, CPWD 2013)**

(a) 6400 W, 800 VAR capacitive

(b) 6400 W, 800 VAR inductive

(c) 5600 W, 3200 VAR capacitive

(d) 5600 W, 3200 VAR inductive

139. Application of Norton's theorem in a circuit results in **(SSC, CPWD 2013)**

(a) a current source and an impedance in parallel

(b) a voltage source and an impedance in series

(c) an ideal voltage source

(d) an ideal current source

140.

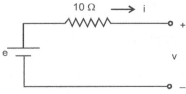

The voltage (v) vs. current (i) curve of the circuit is shown below: **(SSC, CPWD 2013)**

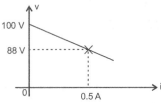

Internal resistance of the source e is

(a) 24 Ω   (b) 4 Ω

(c) 10 Ω   (d) 14 Ω

141. Value of the load impedance $\overline{Z}_L$ for which the load consumes maximum power is

(SSC, CPWD 2013)

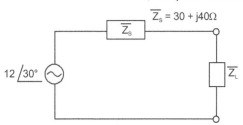

(a) 50 Ω at a power factor of 0.6 lead

(b) 50 Ω at a power factor of 0.6 lag

(c) 30 Ω at a power factor of unity

(d) None of the above

142. Three equal impedances are first connected in delta across a 3-phase balanced supply. If the same impedances are connected in star across the same supply **(SSC, CPWD 2013)**

(a) phase currents will be $\frac{1}{3}$ of the previous value.

(b) line currents will be $\frac{1}{3}$ of the previous value.

(c) power consumed will be $\frac{1}{3}$ of the previous value

(d) power consumed will be 3 times the previous value

143. The average value of the voltage weave $v = 110 + 175 \sin(314t - 25°)$ volts is

(SSC, CPWD 2013)

(a) 110 V   (b) 175 V

(c) 165.75 V   (d) 206.7 V

144. A current from an ac source bifurcates into two branches A and B in parallel. Branch A is an inductor with 30 μH inductance and 1 Ω resistance. Branch B is another inductor with inductance L and 1.5 Ω resistance. For the ratio of currents in the branches to be independent of supply frequency, value of L should be

(a) 30.5 μH

(b) 20 μH

(c) 45 μH

(d) 29.5 μH   **(SSC, CPWD 2013)**

145. Three inductors each of 60 mH are connected in delta. The value of inductance of each arm of the equivalent star connection is **(SSC, CPWD 2013)**

(a) 10 mH   (b) 15 mH

(c) 20 mH   (d) 30 mH

146. The magnetic field energy in an inductor changes from maximum value to minimum value in 5 m sec when connected to an ac source. The frequency of the source in Hz is

(a) 500   (b) 200

(c) 50   (d) 20   **(SSC, CPWD 2013)**

147. A voltage source having an open-circuit voltage of 150 V and internal resistance of 75 Ω, is equivalent to a current source of

(SSC, CPWD 2013)

(a) 2 A in series with 75 Ω

(b) 2 A in parallel with 37.5 Ω

(c) 2 A in parallel with 75 Ω

(d) 1 A in parallel with 150 Ω

148. An inductor with a ferromagnetic core is supplied from a sinusoidal voltage source with frequency 'f'. The current drawn by the inductor will be

(SSC, CPWD 2013)

(a) sinusoidal with frequency 'f'

(b) sinusoidal with frequency '2f'

(c) a sawtooth wave

(d) non-sinusoidal with frequency 'f'

149. In the circuit as shown, voltage measured between A, B is found to be 70 V. Value of M is

(SSC, CPWD 2013)

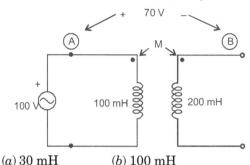

    (*a*) 30 mH   (*b*) 100 mH

    (*c*) 200 mH   (*d*) 70 mH

150. Two coupled coils, connected in series, have and equivalent inductance of 16 mH or 8 mH depending on the connection. The mutual inductance between the coils is

(SSC, CPWD 2013)

    (*a*) 12 mH   (*b*) $8\sqrt{2}$ mH

    (*c*) 4 mH   (*d*) 2 mH

151. Tesla is the unit of   **(SSC, CPWD 2013)**

    (*a*) electric flux density

    (*b*) magnetic field intensity

    (*c*) electric field intensity

    (*d*) magnetic flux density

152. Which one of the following is a valid value of coefficient of coupling between two inductors?

    (*a*) 1.414   (*b*) 0.9

    (*c*) 1.732   (*d*) 17.32 **(SSC, CPWD 2013)**

153. The Ebers - Moll model is applicable to :

    (*a*) JFET

    (*b*) BJT

    (*c*) NMOS transistor

    (*d*) UJT   **(SSC, CPWD 2014)**

154. A d.c. voltmeter has a sensitivity of 1000 Ω/watt. When it measure half full scale in 100 V range, the current through the voltmeter will be :

    (*a*) 50 mA   (*b*) 100 mA

    (*c*) 1mA   (*d*) 0.5mA**(SSC, CPWD 2014)**

155. The power factor of the circuit shown in figure :

(SSC, CPWD 2014)

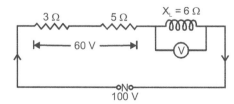

    (*a*) 0.75 lagging   (*b*) 0.6 lagging

    (*c*) 0.3 lagging   (*d*) 0.8 lagging

156. The power factor of an a.c. circuit is given by :

(SSC, CPWD 2014)

    (*a*) $\dfrac{R}{Z}$ (*b*) $\dfrac{X_L}{R}$

    (*c*) $\dfrac{Z}{R}$ (*d*) $\dfrac{R}{X_L}$

157. As compared to full - wave rectifier using two diodes, the four diode bridge rectifier has the dominant advantage of :   **(SSC, CPWD 2014)**

    (*a*) higher efficiency

    (*b*) higher current carrying capacity

    (*c*) lower peak inverse voltage requirement

    (*d*) lower ripple factor

158. The Biot-Savart's law is a general modification of :   **(SSC, CPWD 2014)**

    (*a*) Faraday's laws (*b*) Kirchhoff's law

    (*c*) Lenzs law   (*d*) Ampere's law

159. The current in reverse bias in P - N junction diode may be :   **(SSC, CPWD 2014)**

    (*a*) between 2A and 5A

    (*b*) few micro or nano amperes

    (*c*) few milli amperes

    (*d*) between 0.2 A and 2A

160. Which of the following is non-linear circuit parameter ?   **(SSC, CPWD 2014)**

    (*a*) Transistor   (*b*) Inductance

    (*c*) Condenser   (*d*) Wire wound resistor

161. The B - H curve is used to find the mmf of this section of the magnetic circuit. The section is :

    (*a*) vacuum   **(SSC, CPWD 2014)**

    (*b*) iron part

    (*c*) air gap

    (*d*) both iron part and air gap

162. A terminal where three or more branches meet is known as :   **(SSC, CPWD 2014)**

    (*a*) mesh   (*b*) node

    (*c*) terminus   (*d*) loop

163. The energy stored in the magnetic field of a solenoid 30 cm long and 3 cm diameter with 1,000 turns of wire carrying current of 10 A is :

(SSC, CPWD 2014)

    (*a*) 1.15 J   (*b*) 0.015 J

    (*c*) 0.15 J   (*d*) 0.5 J

164. Find the current through 5 Ω resistor :

(SSC, CPWD 2014)

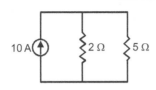

   (a) 3.5 A   (b) 7.15 A

   (c) 5 A   (d) 2.85 A

165. If a 10 – μF capacitor is connected to a voltage source with $v(t) = 50 \sin 2000\, t$ V, then the current through the capacitor is _____ A.

(SSC, CPWD 2014)

   (a) $10^6 \cos 2000\, t$ (b) $5 \times 10^{-4} \cos 2000\, t$

   (c) $\cos 2000\, t$ (d) $500 \cos 2000\, t$

166. In a series resonance circuit, the impedance at half power frequencies is : **(SSC, CPWD 2014)**

   (a) 2R   (b) $\dfrac{R}{\sqrt{2}}$

   (c) $\sqrt{2}\, R$ (d) $\dfrac{R}{2}$

167. A circuit with a resistor, inductor and capacitor in series is resonant of fo Hz. If all the component values are now doubled the new resonant frequency is : **(SSC, CPWD 2014)**

   (a) $\dfrac{f_o}{4}$ (b) $2f_o$

   (c) f_o (d) $\dfrac{f_o}{2}$

168. A 2 cm long coil has 10 turns and carries a current of 750 mA. The magnetising force of the coil is :

(SSC, CPWD 2014)

   (a) 375 AT/m   (b) 225 AT/m

   (c) 675 AT/m   (d) 450 AT/m

169. Total capacitance between the points L and M in figure is : **(SSC, CPWD 2014)**

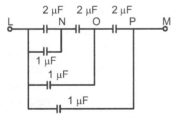

   (a) 4.05 μF   (b) 1.45 μF

   (c) 1.85 μF   (d) 2.05 μF

170. EMF induced in a coil rotating in a uniform magnetic field will be maximum when the :

(SSC, CPWD 2014)

   (a) Rate of cutting flux by the coil sides is minimum.

   (b) Flux linking with the coil is maximum.

   (c) Rate of change of flux linkage is minimum.

   (d) Rate of change of flux linkage is maximum.

171. The mutual inductance between two unity coupled coils of 9 H and 4 H will be :

(SSC, CPWD 2014)

   (a) 36 H   (b) 2.2 H

   (c) 6H   (d) 13 H

172. Three resistors, each of 'R' Ω are connected in star. What is the value of equivalent delta connected resistors ? **(SSC, CPWD 2014)**

   (a) 3 RΩ   (b) $\dfrac{R}{2}\Omega$

   (c) 2 RΩ   (d) $\dfrac{R}{3}\Omega$

173. Super position theorem can be applied only to :

(SSC, CPWD 2014)

   (a) bilateral networks

   (b) linear networks

   (c) non-linear networks

   (d) linear bilateral networks

174. The magnetic potential difference in a magnetic circuit is given by : **(SSC, CPWD 2014)**

   (a) B l H   (b) H J l

   (c) B l (d) H l

175. Find R_3 for the circuit shown in figure :

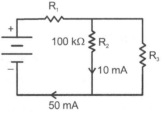

   (a) 25 mega ohm

   (b) 25milli ohm

   (c) 25 ohm

   (d) 25 kilo ohm   **(SSC, CPWD 2014)**

176. Using Millman's theorem, find the current through the load resistance R_L of 3 Ω resistance shown below : **(SSC, CPWD 2014)**

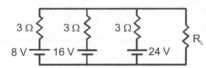

(a) 12A   (b) 4A

(c) 6A   (d) 8A

177. An ideal voltage source should have :

(SSC, CPWD 2014)

(a) infinite source resistance

(b) large value of emf

(c) small value of emf

(d) zero source resistance

178. Consider a constant uniform magnetic field. A conductor moves across this field at a constant velocity. The emf induced in the conductor is termed as :   **(SSC, CPWD 2014)**

(a) Self-Induced emf

(b) Induced emf

(c) Statically Induced emf

(d) Dynamically Induced emf

179. A magnetic circuit carries a flux ϕ_i in the iron part and a flux ϕ_g in the air gap. Then leakage co-efficient   **(SSC, CPWD 2014)**

(a) $\phi_i - \phi_g$ (b) $\dfrac{\phi_i}{\phi_g}$

(c) $\dfrac{\phi_g}{\phi_i}$ (d) $\phi_g \times \phi_i$

180. Thevenin's equivalent voltage and resistance between the terminal A and B for network of given figure is :   **(SSC, CPWD 2014)**

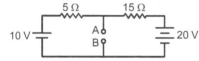

(a) 2.5 V, 12.5 Ω   (b) 2.5 V, 3.75 Ω

(c) 12.5 V, 3.75 Ω   (d) 12.5 V, 2.5 Ω

181. The R_{eq} for the circuit shown in figure is

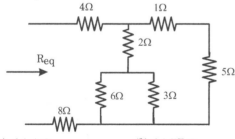

(a) 14.4 Ω   (b) 14.57 Ω

(c) 15.27 Ω   (d) 15.88 Ω

(SSC CPWD 2014)

182. The SI unit of conductivity is

(SSC CPWD 2014)

(a) ohm-m   (b) ohm/m

(c) mho-m   (d) mho/m

183. Calculate the voltage drop across 14.5 Ω resistance.   **(SSC CPWD 2014)**

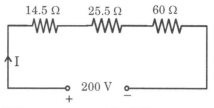

(a) 14.5 V   (b) 18 V

(c) 29 V   (d) 30.5 V

184. For the network shown in the figure, the value of current in 8 Ω resistor is   **(SSC CPWD 2014)**

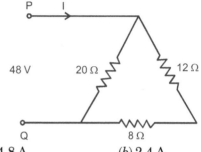

(a) 4.8 A   (b) 2.4 A

(c) 1.5 A   (d) 1.2 A

185. Tesla is same as   **(SSC CPWD 2014)**

(a) Weber/meter   (b) Weber/(meter)^2

(c) Farad/meter   (d) Henry/(meter)^2

186. The unit of volume resistivity is

(a) ohm-m^3/m^2 **(SSC CPWD 2014)**

(b) ohm-m^2/m

(c) ohm-gram-m/gram

(d) ohm-m^4/m^3

187. Four resistance 2 Ω, 4 Ω, 5 Ω, 20 Ω are connected in parallel. Their combined resistance is

(a) 1 Ω   **(SSC CPWD 2014)**

(b) 2 Ω

(c) 4 Ω

(d) 5 Ω

188. In the figure, the value of R is

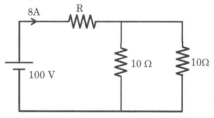

(a) 2.5 Ω   **(SSC CPWD 2014)**

(b) 5.0 Ω

(c) 7.5 Ω

(d) 10.0 Ω

189. For the circuit shown in figure, when $V_s = 0$, $I = 3A$. When $V_s = 200$ V, what will be the value of I ?

(SSC CPWD 2014)

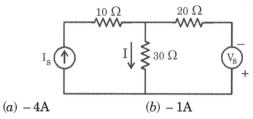

(a) – 4A (b) – 1A
(c) 1 A (d) 7 A

190. For the linear circuit shown in figure,
when R = ∞, V = 20 V; **(SSC CPWD 2014)**
when R = 0, I = 4 A;
When R = 5 Ω, the current I is

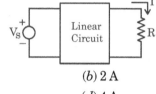

(a) 1 A (b) 2 A
(c) 3 A (d) 4 A

191. The current I in the circuit shown in the figure is

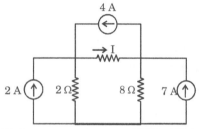

(a) – 3.67 A **(SSC CPWD 2014)**
(b) – 1 A
(c) 4 A
(d) 6 A

192. A resistance R is measured by ammeter-voltmeter method. The voltmeter reading is 200 V and its internal resistance is 2 K. If the ammeter reading is found to be 2 A, then value of R is

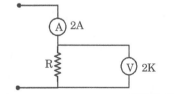

(a) 105.3 Ω **(SSC CPWD 2014)**
(b) 100.0 Ω
(c) 95.3 Ω
(d) 90.3 Ω

193. The circuit shown in the given figure is equivalent to a load of **(SSC CPWD 2014)**

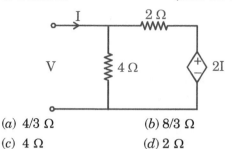

(a) 4/3 Ω (b) 8/3 Ω
(c) 4 Ω (d) 2 Ω

194. Energy stored in an inductor is given by

(SSC CPWD 2014)

(a) $\frac{1}{\sqrt{2}}(LI)^2$ (b) $\frac{1}{2}L^2I$

(c) $\frac{1}{\sqrt{LI}}$ (d) $\frac{1}{2}LI^2$

195. A coil with a certain number of turns has a specified time constant. If the number of turns is doubled, its time constant would

(SSC CPWD 2014)

(a) remain unaffected (b) become double
(c) become four-fold (d) get halved

196. Hysteresis is the phenomenon in the magnetic circuit by which

(a) H lags behind B **(SSC CPWD 2014)**
(b) B lags behind H
(c) B and H are always same
(d) setting up a constant flux is done

197. The flux through each turn of a 100-turn coil is $(t^3 - 2t)$ mWh, where 't' is in seconds. Find the magnitude of the induced emf at $t = 2$ s.

(a) 1 V **(SSC CPWD 2014)**
(b) 0.8 V
(c) 0.4 V
(d) 0.2 V

198. A circuit has inductance of 2 H. If the circuit current changes at the rate of 10 A/sec, then self-induced emf is **(SSC CPWD 2014)**

(a) 5 V (b) 0.2 V
(c) 20 V (d) 10 V

199. The B-H curve for ――― will be a straight line passing through the origin. **(SSC CPWD 2014)**

(a) air (b) soft iron
(c) hardened steel (d) silicon steel

200. Magnetic lines of force coming from a magnet
   (*a*) intersect at infinity   **(SSC CPWD 2014)**
   (*b*) intersect within the magnet
   (*c*) cannot intersect at all
   (*d*) cancel at pole faces

201. The main advantage of temporary magnets is that we can   **(SSC CPWD 2014)**
   (*a*) change the magnetic flux
   (*b*) use any magnetic material
   (*c*) decrease the hysteresis loss
   (*d*) magnetize without any source

202. The magnetic material used in permanent magnets is   **(SSC CPWD 2014)**
   (*a*) iron   (*b*) soft steel
   (*c*) nickel   (*d*) hardened steel

203. For the circuit shown in figure, the voltage across the capacitor during steady state condition is

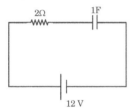

   (*a*) 0 V   (*b*) 4 V
   (*c*) 6 V   (*d*) 12 V
                           (SSC CPWD 2014)

204. Find R_{AB} for the circuit shown in figure.

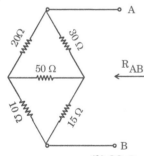

   (*a*) 18 Ω   (*b*) 30 Ω
   (*c*) 45 Ω   (*d*) 68 Ω
                           (SSC CPWD 2014)

205. Calculate the total susceptance of the circuit shown in figure.   **(SSC CPWD 2014)**

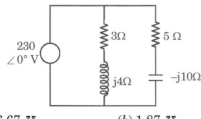

   (*a*) 6.67 ℧   (*b*) 1.87 ℧
   (*c*) 0.16 ℧   (*d*) 0.08 ℧

206. The Q-factor of a parallel resonant circuit is given by   **(SSC CPWD 2014)**
   (*a*) $\dfrac{1}{R}\sqrt{\dfrac{L}{C}}$ (*b*) $\dfrac{1}{R}\sqrt{\dfrac{C}{L}}$
   (*c*) $\dfrac{1}{R}\sqrt{1/LC}$ (*d*) $\dfrac{R}{\sqrt{LC}}$

207. In an R-L series circuit, the phase difference between applied voltage and circuit current will increase if   **(SSC CPWD 2014)**
   (*a*) X_L is increased
   (*b*) R is increased
   (*c*) X_L is decreased
   (*d*) supply frequency is decreased

208. Two sinusoidal currents are given by the equations $i_1 = 50 \sin\left(\omega t + \dfrac{\pi}{4}\right)$ and $i_2 = 25 \sin\left(\omega t - \dfrac{\pi}{6}\right)$.
   The phase difference between them is —— degrees.   **(SSC CPWD 2014)**
   (*a*) 15   (*b*) 30
   (*c*) 45   (*d*) 75

209. A supply voltage of 230 V, 50 Hz is fed to a residential building. Write down its equation for instantaneous value.
   (*a*) 163 sin 314.16 t **(SSC CPWD 2014)**
   (*b*) 230 sin 314.16 t
   (*c*) 325 sin 314.16 t
   (*d*) 361 sin 314.16 t

210. In moving iron instruments, the iron moves in a direction to cause   **(SSC CPWD 2014)**
   (*a*) coil inductance to be constant
   (*b*) mutual inductance to be minimum
   (*c*) minimum reluctance path
   (*d*) decrease in the flux passing through it

211. The material to be used in the manufacture a standard resistor should be of
   (*a*) low resistivity   **(SSC CPWD 2014)**
   (*b*) high resistivity and low temperature is coefficient
   (*c*) high temperature coefficient
   (*d*) low resistivity and high temperature coefficient

212. Fleming's left hand rule is applicable to
   (*a*) DC generator
   (*b*) DC motor
   (*c*) Alternator
   (*d*) Transformer   **(SSC CPWD 2014)**

213. Dielectric loss is proportional to

(a) [frequency]$^{1/2}$

(b) frequency

(c) frequency^2

(d) frequency^3 **(SSC CPWD 2014)**

214. In a CE (common emitter) transistor, V_{CC} = 12 V and the zero signal collector current is 1 mA. Determine the operating point when collector load (R_c) is 6 kΩ. **(SSC CPWD 2014)**

(a) 6 V, 1 mA   (b) 6 V, 2 mA

(c) 12 V, 1 mA   (d) 12 V, 2 mA

215. An AC supply of 230 V is applied to half-wave rectifier through transformer of turns ratio 10 : 1 as shown in figure. Determine the peak inverse voltage across the diode. **(SSC CPWD 2014)**

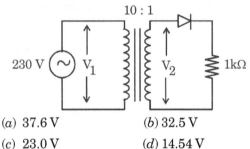

(a) 37.6 V   (b) 32.5 V

(c) 23.0 V   (d) 14.54 V

216. For the circuit shown below, find the resistance between points P & Q. **(SSC CPWD 2015)**

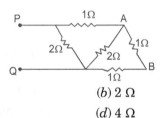

(a) 1Ω (b) 2 Ω

(c) 3 Ω (d) 4 Ω

217. In a pure inductive circuit if the supply frequency is reduced to 1/2, the current will?

(a) be four times as high   **(SSC CPWD 2015)**

(b) be doubled

(c) be reduced by half

(d) be reduced to one fourth

218. When a source is delivering maximum power to the load, the efficiency will be?

(SSC CPWD 2015)

(a) below 50%   (b) above 50%

(c) 50%   (d) maximum

219. In the Maxwell bridge as shown in the figure below the values of resistance Rx and inductance Lx of a coil are to be calculated after balancing the bridge. The component values are shown in the figure at balance. The values of Rx and Lx will respectively be: **(SSC CPWD 2015)**

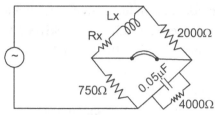

(a) 37.5 ohm, 75 mH

(b) 75 ohm, 75 mH

(c) 375 ohm, 75 mH

(d) 75 ohm, 150 mH

220. A node in a circuit is defined as a

(a) closed path   **(SSC CPWD 2015)**

(b) group of interconnected elements

(c) open terminal of an element

(d) junction of two or more elements

221. The area of the hysteresis loop will be least for one of the following materials. It is?

(a) wrought iron   **(SSC CPWD 2015)**

(b) silicon steel

(c) hard steel

(d) soft iron

222. The voltage across the 1kΩ resistor of the network shown in the given figure is

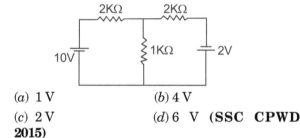

(a) 1 V   (b) 4 V

(c) 2 V   (d) 6 V **(SSC CPWD 2015)**

223. For the circuit shown in figure, the Norton's equivalent current source at terminals A & B is given by: **(SSC CPWD 2015)**

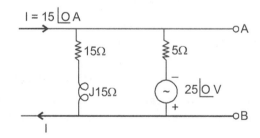

(a) 20 $\angle$0 A   (b) 10 $\angle$0 A

(c) 14 $\angle$36.86 A   (d) 16 $\angle$36.86 A

224. Thevenin's theorem cannot be applied to:

(a) passive circuit

(b) active circuit

(c) nonlinear circuit

(d) linear circuit   **(SSC CPWD 2015)**

225. To operate properly a transistor's base- emitter junction must be forward biased with reverse bias applied to which junction? **(SSC CPWD 2015)**

    (a) Base-collector   (b) Collector-emitter

    (c) Base-emitter   (d) Collector-base

226. A linear circuit is one whose perameters:

    (a) None of the options   **(SSC CPWD 2015)**

    (b) change with change in current

    (c) change with change in voltage

    (d) do not change with voltage and current

227. The unit for permeability is:

    (a) $\dfrac{\text{Wb}}{\text{At} \times \text{m}}$ (b) $\dfrac{\text{At}}{\text{m}}$

    (c) Wb   (d) $\dfrac{\text{At}}{\text{Wb}}$

                                        (SSC CPWD 2015)

228. The Superposition theorem is used when the circuit contains: **(SSC CPWD 2015)**

    (a) a single voltage source

    (b) passive elements only

    (c) active elements only

    (d) a number of voltge sources

229. If the number of turns of a coil is increased, its inductance. **(SSC CPWD 2015)**

    (a) none of the options   (b) is increased

    (c) is decreased   (d) remains the same

230. A dc voltmeter has a sensitivity of 1000 Ω/volt. When it measures half full scale in 100V range, the current through the voltmeter will be?

    (a) 50 mA   (b) 1 mA

    (c) 0.5 mA   (d) 100 mA

                                        (SSC CPWD 2015)

231. Mutual inductance between two coils is 4 H. If current in one coil changes at the rate of 2A/sec, then emf induced in the other coil is?

    (a) 8 V   (b) 2 V

    (c) 0.5 V   (d) 5.0 V

                                        (SSC CPWD 2015)

232. The e.m.f. induced in a coil of N turns is given by: **(SSC CPWD 2015)**

    (a) $N\dfrac{d\phi}{dt}$ (b) $-N\dfrac{d\phi}{dt}$

    (c) $\dfrac{d\phi}{dt}$ (d) $N\dfrac{dt}{d\phi}$

233. To prepare a P type semiconducting material the impurities to be added to silicon are?

    (a) Boron, Gallium

    (b) Arsenic, Antimony

    (c) Gallium, Arsenic

    (d) Gallium, Phosphorous **(SSC CPWD 2015)**

234. A bar of Iron I cm² in cross section has 10^{-4} wb of magnetic flux in it. If μr = 2000. What is the magnetic field intensity in the bar?

    (a) $796 \times 10^3 \dfrac{\text{AT}}{\text{m}}$

    (b) $398 \dfrac{\text{AT}}{\text{m}}$

    (c) $398 \times 10^{-4} \dfrac{\text{AT}}{\text{m}}$

    (d) $398 \times 10^4 \dfrac{\text{AT}}{\text{m}}$ **(SSC CPWD 2015)**

235. An amplifier has a gain of 10,000 expressed in decibels the gain is? **(SSC CPWD 2015)**

    (a) 10   (b) 40

    (c) 100   (d) 80

236. The current 'I' in the electric circuit shown below is? **(SSC CPWD 2015)**

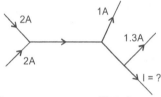

    (a) 3.7 A   (b) 1 A

    (c) 2.7 A   (d) 1.7 A

237. If two capacitances C_1 and C_2 are connected in parallel then the equivalent capacitance is given by **(SSC CPWD 2015)**

    (a) C1 C2   (b) $\dfrac{C_1 C_2}{C_1 + C_2}$

    (c) C1 + C2   (d) C1 | C2

238. If the co-efficient of coupling between two coils is increased, mutual inductance between the coils

    (a) changes depend on current only

    (b) is increased

    (c) is decreased

    (d) remains unchanged   **(SSC CPWD 2015)**

239. When a series RL circuit is connected to a voltage source V at t = 0, the current passing through the inductor L at t = 0+ is

    (a) infinite   (b) $\dfrac{V}{L}$

    (c) zero   (d) $\dfrac{V}{R}$

                                        (SSC CPWD 2015)

ANSWERS

EXERCISE – I

1. (d)	2. (a)	3. (a)	4. (c)	5. (b)	6. (a)	7. (b)	8. (b)	9. (a)	10. (a)
11. (a)	12. (d)	13. (a)	14. (d)	15. (a)	16. (c)	17. (c)	18. (c)	19. (a)	20. (c)
21. (b)	22. (d)	23. (a)	24. (a)	25. (a)	26. (a)	27. (c)	28. (b)	29. (a)	30. (c)
31. (a)	32. (d)	33. (a)	34. (c)	35. (a)	36. (d)	37. (c)	38. (a)	39. (b)	40. (b)
41. (a)	42. (b)	43. (a)	44. (c)	45. (a)	46. (a)	47. (b)	48. (c)	49. (b)	50. (c)
51. (c)	52. (a)	53. (b)	54. (b)						

EXERCISE – II

1. (c)	2. (c)	3. (c)	4. (b)	5. (a)	6. (b)	7. (c)	8. (c)	9. (c)	10. (c)
11. (d)	12. (d)	13. (a)	14. (a)	15. (a)	16. (d)	17. (c)	18. (c)	19. (a)	20. (c)
21. (c)	22. (d)	23. (b)	24. (b)	25. (a)	26. (d)	27. (d)	28. (c)	29. (a)	30. (a)
31. (d)	32. (a)	33. (a)	34. (a)	35. (d)	36. (b)	37. (a)	38. (b)	39. (a)	40. (a)
41. (c)	42. (b)	43. (b)	44. (a)	45. (d)	46. (a)	47. (d)	48. (b)	49. (b)	50. (c)
51. (b)	52. (b)	53. (d)	54. (d)	55. (d)	56. (a)	57. (b)	58. (d)	59. (b)	60. (b)
61. (c)	62. (c)	63. (a)	64. (a)	65. (d)	66. (a)	67. (c)	68. (c)	69. (d)	70. (a)
71. (d)	72. (b)	73. (a)	74. (b)	75. (a,d)	76. (b)	77. (d)	78. (c)	79. (c)	80. (b)
81. (b)	82. (d)	83. (c)	84. (a)	85. (a)	86. (c)	87. (d)	88. (c)	89. (b)	90. (a)
91. (c)	92. (a)	93. (a)	94. (d)	95. (b)	96. (b)	97. (d)	98. (a)	99. (b)	100. (d)
101. (a)	102. (a)	103. (c)	104. (d)	105. (c)	106. (d)	107. (b)	108. (b)	109. (c)	110. (c)
111. (b)	112. (b)	113. (a)	114. (d)	115. (a)	116. (a)	117. (d)	118. (a)	119. (c)	120. (c)
121. (d)	122. (b)	123. (c)	124. (d)	125. (d)	126. (b)	127. (b)	128. (b)	129. (d)	130. (a)
131. (b)	132. (b)	133. (b)	134. (b)	135. (d)	136. (a)	137. (a)	138. (d)	139. (a)	140. (d)
141. (a)	142. (c)	143. (a)	144. (c)	145. (c)	146. (c)	147. (c)	148. (d)	149. (a)	150. (d)
151. (d)	152. (b)	153. (b)	154. (a)	155. (d)	156. (a)	157. (c)	158. (d)	159. (b)	160. (a)
161. (b)	162. (b)	163. (c)	164. (d)	165. (c)	166. (c)	167. (d)	168. (a)	169. (d)	170. (d)
171. (c)	172. (a)	173. (d)	174. (d)	175. (d)	176. (d)	177. (d)	178. (d)	179. (b)	180. (c)
181. (a)	182. (d)	183. (c)	184. (b)	185. (b)	186. (a)	187. (a)	188. (c)	189. (b)	190. (b)
191. (b)	192. (a)	193. (b)	194. (d)	195. (b)	196. (b)	197. (a)	198. (c)	199. (a)	200. (c)
201. (a)	202. (d)	203. (d)	204. (a)	205. (d)	206. (a)	207. (a)	208. (d)	209. (c)	210. (c)
211. (b)	212. (b)	213. (b)	214. (a)	215. (b)	216. (a)	217. (b)	218. (c)	219. (c)	220. (d)
221. (b)	222. (c)	223. (*)	224. (c)	225. (d)	226. (d)	227. (a)	228. (d)	229. (a)	230. (c)
231. (a)	232. (b)	233. (a)	234. (b)	235. (b)	236. (d)	237. (c)	238. (b)	239. (c)	

2

CHAPTER

D.C. Machines

TYPE OF DC MOTORS

Similar to dc generators, the dc motors may also be put into the following three categories on the basis of field excitation:

1. *Shunt motor* – field winding in shunt with the armature
2. *Series motor* – field winding in series with the armature
3. *Compound motor* – one fielding winding in series with armature and another in shunt

1. Shunt Motor.

Field winding is placed in shunt with the armature. This winding draws a separate current I_{sh} from the mains. The field winding consists of a large number of fine wires on each pole. Usually windings on all the poles are connected in series.

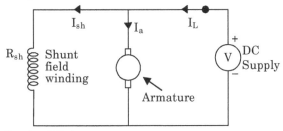

2. Series Motor.

The field winding is placed in series with the armature. Thus the armature current I_a itself flows through the field windings. Series field winding consists of a few turns of thick copper wire on each pole and all these windings on different poles are connected in series.

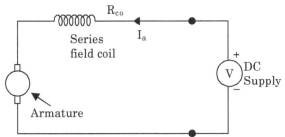

3. Compound Motor.

Compound motor uses two field windings. The series winding is placed in series with the supply and the armature shown in figure. It consists of a few turns of thick copper wire on each pole, all connected in series. The shunt winding is placed in parallel with the armature as shown in figure. The shunt field

winding consists of a large number of fine wire on each pole, all connected in series.

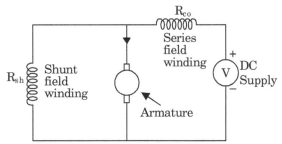

PRINCIPLE OF WORKING OF A DC MOTOR

A dc motor is a machine which converts dc power into mechanical power. Its operation is based on the principle that when a current carrying conductor is placed in a magnetic field, the conductor experiences a mechanical force. The direction of this force is given by Fleming's left hand rule and the magnetic force F is given by

$$F = BI\,l \text{ newtons.}$$

Construction of a dc motor is basically similar to a dc generator. Hence the same dc machine may be used either as a dc generator or a dc motor. Finally like dc generator, dc motors are also series wound, shunt wound and compound wound.

Production of Torque in a dc Motor. Figure shows a part of a multiple dc motor. When the field magnets are excited and current is sent through the armature conductors, then the conductors experience a force tending to rotate the armature. Let the armature conductors under north pole carry current in the direction normal to the surface of paper in figure and pointing into the paper as shown by the crosses. Similarly let conductors under south pole carry current in the direction normal to the surface of paper and pointing out as shown by the dots. Application of Fleming's left hand rule gives the direction of the force exerted on each conductor.

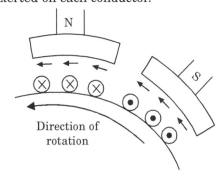

Direction of rotation

This direction is anticlockwise as shown by the small arrows placed above each conductor. This force exerted on armature conductor tends to rotate the armature in the anticlockwise direction as shown in figure. These forces on conductor add up to produce the driving torque, which causes rotation of the armature.

Function of Commutator. Function of commutator in a dc motor is the same as in dc generator. Thus it reverses the current in each conductor as it passes from one pole to another. This results in a continuous and unidirectional torque.

BACK EMF

In a dc motor, as the armature rotates, its conductors also rotate and cut the flux of the poles. Hence as per laws of electromagnetic induction, emf is induced in the conductors. As per Fleming's right hand rule, the direction of this emf is opposite to the applied voltage. Hence this emf is called the counter emf or *back emf* V_b. Obviously then the applied voltage V has to drive armature current I_a in the presence of opposing back emf V_b. The power required to overcome this opposition is $V_b . I_a$.

Magnitude of back emf may be calculated using the same emf equation as used for dc generator.

$$\text{Back emf} \qquad V_b = \frac{\phi NZ}{60} . \frac{P}{A} \text{ volt}$$

where ϕ N, Z, P and A have the same meanings as in dc generator.

Presence of back emf makes a dc motor self-regulating i.e. it makes motor to draw the armature current just sufficient to develop the torque needed by the load. Back emf among other factors, depends on the armature speed. If speed is high, V_b is large and armature current I_a being equal to $(V - V_b)/R_a$ is small. On the other hand, if speed is low, back emf V_b is small and armature current is large resulting is larger torque. Thus we find that like a governor, the back emf makes a motor self regulating, permitting it to draw the current just necessary for torque needed.

DC GENERATOR

Function. A dc generator is an electromagnetic machine, which converts mechanical energy into dc electrical energy.

Principle. Whenever magnetic flux is cut by a conductor, an emf is induced in the conductor as per Faraday's law of electromagnetic induction. This voltage so induced is basically an a.c. voltage. It is made unidirectional with the help of commutator and brushes. This emf causes flow of current in the external circuit if the circuit is closed.

Essential Parts of a DC Generator

(*i*) Magnetic field created by electromagnet

(*ii*) Conductors housed in armature slots

(*iii*) Motion of conductors cutting the magnetic field

(*iv*) Commutator and brushes to collect the voltage and convert it into unidirectional voltage.

Difference in the Structures of DC and AC Generators. In a dc generator, magnetic field is stationary and the conductors move through the field. In an a.c. generator, conductors are stationary and the magnetic fields move.

SPLIT RING LOOP GENERATOR

Fig. (a) gives the basic structure. A single turn rectangular coil ABCD rotates about its own axis within the magnetic field created by either permanent magnet or an electromagnet. The two terminals of the coil are connected to split rings made out of a conducting cylinder cut into two halves or segments insulated from each other by a thin sheet of an insulating material typically mica. Coil terminals are joined to these segments on which rest the carbon or copper brushes as shown in Fig. (*a*) These brushes collect the voltage induced in the coil and to apply it to the external load resistor R_L. The magnets are called the field magnets since they create the magnetic field and similarly call the rotating coil as the armature.

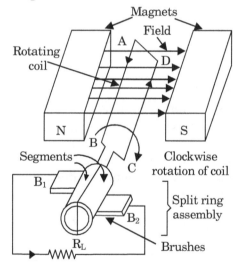

(a) Split ring loop generator

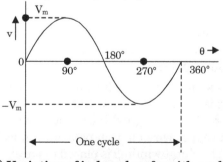

(b) Variation of induced emf v with angle θ coil

Smoothening of Output Voltage and Current. Output voltage waveform is not smooth and involves large variations. This defect may be overcome to a large extent by dividing the commutator ring into 4 parts connected to the coil terminals. For output voltage to be quite smooth, a brush is connected to a segment for only one-fourth revolution i.e. for 90 degrees.

Classification of Transformers base on Construction

Transformers may be classified into the following three types depending on the type of laminated core:

1. *Core type transformer* with single magnetic circuit

2. *Shell type transformer* with double magnetic circuit

3. *Berry type transformer* with distributed magnetic circuit

1. **Core Type Transformer.** Fig(*a*) shows the general shape of core type transformer. The core is built up of iron or alloyed steel sheets or laminations assembled to provide a continuous magnetic path with minimum air gap. Laminated structure is used to reduce the eddy current losses. Average thickness of sheet is 0.35 mm for a frequency of 50 Hz. Laminations are insulated from each other by a thin coat of varnish or oxide layer. Fig (*b*) shows a typical method of arranging the core strips. Here the joints in alternate layers are staggered in order to avoid the presence of narrow gap right through the cross-section of the core. Such a joint is called an *imbricated joint.*

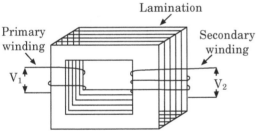

(a) Core type transformer

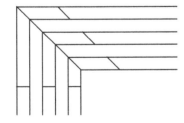

(b) Imbricated joints

In small size transformers, core has rectangular cross-section. However, in large transformers, it is preferred to use an approximately circular cross-section since such a section has the smallest perimeter for a given area and hence it requires less copper in the form of wire, than the rectangular section. In very large transformers, strips may be used in packets with duct in between. These ducts help in ventilation.

In the simplified diagram of Fig (*a*) the primary and the secondary windings are placed on the opposite limbs of the core. However, in practice, the two windings are interleaved to reduce leakage flux. Thus half of the primary winding and half of the secondary winding are placed on each limb either side by side or concentrically with high voltage winding surrounding the low voltage winding with insulation in between the layers and heavy insulation between the windings.

2. **Shell Type Transformers.** Figure shows the section of the laminated core. This section has double magnetic circuit. Shell type transformerdiffers from the core type in that it has two magnetic circuits instead of one. Both the primary and secondary windings are placed on the central limb. Further in core type transformer, the two winding ususally multilayered, almost fully surround the core while in shell type transformer, the two outer section of the core almost fully surround the windings.

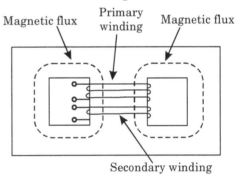

3. **Berry type transformer.** It is basically shell type transformer but in this case, the core consists of laminations arranged in groups, which radiate out from the centre.

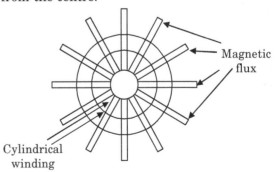

Berry type transformer

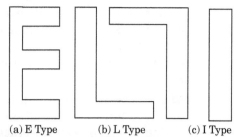

(a) E Type   (b) L Type   (c) I Type

Shapes of Laminations. Individual laminations in all types of transformers are usually cut in the form of long strips of E, L and I shapes

Placement of Windings . The primary and the secondary windings may be either of

(i) *cylindrical or concentric type* or

(ii) *sandwich type*

Fig. (a) shows coaxial windings while Fig. (b) shows sandwich type windings where primary and secondary windings are placed side by side. The concentric type windings are used mainly on core type transformers while *sandwich type* windings are used mainly on shell type transformers.

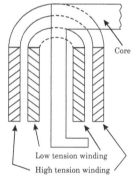

(a) Concentric or cylindrical type windings

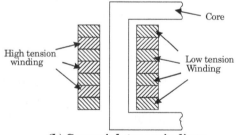

(b) Sanswich type windings

CONSTRUCTION OF A PRACTICAL DC GENERATOR

Basic structure of a commercial dc generator consists of following basic parts:

1. **Field System**
   (i)   Metallic frame or yoke
   (ii) Pole cores and pole shoes
   (iii) Field coils or pole coils
2. Armature core
3. Armature winding
4. Commutator
5. Brushes and bearings

Out of these, the yoke, pole core and pole shoes, and armature core constitute the magnetic circuit while the pole coils, armature winding, commutator and brushes form the electrical circuit.

IMPORTANT TERMS CONCERNING ARMATURE WINDING

Pole Pitch. It is generally defined as the number of armature slots per pole. Thus if there are 4 poles and 48 conductor slots, then pole pitch is 48/4 = 12.

Conductor. By conductor is meant the metallic wire housed in the conductor slot in the armature and in which the emf is induced.

Coil Pitch (Coil Span)Y_s. It is the distance between the two sides of a coil measured in terms of armatures slots.

If the coil pitch is equal to the pole pitch, the winding is said to be *full-pitched*. In such a case, coil span is 180° electrical degrees and the coil sides lie under opposite poles. Then the induced emfs in the coil sides are in phase and additive and maximum emf is induced in the coil, being equal to twice that in each coil side. Thus if there are 4 poles and 40 slots, the coil span is 40/4 = 10 slots.

If the coil pitch is less than the pole pitch, the winding is said to be *fractional pitched*. In such a coil, the emfs induced in the two coil sides are not in phase and do not fully add up. Output emf of the coil, being the vector sum of emf's of the two coil sides, is less than that obtained in full-pitched coil. In commercial dc generators, coil pitch as low as 0.8 of pole pitch is used to cause saving in copper of the end connections and for improving commutation.

Pitch of a Winding (Y). This the distance (in terms armature slots) around the armature between two successive conductors which are directly connected together or the distance between the beginning of two consecutive turns.

Back Pitch (Y_B) . It is the distance (in terms of armature slots), which a coil advances on the back of the armature. Thus if element 1 is connected on the back of armature to element 7, then $Y_B = 7 - 1 = 6$.

Front Pitch (Y_F). It is the number of armature conductors spanned by a coil on the front or the commutator end of an armature. Thus if element 7 is connected to element 3 on the front end of the armature, then the front pitch $Y_F = 7 - 3 = 4$.

Resultant Pitch (Y_R). It is the distance between the beginning of one coil and the beginning of the next coil to which it is connected.

Commutator Pitch (Y_C) . It is distance (in terms of commutator bars or segments) between the segments to which the two ends of a coil are connected.

Single Layer Winding. It is the armature winding in which only one conductor or one coil side is placed in each armature slot. These are not used popularly.

Multilayer Winding. It is the armature winding in which two or more conductors or coil sides are placed in each armature slot, usually in two layers.

LAP AND WAVE WINDINGS

The lap and wave windings differ regarding the arrangement of the end connection at the front or commutator end of armature.

Features of Common to Lap or Wave Windings

(*i*) Front pitch and back pitch are each approximately equal to the pole pitch i.e. windings should be full pitched.

(*ii*) Both front and back pitches should be odd, otherwise it is difficult to place former wound coils properly on the armature.

(*iii*) Number of commutator segment is equal to the number of slots because the front ends of conductors are jointed to the segments in pairs.

(*iv*) The winding must close upon itself.

Lap Winding. In lap winding, the finishing end of one coil is connected to a commutator segment and to the starting end of the adjacent coil situated under the same pole and so on till all the coils have been connected. Fig.(*a*) gives the arrangement for single turn coils. The name lap winding is used because the winding doubles up or laps back with its succeeding coils.

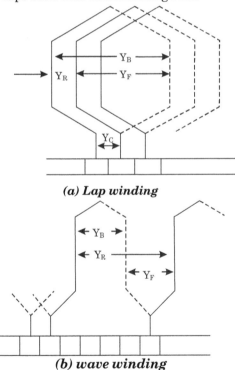

(a) Lap winding

(b) wave winding

Wave Winding. In wave winding, a conductor (or coil side) under one pole is connected at the back to a conductor, which occupies an almost corresponding position under the next pole. Fig (*b*) shows the arrangement for single turn coils.

Relative Performance of Lap and Wave Windings

Merits of Wave Winding.

(*i*) More emf than lap winding for a given number of poles and armature conductors. Thus for the same emf, wave winding requires smaller number of conductors resulting in lower winding cost and more efficient utilization of space in armature slots.

(*ii*) Equalizing connections are necessary.

Limitation of Wave Winding. It is suitable for low current high voltage (600 volts) generators.

Merit of Lap Winding. Since it uses more number of parallel paths, it is useful for large current, low voltage generators.

Armature Resistance R_a. It is the resistance between the armature terminals and includes the resistance of armature conductors and brushes. It is generally small and depends on

(*a*) Number and size of armture conductors

(*b*) Type of armature winding

(*c*) Contact resistance between carbon brushes and the commutator.

TYPES OF DC GENERATOR

DC generators are generally classified according to the method used for field excitation. Thus dc generators may be classified as:

1. **Separately Excited Generator.** In this generator, the fieldelectromagnet is energized from an external independent source such as a battery or a separate small dc generator called the exciter.

2. **Self Excited Generator.** In this generator, the current through the field electromagnetic is supplied from the generator output itself. Self excited generator may be put into three categories depending on where the field coil is placed in series, in parallel or both.

   (*i*) **Series Wound Self-excited Generator.** In this generator, the field windings are placed in series the armature conductors . As a result, the entire armature current I_a flows through the field coil and the load. Since the field windings carry the full load current, they consist of only a few turns of thick wire or strips having low resistance.

   (*ii*) **Shunt Wound Self Excited Generator.** In this generator, the field windings are placed in shunt, i.e. in parallel with the armature conductors with the result that the full generator voltage gets applied across the windings. The shunt field winding uses large number of turns of fine wire. The coil resistance is, therefore, high. As a result only a small part of armature current flows through the field windings.

(iii) Compound Wound Self Excited Generator.
In this generator, there are two sets of field windings on each pole, one in series and the other in parallel with the armature.

Compound wound generators may be of two types :

(a) Short Shunt Compound Wound Generator. The shunt coil is placed directly across the armature while series coil is placed in series with the load.

(b) Long Shunt Compound Wound Generator.
The shunt coil is placed in parallel with both armature and the series coil.

In a compound wound generator, the shunt field is stronger than the series field. When the series field aids the shunt field, the generator is said to be commutatively compounded. On the other hand, if series field oppose the shunt field, the generator is said to be differentially compounded.

EFFICIENCY OF GENERATOR

Out of the total input mechanical power, a part is lost as iron losses and friction losses. The balance power constitutes the electrical power $V_g I_a$ developed in the armature as shown in figure. Out of the total electric power developed in armature, a part is loss as copper losses while the balance of electric power is available at the output.

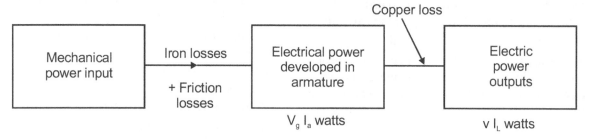

Power losses in a dc generator

Mechanical Efficiency : η_m = Electrical power generated in armature = $\dfrac{V_g I_a}{\text{output of driving engine}}$

Electrical Efficiency : $\eta_e = \dfrac{\text{Electrical power at the output}}{\text{Electrical power generated in armature}} = \dfrac{VI_L}{V_g I_a}$

Overall Efficiency or Commercial Efficiency :

$$\eta_c = \dfrac{\text{Electrical power at the output}}{\text{Mechanical power input to Machine}} = \dfrac{VI_L}{\text{output of driving engine}}$$

Evidently $\eta_c = \eta_m \times \eta_c$. In a good quality generator, overall efficiency may be as high as 95%.

DC GENERATOR CHARACTERISTICS

Following are the important characteristics of a dc generator :

(i) Open Circuit Characteristics V_g - I_f. This curve plots open circuit or no load generated emf V_g against field current I_f at a constant armature speed. This characteristic is basically the magnetization curve of the material of the electromagnets. The shape of this characteristic is practically the same for all generators whether self excited or separately excited.

(ii) Internal or Total Characteristic (V_g - I_a). This plots the emf V_g actually induced in the armature (after allowing for the magnetizing effect of armature reaction) against the armature current I_a. When the generator is supplying load to the external circuit, the total flux gets reduced due to the armature reaction. Hence actually generated emf V_g is less than the emf V_{go} generated under no load condition.

(iii) External Characteristic (V_L – I_L). It plots the terminal voltage V_L against load current I_L. This characteristic is also called the *performance characteristic* or the *voltage regulation characteristic*.

EXERCISE – I

1. Carbon brushes are used in electric motors to
   (a) prevent sparking during commu-tation
   (b) provide a path for flow of current
   (c) brush off carbon deposits on the commutator
   (d) none of these

2. Interpoles in dc motors are used for
   (a) increasing the speed of motor
   (b) reducing sparking at the commu-tator
   (c) decreasing the counter emf
   (d) converting armature current to dc

3. The air gap between stator and armature of an electric motor is kept as small as possible
   (a) to get a stronger magnetic field
   (b) to improve the air circulation
   (c) to reach a higher speed of rotation
   (d) to make the rotation easier

4. Small dc motors upto 5 HP usually have
   (a) 2 poles   (b) 4 poles
   (c) 6 poles   (d) 8 poles

5. A dc motor can be easily identified by
   (a) yoke   (b) size of conductor
   (c) commutator   (d) winding

6. In dc motor, the rotor is
   (a) welded to the shaft
   (b) keyed to the shaft
   (c) soldered to the shaft
   (d) bolted to the shaft

7. In a dc motor, pole shoes are fixed to the magnet core by
   (a) set of screws   (b) key
   (c) soldering   (d) welding

8. The armature of a dc motor is laminated
   (a) to reduce hysteresis loss
   (b) to reduce eddy current loss
   (c) to reduce the cost of core
   (d) to reduce the mass of the armature

9. The value of diverter resistance for a series dc motor is of the order of
   (a) 0.1Ω (b) 2Ω
   (c) 20Ω (d) 400Ω

10. The resistance of the field regulator of a dc shunt motor is of order of
    (a) 0.1Ω (b) 1Ω
    (c) 10Ω (d) 100Ω

11. The dc compound motors are generally
    (a) cumulative compound
    (b) differential compound
    (c) level compound
    (d) none of these

12. The resistance of the starter of a 220 v, 5 HP dc shunt motor is of the order of
    (a) 0.01Ω (b) 0.1Ω
    (c) 1Ω (d) 10Ω

13. In a dc motor, unidirectional torque is produced with the help of
    (a) brushes   (b) commutator
    (c) end plates   (d) both (a) and (b)

14. The back emf of a dc motor
    (a) adds to the supply voltage
    (b) regulates its armature voltage
    (c) helps in energy conversion
    (d) usually exceeds the supply voltage

15. In a dc motor, the ratio of back emf to supply emf is an indication of its
    (a) efficiency
    (b) speed regulation
    (c) starting torque
    (d) running torque

16. The mechanical power developed by the armature of a dc motor is equal to
    (a) power input minus copper loss
    (b) armature current multiplied by back emf
    (c) armature current multiplied by supply emf
    (d) power input minus mechanical losses

17. The armature torque of a dc motor is a function of its
    (a) field flux alone
    (b) armature current alone
    (c) speed alone
    (d) both field flux and armature current

18. The shaft torque of a dc motor is less than its armature torque because of
    (a) copper losses
    (b) mechanical losses
    (c) back emf
    (d) rotational losses

19. Under constant load condition, the speed of a dc motor is effected by
    (a) field flux alone
    (b) armature current alone
    (c) back emf
    (d) both armature current and field flux

20. If the load on a dc shunt motor is increased, its speed decreases primarily due to
    (a) increase in its flux
    (b) decrease in back emf
    (c) increase in armature current
    (d) decrease in brush drop

21. If the pole flux of a dc motor approaches zero, its speed will
    (a) approach zero
    (b) approach infinity
    (c) not change
    (d) approach a stable value between zero and infinity

22. As the load on a dc shunt motor is increased, its speed
    (a) increases proportionately
    (b) remains constant
    (c) increases slightly
    (d) reduces slightly

23. When load is removed, which of the following dc motors will run at excessively high speed ?
    (a) shunt motor
    (b) series motor
    (c) cumulative compound motor
    (d) differential compound motor

24. Speed of a dc motor may be varied by varying
    (a) field current
    (b) applied voltage
    (c) resistance in series with armature
    (d) any of these

25. In a dc motor, maximum power is developed when supply voltage is equal to
    (a) $\frac{1}{2}$ back emf
    (b) $\sqrt{2}$ back emf
    (c) 2 back emf
    (d) $\frac{1}{\sqrt{2}}$ back emf

26. The speed of a series wound dc motor
    (a) can be controlled by shunt field regulator
    (b) can not be controlled by diverter
    (c) increases as flux decreases
    (d) increases as armature circuit resistance increases

27. The speed of a dc motor is
    (a) always constant
    (b) directly proportional to back emf
    (c) directly proportional to flux
    (d) inversely proportional to the product of back emf and flux.

28. The highest speed attained by a dc shunt motor at rated flux is
    (a) infinity
    (b) higher than no load speed
    (c) equal to the no load speed
    (d) lower than the no load speed

29. The speed of a dc shunt motor is required to be more than full load speed. This may be achieved by
    (a) increasing the armature current
    (b) decreasing the armature current
    (c) increasing the excitation current
    (d) reducing the field current

30. If the speed of a dc shunt motor increases, the back emf
    (a) increases
    (b) decreases
    (c) remains unchanged
    (d) first increases and then decreases

31. For a dc motor operating under condition of maximum transfer of power, the efficiency of the motor is
    (a) 100%   (b) about 90%
    (c) 75%   (d) less that 50%

32. DC motors are considered most suitable for the applications in
    (a) fans   (b) water pumps
    (c) traction (d) flour mills

33. Which of the following dc motors will have least percentage increase in input current for a given percentage increase in torque ?
    (a) series motor
    (b) shunt motor
    (c) separately excited motor
    (d) cumulatively compound motor

34. Which dc motor will have highest precentage increase in input current for a given percentage increase in torque ?
    (a) series motor
    (b) shunt motor
    (c) cumulatively compound motor
    (d) separately excited motor

35. In a dc series motor, the shaft torque is less than the armature torque due to

(a) eddy current losses

(b) stray losses

(c) hysteresis losses

(d) copper losses

36. If the applied voltage to a dc shunt motor is halved and the load torque doubled, the armature current will be

(a) unaltered   (b) zero

(c) doubled   (d) halved

37. The starting resistance of a dc motor is usually

(a) infinitely large   (b) large

(c) about 100Ω (d) small

38. Which of the following dc motor has approximately constant speed ?

(a) series motor

(b) shunt motor

(c) cumulatively compound motor

(d) differentially compound motor

39. The back emf of a dc motor depends on

(a) field flux   (b) shape of conductors

(c) type of slip rings   (d) brush material

40. The back emf of dc motor depends on

(a) armature speed N

(b) field fllux ϕ

(c) number of armature conductors

(d) all of these

41. In a dc machine dull yellow spark indicates

(a) winding fault

(b) excessive brush wear

(c) excessive noise

(d) none of these

42. If the supply voltage to a shunt motor is increased by 25%, which of the following will decrease ?

(a) starting torque

(b) full load speed

(c) full load current

(d) none of these

43. In dc motor, which of the following part can withstand the maximum rise in temperature ?

(a) armature winding

(b) field winding

(c) commutator winding

(d) slip rings

44. A dc shunt motor has external resistance R_1 in the field circuit and resistance R_2 in the armature circuit. The starting armature current for the motor will be minimum when

(a) R_1 is minimum and R_2 is maximum

(b) R_1 maximum and R_2 is minimum

(c) both R_1 and R_2 are maximum

(d) both R_1 and R_2 are minimum

45. Two dc series motors are mechanically coupled. One machine runs as motor and the other as generator. The iron losses of the two machines will be identical when

(a) both have the same excitation

(b) both have the same speed

(c) both have the same back emf

(d) both operate at the same voltage

46. The brush voltage drops in dc motors in / of the order of

(a) 2 V   (b) 10 V

(c) 20 V   (d) 40 V

47. Frog leg winding is

(a) same as simplex winding

(b) same as duplex winding

(c) combined lap and wave windings on a single rotor

(d) duplex wave winding on a single rotor

48. In a compound dc motor, the shunt field winding as compared to series winding will have

(a) more turns of smaller diameter

(b) less turns of larger diameter

(c) more turns of larger diameter

(d) less turns of smaller diameter

49. The flux is maximum in following unit of a dc motor

(a) yoke

(b) leading end of pole shoe

(c) trailing end of pole shoe

(d) any of the above

50. In dc motor, the amount of flux leakage depends on

(a) length of air gap

(b) shape of the magnet core

(c) flux density used in core and teeth

(d) all of these

51. In a dc motor, the flux leakage coefficient is typically
(a) 0.5 to 0.7   (b) 0.8 to 1.0
(c) 1.1 to 1.3   (d) 1.4 to 1.6

52. The direction of rotation of a dc motor can be reversed by reversing the connection to
(a) armature   (b) series field
(c) shunt field   (d) any of the above

53. The current flowing in conductors of a dc motor is
(a) ac   (b) dc
(c) ac as well as dc (d) transient

54. Torque of a motor is
(a) force in N-m acting on the rotor
(b) product of tangential force on the rotor and its radius
(c) the electrical power in kW
(d) power given to the load

55. The output power of any electrical motor is taken from
(a) the armature
(b) the conductors
(c) the coupling mounted on the shaft
(d) the poles

56. Which of the following statements about a series motor is correct
(a) It can run easily without load.
(b) It has poor torque.
(c) It has an almost constant speed.
(d) Its field winding consists of small number of thick wires.

57. The speed of a series dc motor at no load is
(a) zero
(b) medium
(c) high
(d) tending to infinity

58. The speed of a dc series motor decreases if the flux in the field winding
(a) remains constant   (b) increases
(c) decreases   (d) none of these

59. The direction of rotation of a dc series motor can be reversed by interchanging
(a) the supply terminals only
(b) the field terminals only
(c) the supply and the field terminals
(d) none of these

60. The armature reaction in a dc motor is attributed to
(a) the effect of magnetic field set up by field current
(b) the effect of magnetic field set up by armature current
(c) copper losses in the armature
(d) the effect of magnetic field set up by back emf

61. When an electric traian is moving down a hill, the dc motor acts as
(a) dc series motor   (b) dc shunt motor
(c) dc series generator (d) dc shunt generator

62. The armature current drawn by a dc motor is proportional to
(a) the speed of the motor
(b) flux required in the moor
(c) torque required
(d) voltage applied to the motor

63. A dc shunt motor is driving a constant torque load with rated excitation. If the field current is reduced to half, then the speed of the motor will become
(a) half
(b) slightly more than half
(c) double
(d) slightly less than double

64. A dc shunt motor is driving a mechanical load at rated voltage and rated excitation. If the load torque becomes double, then the speed of the motor
(a) increases slightly
(b) decreases slightly
(c) becomes double
(d) becomes half

65. A dc series motor is running with a diverter connected across its field winding. If the diverter resistance is increased, then the speed of the motor
(a) decreases/increase
(b) increase
(c) remains unchanged
(d) becomes very high

66. A dc series motor is running at rated speed. If a resistance is placed in series, the speed of the motor
(a) increases
(b) decreases
(c) remains unchanged
(d) increases very much

67. In a dc shunt motor, field excitation is kept at maximum value during starting to
(a) increase acceleration time
(b) reduce armature heating
(c) prevent voltage dip in the supply mains
(d) decrease starting torque

68. The back emf Vb of a dc motor
(a) opposes the applied voltage
(b) assists the applied voltage
(c) does not influence the applied voltage
(d) none of these

69. All d.c. machines are characterized by
(a) electric brushes   (b) armature
(c) commutator   (d) magnetic poles

70. Armature voltage control is suitable if d.c. machine is driven at constant
(a) torque   (b) magnetic field
(c) speed   (d) current

71. Current normally used to excite synchronous and d.c. generators is
(a) D.C.   (b) A.C. single phase
(c) A.C. two phase   (d) A.C. three phase

72. In all electric machines, basic action taking place is
(a) motor action   (b) generator action
(c) both (a) and (b)   (d) all of these

73. In case of a motor
(a) only motor action takes place
(b) motor action precedes generator action
(c) generator action precedes motor action
(d) both take place precedes simultaneously

74. All rotating machines are basically
(a) D.C. machines
(b) A.C. machines
(c) electro-mechanical convertors
(d) heat converters

75. All machines have the structure such that
(a) armature is rotating and field is fixed
(b) field is rotating and armature is fixed
(c) either (a) or (b)
(d) none of these

76. All electrical machines have poles with
(a) a hetro-polar structure
(b) a horse shoe structure
(c) (a) above (b)
(d) none of these

77. Maximum number of brushes which can be used in a machine is
(a) 2
(b) 4
(c) 6
(d) number of poles in the machine or 2

78. Which of the following motors has high starting torque?
(a) D.C. shunt motor
(b) Induction motor
(c) D.C. series motor
(d) A.C. series motor

79. What is the standard direction of a motor?
(a) clockwise   (b) anti-clockwise
(c) none of these   (d) either (a) or (b)

80. Left hand rule is applicable to
(a) motor
(b) generator
(c) transformer
(d) mercury are rectifier

81. Effect of armature flux on the main flux in a d.c. motor is that
(a) it inclines lines of force through the air gap such that they do not remain radial.
(b) it makes distribution of the flux density across both sections unequal
(c) both (a) and (b)
(d) none of these

82. Speed of d.c. series motor at no load is
(a) infinity   (b) 3000 rpm
(c) 1500 rpm   (d) zero

83. Function of the commutator in a d.c. machine is
(a) for easy speed control
(b) to improve commutation
(c) to change a.c. to d.c.
(d) to change alternating voltage to direct voltage

84. If back e.m.f. suddenly disappears in a d.c. motor
(a) nothing will happen
(b) windings will burn due to high armature current
(c) motor will start acting as a generator
(d) motor will stop

85. Direction of rotation of a d.c. series motor can be changed by interchanging
(a) voltage terminals   (b) field terminals
(c) both (a) and (b)   (d) none of these

86. If a d.c. motor is connected across a.c. supply, the motor will

(a) run at normal speed

(b) run at lower speed

(c) burn

(d) run continuosly but for sparking at brushes

87. Voltage applied across the shunt motor has to

(a) overcome the back emf

(b) supply armature ohmic drop

(c) supply fied ohmic drop

(d) both (a) and (b)

88. If back emf of a d.c. motor is doubled while its speed is also doubled, then torque developed by the machine will

(a) remain same   (b) become four times

(c) double   (d) becomes half

89. If field of d.c. shunt motor is opened, then

(a) current in the armature will increase

(b) it will run at its normal speed

(c) speed of motor will be reduced

(d) speed of motor will be high

90. For a series motor, field flux is

(a) constant

(b) proportional to armature current

(c) proportional to temperature

(d) inversely proportional to armature current

91. Field flux is constant in

(a) series motor   (b) compound motor

(c) shunt motor   (d) none of these

92. Dummy coil in a d.c. machine is used to

(a) eliminate reactance voltage

(b) eliminate armature reaction

(c) for mechanical balance of armature

(d) none of these

93. Four point in d.c. motor is used

(a) to decrease the field current

(b) to increase the field current

(c) not to affect the current through hold on coil even if any change in field current takes place

(d) none of these

94. Torque speed characteristic of a series motor is

(a) linear

(b) parabola

(c) rectangular hyperbola

(d) none of these

95. Shunt motor has

(a) widely varying speed

(b) constant speed

(c) low speed at high loads and high speed at low loads

(d) low speed at low loads and high speed at high loads

96. In series-paralled control method when two d.c. series motors are connected in series, speed of the set is

(a) same as in parallel

(b) rated speed of any of the motors

(c) half of the speed of the motors

(d) one fourth of the speed of the motors

97. Torque produced by series combination of two d.c. series motor is

(a) four times the torque when they are connected in parallel

(b) equal to the torque when they are connected in parallel

(c) twice the torque when they are connected in parallel

(d) half the torque when they are connected in parallel

98. For most of the application purpose

(a) series motor is used

(b) shunt motor is used

(c) compound motor is used

(d) depends on requirement

99. Use of the starter in d.c. motors is necessary becaues

(a) to overcome back emf

(b) they are not self starting

(c) to limit the high intial current by inserting high resistance

(d) none of these

100. Speed of the d.c. motor can be varied by

(a) varying field current

(b) varying armature resistance

(c) varying supply voltage

(d) either (b) or (c)

101. As the load is increased, speed of d.c. shunt motor will

(a) reduce slightly

(b) increase slightly

(c) remains constant

(d) none of these

102. Field flux of d.c. motor can be controlled to
 (a) steady speed
 (b) speeds above rated speed
 (c) speeds below rated speed
 (d) speeds above and below rated speed

103. If field current of a shunt motor is changed, then
 (a) horse power remains constant but torque will change
 (b) torque remains constant but h.p will change
 (c) both will change
 (d) both remains constant

104. Synchronous reactance is defined as reactance
 (a) due to leakage flux
 (b) of synchronous machine
 (c) due to armature reaction of the machine
 (d) due to armature reaction and leakage of flux both

105. Armature winding of a series motor is excited
 (a) inductively
 (b) resistively
 (c) conductively
 (d) none of these

106. Speed of a d.c. motor depends upon
 (a) armature resistance
 (b) field flux
 (c) applied voltage
 (d) all of these

107. In the field flux method of speed control
 (a) speeds above normal speed can be attained
 (b) speeds below normal speed can be attained
 (c) any speed can be attained
 (d) none of these

108. Dynamic braking is generally used for
 (a) series motors
 (b) shunt motors
 (c) compound motors
 (d) all of these

109. Stalling current is the maximum value of
 (a) field current for which speed is maximum
 (b) load current for which speed is zero
 (c) diverter current for which speed is maximum
 (d) load current for which speed is maximum

110. Torque developed in d.c. motor depends on
 (a) magnetic field
 (b) armature
 (c) speed
 (d) both (a) and (b)

111. Which method of speed control has minimum efficiency?
 (a) armature control method
 (b) voltage control method
 (c) field control method
 (d) none of these

112. In ward-Leonard system, minimum number of machines required are
 (a) two
 (b) three
 (c) four
 (d) five

113. Ward-Leonard method is basically a
 (a) field control method
 (b) field diverter method
 (c) voltage control method
 (d) armature resistance control method

114. Disadvantage of ward-Leonard system is
 (a) its high initial cost
 (b) increased maintenance cost
 (c) its low efficiency at light loads
 (d) all of them

115. Speed regulation of a d.c. motor can be ideally achieved with
 (a) no excitation to the field of the motor
 (b) constant excitation to the field of the motor
 (c) variable excitation to the field of the motor
 (d) A.C. excitation to the field of the motor

116. Disadvantage of the field-control method of speed control is
 (a) its low efficiency
 (b) that speeds above normal speed can be achieved
 (c) that commutation becomes unsatisfactory
 (d) none of these

117. If plugging is applied to series motor for a long time, then
 (a) motor will burn
 (b) motor will stop
 (c) it will start revolving in other direction at low speed
 (d) none of these

118. In case of regenerative braking, the motor
 (a) dissipates energy in armature circuit
 (b) dissipates energy in field circuit
 (c) both (a) and (b)
 (d) supply energy to source

119. The operation of an electric motor or generator is based on

(a) the law of electromagnetic induction

(b) interaction between magnetic field and current carrying conductor

(c) interaction between two electric fields

(d) interaction between magnetic field and electric field

120. All rotating electric machines are basically

(a) d.c. machines

(b) a.c. machines

(c) electro-mechanical convertors

(d) machines using electromagnetic induction

121. All rotating electrical machines have

(a) rotating armature and fixed field

(b) rotating field and fixed armature

(c) either (a) or (b)

(d) none of these

122. In any dc generators, the emf generated in the armature is maximum when

(a) rate of change of flux linkage is minimum

(b) rate of change of flux linkage is maximum

(c) flux linkage with conductors is maximum

(d) flux linkage with conductors is minimum

123. All dc machines are characterized by

(a) armature   (b) commutator

(c) magnetic poles   (d) electric brushes

124. $V \times B = e$ is the equation of the electrical machines which

(a) is a dc machines

(b) has magnetic poles

(c) works as a motor

(d) converts mechanical energy into electrical energy

125. The function of commutator in a dc machine is

(a) to improve commutation

(b) to change dc voltage into dc voltage

(c) to change ac voltage into dc voltage

(d) to provide easy speed control

126. Under commutation in a dc machine gives rise to

(a) sparking at the leading edge of the brush

(b) sparking at the trailing edge of the brush

(c) no sparking at all

(d) sparking at the middle of the brush

127. In a dc generator, if the brushes are given a small amount of forward shift, the effect of armature reaction is

(a) totally demagnetising

(b) totally magnetising

(c) partly demagnetising and partly cross-magnetising

(d) totally cross-magnetising

128. A conductor is rotating within a magnetic field. At which of the following positions do the zero voltages occur ?

(a) along the axis of the magnetic field

(b) at right angles to the axis of the magnetic field

(c) at 45° with the axis of the magnetic field

(d) none of these

129. In a dc machine, the laminated parts are the armature core and

(a) base   (b) yoke

(c) shaft   (d) pole shoes

130. The commutator in dc machine works as

(a) mechanical inverter

(b) mechanical rectifier

(c) energy converter

(d) either (a) or (b)

131. Which of the following forms an energy converter?

(a) piezo-electric effect

(b) magneto-striction effect

(c) Hall effect

(d) all of these

132. Commutation is possible in dc machines

(a) only when the field is rotating in the armature

(b) only when the armature is rotating in the field

(c) either (a) or (b)

(d) none of these

133. Which of the following parts helps the commutation process ?

(a) interpoles

(b) compensating winding

(c) pole shoes

(d) all of these

134. Commutation segments in a dc machine are separated by thin layers of

(a) synthetic rubber

(b) mica

(c) paper

(d) PVC

135. Commutation in a dc machine may be improved by
  (a) reducing to number of turns in the armature and segments of commu-tator
  (b) increasing the resistances of brushes
  (c) neutralizing the reactance voltage by producing a reverse emf in the coil undergoing commutation
  (d) all of these

136. In the commutation process in a dc machine, which of the following quantity reverses ?
  (a) the voltage
  (b) the current
  (c) both voltage and current
  (d) none of these

137. Increase in the number of com-mutator segments of a dc machine results in
  (a) increase in the total output power
  (b) decrease in the total output power
  (c) increase in the magnitude of output voltage
  (d) smoothening of the shape of output dc wave

138. Each commutator segment is connected to the armature conductor by means of
  (a) insulator
  (b) copper lug
  (c) resistance wire
  (d) carbon brush

139. Brushes for commutator are made of
  (a) copper
  (b) aluminium
  (c) carbon
  (d) synthetic rubber

140. In a dc generator, brushes are always placed
  (a) along geometrical neutral axis (GNA)
  (b) along magnetic neutral axis (MNA)
  (c) along bisector of GNA and MNA
  (d) arbitrarily

141. In dc generators, brushes remain in contact with the conductors which lie
  (a) under north pole
  (b) under south pole
  (c) in the interpolar region
  (d) arbitrarily

142. In a dc generator, sparking between brushes and commutator surface may be due to
  (a) overcommutation
  (b) undercommutation
  (c) to rapid reversal of current
  (d) any of these

143. In a dc generator, rapid brush wear may be due to
  (a) rough commutator surface
  (b) severe sparking
  (c) imperfect contact with commutator
  (d) any of these

144. In a dc machine commutator, pre-ssure on the brush is usually
  (a) less than 1 kg/cm^2
  (b) about 3 kg/cm^2
  (c) about 5 kg/cm^2
  (d) about 10 kg/cm^2

145. Brushes for commutators for 220 V dc generator are generally made of
  (a) copper
  (b) carbon copper
  (c) electrographite
  (d) graphited copper

146. Carbon brushes are used in dc machines to
  (a) brush off carbon deposits in the commutator
  (b) provide a path for flow of current
  (c) prevent overheating of armature winding
  (d) prevent sparking during commu-tation

147. Commutator of a dc machine acts as a
  (a) fullwave rectifier
  (b) halfwave rectifier
  (c) inverter
  (d) controlled rectifier

148. The commutator pitch of a quadruplex lap winding in a dc generator is
  (a) 1
  (b) 2
  (c) 4
  (d) 8

149. The maximum number of brushes which may be used in an electrical machine is equal to
  (a) number of poles in the machine
  (b) 2
  (c) 4
  (d) either (a) or (b)

150. In a dc generator, sparking at brushes results due to
  (a) winding distribution
  (b) armature reactance
  (c) high constant resistance of the brushes
  (d) reactance voltage in coil undergoing commutation

151. Equalizer rings in lap wound armatures are used to
  (a) get sparklers commutation
  (b) avoid unequal current distribution at brushes
  (c) both (a) and (b)
  (d) to neutralize the armature reaction

152. Which winding on dc generators is preferred for generating large current ?

(a) lap winding

(b) progressive wave winding

(c) retrogressive wave winding

(d) all winding give similar results

153. Equalizer rings can be used by

(a) lap wound armatures only

(b) wave wound armatures only

(c) both lap and wave wound armatures

(d) none of these

154. The function of equalizing ring in lap wound dc generator is

(a) to avoid short circuit current

(b) to neutralize the armature reaction

(c) to help get sparklers commutation

(d) to increase the efficiency of the machine

155. In a ring wound commutator, the brush width equals the width of

(a) one commutator segment and one mica insulation

(b) one commutator segment and two mica insulations

(c) two commutator segments and two mica insulations

(d) two commutator segments and one mica insulation

156. In a dc machine without interpoles, to get improved commutation, the brush shift angle must be

(a) varied with change in load

(b) kept constant

(c) zero degree

(d) none of the above

157. In a dc generator, the polarity of the interpole is

(a) always N

(b) always S

(c) same as the main pole ahead

(d) same as the main pole behind

158. In a dc generator, compared to the air gap under field poles, the interpole air gap is made

(a) larger

(b) smaller

(c) the same

(d) much smaller

159. The function of using compensating winding in dc machines is to neutra-lize the

(a) armature reaction in the interpole zone

(b) armature reaction in the commu-tating zone

(c) armature reaction under the pole faces

(d) cross-magnetizing armature reaction

160. The yoke of a dc generator is made of cast iron because

(a) it is cheaper

(b) it completes the magnetic path

(c) it gives mechanical protection to the machine

(d) all of these

161. The conductors of the compensating winding are housed

(a) entirely in the armature slots

(b) entirely in the slots in the pole faces

(c) partly in armature slots and partly in slots in pole faces

(d) around the pole core

162. The armature mmf waveform in a dc machine is

(a) pulsating

(b) rectangular

(c) triangular

(d) sinusoidal

163. Armature magnetic field in a dc generator produces which of the following effect ?

(a) It demagnetizes or reduces the main flux

(b) It cross-magnetizes the main flux

(c) It magnetizes or reinforces the main flux

(d) Both (a) and (a)

164. In a dc generator, in armature conductor along MNA

(a) maximum current is produced

(b) maximum emf is produced

(c) minimum emf is produced

(d) minimum current is produced

165. A dc shunt generator driven at normal speed in the normal direction fails to build up armature voltage because

(a) the resistance of the armature is high

(b) there is no residual magnetism

(c) the field current is too small

(d) none of these

where ϕ is the flux and N is the speed

166. In a dc machine, the armature mmf is always directed along the
    (a) polar axis
    (b) brush axis
    (c) interpolar axis
    (d) none of these

167. In dc machines, armature windings are placed on the rotor because of the necessity for
    (a) electromechanical energy conversion
    (b) generation of voltage
    (c) commutation
    (d) development of torque

168. Armature in a dc machine is made of laminated steel instead of wood because it has
    (a) low permeability
    (b) high permeability
    (c) more mechanical strength
    (d) more mechanical strength and high permeability

169. Copper losses in armature of dc generator amount to which of the following percentage of full load losses ?
    (a) 5 to 10%
    (b) 10 to 20%
    (c) 20 to 30%
    (d) 30 to 40%

170. Stray losses in a dc generator are the same as
    (a) mechanical losses
    (b) magnetic losses
    (c) both (a) and (b) added together
    (d) none of these

171. Standing or constant losses of a dc generator are
    (a) field losses of shunt generator
    (b) armature losses of a compound generator
    (c) stray losses
    (d) both (a) and (b) added together

172. Out of the following four sources of losses in a dc generator which one is minimum ?
    (a) copper losses
    (b) hysteresis losses
    (c) eddy current losses
    (d) windage losses

173. Overall efficiency of dc generators is usually of the order of
    (a) 60 to 70 %
    (b) 70 to 80%
    (c) 80 to 90 %
    (d) 85 to 95 %

174. DC shunt generator has terminal voltage versus load current characteristic which is
    (a) constant
    (b) slightly drooping
    (c) slightly rising
    (d) highly drooping

175. Which of the following type of dc generator gives constant output voltage at all loads ?
    (a) shunt generator
    (b) series generator
    (c) shot shunt compound generator
    (d) level compound generator

176. The terminal voltage of dc shunt generator drops on load because of
    (a) armature reaction
    (b) armature resistance
    (c) weakening of the field due to armature reaction
    (d) all of these

177. If the load on an overcompounded dc generator is reduced, the terminal voltage
    (a) increases
    (b) decreases
    (c) remains unchanged
    (d) may increase or decrease

178. Main reason for break point in the load characteristic of a dc generator is
    (a) armature drop
    (b) armature reaction
    (c) both (a) and (b)
    (d) none of these

179. The internal characteristic of generator is the curve between
    (a) armature current and generated emf
    (b) load current and terminal voltage
    (c) field current and no load voltage
    (d) armature current and IR drop

180. The load characteristic of a gene-rator is the curve between
    (a) load voltage and field current
    (b) generated emf and armature current
    (c) load current and terminal voltage
    (d) load current and voltage drop in armature winding

181. An ideal dc generator has regulation of
    (a) zero
    (b) 20%
    (c) 30%
    (d) 40%

182. Equalizer connections are required when paralleling two
    (a) bipolar generators
    (b) shunt generators
    (c) series generators
    (d) compound generators

183. Generators are often run in parallel because it
    (a) keeps stability of supply
    (b) gives facility of repair which results in fewer breakdown
    (c) gives facility of an additional unit to be installed as and when required
    (d) all of these

184. Two dc shunt generators are operating in parallel. If it is desired to shut down one of the generators
    (a) its main switch is suddenly opened
    (b) its field current is gradually reduced
    (c) the input to its prime mover is suddenly reduced to zero
    (d) none of these

185. In dc generator, the principal reasons for delay in the reversal of current is
    (a) reactance voltage
    (b) the capacitor action with two segments as electrodes and mica as the dielectric
    (c) the air gap between the brushes and the commutator surface
    (d) none of these

186. The critical resistance of dc generator is the resistance of
    (a) field   (b) brush
    (c) armature   (d) compensating pole

187. One method of neutralizing the armature reaction in a dc generator is to
    (a) shift the brushes in lagging direction of rotation
    (b) shift the brushes in leading direction of rotation
    (c) interchange the terminals at the brushes
    (d) none of these

188. The critical resistance of a dc gene-rator can be increased by
    (a) increasing the field current
    (b) increasing its speed
    (c) increasing the armature resistance
    (d) all of these

189. A series dc generator does not build up voltage. The reason is
    (a) short circuited terminals
    (b) reversed terminal of field winding
    (c) reversed terminal of armature winding
    (d) disconnected load

190. Residual magnetism is necessary in
    (a) self excited generator
    (b) separately excited generator
    (c) both (a) and (b)
    (d) none of these

191. If number of poles in a lap wounded generator is increased by a factor 2, then generated emf will
    (a) increase by a factor of 4
    (b) remain same
    (c) increase by a factor 2
    (d) decrease by a factor 2

192. Which of the following accounts for smallest part of full load losses?
    (a) magnetic losses
    (b) mechanical losses
    (c) field copper loss
    (d) armature copper loss

193. Stray losses in a d.c. generator are same as
    (a) mechanical losses
    (b) magnetic losses
    (c) windage losses
    (d) both (a) and (b)

194. Efficiency of a d.c. shunt generator is maximum when
    (a) stray losses are equal to copper losses
    (b) magnetic losses are equal to mechanical losses
    (c) armature copper losses are equal to constant losses
    (d) field copper losses are equal to constant losses

195. Constant losses of a d.c. generator are defined as
    (a) stray losses
    (b) field losses of shunt generator
    (c) armature losses of a compound generator
    (d) both (b) and (c)

196. Equilizer ring in the lap winding of d.c. generator are used to
    (a) avoid overhang
    (b) avoid noise
    (c) avoid harmonics
    (d) avoid unequal distribution of current at brushes

197. D.C. generator have normally an over-all efficiency of the order of
    (a) 85 — 95%   (b) 75 — 85%
    (c) 65 — 75%   (d) 55 — 65%

198. Sparking at the brushes in the d.c. generator is due to
(a) high resistance of the brushes
(b) reactance voltage
(c) armature reaction
(d) quick reversal of current in the coil

199. Armature magnetic field has the effect that it
(a) cross magnetizes it
(b) demagnetizes it
(c) strengthens the main flux
(d) both (a) and (b)

200. Brushes are always placed along
(a) Geometrical neutral axis
(b) Magnetic neutral axis
(c) perpendicular to magnetic neutral axis
(d) none of these

201. Interpoles in the armature of d.c. generator are used to
(a) neutralize the reactance voltage only
(b) neutralize the reactance voltage and cross-magnetization effect of armature reaction
(c) neutralize demagnetization effect
(d) none of these

202. Function of compensating winding is to neutralize
(a) cross-magnetization effect of armature reaction
(b) demagnetization effect of armature reaction
(c) reactance voltage
(d) all of these

203. Critical resistance of the d.c. generator is the resistance of
(a) field   (b) load
(c) brushes   (d) armature

204. In the commutation process
(a) current is reversed
(b) voltage is reversed
(c) both current and voltage are reversed
(d) none of these

205. Difference between interpoles and compensation winding is that
(a) interpoles additionally supply mmf for counter acting the reactance voltage induced in the coil under going commutalion
(b) action of interpoles is localized
(c) interpoles also helps in equalizing distribution of current in brushes
(d) both (a) and (b)

206. Generator is called flat compounded if
(a) rated voltage is less than no load voltage
(b) series field AT produces same voltage at rated and no load
(c) series field AT produces rated voltage greater than no load
(d) series field AT produces rated voltage less than no load

207. Commutation process can be improved by
(a) increasing the resistance of the brushes
(b) reducing the number of turns in armature coil
(c) neutralizing reactance voltage
(d) all of these

208. When two d.c. series generators are running in parallel, equalizer bar is used
(a) to increase the series flux
(b) because both will pass equal currents to the load
(c) to reduce combined effect of armature reaction of both
(d) to increase speed and hence generated emf.

209. In d.c. generator, if field winding attains critical resistance then it will
(a) not develop voltage at all
(b) generate maximum power
(c) generate maximum voltage
(d) none of these

210. For paralleling two d.c. generators, their
(a) polarities must be same
(b) phase sequence must be same
(c) polarities and voltage must be same
(d) both (b) and (c)

211. Equalizer rings can be used by
(a) lap wound armature
(b) wave wound armature
(c) both (a) and (b)
(d) none of these

212. Generators are often run in parallel because of
(a) greater reliabilty
(b) greater efficiency
(c) meeting more load demands
(d) all of these

213. External characteristics of a d.c. generator can be obtained by
(a) internal characteristic
(b) no load saturation characteristic
(c) both (a) and (b)
(d) none of these

214. Commutator machines can be of the type of
(a) d.c. machines
(b) a.c. machines
(c) universal machines
(d) all of these

215. Which of the following is most suitable for parallel operation?
(a) series generator
(b) shunt generator
(c) compound generator
(d) any one of them

216. Critical resistance is resistance of the field winding of a generator
(a) at which it develops maximum voltage
(b) at which it supply maximum power
(c) beyond which it can not develop any voltage
(d) at which the speed of generator is infinity

217. With the increase of field winding of a d.c. generator, terminal voltage will
(a) decrease
(b) increase
(c) remain same
(d) none of these

218. A shunt generator do not build up any voltage at no load because
(a) shunt coil may be connected in reverse direction
(b) there is no residual magnetism in the poles
(c) its shunt field resistance is more than critical resistance
(d) any one of the above

219. Drop in the terminal voltage of a shunt generator under load conditions is due to
(a) armature resistance drop
(b) armature reaction
(c) decrease in field current
(d) all of them

220. Lap winding in a lap wound d.c. generator is provided because it
(a) makes the current distribution at brushes equal to avoid sparks
(b) helps the noiseless operation of the machine
(c) provides a path for the circulation of unbalanced current
(d) provides mechanical strength for the winding of the armature

221. Main reason of drop due to armature reaction in a d.c. generator is
(a) armature flux due to armature current
(b) load current
(c) shunt and series field current
(d) none of these

222. If there is no saturation of flux in the poles of a d.c. generator, then it will
(a) not run
(b) burn due to extraordinarily high potential building up in the armature
(c) not build up any voltage
(d) run under unstable operating conditions.

223. In an over compounded generator, field turns are adjusted such that no load voltage is
(a) equal to the rated load voltage
(b) greater than rated load voltage
(c) less than rated load voltage
(d) none of these

224. If a.c. voltage is applied on the field of d.c. generator, then output will be
(a) d.c. voltage
(b) a.c. voltage
(c) no output
(d) none of these

225. A series generator, any voltage may not build up because
(a) field winding is revervsed
(b) load is connected
(c) very high load is connected
(d) none of these

226. Which generators are in hotels and office building?
(a) under-compounded generators
(b) over-compounded generators
(c) flat-compounded generators
(d) none of these

227. Critical resistance of a d.c. generator can be increased by
(a) increasing its speed
(b) decreasing its armature resistance
(c) decreasing its speed
(d) none of these

228. Over-compounded generator is used for
(a) long distance transmission
(b) short distance transmission
(c) medium distance transmission
(d) none of these

EXERCISE – II

1. Which one of the following is **not** a part of typical TV receiver ? **(RRB 2012)**

   (a) Sweep signal generator

   (b) Envelope detector

   (c) Video amplifier

   (d) Pre-emphasis circuit

2. A DC chopper is used in regenerative braking mode of a dc series motor. The dc supply is 600 V, the duty cycle is 70%. The average value of armature current is 100 A. It is continuous and ripple free. What is the value of power fedback to the supply ?

   (a) 3 kW   (b) 9 kW

   (c) 18 kW   (d) 35 kW **(RRB 2012)**

3. A cumulatively compound dc motor runs at full load speed of 720 rpm. Now if the series field of the motor is short circuited, then the full load speed will be **(RRB 2012)**

   (a) still 720 rpm

   (b) more than 720 rpm

   (c) less than 720 rpm

   (d) zero

4. When the direction of power flow reverses, a differentially compounded motor becomes

   (a) differentially compounded generator

   (b) cumulatively compounded generator

   (c) a shunt generator

   (d) a series generator   **(RRB 2012)**

5. Torque of a motor is

   (a) force in N-m acting on the rotor

   (b) product of tangential force on the rotor and its radius

   (c) the electrical power in kW

   (d) power given to the load   **(RRB 2012)**

6. A d.c. shunt motor is excited from an alternating power frequency voltage source. Its brush–axis is rotated by an angle α from the geometrical neutral axis. The torque developed will be proportional to which one of the following?

   (a) sin α   (b) cos α

   (c) tan α   (d) cos 2α

   (RRB 2012)

7. In dc motor, the rotor is

   (a) welded to the shaft

   (b) keyed to the shaft

   (c) soldered to the shaft

   (d) bolted to the shaft   **(RRB)**

8. Under constant load condition, the speed of a dc motor is effected by **(RRB)**

   (a) field flux alone

   (b) armature current alone

   (c) back emf

   (d) both armature current and field flux

9. If 220 V dc series motor is connected to a 220 V ac supply, then at will **(RRB)**

   (a) not run

   (b) burn out

   (c) run smoothly

   (d) run with less efficiency and high sparking

10. In dc generator, the principal reasons for delay in the reversal of current is

    (a) reactance voltage

    (b) the capacitor action with two segments as electrodes and mica as the dielectric

    (c) the air gap between the brushes and the commutator surface

    (d) none of these   **(RRB)**

11. Equilizer ring in the lap winding of d.c. generator are used to

    (a) avoid overhang

    (b) avoid noise

    (c) avoid harmonics

    (d) avoid unequal distribution of current at brushes   **(RRB)**

12. In d.c. generator, if field winding attains critical resistance then it will

    (a) not develop voltage at all

    (b) generate maximum power

    (c) generate maximum voltage

    (d) none of these   **(RRB)**

13. Which of the following is most suitable for parallel operation?

    (a) series generator

    (b) shunt generator

    (c) compound generator

    (d) any one of them   **(RRB)**

14. Which generators are in hotels and office building?

    (a) under-compounded generators

    (b) over-compounded generators

    (c) flat-compounded generators

    (d) none of these   **(RRB)**

15. For the same rating which of the following motors has the highest starting torque ?

(a) Universal motor

(b) Split phase motor

(c) Synchronous motor

(d) all have identical starting torque   **(RRB)**

16. Carbon brushes are used in electric motors to

(a) prevent sparking during commutator

(b) provide a path for flow of current

(c) brush off carbon deposits on the commutator

(d) none of these   **(RRB)**

17. If the load on a dc shunt motor is increased, its speed decreases primarily due to   **(RRB)**

(a) increase in its flux

(b) decrease in back emf

(c) increase in armature current

(d) decrease in brush drop

18. The speed of a series dc motor at no load is

(a) zero

(b) medium

(c) high

(d) tending to infinity   **(RRB)**

19. Dummy coil in a d.c. machine is used to

(a) eliminate reactance voltage

(b) eliminate armature reaction

(c) for mechanical balance of armature

(d) none of these   **(RRB)**

20. The pitch factor in rotating electrical machines is defined as the ratio of the resultant emf of a

(a) full pitched coil to that of a chorded coil

(b) full pitch to the phase emf

(c) chorded coil to the phase emf

(d) chorded coil to that of a full pitched coil **(RRB)**

21. Generators kept for spinning reserve are

(a) not in operation

(b) kept running on light loads

(c) kept running on heavy loads

(d) none of these   **(RRB)**

22. Carbon brushes are used in electric motors to

(a) prevent sparking during commu-tation

(b) provide a path for flow of current

(c) brush off carbon deposits on the commutator

(d) none of these   **(DMRC 2013)**

23. Under constant load condition, the speed of a dc motor is effected by   **(DMRC 2013)**

(a) field flux alone

(b) armature current alone

(c) back emf

(d) both armature current and field flux

24. DC motors are considered most suitable for the applications in   **(DMRC 2013)**

(a) fans

(b) water pumps

(c) traction

(d) flour mills

25. If 220 V dc series motor is connected to a 220 V ac supply, then at will   **(DMRC 2013)**

(a) not run

(b) burn out

(c) run smoothly

(d) run with less efficiency and high sparking

26. If the back emf of a dc motor suddenly vanishes

(a) the motor will run faster

(b) the motor will start hunting

(c) the efficiency of the motor will increase

(d) the motor will burn out   **(DMRC 2013)**

27. Torque of a motor is

(a) force in N-m acting on the rotor

(b) product of tangential force on the rotor and its radius

(c) the electrical power in kW

(d) power given to the load   **(DMRC 2013)**

28. Two dc series motors connected in series are driving the same mechanical load. If now the motors are connected in parallel, the speed becomes   **(DMRC 2013)**

(a) slightly more than double

(b) slightly less than double

(c) slightly more than half

(d) slightly less than half

29. Speed regulation of a d.c. motor can be ideally achieved with   **(DMRC 2013)**

(a) no excitation to the field of the motor

(b) constant excitation to the field of the motor

(c) variable excitation to the field of the motor

(d) A.C. excitation to the field of the motor

30. Which of the following type of dc generator gives constant output voltage at all loads ?

    (a) shunt generator

    (b) series generator

    (c) shot shunt compound generator

    (d) level compound generator **(DMRC 2013)**

31. Equilizer ring in the lap winding of d.c. generator are used to **(DMRC 2013)**

    (a) avoid overhang

    (b) avoid noise

    (c) avoid harmonics

    (d) avoid unequal distribution of current at brushes

32. Cogging of motor implies that motor

    (a) runs at very low speed

    (b) runs at low speed and then stops

    (c) refuses to start at no load

    (d) refuses to start at load **(DMRC 2013)**

33. The drive generally used for lathe machines are

    (a) squirrel cage induction motors

    (b) synchronous motors

    (c) slip ring induction motors

    (d) dc shunt motors **(DMRC 2013)**

34. Which of the following single phase motors is cheapest ? **(DMRC 2013)**

    (a) Capacitor start motor

    (b) Capacitor run motor

    (c) Reluctance motor

    (d) All have almost the same cost

35. Which of the following single phase motors is relaively free from mechanical and magnetic vibration? **(DMRC 2013)**

    (a) Reluctance motor

    (b) Hysteresis motor

    (c) Universal motor

    (d) Shaded pole motor

36. The motor used in ceiling fans is

    (SSC, CPWD 2008)

    (a) Resistance split phase motor

    (b) Capacitor start motor

    (c) Capacitor start capacitor run motor

    (d) Slip ring motor

37. For battery charging, which of the following DC generators is used? **(SSC, CPWD 2008)**

    (a) DC series generator

    (b) DC shunt generator

    (c) Short shunt compound generator

    (d) Long shunt compound generator

38. The no load speed of DC series motor is

    (a) very small

    (b) medium

    (c) very high

    (d) small **(SSC, CPWD 2008)**

39. A 4 pole, 1200 rpm DC lap wound generator has 1520 conductors. If the flux per pole is 0.01 weber, the emf of generator is **(SSC, CPWD 2010)**

    (a) 608 volts   (b) 304 volts

    (c) 152 volts   (d) 76 volts

40. The condition for a maximum power output from dc motor is **(SSC, CPWD 2010)**

    (a) $E_b = V$ (b) $E_b = \dfrac{V}{2}$

    (c) $E_b = 0$ (d) $E_b = \dfrac{V}{\sqrt{2}}$

41. In Swinburne's method of testing dc machines, the shunt machine is run as a **(SSC, CPWD 2011)**

    (a) motor at full load at rated speed and rated voltage

    (b) generator at full load at rated speed and rated voltage

    (c) generator at no load at rated speed and rated voltage

    (d) motor at no load at rated speed and rated voltage

42. The brushes of a dc machine should be physically placed on the **(SSC, CPWD 2011)**

    (a) armature in the polar axis

    (b) armature in the interpolar axis

    (c) commutation in the polar axis

    (d) commutator in the interpolar axis

43. A dc shunt generator is delivering 500 A at 220 V. The shunt field current is 10 A. The armature resistance is 0.01 Ω. The stray power is 5000 W. The efficiency of the generator is

    (SSC, CPWD 2011)

    (a) 91.09%   (b) 95.82%

    (c) 95.64%   (d) 91.82%

44. The motor characteristics best suited for traction purpose are those of **(SSC, CPWD 2012)**

(a) D.c. series motor

(b) Synchronous motor

(c) Induction motor

(d) D.c. shunt motor

45. A lap wound dc generator having 250 armature conductor runs at 1200 rpm. If the generated emf is 200 V, then the operating flux of the dc generator is **(SSC, CPWD 2012)**

(a) 0.08 wb   (b) 0.04 wb

(c) 0.06 wb   (d) 0.02 wb

46. The highest speed attainable by d.c. shunt motor is **(SSC, CPWD 2012)**

(a) Much higher than no-load speed

(b) Much lower than no-load speed

(c) Ideally infinite

(d) Equal to no-load speed

47. The direction of rotation of a d.c. shunt motor can be reversed by interchanging **(SSC, CPWD 2012)**

(a) The armature terminals only

(b) Either field or armature terminals

(c) The supply terminals

(d) The field terminals only

48. Pole of d.c. machines are often laminated to reduce **(SSC, CPWD 2012)**

(a) Eddy current loss

(b) Iron weight

(c) Armature reaction

(d) Hysteresis loss

49. Universal motor is a _____ motor.

(a) Series

(b) Single phase induction

(c) Synchronous

(d) Shunt **(SSC, CPWD 2012)**

50. Which of the following motors can work satisfactorily on both AC and DC ?

(a) Series motor

(b) Shunt motor

(c) Induction motor

(d) Synchronous motor **(SSC, CPWD 2012)**

51. The load characteristic of dc shunt generator is determined by **(SSC, CPWD 2013)**

(a) the voltage drop in armature resistance

(b) the voltage drop due to armature reaction, voltage drop due to decreased field current and voltage drop in armature resistance

(c) the voltage drop due to armature reaction and voltage drop in armature resistance.

(d) the voltage drop due to armature reaction, voltage drop due to decreased field current and voltage drops in armature resistance and field resistance

52. How many watt-seconds are supplied by a motor developing 2 hp (British) for 5 hours? **(SSC, CPWD 2013)**

(a) 2.6856×10^7 watt-seconds

(b) 4.476×10^5 watt-seconds

(c) 2.646×10^7 watt-seconds

(d) 6.3943×10^6 watt-seconds

53. A 4-pole generator is running at 1200 rpm. The frequency and time period of the emf generated is its coils are respectively **(SSC, CPWD 2013)**

(a) 50 Hz, 0.02 sec.

(b) 40 Hz, 0.025 sec.

(c) 300 Hz, 0.00333 sec.

(d) 2400 Hz, $\dfrac{1}{2400}$ sec.

54. If the supply polarity to the armature terminals of a separately excited d.c. motor is reversed, the motor will run under. **(SSC, CPWD 2013)**

(a) Plugging condition

(b) Regenerative braking condition

(c) Dynamic braking condition

(d) Normal motoring condition

55. A dc series motor has an armature resistance of 0.06 Ω and series field resistance of 0.08 Ω. The motor is connected to a 400 V supply. The line current is 20 A when the speed of the machine is 1100 rpm. when the line current is 50 A and the excitation is increased by 30%, speed of the machine in rpm is **(SSC, CPWD 2013)**

(a) 1100   (b) 1003

(c) 837   (d) 938

56. The speed-torque characteristic of a dc series motor operating from a constant voltage supply is **(SSC, CPWD 2013)**

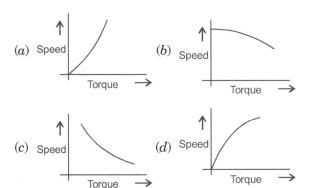

57. A universal motor is one which **(SSC, CPWD 2013)**

(a) can run on any value of supply voltage

(b) has infinitely varying speed

(c) can operate on ac as well as dc voltage

(d) can work as single-phase or three-phases motor

58. The commutator in a d.c. machine acts as **(SSC, CPWD 2013)**

(a) a mechanical inverter

(b) a mechanical rectifier

(c) current controller

(d) either (a) or (b)

59. The purpose of using dummy coil in d.c. machines is to **(SSC, CPWD 2013)**

(a) eliminate harmonics developed in the machine

(b) eliminate armature reaction

(c) bring mechanical balance of the armature

(d) bring mechanical balance of the body of the motor

60. For a 6-pole d.c. machine with wave wound armature, the number of brushes required is **(SSC, CPWD 2013)**

(a) 2   (b) 4

(c) 6   (d) 12

61. Function of interpoles in a d.c. machine is to **(SSC, CPWD 2013)**

(a) reduce field winding heating

(b) improve commutation

(c) compensate for air-gap variation

(d) reduce losses

62. The commutator segments of d.c. machine are made of **(SSC, CPWD 2013)**

(a) tungsten   (b) hard-drawn copper

(c) soft copper   (d) electrolytic copper

63. Which of the following motors can be run on A.C. as well as D.C. supply ? **(SSC, CPWD 2014)**

(a) Reluctance motor

(b) Universal motor

(c) Repulsion motor

(d) synchronous   motor

64. A 150 V d.c. motor of armature resistance 0.4 Ω has back emf of 142 V. The armature current is : **(SSC, CPWD 2014)**

(a) 100 A   (b) 10 A

(c) 20 A   (d) 150 A

65. The rated speed of a given d.c. shunt motor is 1050 r.p.m. To run this machine at 1200 r.p.m the following speed control scheme will be used : **(SSC, CPWD 2014)**

(a) Varying frequency

(b) Armature circuit resistance control

(c) Field resistance control

(d) Ward-Leonard control

66. In which single – phase motor, the rotor has no teeth or winding ? **(SSC, CPWD 2014)**

(a) Universal motor

(b) Split phase motor

(c) Reluctance motor

(d) Hysteresis motor

67. Two $d.c$ series motors connected in series draw current I from supply and run at speed N. When the same two motors are connected in parallel taking current I from the supply, the speed of each motor will be : **(SSC, CPWD 2014)**

(a) $\dfrac{N}{2}$ (b) N

(c) 2N   (d) 4N

68. Which of the following motor has high starting torque ? **(SSC, CPWD 2014)**

(a) synchronous motor

(b) a.c. series motor

(c) d.c. series motor

(d) induction motor

69. Commutation conditions at full load for large DC machines can be efficiently checked by the

    (a) Brake test   (SSC CPWD 2014)
    (b) Swinburne's test
    (c) Hopkinson's test
    (d) Field test

70. The emf induced in a DC shunt generator is 230 V. The armature resistance is 0.1 Ω. If the armature current is 200 A, the terminal voltage will be

    (a) 200 V
    (b) 210 V
    (c) 230 V
    (d) 250 V   (SSC CPWD 2014)

71. The commutator of a DC generator acts as,

    (a) an amplifier
    (b) a rectifier
    (c) a load
    (d) a multiplier   (SSC CPWD 2014)

72. A vacuum cleaner employs —— motor.

    (a) resistance split phase
    (b) capacitor start
    (c) shaded pole
    (d) single phase series   (SSC CPWD 2014)

73. Which of the following applications needs frequent starting and stopping of electric motor ?
                            (SSC CPWD 2014)

    (a) Air-conditioner
    (b) Lifts and hoists
    (c) Grinding mill
    (d) Paper mill

74. As the load is increased, the speed of a dc shunt motor

    (a) Remains constant
    (b) Increases proportionately
    (c) Reduces slightly
    (d) Increases slightly   (SSC CPWD 2015)

75. Locked rotor current of a shaded pole motor is

    (a) less than full load current (SSC CPWD 2015)
    (b) equal to full load current
    (c) several times the full load current
    (d) slightly more than full load current

76. Which of the following motors is preferred for tape-recorders?

    (a) Hysteresis motor
    (b) Two value capacitor motor
    (c) Universal motor
    (d) Shaded pole motor

77. The motor used on small lathes is usually?

    (a) D.C. shunt motor / D.C.
    (b) 3-phase synchronous metor
    (c) Single phase capacitor run motor
    (d) Universal motor   (SSC CPWD 2015)

78. The Ta Vs Ia graph of a dc series motor is a

    (a) Straight line throughout
    (b) Parabola from no load to over load
    (c) Parabola throughout
    (d) Parabola up to full load and straight line at over load   (SSC CPWD 2015)

79. Which of the following motor is non-self starting?

    (a) DC series motor
    (b) Slip ring induction motor
    (c) Synchronous motor
    (d) Squirrel cage induction motor

                            (SSC CPWD 2015)

ANSWERS

EXERCISE – I

1.(b)	2.(b)	3.(a)	4.(a)	5.(c)	6.(b)	7.(a)	8.(b)	9.(a)	10.(d)
11.(a)	12.(d)	13.(d)	14.(c)	15.(a)	16.(b)	17.(d)	18.(d)	19.(a)	20.(b)
21.(b)	22.(d)	23.(b)	24.(d)	25.(c)	26.(c)	27.(b)	28.(c)	29.(d)	30.(a)
31.(d)	32.(c)	33.(a)	34.(b)	35.(b)	36.(c)	37.(d)	38.(b)	39.(a)	40.(d)
41.(d)	42.(b)	43.(b)	44.(a)	45.(a)	46.(a)	47.(c)	48.(a)	49.(a)	50.(d)
51.(c)	52.(a)	53.(a)	54.(b)	55.(c)	56.(d)	57.(d)	58.(b)	59.(b)	60.(b)
61.(c)	62.(c)	63.(d)	64.(b)	65.(a)	66.(b)	67.(b)	68.(a)	69.(c)	70.(a)
71.(a)	72.(c)	73.(b)	74.(c)	75.(a)	76.(a)	77.(d)	78.(c)	79.(b)	80.(a)
81.(c)	82.(a)	83.(d)	84.(b)	85.(c)	86.(c)	87.(d)	88.(a)	89.(d)	90.(b)
91.(a)	92.(c)	93.(c)	94.(c)	95.(b)	96.(d)	97.(a)	98.(d)	99.(c)	100.(d)
101.(a)	102.(b)	103.(a)	104.(d)	105.(c)	106.(d)	107.(a)	108.(d)	109.(b)	110.(d)
111.(a)	112.(b)	113.(c)	114.(d)	115.(b)	116.(c)	117.(c)	118.(d)	119.(b)	120.(c)
121.(a)	122.(b)	123.(b)	124.(d)	125.(c)	126.(b)	127.(c)	128.(a)	129.(d)	130.(b)
131.(d)	132.(b)	133.(a)	134.(b)	135.(d)	136.(b)	137.(d)	138.(b)	139.(c)	140.(b)
141.(c)	142.(d)	143.(d)	144.(a)	145.(c)	146.(b)	147.(a)	148.(c)	149.(d)	150.(d)
151.(c)	152.(a)	153.(a)	154.(c)	155.(a)	156.(a)	157.(c)	158.(a)	159.(c)	160.(d)
161.(b)	162.(c)	163.(d)	164.(c)	165.(b)	166.(b)	167.(c)	168.(d)	169.(d)	170.(c)
171.(d)	172.(d)	173.(d)	174.(d)	175.(d)	176.(d)	177.(b)	178.(b)	179.(a)	180.(c)
181.(a)	182.(d)	183.(d)	184.(b)	185.(a)	186.(a)	187.(b)	188.(b)	189.(a)	190.(a)
191.(b)	192.(b)	193.(d)	194.(c)	195.(d)	196.(d)	197.(a)	198.(b)	199.(d)	200.(b)
201.(b)	202.(b)	203.(a)	204.(a)	205.(d)	206.(b)	207.(d)	208.(b)	209.(a)	210.(d)
211.(a)	212.(d)	213.(c)	214.(d)	215.(b)	216.(c)	217.(b)	218.(d)	219.(d)	220.(a)
221.(a)	222.(c)	223.(c)	224.(b)	225.(b)	226.(c)	227.(a)	228.(a)		

EXERCISE – II

1.(b)	**2.**(c)	**3.**(c)	**4.**(b)	**5.**(b)	**6.**(b)	**7.**(b)	**8.**(b)	**9.**(d)	**10.**(a)
11.(d)	**12.**(a)	**13.**(b)	**14.**(c)	**15.**(a)	**16.**(b)	**17.**(b)	**18.**(d)	**19.**(c)	**20.**(d)
21.(b)	**22.**(b)	**23.**(a)	**24.**(c)	**25.**(d)	**26.**(d)	**27.**(b)	**28.**(a)	**29.**(b)	**30.**(d)
31.(d)	**32.**(c)	**33.**(a)	**34.**(a)	**35.**(b)	**36.**(c)	**37.**(b)	**38.**(c)	**39.**(b)	**40.**(b)
41.(d)	**42.**(c)	**43.**(c)	**44.**(a)	**45.**(b)	**46.**(d)	**47.**(b)	**48.**(a)	**49.**(a)	**50.**(a)
51.(b)	**52.**(a)	**53.**(b)	**54.**(a)	**55.**(c)	**56.**(c)	**57.**(c)	**58.**(d)	**59.**(c)	**60.**(a)
61.(b)	**62.**(b)	**63.**(b)	**64.**(c)	**65.**(c)	**66.**(d)	**67.**(d)	**68.**(c)	**69.**(c)	**70.**(b)
71.(b)	**72.**(d)	**73.**(b)	**74.**(c)	**75.**(c)	**76.**(a)	**77.**(a)	**78.**(b)	**79.**(c)	

■■

Transformers

Transformer is a static electrical apparatus which converts electrical energy from higher voltage to lower voltage or *vice versa* at the same supply frequency.

Types of transformers :

1. Core type
2. Shell type
3. Berry type

TRANSFORMERS AND DC MACHINES

Principle of Operation of a Transformer

A transformer basically consists of two separate windings, called the *primary winding and the secondary winding,* magnetically coupled with each other through low reluctance magnetic circuit. On connecting the primary winding to an a.c. source as shown below in figure an a.c. current I_1 flows through the primary winding producing an a.c. magnetic flux in the neighbourhood of the coil. A part of this magnetic flux links with the secondary winding producing an a.c. voltage E_2 across the secondary winding. Thus basically the voltage across the secondary winding is produced through the mechanism of mutual induction. If the output terminals of secondary are connected to a load impedance, currnt I_2 flows in the secondary winding and the load impedance and thus electrical energy is transferred entirely from primary to the secondary through the magnetic coupling. To provide high magnetic flux linkage between the two windings, a flow reluctance magnetic path is provided, typically using laminated steel core.

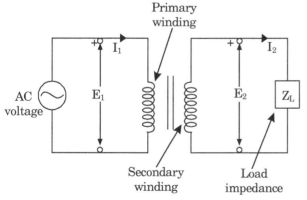

Basic circuit of a transformer

Voltage Transformation Ratio k. As a result on an ac voltage applied to the primary of the transformer, let E_1 volts (rms) be developed across the primary winding and let E_2 volts (rms) be developed across the secondary winding. Then the ratio E_2/E_1 is called the transformation ratio, usually denoted by k.

Thus voltage transformation ratio

$$k = \frac{\text{voltage induced across the secondary}}{\text{voltage induced across the primary}} = \frac{E_2}{E_1}$$

Thus magnitude of the voltage on the primary side gets multiplied by the factor k. This voltage transformer ratio k may be less than one, equal to one or more than 1. If $k < 1$, the transformer is called *step-down* transformer while if $k > 1$, the transformer is called *step-up* transformer.

Further it may be noted that only the magnitude of the voltage changes while the frequency and wave shape remain unchanged. Thus the main features of transformer are :

(*i*) It transfers electric energy from primary to the secondary side.

(*ii*) Voltage and current on the secondary side, in general, differ from those on the primary side.

(*iii*) There is no change in frequency.

(*iv*) Energy is transferred through electromagnetic induction.

Principle of transformers

Energy is transferred at the same frequency from primary winding to secondary winding by means of electromagnetic induction. The flux Φ links not only with the secondary winding but also with the primary winding, thus producing self-induced emf in primary winding which limits the primary current.

Transformer must not be connected to a dc source. If primary winding is connected to dc supply mains, flux produced will not vary but remain constant in magnitude and therefore no emf will be induced in secondary winding except at the moment of switching on. Also there will be no back back emf induced in the primary winding. Therefore a heavy current will be drawn from the supply which may result in the burning of the winding.

Transformer Losses. Losses occuring in the transformer are :

1. *Iron losses* (P_i) :

   These are independent of load which occur due to pulsation of flux in the core.

2. *Copper losses* (P_c) :

   These occur due to ohmic resistance of the transformer winding. The purpose of open-circuit test is to determine the iron loss and no-load current.

Open Circuit and Short Circuits Tests. In open-circuit test, secondary is open circuit, and normal voltage is applied to the primary winding of the transformer.

Short-circuit test is performed to determine the full load copper losses by short circuiting the secondary of the transformer.

Equivalent Resistance and Reactance. Equivalent resistance of the transformer as referred to primary R_{01} or as referred to secondary, R_{02} are :

$$R_{01} = r_1 + r_2/K^2$$
or $$R_{02} = r_2 + K^2 r_1$$

Equivalent reactance of transformer as referred to primary, X_{01} or as referred to secondary, X_{02} are :

$$X_{01} = x_1 + x_2/K^2$$
$$X_{02} = x_2 + K^2 x_1$$

where r_1, r_2, x_1, x_2 are the resistance and reactance of primary and secondary windings K being the transformation ratio.

Efficiency of Transformer. The parameter is given by :

$$\eta = \frac{V_2 I_2 \cos\phi}{V_2 I_2 \cos\phi + P_i + x^2 P_c}$$

where V_2 is the secondary terminal voltage, I_2 secondary load current, $\cos\phi$ is the power factor of load, and x is the fraction of the load.

Voltage Regulation. This is defined as
Percentage regulation

$$= \left(\frac{I_2 R_{02} \cos\phi \pm I_2 X_{02} \sin\phi}{V_{02}}\right) \times 100$$

where R_{02} and X_{02} are total resistance and reactance of transformer referred to the secondary.

Moreover, + sign to be used for inductive load, and - sign to be used for capacitive load.

Condition for Maximum Efficiency.
Iron losses includes both hysteresis loss and eddy current loss and is practically the same at all loads. Output current at which maximum efficiency occurs

is given by $= $ Full load $\sqrt{\dfrac{\text{Iron Loss}}{\text{F.L. copper loss}}}$

All day efficiency.

$$All\ day\ efficiency = \frac{\text{Output in kWh}}{\text{Input in kWh}} \text{ (for 24 hours.)}$$

The distribution transformers are designed to keep core losses minimum and copper losses are relatively less.

Parallel Operation. *The conditions for successful parallel operation of the single phase transformers are :*

1. The primary and secondary windings should be suitable for supply voltage and frequency.
2. The transformers should be properly connected with regard to polarity.
3. The transformation ratio should be identical.
4. The percentage impedance should be equal.

Scott Connection. It is used to accomplish three-phase to three-phase and three-phase to two-phase transformation.

Stat-star connection is not suitable and economical for small high voltage transformation.

EXERCISE – I

1. A transformer transforms
   (a) frequency
   (b) voltage
   (c) current
   (d) both voltage and current

2. A transformer does not change the following
   (a) voltage
   (b) frequency
   (c) waveform
   (d) both frequency and waveform

3. A transformer provides a path for magnetic flux of
   (a) high conductivity
   (b) high reluctance
   (c) low reluctance
   (d) low conductivity

4. An ordinary transformer works on
   (a) a.c
   (b) d.c
   (c) both a.c. and d.c.
   (d) pulsating d.c.

5. An ideal transformer is one which has
   (a) a common core for its primary and secondary windings
   (b) core of stainless steel and winding of pure copper wire
   (c) no losses and magnetic leakage
   (d) interleaved primary and secondary windings

6. The transformer core is generally made of
   (a) alumimium   (b) silicon steel
   (c) copper   (d) wood

7. Which of the following is minimized by laminating the core of a transformer ?
   (a) hysteresis loss
   (b) eddy current loss
   (c) heat loss
   (d) all of these

8. Thickness of laminations of trans-former core is usually of the order of
   (a) 0.35 mm to 0.5 mm
   (b) 3.5 mm to 5 mm
   (c) 35 mm to 50 mm
   (d) 5 mm to 10 mm

9. The main purpose of using core in a transformer is to
   (a) prevent eddy current losses
   (b) prevent hysteresis losses
   (c) decrease reluctance of the common magnetic circuit
   (d) decrease iron losses

10. Transformer works on the principle of
    (a) mutual induction
    (b) self induction
    (c) Faraday's law of electromagnetic induction
    (d) self and mutual induction both

11. If dc voltage is applied to the primary of a transformer it may
    (a) work
    (b) not work
    (c) burn the winding
    (d) give lower voltage on the secondary side

12. Which of the following will improve the mutual coupling between primary and secondary of a transformer ?
    (a) high reluctance magnetic core
    (b) transformer oil of high breakdown voltage
    (c) winding material of high resistivity
    (d) low reluctance magnetic core

13. Which type of core is used for a high frequency transformer
    (a) open iron core
    (b) air core
    (c) closed iron core
    (d) none of these

14. Transformer oil used in tranformer provides
    (a) insulation and cooling
    (b) cooling and lubrication
    (c) lubricaiton and insulation
    (d) insulation, cooling and lubrication

15. Enamel layer is coated over the lamination of a transformer core to
    (a) decrease the hum
    (b) attain adhesion between the lamination
    (c) insulate the laminations from each other
    (d) prevent corosion of laminations

16. The size of transformer core depends on
    (a) frequency
    (b) area of the core
    (c) flux density of core material
    (d) both (a) and (c)

17. In power tranformers, breather is used to
    (a) extract moisture from the air
    (b) take insulating oil from the con-servator
    (c) provide cooling to the windings
    (d) provide insulation to the windings

18. In a transformer, conservator con-sists of
    (a) an air tight metal drum fixed at the top of the tank
    (b) drum placed at the bottom of the tank
    (c) overload protection circuit
    (d) none of these

19. In a transformer, the resistance between its primary and secondary should be
    (a) zero   (b) infinite
    (c) about 1 MΩ   (d) about 100 MΩ

20. For large power tranformer, best utilization of available core space can be made by using
    (a) rectangular core section
    (b) square core section
    (c) stepped core section
    (d) none of these

21. Five limb core construction of a transformer has advantage over three limb core construction that
    (a) eddy current loss is less
    (b) magnetic reluctance of the three phases can be balanced
    (c) hysteresis loss is less
    (d) permeability is higher

22. In a transformer, low voltage windings are placed nearer to the core in the case of concentric windings because it reduces
    (a) hysteresis loss
    (b) eddy current loss
    (c) insulation requirement
    (d) leakage fluxes

23. Transformer windings are tapped in the middle because
    (a) it reduces insulation requirement
    (b) it eliminates axial forces on the windings
    (c) it eliminates radial forces on the windings
    (d) none of these

24. The primary and secondary induced emfs E_1 and E_2 in two-winding transformer are always
    (a) equal in magnitude
    (b) antiphase with each other
    (c) in phase with each other
    (d) determined by load on transformer secondary

25. An step-up transformer increases
    (a) voltage   (b) current
    (c) frequency   (d) power

26. Eddy current losses in a transformer core may be reduced by
    (a) reducing the thickness of lami-nations
    (b) increasing the thickness of lami-nations
    (c) increasing the air gap in the magnetic circuit
    (d) reducing the air gap in the magnetic circuit

27. In a tranformer, the oil must be free from
    (a) odour   (b) sulphur
    (c) moisture   (d) both (b) and (c)

28. In a tranformer, the magnetic coupling between the primary and secondary circuits can be increased by
    (a) increasing the number of turns
    (b) using soft material for windings
    (c) using magnetic core of low reluc-tance
    (d) using tranformer oil of better quaitliy

29. If the flux density in the core of a tranformer is increased
    (a) the frequency the secondary winding voltage increases
    (b) waveshape of the secondary winding voltage gets distorted
    (c) size of the transformer can be reduced
    (d) eddy current losses increase

30. The power factor in a transformer
    (a) is always unit
    (b) is always leading
    (c) is always lagging
    (d) depends on the power factor of load

31. Which of the following tranformers will be largest is size ?
    (a) 1 kVA, 50 Hz
    (b) 1 kVA, 60 Hz
    (c) 1 kVA, 100 Hz
    (d) 1 kVA, 500 Hz

32. Which of the following materials is used to absorb moisture from air entering the transformer ?
    (a) sodium chloride   (b) silica sand
    (c) felt pad   (d) silical gel

33. Which of the following acts as a protection against high voltage surges due to lightening and switching ?
    (a) breather
    (b) conservator
    (c) horn gaps
    (d) thermal overload relays

34. A tap changer is used on a trans-former for
    (a) adjustments in primary voltage
    (b) adjustments in secondary voltage
    (c) adjustments in both primary and secondary voltages
    (d) adjustment in power factor

35. Overcurrents in a transformer affect
    (a) insulation life   (b) temperature rise
    (c) mechanical stress   (d) all of these

36. Highest rating tranformers are likely to find application in
    (a) distribution   (b) generation
    (c) substation   (d) transmission

37. Transformer ratings are usually expressed in terms of
    (a) volts   (b) k Wh
    (c) kVA   (d) kW

38. The noise in a tranformer due to vibration of laminations set by magnetic forces, is called
    (a) flicker noise
    (b) humming noise
    (c) transit-time noise
    (d) agitation noise

39. The maximum load that a power transformer can carry is limited by its
    (a) voltage ratio
    (b) copper loss
    (c) temperature noise
    (d) dielectric strength of oil

40. In a three-phase transformer, the phase difference between the pri-mary voltage and the induced secondary winding voltage is
    (a) 90°   (b) 120°
    (c) 180°   (d) 270°

41. The inductive reactance of a trans-former depends on
    (a) electromotive force
    (b) magnetomotive force
    (c) magnetic flux
    (d) leakage flux

42. When the secondary of the trans-former is loaded, the flux in the transformer constant will
    (a) remain same.
    (b) be directly proportional to secondary current
    (c) be directly proportional to the current drawn by primary winding
    (d) none of these

43. When the secondary of a transformer is loaded, the current in the primary side will
    (a) not be effected
    (b) increase
    (c) decrease
    (d) be the sum of no-load current and excess current drawn due to the secondary current

44. Electric power is transferred from one coil to the other coil in a transformer
    (a) electrically
    (b) electromagnetically
    (c) magnetically
    (d) physically

45. A transformer operates
    (a) always at unity power factor
    (b) has its own constant power factor
    (c) at a power factor always below 0.8
    (d) at power factor depending on the power factor of the load

46. In an ideal transformer on no-load, the primary applied voltage is balanced by
    (a) the secondary voltage
    (b) drop across resistances and reac-tances
    (c) secondary induced emf
    (d) primary induced emf

47. In a transformer, the no load current in terms of full load current is of the order of
    (a) 1 to 3%   (b) 3 to 10%
    (c) 10 to 20%   (d) 20 to 30%

48. In a transformer, the magnitude of the mutual flux is
    (a) low at low loads and high at high loads
    (b) high at low loads and low at high loads
    (c) same at all loads
    (d) varies at low loads and constant at high loads

49. Use of higher flux density in trans-former design
  (a) increases the weight per kVA
  (b) decreases the weight per kVA
  (c) increases the weight per kW
  (d) decreases the weight per kW

50. The efficiency of transformer compared with that of electric motors of the same rating is
  (a) about the same   (b) much smaller
  (c) slightly higher   (d) much higher

51. The no load current taken by a transformer lags the applied voltage approximately by
  (a) 80°   (b) 60°
  (c) 45°   (d) 30°

52. An ideal transformer is one which
  (a) has no losses and magnetic leakage
  (b) has core of stainelss steel
  (c) has inter leaved primary and secondary windings
  (d) has a common core for its primary and secondary windings

53. In a two winding transformer, the primary and the secondary induced emfs E1 and E2 are always
  (a) in phase with each other
  (b) antiphase with each other
  (c) equal in magnitude
  (d) of different frequency

54. Distribution transformers are designed to have maximum efficiency at about
  (a) no load   (b) 50% of full load
  (c) full load   (d) 75% of full load

55. Use of silicon steel for laminations in a transformer reduces
  (a) eddy current losses
  (b) hysteresis losses
  (c) both eddy current and hysteresis losses
  (d) noise generated in the transformer

56. Cross-over windings are used for
  (a) high voltage winding of small rating transformer
  (b) low voltage winding of small rating transformer
  (c) high voltage winding rating of large transformer
  (d) low voltage winding of large rating transformer

57. Advantage of putting tappings at the phase ends of a transformer is
  (a) fine variation of voltage
  (b) ease of operation
  (c) reduction in number of bearings
  (d) better regulation

58. The yoke sections of transformers using hot-rolled laminations is made about 15% larger than that of the core in order to
  (a) reduce copper loss
  (b) increase the size of transformer
  (c) provide better cooling
  (d) reduce iron loss in yoke and magnetising current

59. The primary and secondary windings of an ordinary transformer always have
  (a) different number of turns
  (b) copper wire of same diameter
  (c) common magnetic circuit
  (d) separate magnetic circuits

60. The leakage flux of a transformer is defined as
  (a) the flux which is linked with both the primary and the secondary windings
  (b) the flux which is linked either only with the primary or only with the secondary
  (c) the flux whose path is exclusively through the air
  (d) none of these

61. Helical coils are very well suited for
  (a) HV winding of large rating trans-former
  (b) HV winding of large rating trans-former
  (c) LV winding of small rating trans-former
  (d) LV winding of large rating trans-former

62. Compared with the secondary of a loaded step-up transformer, the primary has
  (a) lower voltage and higher current
  (b) higher voltage and lower current
  (c) lower voltage and lower current
  (d) higher voltage and higher current

63. Special silicon steel is used for the laminations of transformer, because it has
  (a) high resistivity and high hysteresis loss
  (b) high resistivity and low hysteresis loss
  (c) low resistivity and high hysteresis loss
  (d) low resistivity and low hysteresis loss

64. The commercial efficiency of a transformer while on open circuit is
    (a) zero
    (b) 100%
    (a) 50 %
    (b) none of these

65. In a transformer, spiral winding is suitable only for windings
    (a) carrying very low current
    (b) carrying very high current
    (c) rated for high voltage
    (d) rated for low voltage

66. In a transformer, continuous disc winding is suitable for
    (a) low voltage winding of small trans-formers
    (b) high voltage winding of small trans-formers
    (c) low voltage winding of large trans-formers
    (d) high voltage winding of large trans-formers

67. For transformation ratio k, the transformer secondary impedance has to be multiplied by the following factor to get its equivalent primary impedance
    (a) k
    (b) 1/k
    (c) k^2
    (d) $1/k^2$

68. The magnetic flux in a transformer follows a path of
    (a) high reluctance
    (b) low reluctance
    (c) high conductivity
    (d) low conductivity

69. In transformers, interlamination insulation is generally provided by
    (a) thick paper
    (b) thin mica sheet
    (c) thin coating varnish
    (d) none of these

70. The resistance of the low voltage winding of a transformer
    (a) is equal to the resistance of the HV winding
    (b) is greater than the resistance of the HV winding
    (c) is less than the resistane of the HV winding
    (d) may be either more or less han the resistance of the HV winding

71. Transfer of energy from primary to the secondary of a transformer results due to
    (a) the difference in the number of primary and secondary turns
    (b) changing currents in the two win-dings
    (c) magnetic flux linkage between the two windings
    (d) all of these

72. The leakage flux in a transformer depends on
    (a) the supply frequency
    (b) load current
    (c) mutual flux
    (d) none of these

73. In a transformer, at every instant, the direction of the secondary current is such as to oppose any change of flux. This is as per
    (a) Lenz's law
    (b) Faraday's law
    (c) Coulomb's law
    (d) Ampere's law

74. As the load in a transformer increa-ses, the mutual flux linkage in the core
    (a) increases
    (b) decreases
    (c) remains unchanged
    (d) first increases and becomes constant

75. The magnetic compting between the primary and the secondary of a transformer may be increased by
    (a) increasing the number of lamina-tions of core
    (b) changing the turns ratio
    (c) using the magnetic core of lower reluctance
    (d) none of these

76. A transformer is connected to a constant voltage supply. As the supply frequency increases, the magnetic flux in the core
    (a) decreases
    (b) increases toward saturation
    (c) becomes zero
    (d) becomes constant

77. Circular coil sections are generally used in transformer because they
    (a) have the toughest mechanical shape
    (b) are easy to wound
    (c) reduce copper losses
    (d) reduce iron losses

78. Good transformer oil should contain water less than
    (a) 4 ppm
    (b) 8 ppm
    (c) 12 ppm
    (d) 20 ppm

79. Stepped core limbs are used to
    (a) reduce iron material and iron losses
    (b) reduce copper material and copper losses
    (c) both (a) and (b)
    (d) increase mechanical strength of the core

80. Ferrite cores have less eddy current losses than iron losses because ferrites have
    (a) low permeability
    (b) high hysteresis
    (c) high resistance
    (d) all of these

81. The secondary of a transformer is never kept open circuited under actual operating conditions to
    (a) provide safety to human beings
    (b) protect the primary circuit
    (c) avoid saturation of core
    (d) avoid high voltage insulation

82. The end winding of a power transformer is given extra insulation to protect it against
    (a) oil leakage
    (b) excessive heating
    (c) travelling wave surges on distri-bution lines
    (d) none of these

83. The reactance of a transformer is determi-ned by its
    (a) leakage flux
    (b) common core flux
    (c) size of the core
    (d) permeability of the core material

84. For getting minimum weight of a transformer, the weight of iron should be
    (a) less than the weight of copper
    (b) greater than the weight of copper
    (c) equal to the weight of copper
    (d) none of these

85. A constant current transformer should not have
    (a) high value of reactance
    (b) a movable secondary winding
    (c) a high value of resistance
    (d) primary and secondary windings surroun-ding the core

86. Eddy current loss in a transformer depends on
    (a) voltage alone
    (b) frequency alone
    (c) thickness of lamination
    (d) all of these

87 Routine efficiency of a transformer depends upon
    (a) load current alone
    (b) power factor of load alone
    (c) both (a) and (b)
    (d) supply frequency

88. Power transformers are usually designed to have maximum efficie-ncy at
    (a) a little more than full load
    (b) near full load
    (c) half load
    (d) quarter load

89. For short circuit and open circuit tests of a transformer, the instru-ments are connected on
    (a) LV side and HV side respectively
    (b) HV side and LV side respectively
    (c) HV side only
    (d) LV side only

90. Two transformers operating in pararllel share the load depending on their
    (a) efficiency   (b) rating
    (c) leakage reactance   (d) per unit impedance

91. Incorrect polarity in parallel operation of two transformers results in
    (a) open circuit
    (b) short circuit
    (c) regeneration of power
    (d) load sharing proportional to their kVA rating

92. In parallel operation of trans-formers, to reduce copper loss
    (a) they should have equal turns ratio
    (b) their phases should be the same
    (c) they should have zero impedance
    (d) none of these

93. Essential condition for parallel operation of two single phase trans-formers is that they should have same
    (a) efficiency
    (b) capacity
    (c) voltage ratio
    (d) polarity

94. In an autotransformer, power is transferred through
    (a) conduction process alone
    (b) induction process alone
    (c) both conduction and induction processes
    (d) mutual coupling

95. If a two-winding step down trans-former is converted into an auto-transformer by using additive polarity, then

(a) the kVA rating gets reduced

(b) the kVA rating gets increased considerably

(c) the kVA rating remain unchanged

(d) none of these

96. The main advantage of an auto-transformer over a two winding transformer is that

(a) is uses only one winding

(b) core losses are reduced

(c) it needs no cooling

(d) it has simple construction

EXERCISE – II

1. Two single phase transformers A and B are connected in parallel, observing all requirements of a parallel operation, except that the induced voltage E_a is slightly greater than E_b; Z_{ea} and Z_{eb} being the equivalent impedances of A and B, both referred to the secondary side.

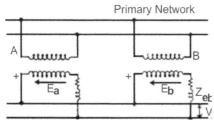

Primary Network

Under this operating condition with the primary bus-bars being energised, a circulating current will flow

(a) only in the secondary windings of A and B

(b) in both the primary and the seconday windings of A and B

(c) in both the primary and the secondary windings of A and B, as well as in the primary side network

(d) in the primary and the secondary windings of A and B, and boost the voltages on the secondary side of both A and B   **(RRB 2012)**

2. What is the phase displacement between primary and secondary voltages for a star-delta, 3-phase transformer connection shown below ?

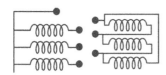

(a) 30^{238}_{92} lagging

(b) 30^{238}_{92} leading

(c) 0^{238}_{92}

(d) 180^{238}_{92} **(RRB 2012)**

3. A ferrite core has lower specific eddy current loss compared to an iron core because the iron core has   **(RRB 2012)**

(a) Higher electrical resistance

(b) Lower electrical resistance

(c) Higher permeability

(d) Lower permeability

4. Two transformers, with equal voltage ratio and negligible excitation current, connected in parallel, share load in the ratio of their kVA rating only, if their p.u. impedances (based on their own kVA) are   **(RRB 2012)**

(a) equal

(b) in the inverse ratio of their ratings

(c) in the direct ratio of their ratings

(d) purely reactive

5. The function of oil in a transformer is to provide

(a) insulation and cooling

(b) protection against lightning

(c) protection against short circuit

(d) lubrication   **(RRB 2012)**

6. If a line of surge impedance Z_0 is terminated in an impedance Z then the reflection for current and voltage surges at the termination are given respectively by   **(RRB 2012)**

(a) $\dfrac{Z_o - Z}{Z_o + Z}, \dfrac{2Z}{Z_o + Z}$

(b) $\dfrac{Z_o - Z}{Z_o + Z}, \dfrac{Z - Z_o}{Z_o + Z}$

(c) $\dfrac{2Z_o}{Z_o + Z}, \dfrac{2Z}{Z_o + Z}$

(d) $\dfrac{2Z_o}{Z_o + Z}, \dfrac{Z - Z_o}{Z_o + Z}$

7. The transformer core is generally made of

(a) alumimium

(b) silicon steel

(c) copper

(d) wood   **(RRB)**

8. Transformer windings are tapped in the middle because

(a) it reduces insulation requirement

(b) it eliminates axial forces on the windings

(c) it eliminates radial forces on the windings

(d) none of these   **(RRB)**

9. A tap changer is used on a trans-former for

(a) adjustments in primary voltage

(b) adjustments in secondary voltage

(c) adjustments in both primary and secondary voltages

(d) adjustment in power factor   **(RRB)**

10. A transformer is connected to a constant voltage supply. As the supply frequency increases, the magnetic flux in the core
    (a) decreases
    (b) increases toward saturation
    (c) becomes zero
    (d) becomes constant **(RRB)**

11. Essential condition for parallel operation of two single phase trans-formers is that they should have same
    (a) efficiency
    (b) capacity
    (c) voltage ratio
    (d) polarity **(RRB)**

12. Eddy current losses in a transformer core may be reduced by **(RRB)**
    (a) reducing the thickness of lami-nations
    (b) increasing the thickness of lami-nations
    (c) increasing the air gap in the magnetic circuit
    (d) reducing the air gap in the magnetic circuit

13. In power tranformers, breather is used to
    (a) extract moisture from the air
    (b) take insulating oil from the con-servator
    (c) provide cooling to the windings
    (d) provide insulation to the windings **(RRB)**

14. Five limb core construction of a transformer has advantage over three limb core construction that
    (a) eddy current loss is less
    (b) magnetic reluctance of the three phases can be balanced
    (c) hysteresis loss is less
    (d) permeability is higher **(RRB)**

15. Which of the following tranformers will be largest is size ? **(RRB)**
    (a) 1 kVA, 50 Hz
    (b) 1 kVA, 60 Hz
    (c) 1 kVA, 100 Hz
    (d) 1 kVA, 500 Hz

16. In a three-phase transformer, the phase difference between the pri-mary voltage and the induced secondary winding voltage is **(RRB)**
    (a) 90°
    (b) 120°
    (c) 180°
    (d) 270°

17. Assuming an ideal transformer, the Thevenin's equivalent voltage and impedance as seen from the terminals x and y for the circuit in figure are

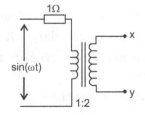

(a) 2 sin(ωt), 4Ω
(b) 1 sin(ωt), 1Ω
(c) 1 sin(ωt), 2Ω
(d) 2 sin(ωt), 0.5Ω
(RRB)

18. A transformer provides a path for magnetic flux of
    (a) high conductivity **(DMRC 2013)**
    (b) high reluctance
    (c) low reluctance
    (d) low conductivity

19. Transformer oil used in tranformer provides
    (a) insulation and cooling **(DMRC 2013)**
    (b) cooling and lubrication
    (c) lubricaiton and insulation
    (d) insulation, cooling and lubrication

20. Eddy current losses in a transformer core may be reduced by
    (a) reducing the thickness of lami-nations
    (b) increasing the thickness of lami-nations
    (c) increasing the air gap in the magnetic circuit
    (d) reducing the air gap in the magnetic circuit **(DMRC 2013)**

21. Highest rating tranformers are likely to find application in
    (a) distribution
    (b) generation
    (c) substation
    (d) transmission **(DMRC 2013)**

22. Compared with the secondary of a loaded step-up transformer, the primary has **(DMRC 2013)**
    (a) lower voltage and higher current
    (b) higher voltage and lower current
    (c) lower voltage and lower current
    (d) higher voltage and higher current

23. In a transformer, at every instant, the direction of the secondary current is such as to oppose any change of flux. This is as per **(DMRC 2013)**
    (a) Lenz's law
    (b) Faraday's law
    (c) Coulomb's law
    (d) Ampere's law

24. Stepped core limbs are used to **(DMRC 2013)**
    (a) reduce iron material and iron losses
    (b) reduce copper material and copper losses
    (c) both (a) and (b)
    (d) increase mechanical strength of the core

25. For short circuit and open circuit tests of a transformer, the instru-ments are connected on
    (a) LV side and HV side respectively
    (b) HV side and LV side respectively
    (c) HV side only
    (d) LV side only   **(DMRC 2013)**

26. Two transformers operating in pararllel share the load depending on their   **(DMRC 2013)**
    (a) efficiency
    (b) rating
    (c) leakage reactance
    (d) per unit impedance

27. In an autotransformer, power is transferred through   **(DMRC 2013)**
    (a) conduction process alone
    (b) induction process alone
    (c) both conduction and induction processes
    (d) mutual coupling

28. The main advantage of an auto-transformer over a two winding transformer is that
    (a) is uses only one winding
    (b) core losses are reduced
    (c) it needs no cooling
    (d) it has simple construction   **(DMRC 2013)**

29. High frequency transformer cores are generally made of   **(DMRC)**
    (a) cast iron   (b) mu-metal
    (c) ferrite   (d) graphite

30. A linear transformer and its T-equivalent circuit are shown in Figure I and Figure II respectively. The values of inductance L_a, L_b and L_c are respectively   **(DMRC)**

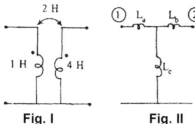

Fig. I	Fig. II

    (a) 1H, –2H and 2H   (b) –1H, 2H and 2H
    (c) 3H, 6H and –2H   (d) 3H, 6H and 2H

31. The transformer used for AC welding sets is   **(SSC, CPWD 2008)**
    (a) booster type   (b) step up type
    (c) steo down type   (d) equal turn ratio type

32. Area of hysteresis loop represents   **(SSC, CPWD 2008)**
    (a) copper loss   (b) eddy current loss
    (c) dielectric loss   (d) hysteresis loss

33. The purpose of the conservator in a transformer is   **(SSC, CPWD 2008)**
    (a) to cool the winding
    (b) to prevent moisture in the transformer
    (c) to prevent short circuit of primary and secondary winding
    (d) to take up contraction and expansion of oil

34. In case of a power transformer, the no load current in terms of rated current is   **(SSC, CPWD 2008)**
    (a) 10 to 20%   (b) 2 to 6%
    (c) 15 to 30%   (d) 30 to 50% and Motor

35. If copper loss of transformer at $\frac{7}{8}$ th full load is 4900 W, then its full load copper loss would be   **(SSC, CPWD 2008)**
    (a) 5600 W   (b) 6400 W
    (c) 373 W   (d) 429 W

36. If a 500 KVA, 200 Hz transformer is operated at 50 Hz, its KVA rating will be   **(SSC, CPWD 2009)**
    (a) 2000 KVA   (b) 125 KVA
    (c) 250 KVA   (d) 1000 KVA

37. The power factor at which transformer operates   **(SSC, CPWD 2009)**
    (a) is unity
    (b) is 0.8 lag
    (c) is 0.8 lead
    (d) depends upon the power factor of the load

38. The efficiency of a 100 KVA transformer is 0.98 at full as well as half load. For this transformer at full load the copper loss **(SSC, CPWD 2009)**
    (a) is less than core loss
    (b) is equal to core loss
    (c) is more than core loss
    (d) All the above

39. Which of the following will improve the mutual coupling between primary and secondary circuit?   **(SSC, CPWD 2009)**
    (a) Transformer oil of high breakdown voltage
    (b) High reluctance magnetic core
    (c) Winding material of high resistivity
    (d) Low reluctance magnetic core

40. High leakage transformers are of

(SSC, CPWD 2009)

(a) small voltage ampere rating

(b) high voltage ampere rating

(c) low voltage rating

(d) high voltage rating

41. Two coupled coils with $L_1 = L_2 = 0.6$ H have a coupling coefficient of $K = 0.8$. The turn

ratio $\dfrac{N_1}{N_2}$ is   (SSC, CPWD 2009)

(a) 4   (b) 2

(c) 1   (d) 0.5

42. A transformer is working at its full load and its efficiency is also maximum. The iron loss is 1000 watts. Then, its copper loss at half of full load will be   (SSC, CPWD 2010)

(a) 250 watt   (b) 300 watt

(c) 400 watt   (d) 500 watt

43. A 2 kVA transformer has iron loss of 150 W and full load copper loss of 250 W. The maximum efficiency of the transformer will occur when the total loss is   (SSC, CPWD 2010)

(a) 500 W   (b) 400 W

(c) 300 W   (d) 275 W

44. The burden of current transformers is expressed in   (SSC, CPWD 2011)

(a) watt

(b) V A

(c) rated secondary current

(d) voltage rating of secondary

45. A 20 kVA, 2000 V / 200 V, 2-winding transformer, when used as an autotransformer, with constant voltage source of 2000 V, is capable of handling.

(SSC, CPWD 2011)

(a) 20 kVA   (b) 220 kVA

(c) 320 kVA   (d) None of these

46. Power transformers are designed such that maximum efficiency occurs at

(SSC, CPWD 2011)

(a) half of the full load

(b) near full load

(c) 1/4th of full load

(d) 3/4th of full load

47. In a 1-phase transformer, the copper loss at full load is 600 Watts. At half of the full load the copper loss will be   (SSC, CPWD 2012)

(a) 150 Watts   (b) 75 Watts

(c) 600 Watts   (d) 300 Watts

48. An autotransformer used with a sodium vapour lamp should have high   (SSC, CPWD 2012)

(a) Winding resistance

(b) Leakage reactance of windings

(c) V A rating

(d) Transformation ratio

49. In an auto-transformer, the number of turns in primary winding is 210 and in secondary winding is 140. If the input current is 60A, the currents in output and in common winding are respectively

(SSC, CPWD 2012)

(a) 40 A, 20 A

(b) 40 A, 100 A

(c) 90 A, 30 A

(d) 90 A, 150 A

50. A 3-phase transformer has its primary connected in delta and secondary in star. Secondary to primary turns ratio per phase is 6. For a primary voltage of 200 V, the secondary voltage would be

(SSC, CPWD 2012)

(a) 2078 V   (b) 693 V

(c) 1200 V   (d) 58 V

51. The iron loss in a 100 KVA transformer is 1 KW and full load copper losses are 2 KW. The maximum efficiency occurs at a load of

(SSC, CPWD 2012)

(a) 100 KVA

(b) 70.7 KVA

(c) 141.4 KVA

(d) 50 KVA

52. For welding purpose, the secondary of transformer used should be capable of carrying

(SSC, CPWD 2013)

(a) high voltage, high current

(b) his voltage, low current

(c) low voltage, high current

(d) low voltage, low current

53. If the frequency of input voltage of a transformer is increased keeping the magnitude of the voltage unchanged, then **(SSC, CPWD 2013)**

(a) both hysteresis loss and eddy current loss in the core will increase

(b) hysteresis loss will increase but eddy current loss will decrease

(c) hysteresis loss will increase but eddy current loss will remain unchaged

(d) hysteresis loss will decrease but eddy current loss will increase

54. A delta - star transformer has a phase to phase voltage transformation ratio of a : 1 [delta phase : star phase]. The line to line voltage ratio of star - delta is given by : **(SSC, CPWD 2014)**

(a) $\dfrac{a}{1}$ (b) $\dfrac{\sqrt{3}}{\sqrt{a}}$

(c) $a\dfrac{\sqrt{3}}{1}$ (d) $\dfrac{\sqrt{3}}{a}$

55. A 10 Ω resistive load is to be impedance matched by a transformer to a source with 6250 Ω of internal resistance. The ratio of primary to secondary turns of transformer should be : **(SSC, CPWD 2014)**

(a) 25   (b) 10

(c) 15   (d) 20

56. In which of the following transformers, is the secondary winding always kept closed ?

(a) Current transformer   **(SSC CPWD 2014)**

(b) Potential transformer

(c) Power transformer

(d) Distribution transformer

57. Low voltage windings are placed nearer to the core in the case of concentric windings because

(a) it reduces hysteresis loss

(b) it reduces eddy current loss

(c) it reduces insulation requirement

(d) it reduces leakage fluxes **(SSC CPWD 2014)**

58. If K is the phase -to-phase voltage ratio, then the line-to-line voltage ratio in a 3-phase Y – Δ transformer is **(SSC CPWD 2014)**

(a) K   (b) $K/\sqrt{3}$

(c) $\sqrt{3}\,K$ (d) $\sqrt{3}/K$

59. In an autotransformer of voltage ratio $\dfrac{V_1}{V_2}$, $V_1 > V_2$, the fraction of power transferred inductively is proportional to

(a) $V_1/(V_1 + V_2)$ **(SSC CPWD 2014)**

(b) V_2/V_1

(c) $(V_1 - V_2)/(V_1 + V_2)$

(d) $(V_1 - V_2)/V_1$

60. Stepped core is used in transformers in order to reduce **(SSC CPWD 2014)**

(a) volume of iron   (b) volume of copper

(c) iron loss   (d) reluctance of core

61. The transformer used in a welding set is

(a) step-up transformer

(b) step-down transformer

(c) constant current transformer

(d) booster transformer   **(SSC CPWD 2014)**

62. The primary and secondary windings of a transformer are wound on the top of each other in order to reduce____?

(a) iron losses

(b) reakage reactance

(c) copper losses

(d) winding resistance   **(SSC CPWD 2015)**

63. The no load primary current I_0 is about _____ of full load primary current of a transformer.

(a) 3-5%

(b) above 40%

(c) 15-30%

(d) 30-40%   **(SSC CPWD 2015)**

ANSWERS

EXERCISE – I

1. (d)	**2.** (d)	**3.** (c)	**4.** (a)	**5.** (c)	**6.** (b)	**7.** (b)	**8.** (a)	**9.** (c)	**10.** (d)
11. (c)	**12.** (d)	**13.** (b)	**14.** (a)	**15.** (c)	**16.** (d)	**17.** (a)	**18.** (a)	**19.** (b)	**20.** (c)
21. (b)	**22.** (c)	**23.** (b)	**24.** (c)	**25.** (a)	**26.** (a)	**27.** (d)	**28.** (c)	**29.** (c)	**30.** (d)
31. (d)	**32.** (d)	**33.** (c)	**34.** (b)	**35.** (d)	**36.** (b)	**37.** (c)	**38.** (b)	**39.** (a)	**40.** (c)
41. (d)	**42.** (a)	**43.** (d)	**44.** (c)	**45.** (d)	**46.** (c)	**47.** (a)	**48.** (c)	**49.** (b)	**50.** (d)
51. (a)	**52.** (a)	**53.** (a)	**54.** (b)	**55.** (b)	**56.** (a)	**57.** (c)	**58.** (d)	**59.** (c)	**60.** (b)
61. (d)	**62.** (a)	**63.** (b)	**64.** (a)	**65.** (b)	**66.** (d)	**67.** (c)	**68.** (b)	**69.** (c)	**70.** (c)
71. (c)	**72.** (b)	**73.** (a)	**74.** (c)	**75.** (c)	**76.** (b)	**77.** (a)	**78.** (b)	**79.** (b)	**80.** (c)
81. (c)	**82.** (c)	**83.** (b)	**84.** (c)	**85.** (c)	**86.** (d)	**87.** (c)	**88.** (c)	**89.** (b)	**90.** (d)
91. (b)	**92.** (a)	**93.** (d)	**94.** (c)	**95.** (b)	**96.** (a)				

EXERCISE – II

1. (c)	**2.** (b)	**3.** (d)	**4.** (a)	**5.** (a)	**6.** (b)	**7.** (b)	**8.** (b)	**9.** (b)	**10.** (b)
11. (d)	**12.** (a)	**13.** (a)	**14.** (b)	**15.** (d)	**16.** (c)	**17.** (a)	**18.** (c)	**19.** (a)	**20.** (a)
21. (b)	**22.** (a)	**23.** (a)	**24.** (b)	**25.** (b)	**26.** (d)	**27.** (c)	**28.** (a)	**29.** (c)	**30.** (b)
31. (c)	**32.** (d)	**33.** (d)	**34.** (b)	**35.** (b)	**36.** (b)	**37.** (d)	**38.** (c)	**39.** (d)	**40.** (a)
41. (c)	**42.** (a)	**43.** (c)	**44.** (b)	**45.** (b)	**46.** (d)	**47.** (a)	**48.** (b)	**49.** (c)	**50.** (a)
51. (b)	**52.** (c)	**53.** (c)	**54.** (d)	**55.** (a)	**56.** (a)	**57.** (c)	**58.** (c)	**59.** (d)	**60.** (b)
61. (b)	**62.** (b)	**63.** (a)							

4

Induction Motors

Induction Motor. It is the most widely used a.c. motor because of its low cost, simple and extremely rugged construction, high efficiency, reasonably good power factor, and simple starting arrangement.

Principle of Operation. When a three-phase stator windings are fed by three-phase supply, a magnetic flux of constant magnitude but rotating at synchronous speed is set up. The flux passes through the air gap, and cuts the stationary rotor conductors. Due to relative speed between rotating magnetic flux and stationary conductors, an emf is induced in the conductors according to Faraday's law of electromagnetic induction and its direction is given by Fleming's right hand rule. Since the rotor conductors are in a closed circuit, rotor current is produced whose direction is such as to oppose the cause which is producing it. Rotor current is produced due to relative speed between rotating flux of stator and stationary rotor conductors. Hence to reduce the relative speed, the rotor starts running in the same direction as that of the flux and tries to catch up with the rotating flux.

Induction motor consists of two parts

1. Stationary part called stator
2. Revolving part called rotor.

It is mainly of two types :

1. Squirrel cage type
2. Wound rotor type

Phase supply produces a rotating magnetic field which rotate at synchronous speed, given by N = $\dfrac{120f}{P}$

An induction motor cannot run at synchronous speed. If it were possible, by some means for the rotor to attain synchronous speed, the rotor would then be standing still with respect to the rotating flux with the result that no emf would be induced in the rotor, no rotor current would flow and therefore there would be no torque developed.

Slip of an induction motor(s) :

$$s = \dfrac{\text{synchronous speed} - \text{rotor speed}}{\text{synchronous speed}}$$

Rotor current frequency,

$$f' = \text{slip} \times \text{supply frequency}$$

Starting torque is maximum when rotor resistance equals rotor reactance *i.e.,* $R_2 = X_2$.

Torque under running conditions is maximum at that value of slip s, which makes rotor reactance per phase equal to rotor resistance per phase.

The slip of an inductor motors can be measured by actual measurement of motor speed or, comparing rotor and stator supply frequencies with d.c. moving coil millivolt-meter, and stroboscopic method.

Rotor copper loss in induction motor = s × rotor input

Synchronous wattage. It is the power transferred across the air-gap to the rotor.

Torque is synchronous watt = rotor input.

No load current is 40%–50% of full load current.

Electrical equivalent of mechanical load on motor

$$= R_2 (1/s - 1).$$

Power output of an induction motor is maximum when equivalent load resistance is equal to the stand-still leakage impedance of the motor.

Double Squirrel Cage Motor. A double squirrel cage motor consists of two independent cages on the same rotor one inside the other. The outer cage consists of a high resistance metal whereas the inner cags has low resistance copper bars. It has high starting torque without sacrificing its electical efficiency under normal running conditions.

SPEED CONTROL OF INDUCTION MOTOR

It can be achieved by following methods :

(*i*) Changing the applied voltage
(*ii*) Changing the applied frequency
(*iii*) Changing the number of stator poles
(*iv*) Injecting an emf in the rotor circuit
(*v*) Cascading, and
(*vi*) Rotor rheostat control

EXERCISE – I

1. In an induction motor, rotor slots are usually not quite parallel to the shaft but are given a slight skew
   (a) to reduce the magnetic hum
   (b) to reduce the locking tendency of the rotor
   (c) both (a) and (b) above
   (d) to increase the speed of the motor

2. In an induction motor, rotor runs at a speed
   (a) equal to the speed of stator field
   (b) lower than the speed of stator field
   (c) higher than the speed of stator field
   (d) having no relation with the speed of stator field

3. When an induction motor runs at rated load and speed, the iron losses are
   (a) negligible
   (b) very heavy
   (c) independent of supply frequency
   (d) independent of supply voltage

4. The emf induced in the rotor of an induction motor is proportional to
   (a) voltage applied to stator
   (b) relative velocity between flux and rotor conductors
   (c) both (a) and (b) above
   (d) slip

5. The starting torque of an indiction motor is maximum when
   (a) rotor resistance equals rotor reactance
   (b) rotor resistance is twice the rotor reactance
   (c) rotor resistance is half the rotor reactance
   (d) rotor resistance is R_2 times the rotor reactance

6. Wattmeter reading in no load test of induction motor gives
   (a) copper losses in the stator
   (b) friction and winding losses
   (c) sum of (a) and (b) above
   (d) total losses in the rotor on no load

7. The slip frequency of an induction motor is
   (a) the frequency of rotor currents
   (b) the frequency of stator currents
   (c) difference of the frequencies of the stator and rotor currents
   (d) sum of the frequencies of the stator and rotor currents

8. At zero in an induction motor
   (a) the motor runs at synchronous speed
   (b) motor runs as a generator
   (c) motor does not run
   (d) slip produced is zero

9. The field of an induction motor rotor rotates relative to the stator at
   (a) rotor speed   (b) synchronous speed
   (c) slip speed   (d) very low speed

10. Starters are used in induction motor because
    (a) its starting torque is high
    (b) it is run against heavy load
    (c) it can not run in reverse direction
    (d) its starting current is five times or more than its rated current

11. By synchronous wattage of an induction motor is meant
    (a) stator input in watts
    (b) rotor output in watts
    (c) rotor input in watts
    (d) shaft output in watts

12. The synchronous speed of an induction motor is defined as
    (a) natural speed at which a magnetic field rotates
    (b) the speed of a synchronous motor
    (c) the speed of an induction motor at no load
    (d) none of these

13. Three-phase induction motor is mainly suitable for which of the following application
    (a) For running different machine tools where several speeds are required
    (b) For running paper machine requiring exact speed control
    (c) For running electric vehicles
    (d) For running rolling mills needing exact speed control

14. The field winding of a three phase synchronous machine is excited by
    (a) single-phase ac supply
    (b) three-phase ac supply
    (c) dc supply
    (d) supply obtained from an inverter

15. When a polyphase induction motor is loaded
  (a) increases and its frequency decreases
  (b) increases and its frequency increases
  (c) decreases and its frequency increases
  (d) decreases and its frequency decreases

16. If in a 3-phase induction motor, two phases open accidently, the motor will
  (a) run at dangerously high speed
  (b) stop
  (c) continue to run depending on load
  (d) none of these

17. A three-phase synchronous machine is a
  (a) singly excited machine
  (b) doubly excited machine
  (c) machine in which three-phase supply is fed to both stator and rotor winding
  (d) none of these

18. Squirrel cage induction motor has
  (a) zero starting torque
  (b) very small starting torque
  (c) medium starting torque
  (d) very high starting torque

19. The purpose of blades in a squirrel cage induction motor is
  (a) to reduce the magnetic resistance of the roor
  (b) to cool the rotor
  (c) to reduce the electrical resistance of rotor cage
  (d) none of these

20. Which of the following is the advantage of double squirrel cage rotor as compared to the round bar cage rotor ?
  (a) larger slip
  (b) lower starting torque
  (c) higher power factor
  (d) higher efficiency

21. On open circuiting the rotor of a squirrel cage induction motor, the rotor
  (a) makes noise
  (b) does not run
  (c) does not run
  (d) runs at dangerously high speed

22. With increase of load, the speed of induction motor operating in the stable region
  (a) increases
  (b) decreases
  (c) remains constant
  (d) increases and then becomes constant

23. In the following motor, external resistance can be added to start the motor
  (a) slip ring induction motor
  (b) squirrel cage induction motor
  (c) salient pole synchronous motor
  (d) wound rotor synchronous motor

24. The disadvantage of starting an induction motor with a star-delta starter is that
  (a) the starting torque is one-third of the torque in case of delta connection
  (b) during starting high losses result
  (c) the starting torque increases and the motor runs with jerks
  (d) none of these

25. Improvement of the power factor in an induction motor results in
  (a) decreased torque
  (b) increased torque
  (c) increased torque current
  (d) increased torque and decreased current due to increased impedance

26. Which of the following function is served by the resistance placed in parallel with one phase of three-phase induction motor ?
  (a) smooth starting
  (b) higher starting torque :
  (c) higher maximum torque
  (d) highly reduced starting torque

27. The rotor output of an induction motor is 15 kW and the slip is 4%. Then the rotor copper loss is
  (a) 600 watts   (b) 300 watts
  (c) 700 watts   (d) 1200 watts

28. In an induction motor, the rotor input is 600 W and slip is 4%. The rotor copper loss is
  (a) 650 W   (b) 600 W
  (c) 625 W   (d) 700 W

29. For smooth starting of three-phase squirrel cage induction motor, the starting method preferred is
  (a) rotor resistance   (b) star-delta
  (c) auto-transformer   (d) stator resistance

30. The power factor of star connected induction motor is 0.5. On being connected in delta, the power factor will ?
  (a) become zero
  (b) remain the same
  (c) reduce
  (d) increase

31. Any odd harmonic in the current of an induction motor will result in magnetic field which
  (*a*) oscillates at harmonic frequency
  (*b*) rotates in backward direction
  (*c*) rotates in forward direction at the harmonic speed
  (*d*) is stationary relative to the field of the fundamental

32. Cogging of motor implies that motor
  (*a*) runs at very low speed
  (*b*) runs at low speed and then stops
  (*c*) refuses to start at no load
  (*d*) refuses to start at load

33. In a double cage induction motor, the inner cage has
  (*a*) low R and low X
  (*b*) low R and high X
  (*c*) high R and high X
  (*d*) high R and low X

34. Number of different speeds that can be obtained from two induction motors in cascade is
  (*a*) 2   (*b*) 3
  (*c*) 4   (*d*) 6

35. Advantage of slip ring induction motor over squirrel cage induction motor is
  (*a*) suitability of higher speeds
  (*b*) higher efficiency
  (*c*) higher power factor
  (*d*) that it can be started using factor resistance

36. The starting torque of a cage rotor induction motor can be increased by using rotor having
  (*a*) low inductance and low resistance
  (*b*) low inductance and high resistance
  (*c*) high inductance and high resistance
  (*d*) high inductance and low resistance

37. Large air gap in an induction motor results in
  (*a*) increased overload capacity
  (*b*) better cooling
  (*c*) reduced pulsation losses
  (*d*) reduced noise

38. Simplest method of eliminating the harmonic induction torque is
  (*a*) skewing
  (*b*) chording
  (*c*) integral slot winding
  (*d*) none of these

39. The drive generally used for lathe machines are
  (*a*) squirrel cage induction motors
  (*b*) synchronous motors
  (*c*) slip ring induction motors
  (*d*) dc shunt motors

40. Motor commonly used for traction purpose is
  (*a*) induction motor   (*b*) dc shunt motor
  (*c*) dc series motor   (*d*) synchronous motor

41. Maximum power developed in a synchronous motor occurs at a coupling angle of
  (*a*) 0°   (*b*) 60°
  (*c*) 90°   (*d*) 120°

42. The back emf set up in the stator of synchronous motor depends on
  (*a*) coupling angle   (*b*) rotor excitation
  (*c*) speed of the rotor (*d*) input to prime mover

43. Synchronous induction motors are mostly used for driving
  (*a*) lathe machines
  (*b*) cranes
  (*c*) rotary compressors
  (*d*) none of these

44. The noise and tooth pulsation losses may be reduced by using
  (*a*) large number of open slots in stator
  (*b*) large number of narrow slots in stator
  (*c*) small number of open slots in stator
  (*d*) small number of narrow slots in stator

45. Which of the following motors is most suitable for best speed control ?
  (*a*) dc series motor   (*b*) dc shunt motor
  (*c*) induction motor   (*d*) synchronous motor

46. If the frequency of input power to an induction motor increases, the rotor copper loss
  (*a*) increases   (*b*) decreases
  (*c*) remains the same (*d*) none of these

47. The stator frame in an induction motor is used
  (*a*) as a return path for the flux
  (*b*) to hold the armature stampings/stator
  (*c*) to protect the whole machine
  (*d*) to provide ventilation to the armature

48. The speed of a three-phase cage-rotor induction motor depends on
  (*a*) frequency of the supply only
  (*b*) number of pole alone
  (*c*) number of poles and frequency of supply
  (*d*) input voltage

49. Dispersion coefficient σ is the ratio of
   (a) magnetising current to supply voltage
   (b) magnetising current to ideal short circuit current
   (c) open circuit voltage to short circuit current for the same excitation
   (d) none of these

50. The fractional slip of an induction motor is to ratio
   (a) rotor Cu loss/rotor input
   (b) stator Cu loss/stator input
   (c) rotor Cu loss/rotor output
   (d) rotor Cu loss/stator Cu loss

51. The complete circle diagram of a 3-phase induction motor can be drawn with the help of
   (a) running-light test alone
   (b) both running-light and blocked-rotor tests
   (c) running-light and blocked-rotor and stator-resistance tests
   (d) blocked rotor test alone.

52. A SCIM runs at constant speed only so long as
   (a) torque developed by it remains constant
   (b) its supply voltage remains constant
   (c) its torque exactly equals the mechanical load
   (d) stator flux remains constant

53. The synchronous speed of a linear induction motor does NOT depend on
   (a) width of pole pitch   (b) number of poles
   (c) supply frequency   (d) any of the above

54. If the stator voltage and frequency of an induction motor are reduced proportionately, its
   (a) locked rotor current is reduced
   (b) torque developed is increased
   (c) magnetising current is decreased
   (d) both (a) and (b)

55. Single phase induction motor can be made self starting by
   (a) adding series combination of capacitor and auxiliary winding in parallel with the main winding
   (b) adding an auxiliary winding in parallel with the main winding
   (c) adding an auxiliary winding in series with a capacitor and the main winding
   (d) none of these

56. All single phase motors have
   (a) very small starting torque
   (b) medium starting torque
   (c) zero starting torque
   (d) large starting torque

57. Single phase motors generally get overheated due to
   (a) overloading
   (b) short windings
   (c) bearing troubles
   (d) any of above

58. If a single phase motor runs slow, it may be due to
   (a) overload   (b) low freuency
   (c) low voltag   (d) any of these

59. Which of the following single phase motors is cheapest ?
   (a) Capacitor start motor
   (b) Capacitor run motor
   (c) Reluctance motor
   (d) All have almost the same cost

60. If a single phase motor runs hot, the probable cause may be
   (a) overload   (b) low voltage
   (c) high voltage   (d) amu pf the abpve

61. Which of the following single phase motors is relaively free from mechanical and magnetic vibration?
   (a) Reluctance motor
   (b) Hysteresis motor
   (c) Universal motor
   (d) Shaded pole motor

62. Which of the following single phase motors does not have constant speed characteristics ?
   (a) Reluctance motor
   (b) Hysteresis motor
   (c) Universal motor
   (d) All of the above

63. For the same rating which of the following motors has the highest starting torque ?
   (a) Universal motor
   (b) Split phase motor
   (c) Synchronous motor
   (d) all have identical starting torque

64. If a single phase motor fails to start, the probable cause may be
   (a) open circuit in auxiliary winding
   (b) open circuit in main winding
   (c) blown fuses
   (d) any of the above

65. The speed of the split phase induction motor can be reversed by reversing the leads of

(a) auxiliary winding

(b) main winding

(c) either (a) or (b)

(d) speed can not be reversed

66. A capacitor start single phase induction motor will usually have power factor of

(a) unity

(b) 0.6 leading

(c) 0.8 leading

(d) 0.6 lagging

EXERCISE – II

1. The supply voltage to an induction motor is reduced by 10%. By what percentage, approximately, will the maximum torque decrease?

(a) 5%   (b) 10%

(c) 20%   (d) 40%   **(RRB 2012)**

2. When a single phase induction motor is excited with single phase a.c. voltage, the magnetic field set up is equivalent to

(a) two fields, rotating in opposite directions with different speeds

(b) two fields, rotating at synchronous speed in opposite directions

(c) two fields, rotating at synchronous speed

(d) two fields rotating in the same direction but at different speeds   **(RRB 2012)**

3. The stator and the rotor of a 3-phase, 4-pole wound-rotor induction motor are excited, respectively, from a 50 Hz and a 30 Hz source of appropriate voltage. Neglecting all losses, what is/are the possible no-load speed/speeds at which the motor would run ?

(a) 1500 rpm and 900 rpm

(b) 2400 rpm and 600 rpm

(c) 2400 rpm only

(d) 600 rpm only   **(RRB 2012)**

4. A wound rotor induction motor runs with a slip of 0.03 when developing full load torque. Its rotor resistance is 0.25 ohm per phase. If an external resistance of 0.50 ohm per phase is connected across the slip rings, what is the slip for full load torque ?

(a) 0.03   (b) 0.06

(c) 0.09   (d) 0.1   **(RRB 2012)**

5. Which of the points on the torque-speed curve of the induction motor represents operation at a slip greater than 1 ?

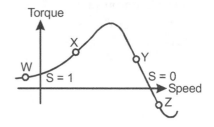

(a) W   (b) X

(c) Y   (d) Z   **(RRB 2012)**

6. The rotor slots are slightly skewed in squirrel-cage induction motor to

(a) increase the strengths of rotor bars

(b) reduce the magnetic hum and locking tendency of rotor

(c) economise on the copper to be used

(d) provide ease of fabrication   **(RRB 2012)**

7. A smaller air gap in a polyphase induction motor helps to

(a) reduce the chances of crawling

(b) increase the starting torque

(c) reduce the chance of cogging

(d) reduce the magnetizing current **(RRB 2012)**

8. Wattmeter reading in no load test of induction motor gives

(a) copper losses in the stator

(b) friction and winding losses

(c) sum of (a) and (b) above

(d) total losses in the rotor on no load   **(RRB)**

9. Squirrel cage induction motor has

(a) zero starting torque

(b) very small starting torque

(c) medium starting torque

(d) very high starting torque   **(RRB)**

10. For smooth starting of three-phase squirrel cage induction motor, the starting method preferred is **(RRB)**
    (a) rotor resistance   (b) star-delta
    (c) auto-transformer   (d) stator resistance

11. If the stator voltage and frequency of an induction motor are reduced proportionately, its
    (a) locked rotor current is reduced
    (b) torque developed is increased
    (c) magnetising current is decreased
    (d) both (a) and (b)   **(RRB)**

12. With increase of load, the speed of induction motor operating in the stable region   **(RRB)**
    (a) increases
    (b) decreases
    (c) remains constant
    (d) increases and then becomes constant

13. The rotor output of an induction motor is 15 kW and the slip is 4%. Then the rotor copper loss is
    (a) 600 watts   (b) 300 watts
    (c) 700 watts   (d) 1200 watts   **(RRB)**

14. In a double cage induction motor, the inner cage has   **(RRB)**
    (a) low R and low X
    (b) low R and high X
    (c) high R and high X
    (d) high R and low X

15. The fractional slip of an induction motor is to ratio
    (a) rotor Cu loss/rotor input
    (b) stator Cu loss/stator input
    (c) rotor Cu loss/rotor output
    (d) rotor Cu loss/stator Cu loss   **(RRB)**

16. A capacitor start single phase induction motor will usually have power factor of   **(RRB)**
    (a) unity   (b) 0.6 leading
    (c) 0.8 leading   (d) 0.6 lagging

17. A three-phase, 4-pole, self excited induction generator is feeding power to a load at a frequency f_1. If the load is partially removed, the frequency becomes f_2. If the speed of the generator is maintained at 1500 rpm in both the cases, then
    (a) $f_1, f_2 > 50$ Hz and $f_1 > f_2$
    (b) $f_1 < 50$ Hz and $f_2 > 50$ Hz
    (c) $f_1, f_2 < 50$ Hz and $f_2 > f_1$
    (d) $f_1 > 50$ Hz and $f_2 < 50$ Hz   **(RRB)**

18. In an induction motor, rotor runs at a speed
    (a) equal to the speed of stator field
    (b) lower than the speed of stator field
    (c) higher than the speed of stator field
    (d) having no relation with the speed of stator field   **(DMRC 2013)**

19. Wattmeter reading in no load test of induction motor gives   **(DMRC 2013)**
    (a) copper losses in the stator
    (b) friction and winding losses
    (c) sum of (a) and (b) above
    (d) total losses in the rotor on no load

20. If in a 3-phase induction motor, two phases open accidently, the motor will   **(DMRC 2013)**
    (a) run at dangerously high speed
    (b) stop
    (c) continue to run depending on load
    (d) none of these

21. A capacitor start single phase induction motor will usually have power factor of **(DMRC 2013)**
    (a) unity
    (b) 0.6 leading
    (c) 0.8 leading
    (d) 0.6 lagging

22. Motor used for elevators is generally   **(SSC, CPWD 2008)**
    (a) synchronous motor   (b) universal motor
    (c) induction motor   (d) reluctance motor

23. The slip of an induction motor under full load condition is about   **(SSC, CPWD 2008)**
    (a) 0.1   (b) 0.03
    (c) 0.2   (d) 0.8

24. The starting torque of a 3-phase induction motor varies as   **(SSC, CPWD 2009)**
    (a) V^2 (b) V
    (c) $\sqrt{V}$ (d) $\dfrac{1}{V}$

25. In a 3-phase induction motor, the mechanical power developed; in terms of air gap power P_g is   **(SSC, CPWD 2009)**
    (a) $(1-S)P_g$ (b) $P_g S$
    (c) $\dfrac{P_g}{1-S}$ (d) $\dfrac{P_g}{S}$

26. In a 3-phase induction motor starting torque will be maximum when **(SSC, CPWD 2010)**

(a) $R_2 = \dfrac{1}{X_2}$

(b) $R_2 = X_2$

(c) $R_2 = X_2^2$

(d) $R_2 = \sqrt{X_2}$

Where R_2 is Rotor resistance and X_2 is rotor reactance.

27. A 4-pole, 3-phase induction motor is running at 4% slip at full load. If the speed of the motor is 750 rpm, the supply frequency is **(SSC, CPWD 2010)**

(a) $16\dfrac{2}{3}$ Hz

(b) 25 Hz

(c) 50 Hz

(d) 60 Hz

28. The ratio of no load current to full load current of a single phase induction motor is **(SSC, CPWD 2011)**

(a) 0.1

(b) 0.2

(c) 0.4

(d) 0.8

29. During starting of a three-phase induction motor, the machine may refuse to start at all. This phenomenon is called **(SSC, CPWD 2011)**

(a) Single phasing

(b) Cogging

(c) Stalling

(d) Crawling

30. In star-delta starting of three-phase induction motor the starting voltage is reduced to **(SSC, CPWD 2012)**

(a) $\sqrt{3}$ times of normal voltage

(b) 3 time of normal voltage

(c) $\dfrac{1}{3}$ times of normal voltage

(d) $\dfrac{1}{\sqrt{3}}$ times of normal voltage

31. If the starting torque of a 3 phase induction motor is T_{st} for DOL starting, that for star-delta starting of the same motor is **(SSC, CPWD 2012)**

(a) $T_{st}/3$

(b) $T_{st}/\sqrt{3}$

(c) $\sqrt{3}\ T_{st}$

(d) $3\ T_{st}$

32. Based on revolving field theory, the forward and backward frequencies of the rotor emf of a 4-pole, 50 Hz, single-phase induction motor when running at 1300 rpm in the same direction of the forward field are respectively **(SSC, CPWD 2012)**

(a) 107.69 Hz, 7.69 Hz

(b) 93.33 Hz, 6.67 Hz

(c) 7.69 Hz, 107.69 Hz

(d) 6.67 Hz, 93.33 Hz

33. Slip of a 3-phase induction motor may be expressed as **(SSC, CPWD 2012)**

(a) Rotor copper loss/rotor core loss

(b) Rotor copper loss/rotor power input

(c) Rotor copper loss/rotor input power

(d) Rotor power input/rotor copper loss.

34. The single phase Induction Motor (IM) which does not have centrifugal switch is **(SSC, CPWD 2013)**

(a) capacitor start single phase IM

(b) resistance split single phase IM

(c) capacitor start capacitor run single phase IM

(d) permanent capacitor run single phase IM

35. if the centrifugal switch of a single-phase resistance split induction motor does not open after starting of motor, the motor **(SSC, CPWD 2013)**

(a) will run above normal speed

(b) will run below normal speed

(c) will draw very small current

(d) will draw high current and get over- heated

36. Which one of the following is a speed control method of three-phase squirrel cage induction motor? **(SSC, CPWD 2013)**

(a) Plugging method

(b) Star-delta switch method

(c) Pole-changing method

(d) Centrifugal clutch method

37. The repulsion-start induction-run motor is used because of : **(SSC, CPWD 2014)**

(a) high starting torque

(b) good power factor

(c) high efficiency

(d) minimum cost

38. The rotor slots, in an induction motor are usually not quite parallel to the shaft because it : **(SSC, CPWD 2014)**

(a) improves the power factor

(b) improves the efficiency

(c) helps the rotor teeth to remain under the stator

(d) helps in reducing the tendency of the rotor teeth to remain under the stator teeth

39. The synchronous speed of a three phase induction motor having 20 polar and connected to a 50 Hz source is : **(SSC, CPWD 2014)**

(a) 1200 rpm   (b) 300 rpm

(c) 600 rpm   (d) 1000 rpm

40. When the rotor of a three phase induction motor is blocked, the slip is : **(SSC, CPWD 2014)**

(a) 1   (b) 0

(c) 0.1   (d) 0.5

41. A 3-phase 4 pole induction motor works on 3-phase 50 c/s supply. If the slip of the motor is 4%. The actual speed will be : **(SSC, CPWD 2014)**

(a) 720 rpm   (b) 1550 rpm

(c) 1460 rpm   (d) 1440 rpm

42. In a 3-phase induction motor crawling happens at **(SSC CPWD 2014)**

(a) any speed

(b) no-load speed

(c) odd multiples of fundamental

(d) even multiples of fundamental

43. A 4-pole, 3-phase induction motor runs at 1440 rpm on a 50 Hz supply. Find the slip speed.

(a) 2940 rpm   **(SSC CPWD 2014)**

(b) 1500 rpm

(c) 1440 rpm

(d) 60 rpm

44. In capacitor start single phase induction motor, the current in the **(SSC CPWD 2014)**

(a) supply lines leads the voltage

(b) starting winding lags the voltage

(c) main winding leads the voltage

(d) starting winding leads the voltage

45. In a single phase induction motor, speed sensitive centrifugal switch is connected in —— winding.

(a) parallel with main

(b) series with main

(c) parallel with starting

(d) series with starting   **(SSC CPWD 2014)**

46. At starting, the current through the starting winding (I_s) of single phase induction motor

(a) lags 'V' by 90°

(b) leads 'V' by 90°

(c) is nearly in phase with 'V'

(d) leads 'V' by 75°   **(SSC CPWD 2014)**

47. In a single phase induction motor at start, the two revolving fields produce

(a) unequal torques in the rotor conductors

(b) no torque in the rotor conductor

(c) equal and opposite torques in the rotor conductors

(d) equal torques in same direction in the rotor conductors   **(SSC CPWD 2014)**

48. The purpose of starting winding in a single-phase induction motor is to ? **(SSC CPWD 2015)**

(a) Produce rotating flux in conjunction with main winding

(b) Limit temperature rise of the machine

(c) Reduce losses

(d) Increase losses

49. If static voltage of a squirrel cage induction motor is reduced to 50 percent of its rated value, torque developed is reduced by how many percentage of its full load value? **(SSC CPWD 2015)**

(a) 50%   (b) 25%

(c) 75%   (d) 57.7%

50. An eight pole wound rotor induction motor operating on 60 Hz supply is driven at 1800 rpm by a prime mover in the opposite direction of revolving magnetic field. The frequency of rotor current is **(SSC CPWD 2015)**

(a) 120 Hz   (b) 180 Hz

(c) 60 Hz   (d) 200 Hz

ANSWERS

EXERCISE – I

1. (c)	**2.** (b)	**3.** (a)	**4.** (c)	**5.** (a)	**6.** (d)	**7.** (a)	**8.** (c)	**9.** (b)	**10.** (d)
11. (c)	**12.** (a)	**13.** (a)	**14.** (c)	**15.** (a)	**16.** (c)	**17.** (c)	**18.** (b)	**19.** (b)	**20.** (b)
21. (c)	**22.** (b)	**23.** (a)	**24.** (a)	**25.** (d)	**26.** (a)	**27.** (a)	**28.** (c)	**29.** (c)	**30.** (c)
31. (b)	**32.** (c)	**33.** (b)	**34.** (c)	**35.** (d)	**36.** (c)	**37.** (c)	**38.** (b)	**39.** (a)	**40.** (c)
41. (c)	**42.** (b)	**43.** (c)	**44.** (b)	**45.** (b)	**46.** (a)	**47.** (a)	**48.** (c)	**49.** (b)	**50.** (a)
51. (c)	**52.** (c)	**53.** (a)	**54.** (d)	**55.** (a)	**56.** (c)	**57.** (d)	**58.** (d)	**59.** (a)	**60.** (d)
61. (b)	**62.** (c)	**63.** (a)	**64.** (d)	**65.** (c)	**66.** (d)				

EXERCISE – II

1. (c)	**2.** (b)	**3.** (b)	**4.** (c)	**5.** (a)	**6.** (b)	**7.** (d)	**8.** (d)	**9.** (b)	**10.** (c)
11. (d)	**12.** (b)	**13.** (a)	**14.** (b)	**15.** (a)	**16.** (d)	**17.** (c)	**18.** (b)	**19.** (d)	**20.** (c)
21. (d)	**22.** (c)	**23.** (b)	**24.** (a)	**25.** (a)	**26.** (b)	**27.** (b)	**28.** (d)	**29.** (b)	**30.** (d)
31. (a)	**32.** (d)	**33.** (b)	**34.** (d)	**35.** (d)	**36.** (c)	**37.** (a)	**38.** (d)	**39.** (b)	**40.** (a)
41. (d)	**42.** (c)	**43.** (d)	**44.** (d)	**45.** (d)	**46.** (c)	**47.** (c)	**48.** (a)	**49.** (d)	**50.** (b)

An alternator consists of a stator and a rotor. The stator provides the armature windings whereas rotor provides the rotating magnetic field.

Basic Principle.

When rotor is rotated by the prime-mover, the stator winding or conductors are cut by the magnetic flux of the rotor magnetic poles. Hence an emf is induced in the stator conductors. The emf generated in the stator conductors is taken out from three leads connected to the stator winding as shown in the figure.

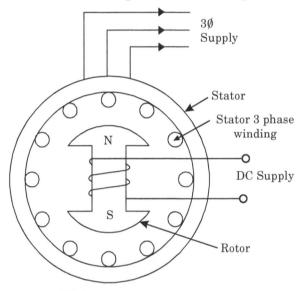

Types of Pole.

The rotors are of two types :

1. **Salient pole type :** It is used for low and medium speed alternators.

2. **Smooth cylindrical type :** It is used for turbo-alternator.

Frequency of alternating current produced is

$$f = \frac{PN}{120}\,\text{Hz},$$

P and N being the no. of poles and speed.

EMF equation of an alternator

$$E = 4.44\ K_c\ K_d\ \Phi\ fT \text{ volts/phase}$$

where K_c coil span factor = $\cos{(\alpha/2)}$, (α is angle by which the coil span falls short),

$$K_d = \text{distribution factor} = \frac{\sin m\beta/2}{m\sin \beta/2},$$

(m is number of slots/pole/phase)

$$\beta = \left(\frac{180°}{\text{No. of slots/pole}}\right)$$

Voltage Regulation. Terminal voltage V is less than open-circuit voltage E_0 because of

(i)   armature drop, IR_a

(ii) synchronous reactance drop IX_s

(iii) armature reaction drop IX_a.

$$\% \text{ Voltage regulation} = \frac{E_0 - V}{V} \times 100$$

Voltage regulation can be found by Synchronous Impedance Method, M.M.F. Method, and Zero Power-Factor method.

SYNCHRONOUS MOTORS

Synchronization

For proper synchronization of alternators, the following conditions must be satisfied :

1. terminal voltage of the incoming alternator must be the same as bus-bar voltage.

2. speed of the incoming machine must be such that its frequency equals bus-bar frequency.

3. phase of the alternator voltage must be identical with the phase of the bus-bar voltage.

Synchronizing current, $I_{sy} = \dfrac{E_r}{Z_s}$

Synchronizing power, $P_{sy} = \alpha E I_{sy}$ watts/phase

Synchronizing torque, $T_{sy} = \dfrac{3 \times 60 \times P_{sy}}{2\pi N_s}$ N m

Synchronous Motor. It is electrically identical with an alternator.

Characteristics of synchronous motors :

(a) It runs at synchronous speed, $N_s = 120f/P$

(b) It is not inherently self-starting.

(c) It is capable of being operated under a wide range of power factors both lagging as well as leading.

Magnitude of armature current varies with excitation. When over-excited, motor runs with leading p.f., and with lagging p.f. when under-excited.

Torque developed by the motor depends on the coupling angle.

In synchronous motor, minimum current corresponds to unity power factor.

Methods of Starting Synchronous Motors.

Since the synchronous motors has no self-starting torque, therefore it is necessary that an external means is to be employed to start the motor.

Various methods are :

1. **D.C. source.** The synchronous motor is coupled to a d.c. compound motor, whose speed is adjusted by a speed regulator. The synchronous motor is then excited and synchronized with the a.c. supply. At the moment of synchronizing the synchronous motor is switched on to a.c. mains and d.c. motor is disconnected from the d.c. supply mains or its field is strengthened until it begins to function as a generator. Otherwise synchronous motor will act as an a.c. motor with d.c. motor as its load.

2. **By means of a.c. Motor.** Synchronous motor with an exciter is coupled with a small induction motor. Before switching the a.c. supply to the synchronous motor it must be synchronized to the bus-bar. The induction motor used for starting should have lesser number of poles than synchronous motor so that it may be capable of bringing the synchronous motor to the synchronous speed. After normal operation has been established, the induction motor is sometimes uncoupled from the synchronous motor.

3. **Self-starting.** The synchronous motor can be made self-starting by providing a special winding on the rotor poles known as *damper winding or squirrel cage winding*. It consists of short-circuited-copper bars embedded in the face of the field pole. A.C. supply given to the stator produces a rotating magnetic field which causes the rotor to rotate. Therefore in the beginning the synchronous motor with damper winding starts as squirrel cage induction motor.

When the motor approaches its synchronous speed, the rotor winding is connected to the exciter winding so that the rotor is magnetically looked by the rotating field of the stator and thus the motor runs as synchronous motor.

HUNTING

When a synchronous motor is connected to a varying load, a condition known as hunting is produced which may also occur if the supply frequency is pulsating (*e.g.* when connected to reciprocating engines). When a synchronous motor is on load, its rotor falls back in phase by a coupling angle δ. As the load is increased progressively, this angle also increases so as to produce more torque, to follow with the increased load. If there is sudden decrease in the load, the motor is immediately pulled up or advanced to a new value corresponding to a new load. But in this process, the rotor overshoots, hence it is again pulled back. In this way the rotor starts oscillating about its new position of equilibrium corresponding to new load. If the time period of these oscillation happens to be equal to natural time period of the machine, the mechanical resonance is set up. The amplitude of these oscillations is built up to a large value and may eventually become so great that the machine is thrown out of synchronism. To stop the build up of these oscillations, circuit dampers are employed which consist of short-copper bars embedded in the faces of the field poles of the motor. The oscillation of the rotor sets up eddy currents in the dampers which flow in such a way so as to suppress the oscillations.

Application of synchronous motors :

1. It is used in power houses and substations in parallel with bus-bars to improve the power-factor.

2. In factories having large number of induction motors or other apparatus operating with lagging power factor, these motors are used in order to improve the power factor.

3. It is used as booster to control the voltage at the end of transmission line by varying its excitation.

4. It is used in rubber, textile and cement mills, and other big industries for power application.

5. It is used to derive continuously operating and constant speed equipment such as centrifugal pumps, blowers, and motor generators.

EXERCISE – I

1. Alternator works on the principle of
   (a) mutual induction
   (b) Faraday's law of electromagnetic induction
   (c) self mutual induction
   (d) self and mutual induction

2. The rotor of alternator has
   (a) no slip rings
   (b) two slip rings
   (c) three slip rings
   (d) four slip rings

3. The generator which gives dc supply to the rotor of an alternator is called
   (a) convertor   (b) exciter
   (c) inverter   (d) rectifier

4. In alternators, salient pole type rotors are generally used with prime movers of
   (a) high speed
   (b) low speed
   (c) medium speed
   (d) any speed

5. In alternators, cylindrical pole type rotors are generally used with prime movers of
   (a) high speed
   (b) low speed
   (c) medium speed
   (d) both low and high speeds

6. The frequency of voltage generated in an alternator depends on
   (a) number of poles
   (b) speed of alternator
   (c) both (a) and (b)
   (d) type of winding

7. Salient pole type rotors are
   (a) larger in diameter and smaller in axial length
   (b) larger in diameter and larger in axial length
   (c) smaller in diameter and larger in axial length
   (d) smaller in diameter and smaller in axial length

8. The emf generated in alternator depends on
   (a) frequency
   (b) flux per pole
   (c) coil span factor
   (d) all of these

9. The number of electrical degrees passed through in one revolution of a four pole synchronous alternator is
   (a) 360°   (b) 720°
   (c) 1440°   (d) 2880°

10. As the speed of an alternator increases, the frequency
    (a) increases
    (b) decreases
    (c) remains constant
    (d) may increase or decrease depending on the power factor

11. An alternator is said to be overexcited when it is operating at
    (a) unity power factor
    (b) leading power factor
    (c) lagging power factor
    (d) either lagging or leading power factor

12. The frequency per pole in an alternator is equal to
    (a) number of poles
    (b) number of armature conductors
    (c) number of pair of poles
    (d) none of these

13. The exciter for a generator is a
    (a) series motor
    (b) shunt motor
    (c) compound motor
    (d) shunt generator

14. The rotor of a salient pole alternator has 12 poles. The number of cycles of emf per revolution would be
    (a) 12   (b) 6
    (c) 3   (d) 4

15. The advantage of salient poles in an alternator is
    (a) reduced noise
    (b) reduced windage loss
    (c) adaptability to low and medium speed operations
    (d) reduced bearing loads and noise

16. In an alternator, when the load increases due to armature reaction, the terminal voltage
    (a) drops
    (b) rises
    (c) remains unchanged
    (d) may drop or rise

17. The exciting field coil of an alternator is generally excited by
    (a) a separate dc generator driven by some source
    (b) a separate ac generator driven by some source
    (c) a dc generator coupled directly to the armature shaft
    (d) a battery

18. The ratio of armature leakage reactance to synchronous reactance of large size modern alternator is about
    (a) 0.05   (b) 0.2
    (c) 0.4   (d) 0.6

19. High speed alternators usually have
    (a) salient pole rotors
    (b) cylindrical rotors
    (c) both salient pole and cylindrical rotors
    (d) none of these

20. Cylindrical rotor alternators have
    (a) large length to diameter ratio
    (b) small length to diameter ratio
    (c) vertical configuration
    (d) none of these

21. To ensure effective cooling, cylindrical rotor alternators use
    (a) radial ducts only
    (b) axial ducts only
    (c) both radial and axial ducts
    (d) forced air cooling

22. The main advantage of using fractional pitch winding in an alternator is to reduce
    (a) amount of copper in the winding
    (b) size of the machine
    (c) harmonics in the generated emf
    (d) cost of the machine

23. The pitch factor in rotating electrical machines is defined as the ratio of the resultant emf of a
    (a) full pitched coil to that of a chorded coil
    (b) full pitch to the phase emf
    (c) chorded coil to the phase emf
    (d) chorded coil to that of a full pitched coil

24. In a rotating electrical machine, the chording angle for eliminating fifth harmonic should be
    (a) 30°   (b) 33°
    (c) 36°   (d) 38°

25. The material used for the manufacture of large turbo-alternator is
    (a) hot rolled grain oriented steel
    (b) cold rolled grain oriented steel
    (c) cast steel
    (d) wrought iron

26. Use of damped winding in alternators results in
    (a) elimination of harmonic effects
    (b) a low resistance path for the currents due to unbalancing of voltage
    (c) oscillations when two alternators operate in parallel
    (d) all of these

27. In a synchronous machine, if the field flux axis ahead of the armature field axis in the direction of rotation, the machine is working as
    (a) asynchronous motor
    (b) asynchronous generator
    (c) synchronous motor
    (d) synchronous generator

28. In an alternator, the armature reaction is completely magnetising when the load power factors is
    (a) unity   (b) 0.07
    (c) zero lagging   (d) zero leading

29. Which of the following is not an integral part of a synchronous generator system ?
    (a) Prime mover
    (b) Excitation system
    (c) Distribution transformer
    (d) Protection system

30. Cross magnetisation in an alternator field results in output which is
    (a) true sinusoidal
    (b) nonsinusoidal
    (c) harmonic free
    (d) none of these

31. In an alternator, in order to reduce the harmonics in the generated emf
    (a) slots are skewed
    (b) salient pole tips are changed
    (c) winding is made well distributed
    (d) all of these

32. Permissible variation in supply frequency of alternators is
    (a) ±1%   (b) ±2%
    (c) ±4%   (d) ±6%

33. Unbalanced 3-phase stator currents in an alternator cause
    (a) heating of rotor
    (b) vibrations
    (c) double frequency currents in the rotor
    (d) all of these

34. In large synchronous generators, protection provided against external faults is
    (a) biased differenctial protection
    (b) sensitive earth fault protection
    (c) inter-turn fault protection
    (d) all of these

35. The following part plays important role in overspeed protection of an alternator
    (a) overcurrent relay
    (b) alarm
    (c) differential protection
    (d) governor

36. In alternators, the distribution factor is defined as the ratio of emfs of
    (a) distributed winding to concentrated winding
    (b) full pitch winding to distributed winding
    (c) distributed winding to full pitch winding
    (d) concentrated winding to distributed winding

37. For the same power rating, an alternator operating at lower voltage will be
    (a) less noisy
    (b) costlier
    (c) larger in size
    (d) more efficient

38. The maximum current that can be supplied by an alternator depends on
    (a) speed of the exciter
    (b) number of poles
    (c) exciter current
    (d) strength of the magnetic field

39. In an alternator, use of short pitch coil of $160°$ will indicate the absence of following harmonic
    (a) third
    (b) fifth
    (c) seventh
    (d) ninth

40. Overheating of windings of an alternator
    (a) reduces generated voltage
    (b) reduces power factor
    (c) reduces life of the machine
    (d) causes no significant evil effect

41. The necessary condition for parallel operation of two alternators is
    (a) terminal voltage should be the same
    (b) frequency should be the same
    (c) phase sequence should be the same
    (d) all of these

42. When two alternators are running in parrallel, if the prime mover of one of the alternators is disconnected, then alternator will
    (a) stop running
    (b) run as a synchronous motor
    (c) run as a generator
    (d) none of these

43. Two alternators are running in parallel. If the driving force of both the alternators is changed, there will be changed in
    (a) frequency
    (b) back emf
    (c) generated voltage
    (d) all of these

44. The rotor of a high speed tubro-alternator is made up of solid steel forging to get
    (a) high mechanical stress
    (b) economy
    (c) reduction of eddy current loss
    (d) reduction of bearing friction

45. In a 3-phase alternator, the unsaturated synchronous reactance of 3Ω per phase. Then saturated synchronous reactance is
    (a) 3Ω (b) $>3\Omega$
    (c) $<3\Omega$ (d) $>> 3\Omega$

46. The rated voltage of alternaors used in power satations is usually
    (a) $11\,kV$ (b) $33\,kV$
    (c) $66\,kV$ (d) $132\,kV$

47. Salient pole machines have
    (a) large number of poles
    (b) small number of poles
    (c) small diameters
    (d) long cores

48. The stator of modern alternators are wound for
    (a) $60°$ phase groups
    (b) $120°$ phase groups
    (c) $180°$ phase groups
    (d) $240°$ phase groups

49. The armature reaction of an alternator influences
  (a) windage losses
  (b) operating speed
  (c) generated voltage per phase
  (d) waveform of generated voltage

50. When an alternator is supplying unity power factor load, the armature reaction will produce
  (a) magnetisation of the main field
  (b) demagnetisation of the main field
  (c) distortion of the main field
  (d) none of these

51. Alternators are generally designed to generate
  (a) fixed frequencies
  (b) variable frequencies
  (c) fixed currents
  (d) fixed power factors

52. In thermal stations, the number of poles used in alternators are usually
  (a) 48   (b) 12
  (c) 24   (d) none

53. In a synchronous alternator, the frequency f in Hz is given by
  (a) $f = \dfrac{PN}{120}$ (b) $f = \dfrac{PN}{60}$
  (c) $f = \dfrac{P}{60N}$ (d) $f = \dfrac{N}{60P}$
  where N is the speed in rpm and P is the number of poles.

54. In a synchronous alternator, armature reaction is solely determined by
  (a) power factor of the load
  (b) amount of current drawn from the alternator
  (c) speed of the prime mover driving the alternator
  (d) none of these

55. For zero power factor leading, the effect of armature reaction in an alternator on the main flux is
  (a) magnetising
  (b) demagnetising
  (c) cross-magnetising
  (d) none of these

56. The emf generated in an alternator due to nth harmonic is
  (a) n times the fundamental emf
  (b) equal to the fundamental emf
  (c) less than the fundamental emf
  (d) zero

57. The armature reaction of an alternator will be cross-magnetising if the power factor of the load is
  (a) zero leading
  (b) less than unity
  (c) unity
  (d) more than unity

58. The effect of cross-magnetizing field in an alternator may be reduced by
  (a) shifting the brush positions
  (b) using interpoles
  (c) using a magnetizing pole
  (d) none of these

59. The following method is best suited for finding the voltage regulation of an alternator
  (a) synchronous impedance method
  (b) Poltier triangle method
  (c) MMF method
  (d) none of these

60. Power factor of an alternator driven by constant prime mover input can be changed by changing its
  (a) speed
  (b) load
  (c) field excitation
  (d) phase sequence

61. In a large alternator, the moving part is
  (a) the poles
  (b) armature
  (c) brushes
  (d) none of these

62. To reverse the phase sequence of voltage generated in an alternator, we should
  (a) reverse the connection of its field winding
  (b) interchange any two of its phase terminals
  (c) both (a) and (b)
  (d) none of these

63. The length l of the rotor of a turbo-alternator and its diameter D are related as below
  (a) $l = D/2$ (b) $l = D$
  (c) $l = 2D$ (d) $l \gg D$

64. If the terminal voltage of an alternator is required to decrease with increase of load, the pf of the load should be
  (a) zero lagging
  (b) zero leading
  (c) unity
  (d) more than unity

65. Short pitch coils are used in alternators
    (a) to reduce the size of the machine
    (b) to reduce the stray losses
    (c) to reduce harmonic output
    (d) to reduce accurate phase shift of 120° between each phase

66. The most accurate method of measuring the hot spot temperature in field winding is
    (a) thermocouple method
    (b) thermometer method
    (c) by measuring the increase in winding resistances
    (d) none of these

67. In case of two alternators running in parallel and perfectly synchronized, the synchronizing power is
    (a) zero   (b) positive
    (c) negative   (d) ideally infinite

68. On keeping the input to the prime mover of an alternator constant and increasing the excitation
    (a) kVA becomes leading
    (b) kVA becomes lagging
    (c) kW will change
    (d) pf of the load remains unaltered

69. If an alternator is operating at a leading power factor, its voltage regulation is
    (a) more than one   (b) equal to zero
    (c) negative   (d) none of these

70. Hunting in synchronous machines can be reduced by using
    (a) damped bars
    (b) flywheel
    (c) machines having suitable synchronization power
    (d) all of these

71. In parallel operation of alternators, the synchronizing power is maximum, if armatures have
    (a) reactances equal to resistance
    (b) reactances less than resistances
    (c) reactances greater than resistances
    (d) none of these

72. For same power rating, the higher voltage alternator is
    (a) larger in size
    (b) smaller in size
    (c) cheaper
    (d) costlier

73. To run two alternators in parallel, the black Amp test is performed to ensure proper
    (a) voltage matching
    (b) frequency matching
    (c) phase difference matching
    (d) phase sequence matching

74. When a single alternator connected to infinite busbar supplies a local load, the change in excitation of the machine results in change of
    (a) power factor
    (b) power output
    (c) input power
    (d) terminal voltage

75. In parallel operation of two alternator, the synchronizing torque comes into operation where there is
    (a) phase difference between the two voltages
    (b) frequency difference between two voltages
    (c) voltage difference between the two voltages
    (d) either (a), (b) or (c)

76. In alternator, during hunting when the speed becomes supersynchronous, the damped bars develop
    (a) reluctance torque
    (b) pseudo-stationary torque
    (c) eddy current torque
    (d) induction generator torque

77. The slip rings employed in a three-phase alternator in hydrostation are insulated for
    (a) full armature voltage
    (b) extra high tension voltage
    (c) low voltage
    (d) very high voltage

78. An alternator is capable of delivering power at a particular frequency. The frequency can be increased by
    (a) increasing the current supplied to the field elecromagnets
    (b) reversing the armature rotation
    (c) increasing armature speed
    (d) reversing the field polarity

79. Distributing the armature winding of alternator in more than one number of slot per pole per phase results in
    (a) economy of material used in winding
    (b) reduction of irregularities produced in waveform
    (c) less weight of the entire armature
    (d) increase of generated emf per phase

80. Regulation of an alternator is likely to be negative in case of
   (a) high speed alternators
   (b) low speed alternators
   (c) lagging power factor of the load
   (d) leading power factor of the load

81. Maximum power in a synchronous machine is obtained when the load angle is
   (a) 0°   (b) 85°
   (c) 120°   (d) 135°

82. One of the advantages of distributing the winding in alternator is to
   (a) reduce noise
   (b) same on copper
   (c) improve voltage waveform
   (d) reduce harmonics

83. In case of a uniformly distributed winding in an alternator, the value of distribution factor is
   (a) 0.995   (b) 0.90
   (c) 0.80   (d) 0.70

84. The voltage of field system for an alternator is usually
   (a) less than 200 V
   (b) between 200 V and 500 V
   (c) 500 V
   (d) above 500 V

85. The following are the experimental data required for Poltier method for finding the voltage regulation of an alternator
   (a) no load curve, short circuit test values
   (b) no load curve, zero power factor curve
   (c) zero power factor curve, short circuit test curve
   (d) none of these

86. Salient-pole rotors are not used for high speed turbo alternators because of
   (a) large eddy loss
   (b) high centrifugal force and windage loss
   (c) excessive bearing friction
   (d) harmful mechanical oscillations

87. The short circuit characteristic of an alternator is
   (a) always linear
   (b) always nonlinear
   (c) sometimes linear and sometimes nonlinear
   (d) none of these

88. In order to reduce the harmonics in the emf generated in an alternator
   (a) slots are skewed
   (b) silent pole tips are chamfered
   (c) winding is well distributed
   (d) all of these

89. The hunting in synchronous machines can be guarded against by
   (a) using a flywheel
   (b) designing the synchronous machine with suitable synchronizing power
   (c) damped bars
   (d) all of these

90. Of the following conditions, the one which does not have to be met by alternators working in parallel is
   (a) terminal voltage of each machine must be the same
   (b) the machines must have the same phase rotation
   (c) the machines must operate at the same frequency
   (d) the machines must have equal ratings

91. The power factors of an alternator is determined by its
   (a) speed   (b) loud
   (c) excitation   (d) prime mover

92. With a load p.f. of unity, the effect of armature reaction on the main-field flux of an alternator is
   (a) distortional
   (b) magnetising
   (c) demagnetising
   (d) nominal

93. Large synchronous machines are constructed with armature winding on the stator because stationary armature winding
   (a) can be insulated satisfactorily for higher voltages
   (b) can be cooled more efficiently
   (c) all of these
   (d) both (a) and (b)

94. Main disadvantage of using short-pitch winding in alternators is that it
   (a) reduces harmonics in the generated voltage
   (b) reduces the total voltage around the armature coils
   (c) produces a symmetry in the three phase windings
   (d) increases Cu of end connections

95. If two machines are running in synchronism and the voltage of one machine is suddenly increased
    (a) the machines will burn
    (b) both machines will stop
    (c) synchronising torque will be produced to restore further synchronism
    (d) none of these

96. Maximum current that can be supplied by an alternator depends on
    (a) speed of the exciter
    (b) number of poles
    (c) exciter current
    (d) strength of the magnetic field.

97. Advantage of using short pitched windings in an alternator is that it
    (a) suppresses the harmonics in generated emf
    (b) reduces the total voltage around the armature coils
    (c) saves copper use in windings
    (d) improves cooling by better circulation of air.

98. When an alternator is running on no load, the power supplied by the prime mover is mainly consumed
    (a) to meet iron losses
    (b) to meet copper losses
    (c) to meet all no load losses
    (d) to produce induced emf in armature winding.

99. Two alternators are running in parallel. If the field on one of the alternator is adjusted, it will
    (a) reduce its speed
    (b) change its load
    (c) change its power
    (d) change its frequency.

100. The advantage of a short pitch winding is
    (a) low noise
    (b) increased inductance
    (c) suppression of harmonics
    (d) reduced eddy currents.

101. The regulation of an alternator is
    (a) the reduction in terminal voltage when alternator is loaded
    (b) the variation of terminal voltage under the conditions of maximum and minimum excitation
    (c) the increase in terminal voltage when load is thrown off
    (d) the change in terminal voltage from lagging power factor to leading power factor.

102. In synchronous generator operating at zero pf lagging, the effect of armature reaction is
    (a) magnetizing
    (b) demagnetizing
    (c) cross-magnetizing
    (d) both magnetizing and cross-magnetizing.

103. Main advantage of distributing the winding in slots is to
    (a) add mechanical strength to the winding
    (b) reduce the amount of copper required
    (c) reduce the harmonics in the generated e.m.f.
    (d) reduce the size of the machine.

104. One turn consists of
    (a) two coilsides
    (b) two conductors
    (c) four conductors
    (d) four coilsides

EXERCISE – II

1. A synchronous motor is operated from a bus voltage of 1.0 pu and is drawing 1.0 pu zero power factor leading current. Its synchronous reactance is 0.5 pu. What is the excitation emf of the motor ?
    (a) 2.0
    (b) 1.5
    (c) 1.0
    (d) 0.5 **(RRB 2012)**

2. What is the value of the load angle when the power output of a salient pole synchronous generator is maximum ? **(RRB 2012)**
    (a) 0°
    (b) 45°
    (c) 90°
    (d) None of these

3. If the field of a synchronous motor is underexcited, the power factor will be **(RRB 2012)**
    (a) lagging
    (b) leading
    (c) unity
    (d) more than unity

4. The synchronous reactance is the
    (a) reactance due to armature reaction of the machine
    (b) reactance due to leakage flux
    (c) combined reactance due to leakage flux and armature reaction
    (d) reactance either due to armature reaction or leakage flux **(RRB 2012)**

5. Consider the following:
   1. Supply voltage
   2. Excitation current
   3. Maximum value of load angle

   The maximum power developed by a synchronous motor is a function of which of the above?
   (a) 1 and 2   (b) 1 and 3
   (c) 2 and 3   (d) 1, 2 and 3
   (RRB 2012)

6. Which one of the following methods gives more accurate result for determination of voltage regulation of an alternator?   **(RRB 2012)**
   (a) m.m.f. method
   (b) Synchronous impedance method
   (c) Potier triangle method
   (d) American Institution Standard method

7. The material used for the manufacture of large turbo-alternator is   **(RRB)**
   (a) hot rolled grain oriented steel
   (b) cold rolled grain oriented steel
   (c) cast steel
   (d) wrought iron

8. Two alternators are connected in parallel. Their KVA and kW load shares can be changed by changing respectively their   **(RRB)**
   (a) driving torque and excitation
   (b) excitation and driving torque
   (c) excitation only
   (d) driving torques only

9. Cross magnetisation in an alternator field results in output which is   **(RRB)**
   (a) true sinusoidal
   (b) nonsinusoidal
   (c) harmonic free
   (d) none of these

10. Permissible variation in supply frequency of alternators is   **(RRB)**
    (a) ±1%   (b) ±2%
    (c) ±4%   (d) ±6%

11. Unbalanced 3-phase stator currents in an alternator cause   **(RRB)**
    (a) heating of rotor
    (b) vibrations
    (c) double frequency currents in the rotor
    (d) all of these

12. The armature reaction of an alternator will be cross-magnetising if the power factor of the load is   **(RRB)**
    (a) zero leading   (b) less than unity
    (c) unity   (d) more than unity

13. Turbo alternators are used in thermal plants is
    (a) stationary field type
    (b) cylindrical rotor type
    (c) salient pole type
    (d) none of these   **(RRB)**

14. Load division between two parallel operating alternators are affected by   **(RRB)**
    (a) more lagging power angle
    (b) change in generated voltage
    (c) change in input to prime mover
    (d) increasing the system frequency

15. Cylindrical rotor alternators have
    (a) large length to diameter ratio
    (b) small length to diameter ratio
    (c) vertical configuration
    (d) none of these   **(DMRC 2013)**

16. In an alternator, in order to reduce the harmonics in the generated emf   **(DMRC 2013)**
    (a) slots are skewed
    (b) salient pole tips are changed
    (c) winding is made well distributed
    (d) all of these

17. In a synchronous alternator, the frequency f in Hz is given by   **(DMRC 2013)**
    (a) $f = \dfrac{PN}{120}$ (b) $f = \dfrac{PN}{60}$
    (c) $f = \dfrac{P}{60N}$ (d) $f = \dfrac{N}{60P}$
    where N is the speed in rpm and P is the number of poles.

18. In synchronous motor, minimum armature current occurs at   **(SSC, CPWD 2008)**
    (a) zero power factor
    (b) leading power factor
    (c) lagging power factor
    (d) unity power factor

19. High speed alternators usually have
    (a) salient pole rotor   **(SSC, CPWD 2008)**
    (b) cylindrical rotor
    (c) both salient pole and cylindrical rotor
    (d) None of the above

20. The field winding of an alternator requires
(SSC, CPWD 2008)
 (a) DC supply
 (b) AC supply
 (c) Pulsating DC
 (d) Any of the above

21. The rotor input when, rotor copper loss in an induction motor is 600 W and slip is 3% is
(SSC, CPWD 2008)
 (a) 18 kW (b) 200 kW
 (c) 20 kW (d) 25 kW

22. The angle between induced emf and terminal voltage on no-load for a single phase alternator is **(SSC, CPWD 2009)**
 (a) 180º (b) 90º
 (c) 0º (d) 270º

23. A salient pole synchronous generator connected to an infinite bus power will deliver maximum power at a power angle of **(SSC, CPWD 2009)**
 (a) δ = 0 (b) δ = 90º
 (c) δ = 45º (d) δ = 30º

24. Starting torque of synchronous motor is
 (a) very low **(SSC, CPWD 2009)**
 (b) zero
 (c) very high
 (d) half-full load torque

25. The negative phase sequence in a 3-phase synchronous motor exists when the motor is
 (a) underload **(SSC, CPWD 2009)**
 (b) overloaded
 (c) supplied with unbalanced voltage
 (d) hot

26. A centre zero ammeter connected in the rotor circle of a 6 pole, 50 Hz induction motor makes 30 oscillations in one minute. The rotor speed is **(SSC, CPWD 2009)**
 (a) 670 rpm (b) 990 rpm
 (c) 1010 rpm (d) 1030 rpm

27. Variation in dc excitation of a synchronous motor causes variation in **(SSC, CPWD 2010)**
 (a) speed of motor
 (b) power factor
 (c) armature current
 (d) both (b) and (c)

28. For a 3-phase, 4-pole, 50 Hz synchronous motor the frequency, no. of poles, and the load torque are all halved. The motor speed will be
(SSC, CPWD 2010)
 (a) 375 rpm (b) 75 rpm
 (c) 1500 rpm (d) 3000 rpm

29. While starting synchronous motor its field winding should be **(SSC, CPWD 2010)**
 (a) kept open
 (b) connected to a dc source
 (c) connected to ac source
 (d) kept shortcircuited

30. Voltage regulation of an alternator may be negative where **(SSC, CPWD 2011)**
 (a) the load power factor is lagging
 (b) the load power factor is leading
 (c) it is loaded beyond its full load capacity
 (d) the machine is run at very low loads

31. V-curves for isolated, 3-phase synchronous motor show **(SSC, CPWD 2011)**
 (a) the variation of mechanical power with field excitation at constant speed
 (b) the variation of armature voltage with field excitation at constant mechanical power
 (c) the variation of armature voltage with mechanical power at constant field excitation
 (d) the variation of armature current with field excitation at constant mechanical power

32. Which one of the following is correct ?
(SSC, CPWD 2011)
 (a) Synchronous motor is supplied with dc voltage in the armature winding
 (b) Synchronous motor is supplied with ac voltage in the field winding
 (c) Synchronous motor is supplied with rectified voltage in the armature winding
 (d) Synchronous motor is supplied with dc voltage in the field winding

33. The pitch factor for a full pitched winding of a synchronous machine is **(SSC, CPWD 2012)**
 (a) 0.5 (b) 0.9
 (c) 0.0 (d) 1.0

34. Which one of the following is correct ?

(SSC, CPWD 2012)

(a) The effect of air gap flux on armature current of a synchronous machine is called armature reaction.

(b) The effect of armature current on main flux of a synchronous machine is called armature reaction.

(c) The effect of armature current on air gap flux of a synchronous machine is called armature reaction

(d) The effect of field current on main flux of a synchronous machine is called armature reaction.

35. Two alternators rated 40 MVA and 60 MVA respectively are working in parallel and supplying a total load of 80 MW. Speed regulation of both the alternators is 5%. The load sharing between them will be   (SSC, CPWD 2012)

(a) 32 MW, 48 MW

(b) 36 MW, 44 MW

(c) 40 MW each

(d) 30 MW, 50 MW

36. A 3-phase synchronous motor is started by utilizing the torque developed in

(SSC, CPWD 2013)

(a) the high-speed steam-turbine

(b) the damper winding on the rotor

(c) the damper winding on the stator

(d) the low-speed water-turbine

37. Alternators are usually designed to generate which type of a.c. voltage?   (SSC, CPWD 2013)

(a) With fixed requency

(b) With variable frequecny

(c) Fixed current

(d) Fixed power factor

38. A 300 kW alternator is driven by a prime mover of speed regulation 4% while the prime mover of another 200 kW alternator has a speed regulation of 3%. When operating in parallel, the total load they can take without any of them being overloaded is   (SSC, CPWD 2013)

(a) 500 kW   (b) 567 kW

(c) 425 kW   (d) 257 kW

39. Hydrogen is used in large alternators mainly to :

(SSC, CPWD 2014)

(a) reduce eddy current losses

(b) reduce distortion of wave form

(c) cool the machine

(d) strengthen the magnetic field

40. A synchronous motor working at leading power factor can be used as :   (SSC, CPWD 2014)

(a) mechanical synchronizer

(b) voltage booster

(c) phase advancer

(d) noise generator

41. For V-curves for a synchronous motor the graph is drawn between :   (SSC, CPWD 2014)

(a) armature current and power factor

(b) field current and armature current

(c) terminal voltage and load factor

(d) power factor and field current

42. Which of the following condition is **NOT** mandatory for alternators working in parallel ?

(SSC, CPWD 2014)

(a) The alternators must have the same phase sequence.

(b) The terminal voltage of each machine must be the same.

(c) The machines must have equal kVA ratings.

(d) The alternators must operate at the same frequency.

43. The positive, negative and zero sequence impedances of 3-phase synchronous generator are j 0.5 pu, j 0.3 pu and j 0.2 pu respectively. When symmetrical fault occurs on the machine terminals. Find the fault current. The generator neutral is grounded through reactance of j 0.1 pu.   (SSC, CPWD 2014)

(a) $-j$ 3.33 pu   (b) $-j$ 1.67 pu

(c) $-j$ 2.0 pu   (d) $-j$ 2.5 pu

44. A synchronous motor can be used as synchronous condenser when it is   (SSC CPWD 2014)

(a) over excited

(b) over loaded

(c) under excited

(d) under loaded

45. Which one of the following methods would give a higher than actual value of regulation of an alternator ? **(SSC CPWD 2014)**

(a) ZPF method   (b) MMF method

(c) EMF method   (d) ASA method

46. If the excitation of an alternator operating in parallel with other alternator is increased above the normal value of excitation, its

(a) power factor becomes more lagging

(b) power factor becomes more leading

(c) output current decreases

(d) output kW decreases   **(SSC CPWD 2014)**

47. In an alternator, the effect of armature reaction is minimum at power factor of

(a) 0.5 lagging

(b) 0.866 lagging

(c) 0.866 leading

(d) unity   **(SSC CPWD 2014)**

48. Damper winding in synchronous motors is used to   **(SSC CPWD 2014)**

(a) suppress hunting

(b) improve power factor

(c) develop reluctance torque

(d) improve the efficiency

49. Turbo alternators have rotors of
(SSC CPWD 2014)

(a) small diameter and long axial length

(b) large diameter and long axial length

(c) large diameter and small axial length

(d) small diameter and small axial length

50. A 10 pole 25 Hz alternator is directly coupled to and is driven by 60 Hz synchronous motor then the number of poles in a synchronous motor are?

(a) 24 poles

(b) 48 poles

(c) 12 poles

(d) None of the options   **(SSC CPWD 2015)**

51. A salient pole synchronous motor is operating at 1/4 full load. If its field current is suddenly switched off, it would? **(SSC CPWD 2015)**

(a) run at super-synchronous speed

(b) stop running

(c) run at sub-synchronous speed

(d) continue to run at synchronous speed

52. An alternator is supplying a load of 300 kw at a power factor of 0.6 lagging. If the power factor is raised to unity, how many more kw can alternator supply?

(a) 300 kw

(b) 100 kw

(c) 150 kw

(d) 200 kw   **(SSC CPWD 2015)**

53. The reactive power generated by a synchronous alternator can be controlled by?

(a) changing the alternator speed

(b) changing the field excitation

(c) changing the terminal voltage

(d) changing the prime move input
(SSC CPWD 2015)

54. Synchronous impedance method of finding voltage regulation of an alternator is called pessimistic method because? **(SSC CPWD 2015)**

(a) it gives regulation value lower than its actual found by direct loading

(b) armature reaction is wholly magnetising

(c) it is simplest to perform and compute

(d) it gives regulation value higher than its actual found by direct loading

ANSWERS

EXERCISE – I

1. (b)	**2.** (b)	**3.** (b)	**4.** (b)	**5.** (a)	**6.** (c)	**7.** (a)	**8.** (d)	**9.** (a)	**10.** (a)
11. (b)	**12.** (c)	**13.** (d)	**14.** (b)	**15.** (c)	**16.** (d)	**17.** (c)	**18.** (b)	**19.** (b)	**20.** (a)
21. (c)	**22.** (c)	**23.** (d)	**24.** (c)	**25.** (d)	**26.** (d)	**27.** (d)	**28.** (d)	**29.** (c)	**30.** (b)
31. (d)	**32.** (b)	**33.** (d)	**34.** (d)	**35.** (d)	**36.** (c)	**37.** (c)	**38.** (d)	**39.** (d)	**40.** (c)
41. (d)	**42.** (c)	**43.** (a)	**44.** (a)	**45.** (c)	**46.** (a)	**47.** (a)	**48.** (a)	**49.** (c)	**50.** (c)
51. (a)	**52.** (d)	**53.** (a)	**54.** (a)	**55.** (a)	**56.** (c)	**57.** (c)	**58.** (a)	**59.** (b)	**60.** (c)
61. (a)	**62.** (c)	**63.** (d)	**64.** (b)	**65.** (c)	**66.** (a)	**67.** (c)	**68.** (b)	**69.** (c)	**70.** (d)
71. (d)	**72.** (b)	**73.** (b)	**74.** (a)	**75.** (d)	**76.** (d)	**77.** (c)	**78.** (c)	**79.** (b)	**80.** (d)
81. (b)	**82.** (c)	**83.** (a)	**84.** (a)	**85.** (b)	**86.** (b)	**87.** (a)	**88.** (d)	**89.** (d)	**90.** (d)
91. (b)	**92.** (a)	**93.** (d)	**94.** (b)	**95.** (c)	**96.** (d)	**97.** (b)	**98.** (c)	**99.** (b)	**100.** (c)
101. (c)	**102.** (b)	**103.** (c)	**104.** (b)						

EXERCISE – II

1. (d)	**2.** (d)	**3.** (a)	**4.** (c)	**5.** (a)	**6.** (c)	**7.** (b)	**8.** (c)	**9.** (b)	**10.** (b)
11. (d)	**12.** (c)	**13.** (b)	**14.** (c)	**15.** (a)	**16.** (d)	**17.** (a)	**18.** (d)	**19.** (b)	**20.** (a)
21. (c)	**22.** (c)	**23.** (b)	**24.** (b)	**25.** (c)	**26.** (b)	**27.** (d)	**28.** (c)	**29.** (d)	**30.** (b)
31. (d)	**32.** (d)	**33.** (d)	**34.** (b)	**35.** (a)	**36.** (b)	**37.** (a)	**38.** (c)	**39.** (c)	**40.** (c)
41. (b)	**42.** (c)	**43.** (b)	**44.** (a)	**45.** (c)	**46.** (a)	**47.** (d)	**48.** (a)	**49.** (a)	**50.** (a)
51. (d)	**52.** (d)	**53.** (b)	**54.** (d)						

6
CHAPTER

Power Generation

HYDRO–ELECTRIC POWER PLANTS

These power plants utilises potential energy of the water at a high level for the generation of electrical energy.

Requirements.

(i) Ample quantity of water at sufficient head

(ii) Suitable site

Amount of power that can be developed depends on

(i) quantity of water available,

(ii) rate at which it is available,

(iii) head

Electrical power developed,

$$P = w \, Q \, H\eta \times 9.81 \times 10^{-3} \text{ kW}$$

where W = specific weight of water in kg/m³,

Q = rate of flow of water in m³/s,

H = height of fall or head in m, and

h = generation efficiency.

In a hydro–electic power station, water head is created by constructing a dam across a river or lake. The pressure head of water or kinetic energy of water is utilised to drive the water turbines coupled to alternators and, therefore generation of electrical power.

Advantages.

(i) These plants are neat and clean, robust, highly reliable, cheapest in operation and maintenance and have got longer life.

(ii) These plants do not need any fuel.

(iii) Can be run up and synchronised in few minutes.

(iv) These have no stand by losses.

Disadvantages.

(i) These needs long area, enormously high construction cost, long time for erection and long transmission lines.

(ii) Reservoir of such a plants submerges huge areas

(iii) Long dry season may affect the power supply.

Selection of Site.

Selected site should have

(i) large catchment area

(ii) high average rain fall

(iii) favourable place for constructing the storage or reservoir.

(iv) land should be cheap in cost and rocky in order to withstand the weight of large building and heavy machinery.

(v) possibility of providing adequate transportation facilities so that the necessary equipment and machinery could be easily transported.

CLASSIFICATION OF HYDRO-ELECTRIC POWER PLANTS

(1) Classification according to the extent of water flow regulation available.

(i) *Run off river power flow :*

These plants without pondage do not store water and uses the water as it comes. Such plants can be built at a considerably low cost but the head available and the amount of power generated are usually very low. During the high flow periods such plants can be employed to supply a substantial portion of base load.

(ii) *Run-off river power plants with pondage :*

These plants with pondage have increased usefulness because of pondage which usually refers to the collection of water behind a dam at the plant and increases the firm capacity for a short-period, say a week or more depending on the size of pondage. Such power plants are comparatively more reliable and its generating capacity is less dependent on available rate of flow of water.

Depending on the flow of stream, these power plants can serve as

(a) Base load plans-during high flow periods.

(b) Peak load plants-during low flow periods.

(iii) *Reservoir power plants :*

These are with reservoirs of sufficiently large size to permit carry-over storage from the wet season to the dry season, and thus to supply firm flwo substantially more than the minimum natural flow. Such plants can be used as base load plants or peak load plants as per requirement. Most of the hydro-electric power plants everywhere in the world are of this type.

(2) Classification according to availability of water head.

(i) *Low head (below 60m) :*

Low head power plant usually consists of a dam across a river. A side way stream diverges from the river at the dam and over this strem the power house is constructed. Later this channel joins the river further down stream. Such a plant uses vertical shaft Francis, propeller or Kaplan turbine. Structure of such a plant is extensive and expensive. Generators used in such plants are of low speed and large diameter.

(ii) *Medium head (above 60m and below 300m) :*

Medium head power plant uses horizontal shaft Francis, propeller or Kaplan turbines. In such a plant water is carried from main reservoir to foreby through open channel and then to turbines through the penstock. the forebay itself serves as the surge tank in this case.

(iii) *High head power plants (above 300m) :*

High head power plant uses Pelton wheels or jet impulse turbines as a prime-movers. In such a plant, the water from the reservoir is carrried through tunnel upto the surge tank and from surge tank to the power house through the penstock. The generators used in such plants are of high speed and small diameter. Penstocks used are of large lengths and comparatively smaller cross-section.

(3) Classification according to the load supplied.

(i) *Base load plants :*

These cater the base load of the system. Such plants have high load factors and continue to run for longer durations. Such plants are usually of large capacity.

(ii) *Peak load plants :*

These are used only when the power demand exceeds the limits of other power plants in the inter-connected system. Diesel engine plant, gas turbine plant or even steam power plants is used as a peak load plant.

(iii) *Pumped storage power plants:*

These uses reversible turbines which operate as turbines for power generation during peak load hours and as pumps for pumping water during peak-off hours.

WATER TURBINES

In hydro-electric power plants, water turbines are used. The water turbines are

(i)   simple in constrution

(ii) highly efficient in operation (about 90% on full load)

(iii) easily controllable

(iv) pick up the load in a very short time

They are built in various size to 10,00,000 hp with speeds varying from 80 rpm to 1,275 rpm depending on their size. Hydraulic turbines may be vertical of horizontal.

The water turbines used as prime movers in hydro-electric power stations.

CLASSIFICATION OF WATER TURBINES

(1) According to the type of flow of water.

(i) *Axial flow turbines :* These have flow of water along the shaft axis such as propeller and Kaplan turbines.

(ii) *Inward radial flow turbines:* These have flow of water along the radius such as Francis turbine.

(iii) *Tangential flow turbines :* These have flow of water along the tangential directions such as Pelton wheel turbine.

(iv) *Mixed flow (radial inlet and axial outlet) turbines :* e.g. Francis turbine.

(2) According to the action of water on moving blades.

(i) *Impulse turbines :* When the entire pressure of water is converted into kinetic energy in a nozzle and the jet thus formed drives the wheel, the turbine is of impulse type,

(ii) *Reaction turbines :* When the water pressure combined with its velocity work on the runner the turbine is known as reaction type turbine.

(3) According to the name of the originator.

(i) *Pelton wheel :* Pelton wheel is an impulse turbine and is used for high head poer plants and their speed is about 1275 rpm.

(ii) *Kaplan turbines :* These are used for medium head power plants and for variable load. Their speed range is 320 to 1000 rpm.

(iii) *Francis reaction turbines:* In these vertical shaft arrangement has proved better and is therefore universally adopted. In case of large sized impulse turbines, horizontal shaft arrangement is mostly adopted.

STEAM POWER PLANTS

In steam power plants, the heat of combustion of fossil fuels (coa, oil or gas) is utilized by the boilers to raise steam at high pressure and temperature. The steam so produced is used in driving the steam turbines or sometimes steam engines coupled to generators and thus in generating electrical energy.

Essential features of power plants.

Boilers, turbines coupled to electrical generators, condensers and large number of auxiliaries. The thermal efficiency of steam power plants is quite low (about 30%) and overall efficiency is about 29%. In steam power plants more than 50 percent of total heat of combustion is lost as heat rejected to the condenser.

Steam power plant basically operates on the Rankine cycle. Coal is burnt in a boiler, which converts water into steam. The stam is expanded in a turbine, which produces mechanical power driving the alternator coupled to the turbine. The steam after expansion in prime mover (turbine) is ususaly condensed in a condenser to be fed into the boiler again.

Arrangement is divided into four main circuits.

(*i*) Fuel and ash circuit

(*ii*) Air and fuel gas circuit

(*iii*) Feed water and steam circuit

(*iv*) Cooling water circuit.

Advantages.

(*i*) Fuel used is cheaper

(*ii*) Less space is required

(*iii*) Low initial cost

(*iv*) Less production cost

(*v*) Ability of responding to rapidly changing loads without difficiult

(*vi*) Capability of working under 25% of over load continuously.

Disadvantages.

(*i*) High maintenance and operating costs.

(*ii*) Pollution of atmosphere.

(*iii*) Requirement of water in huge quantity,

(*iv*) Handling of coal and disposal of ash-quite difficult,

(*v*) Long time requirement for erection and put into action.

Selection of Site

Factors considered for site selection of steam power plants are

(*i*) Nearnerss to load centre

(*ii*) Supply of water

(*iii*) Availability of coal

(*iv*) Availability of land at a reasonable price

(*v*) Type of availability of land

(*vi*) Transportation facilities

(*vii*) Availability of labours

(*viii*) Distance from populated area.

FUELS

Fuels may be classified as

(*i*) Solid

(*ii*) Liquid

(*iii*) Gaseous

Fuels may also be classified as

(*i*) Natural fuels

(*ii*) Prepared fuels

Fuels commonly used for combustion in the thermal power plants are

(*i*) Coal

(*ii*) Oil

(*iii*) Gas.

Gaseous fuel is rarely economical except when the power plant is located near natural gas field or gas manufacturing industries. Oil is used only where it is plentiful and cheap. Coal is the most commonly used fuel in thermal power plants.

Plant Efficiency

Efficiency of thermal power plants is quite low. The overall plant efficiency is not more than 40% but for majority of plants it is between 25 and 30%.

NUCLEAR POWER PLANTS

These plants are not well suited for varying loads since the reactor does not respond to the load fluctuation efficiently. They are usually operated at a load factor not below 80%

Advantages.

(*i*) Low fuel requirement resulting in low fuel cost and no problem of transportation and storage,

(*ii*) Less area requirement

(*iii*) Most economical in large capacity

(*iv*) Conservation of coal, oil etc

(*v*) Extremely flexible output control.

Disadvantages.

(*i*) Very high initial capital cost

(*ii*) Greater technical know how requirements in erection and commissioning

(*iii*) Possibility of occurrence of a dangerous amount of radio-active pollution

(*iv*) High mainteance cost owing to lack of standardisation

(*v*) High maintenance

(*vi*) Problem of disposal of the products, which are radio-active.

Selection of Site

Factors considered for site selection of nuclear power plants

(*i*) Nearness to load centre

(*ii*) Availability of water supply

(*iii*)Distance from populated area

(*iv*)Transportation facilities during erection period

(*v*) Type of land

(*vi*)Availability of space for disposal of waste.

Atomic Fuels

(*i*) Uranium (U$_{235}$)

(*ii*) Thorium (Th$_{232}$)

(*iii*)Plutonium (Pu$_{239}$)

NUCLEAR REACTOR

It is that part of nuclear power plant where nuclear fuel is subjected to nuclear fission and the energy released in the process is utilised to heat the coolant which may in turn generate steam to be used in gas turbine.

A nuclear reactor consists of

(*i*) *Reactor core :* These contains a number of fuel rods made of fissile material

(*ii*) Moderator material in the reactor core is provided to moderate, or reduce the neutron speeds to a value that increases the possibility of fission occurring.

(*iii*) *Reflector :* These completely surrounds the reactor core within the thermal shielding arrangement and bounces back most of the neutrons that escape from the fuel core. This conserves the nuclear fuel, as the low speed neutrons thus returned are useful in continuing the chain reaction.

(*iv*) *Thermal shielding :* This is provided to prevent the reactor wall from getting heated,. Coolant flows over the shielding to take away the heat.

(*v*) *Control rods :* Meant for regulating the fissioning in the reactor by absorbing the excess neutrons and. These are made of boron and are inserted into the reactor core from the top of the reactor vessel.

(*vi*) *Reactor vessel :* It is a tank encloses the reactor core, reflector and the thermal shielding and provides the entrance and exit for the coolant and also the passage for its flow through and around the reactor core.

(*vii*)*Coolant.* It is a medium through which heat generated in the reactor is transferred to the heat exhanger for further utilisation in power generation.

Classification of Nuclear Reactors

(1) According to the applications.

(*i*) Research and development reactors (used for testing new reactor designs and research)

(*ii*) Production reactors (used for converting fertile materials into fissile materials)

(*iii*)Power reactors (used for generation of electrical energy)

(2) According to the type of fission.

(*i*) Fast

(*ii*) Slow

(*iii*)Intermediate reactors.

(3) According to the type of fuel used.

(*i*) Natural uranium

(*ii*) Enriched uranium

(*iii*)Plutonium

(4) According to the state of fuels used.

(*i*) Solid

(*ii*) Liquid

(5) According to the fuel cycel.

(*i*) Burner

(*ii*) Converter

(*iii*)Breeder

(6) According to the arrangement of fissile and fertile material.

(*i*) One region (fissile and fertile material mixed)

(*ii*)Two region (fissile and fertiale material separate) reactors.

(7) According to the arrangement of fuel and the moderator.

(*i*) Homogeneous

(*ii*) Heterogeneous

(8) According to the moderator materials used.

(*i*) Heavy water

(*ii*) Graphite

(*iii*)Ordinary water

(*iv*)Beryllium or organic reactors

(9) According to the cooling system employed.

(*i*) Direct

(*ii*) Indirect reactors.

(10) According to the coolants used.

(*i*) Gas

(*ii*) Water

(*iii*)Heavy water

(*iv*)Liquid metal reactors

TYPES OF POWER REACTORS

(1) Pressurized Water Reactor (PWR).

Such a reactor is a thermal reactor and uses zirconium clad enriched uranium fuel.

Advantages

(i) Compactness

(ii) Possibility of breeding plutonium

(iii) Isolation of radioactive material from the main steam system

(iv) Cheap light water can be used as coolant-cum-moderator

(v) High power-density

Disadvantages

(i) Use of high pressure water system

(ii) Formation of low temeperature (250°C) steam

(iii) Use of expensive cladding material for corrosion prevention

(iv) High losses from heat exchanger

(v) High power consumption of auxiliaries

(vi) Poor thermal efficienty (20%).

(2) Boiling Water Reactor (BWR).

This is the simplest type of water reactor.

Advantages

(i) Small size pressure vessel

(ii) High steam pressure

(iii) Simple construction

(iv) Elimination of heat exchanger circuit resulting in reduction of cost and gain in thermal efficiency

(3) Gas Cooled Reactor.

This type of reactor employs a gas (CO_2 or helium) in place of water as the coolant and graphite as the moderator.

Advantages.

(i) Less severe corrosion problems

(ii) Possibility of use of natural uranium as fuel

(iii) Greater safety in comparison with water cooled reactors

Disdvantages.

Large energy consumption by gas blowers which may consume as much as 20% of the energy generated.

DIESEL-ELECTRIC POWER PLANTS

Diesel electric power plant is a power plant in which a diesel engine is used as the prime-mover for the generation of electric energy.

Advantages.

(i) Layout, design and construction of foundation and building is simple and cheap

(ii) Procurement, installation and commissioning quick

(iii) Flexibility in location

(iv) Simple design and installation

(v) Less space requirement because of minimum auxiliaries

(vi) No stand by losses

(vii) Limited cooling water requirement

(viii) High operation efficiency irrespective of load

(ix) Less fire hazard

(x) Can be started and put on load quickly

(xi) Can respond to varying loads without any difficulty

(xii) Need less space for fuel storage

(xiii) Free from ash handling problem

(xiv) Overall capital cost including installation per unit of installed capacity is lesser

(xv) Simple in operation

Disadvantages.

(i) Limited diesel unit capacity

(ii) Serious problem of noise from the exhaust

(iii) High maintenance and lubrication cost

(iv) High fuel cost

(v) Cannot supply over loads continuously.

Selection of site

Factors considered for site selection of diesel power plants are

(i) Availability of water supply

(ii) Availability of fuel

(iii) Availability of transportation facilities

(iv) Distance from populated area

(v) Availability of land

(vi) High bearing capacity to withstand the load of the plant

(vii) Vibrations transmitted to the foundation from compressors and diesel engines.

Elements of Diesel Electric Power Plants

(i) Diesel engine

(ii) Engine air intake (including air filters, ducts and supercharger (integral with the engine)

(iii) Engine fuel system (including fuel storage tanks, fuel transfer pumps) *(iv)* Engine exhaust system (including silencers and connecting ducts.)

(v) Engine cooling system (including cooling pumps, cooling towers or spray ponds)

(vi) Engine lubricating oil system (including lurbricating oil pumps, oil tanks, filters ,coolers, purifiers and connecting pipe work.)

(vii) Engine starting equipment (including batter, compressed air supply.)

GAS TURBINE ELECTRIC POWER PLANTS

Gas turbine electric power plant is a power plant in which a gas turbine is used as the prime-mover for the generation of electrical energy.

Advantages.

(i) Simplicity of design and installation

(ii) High realiability

(iii) Simple lubrication system

(iv) Clean exhaust requiring no stack

(v) Compactness

(vi) Low initial cost

(vii) Requiring small building space and light foundations requiring little cooling water.

(viii) Delivery and installation time for such power plants is much less

(ix) Can be started quickly

(x) Can be put to share full load within a few minutes

(xi) Efficiency can be improved considerably by using heat economy devices.

(xii) Gas turbines may be operated by remote control and need little or no personnel while operating and while shutdown maintance costs is low.

Disadvantages.

(i) Inability of using coal or heavy residual petroleum as fuel

(ii) Low net output low overall efficiency

(iii) Noisy operation

(iv) High specific fuel consumption

(v) Limited unit capacity

Selection of Site

Factors considered for the site selection of gas turbine power plants are follows.

(i) Distance from load centre

(ii) Availability of land at reasonable rate

(iii) Availability of fuel at reasonable rate

(iv) Availability of transportation facilities

(v) Distance from populted area

(vi) Type of land

Fuels For Gas Turbines

A vartiety of fuels (solid, liquid and gaseous) are available for use in gas turbines. The petroleum fuels such as kerosene, gas oil diesel oil, residual oil, are quite suitable for use in gas turbines. Natural gas which is mainly methane, has a very high calorific value and is generally used for auxiliary power generation in oil fields.

OPEN AND CLOSED GAS CYCLE TURBINE POWER PLANT.

Open cycle gas turbine power plant.

In these, the fuel is mixed with air in the combustion chamber and the combustion gases are expanded in the gas turbine, which causes erosion and corrosion of turbine blades and, therefore, it becomes essential to use fuel of superior quality in the combustion chamber. This draw-back is overcome in case closed cycle power plant is adopted, in which fuel is not mixed with the working medium (air or any other gas such as helium, argon, hydrogen and neon).

Closed cycle gas turbine power plant.

In these plants, the medium is heated externally and is continuously circulated through the compressors, heat exchangers, intercoolers, reheaters and gas coolers. Load variation is affected by controlling the absolute pressure and the mass flow of the circulating air.

Combination gas turbine power plants.

The gas turbine power plants are mainly used for supplying peak loads in other types of power plants e.g. in steam and hydro-electric power plants. The heat content of gas turbine exhaust is quite substantial. A combination gas turbine-steam turbine cycle aims at improving the overall plant efficiency by using the heat of exhaust gases from the gas turbine as a heat source for a steam plant cycle.

Arrangements of combination cycles generally employed

(i) Use of exhaust gases of gas turbine power plant for heating of feed water

(ii) Use of exhaust gases from turbine as combustion air in steam boiler

(iii) Use of gases from a supercharged boiler for expansion in gas turbine

Advantages

(i) Saving in exhaust heat of the gas turbine resulting in increase of its heat rate

(ii) Reduction in stack emissions

(iii) Reduction in space requirement

(*iv*) Reduction in requirements of condensing water by 60% as compared to fossil fuel plant of given capacity

(*v*) Reduction in starting time

Uses.

(*i*) For supplying peak loads in other types of power plants (steam and hydro plants) because of their higher fuel costs and low initial costs

(*ii*) For driving auxiliaries in other power plants

(*iii*) As standby power plants in hydro-power plants

(*iv*) To operate as combination plants with conventional steam boilers and as base-load plants where fuel oil or natural gases are cheap and easily available, water supply is scarce

(*v*) Load factor is very low, say 15-18 %.

NON-CONVENTIONAL METHODS OF POWER GENERATION

(*i*) Magneto-hydrodynamic (MHD) power generation

(*ii*) Solar cells

(*iii*) Fuel cells

(*iv*) Thermo-electric generator

(*v*) Thermionic convertor

(*vi*) Solar power generation, wind power generation

(*vii*) Geo-thermal energy generation

(*viii*) Tidal power generation

(*i*) Magneto-Hydro-Dynamic (MHD) power generation.

The basic principle of MHD generation is the same as that of a conventional electrical generator, i.e motion of a conductor through a magnetic field induces an emf in it. In MHD generation, electrical energy is directly generated from hot combustion gases produced by the combustion of the fuel without moving parts. MHD generator is heat engine operating on a turbine cycle and transforming the internal energy of gas directly into electrical energy.

Advantages.

(*i*) High conversion efficiency (about 50%)

(*ii*) High capital costs

(*iii*) More realiable having no moving part

(*iv*) More efficient heat utilisation reduces the amount of heat discharged to environments and so the amount of cooling water required is reduced.

(*ii*) Thermionic convertor.

In such a device, electrons act as the working fluid in place of a vapour or gas.

These electrons are driven by heat energy across a potential difference to produce electrical energy.

(*iii*) Fuel cells.

A fuel cell is a device in which chemical energy is directly converted into electrical energy. In fuel cells, chemical energy of the reactants is converted into electrical energy as an isothermal process. Thus heat is not involved in the conversion process and a high conversion efficiency is possible.

BASE LOAD AND PEAK LOAD

The unvarying load, which occurs almost the whole day on the power plant is called the base load whereas the various peak demands of the load over and above the base load of the power plant is called the peak loads.

Power plants to be employed as base power plants should have

(*i*) low operating cost

(*ii*) capability of working continuously for the long periods

(*iii*) requirement of few operating personnel and their repairs should be economical and speedy.

The power plants to be employed as peak power plants should have the capability of quick start, synchronisation and taking up of system load and quick response to load variation.

The hydro-power plants should be employed for base load operation as far as possible because of their higher capital cost. However during the periods of draught, the hydro-plants may be used as peak load plants. A steam power plant gives minimum cost of generation per unit when used as base load plant. However, in order to save fuel it may be used as peak load plant. Nuclear power plants are suitable only for base load operation at high load factors exceeding 0.8. Gas turbine power plants are suitable for supplying peak loads and diesel power plants play a very little role in bulk power generation because of their uneconomical operating costs.

INTERCONNECTION OF POWER STATIONS

Several generating stations connected to each other form an interconnected system.

Advantages.

(*i*) Reduced reserve plant capacity in the system as a whole, improved load factor

(ii) Diversity factor and operation efficiency

(iii) Increased reliability of supply and effective capacity of the whole system

(iv) Reduced capital cost per kW

(v) Economical operation of power plants.

COSTS OF POWER GENERATION

Total annual cost incurred in the power generation is given by

$$E = a + b \, kw + c \, kwh$$

where a, b, and c are constants.

Fixed and semi-fixed cost being independent of the amount of energy generated is also called "standing cost."

In deciding any scheme for any given service, the choice must be such that the total operating cost (sum of annual fixed cost, semi-fixed cost and operating cost) be minimum.

Classification of costs.

(1) *Fixed cost.*

This cost is independent of maximum demand and energy output. It is due to

(i)   annual cost of central organisation

(ii) interest on the capital cost of land (especially if some land is held for furture development)

(iii) salaries of high officials

(2) *Semi-fixed cost.*

This cost depends upon the maximum demand but is independent of energy output. The semi-fixed cost is due to

(i)   annual interest and depreciation on the capital cost of the generating plant

(ii) transmission and distribution network

(iii) building and other civil engineering works

(iv) all types of taxes and insurance charges

(v)   salaries of management and clerical staff.

(3) *Running or operating cost.*

This cost depends upon

(i)   number of hours the plants is in operation or

(ii) number of units of electrical energy generated

The running or operating cost is due to

(i)   annual cost of fuel

(ii) lubricating oil

(iii) water

(iv) maintenance and repair cost of equipment

(v)   wages and salaries of operational and maintenance staff and salaries of supervisory staff engaged on the running of the plant.

ECONOMICS OF GENERATION

The generation of electrical energy economically depends on the type, location and the rating of generating stations. The generating stations may be steam, hydro, diesel or other type. The power stations should be as near as possible to the centre of the loads so that the transmission cost and losses are minimum. The other consideration for the design of the power station are reliability, minimum capital and operating costs.

Considerations deciding the type and rating of generating plant:

(i) *Load curves.*

The load on the power station varies from time to time. The daily variations in load on the power station from time to time-hourly or half hourly can be plotted on a graph taking load on y-axis and time on x-axis. The curve so obtained is known as *daily load curve*. From the daily load curves of a particular month, the monthly load curve can be plotted by calculating the average value of power at a particular time of the day. Simiarly if we consider such monthly load curves of a particular year, and from the average value of power at a particular time of the day, the annual load curve can be obtained.

Informations obtained by the load curves

(a) Variation of the load during different hours of the day

(b) Area under the curve represents the total number of units generated in a day.

(c) Peak of the curve represents the maximum demand on the station on a particular day.

(d) Area under the load curve divided by the number of hours represents the average load on the power station.

(e) Ratio of the area under the load curve to the total area of the rectangle in which it is contained gives the load factor.

(ii) *Load duration curve.*

This type of curve indicates the variation of load, but with the loads arranged in descending order of magnitude i.e. the greatest load on the left, lesser loads towards the right and the least load at the extreme right. This curve gives the number of hours for which a particular load lasts during the day. The area under this curve like load curve or chronological curve gives the total number of units generated for the period considered. From this curve the load factor of the station can also be determined. From these curves, the distribution of load between various generating units can also be predicted.

(iii) **Mass curve.**

This curve is plotted with units (kWh) as ordinate and time as abscissa. Thus a mass curve gives the total energy consumed by the load upto a particular time a day.

(iv) **Connected load.**

The sum of continuous ratings of all the electrical equipment connected to the supply is known as connected load.

(v) **Maximum demand.**

It is not necessary that all the connected load be switched to a system at a time. The greatest of all "short time interval averaged" (15 minutes or $\frac{1}{2}$ hour or 1 hour) during a given period   a day, a month or a year), on the power station is called the maximum demand. It is sometimes also called as system peak. It is the maximum demand which determines the size and cost of the installation.

(vi) **Demand factor.**

The ratio of actual maximum demand on the system to the total rated load connected to the system is called the demand factor. It is always less than unity.

(vii) **Average load or demand.**

The average load or demand on the power station is the average of loads occurring at the various events.

(viii) **Load factor.**

The ratio of average load to the maximum demand during a certain period of time such as a day or a month or a year is called the load factor. Since average load is always less than the maximum demand, load factor is therefore, always less than unity.

(ix) **Diversity factor.**

The maximum demands of all the consumers supplied from an installation do not occur usually at the same time. Maximum demand on the installation is, thus always less than the sum of individual maximum demands of all consumers connected to it.

The ratio of sum of the individual maximum demands of all the consumers supplied by it to the maximum demand of the power station is called the *diversity factor*. It is always greater than unity.

(x) **Capacity factor or Plant factor.**

Every plant has to have a reserve capacity so as to take care of the future expansion and increase in load and therefore total installed capacity of the plant is usually greater than that actually required (maximum demand). Capacity (or plant) factor is defined as the ratio of the average load to the rated capacity of the power plant.

(xi) **Utilisation factor.**

It is a measure or the utility of the power plant capacity and is the ratio of maximum demand to the rated capacity of the power plant. It is always less than unity.

(xii) **Plant operating factor or plant use factor.**

It is defined as the ratio of actual energy generated during a given period (say a year) to the product of capacity of the plant and the number of hours the plant has been actually in operation during the period.

(xiii) **Installed capacity.**

The total of station capacities available to supply the system load is called the installed capacity.

(xiv) **Firm power.**

It is the power intended to be always available (even under emergency conditions).

(xv) **Cold reserve.**

It is that portion of the installed reserve kept in operable conditions and available for service, but not normally ready for immediate loading.

(xvi) **Hot reserve.**

It usually refers to boiler excess capacity, which is kept hot and with steam pressure, ready for use.

(xvii) **Operating reserve.**

It refers to capacity in service in excess of peak load.

(xviii) **Spinning reserve.**

It is the generating capacity connected to the bus and ready to take load.

Significance of Load factor and Diversity factor.

Higher the values of load factor and diversity factors, lower will be the over all cost per unit generated.

The capital cost of the power station depends upon the capacity of the power station. Lower the maximum demand of the power station, lower is the capacity required and therefore lower is the capital cost of the plant. With a given number of consumers higher the diversity factor of their loads, smaller will be the capacity of the plant required and consequently the fixed charges due to capital investment will be much reduced.

Similarly higher load factor means more average load or more number of units generated for a given maximum demand and therefore overall cost per unit of electrical energy generated is reduced due to distribution of standing charges which are proportional to maximum demand and independent of number of units generated.

Thus the suppliers should always try to improve the load factor as well as diversity factor by inducing the consumers to use the electrical energy during off peak hours and they may be charged at lower rates for such schemes.

TARIFF

Tariff means the schedule of rates framed for supply of electrical energy to the various categories of consumers.

All types of tariffs must cover the recovery of costs of

(i)   capital investment in generating, transmitting and distributing equipment

(ii)   operation, supplies and maintenance of equipment and

(iii) metering equipment, billing, collection and miscellaneous serivces and

(iv) a satisfactory return on the total capital investment.

COMMON TYPES OF TARIFFS

(i) *Flat demand tariff.*

This is one of the earliest forms of tariffs used for charging the consumers for electrical energy consumption. This tariff is expressed as

energy charges, y = Rs. ax

where a = rate per lamp or kW of connected load and

x = number of lamps or load connected in kw.

In this types of tariff, the metering equipmetn, meter reading, billing, and accounting costs are eliminated.

(ii) *Simple tariff.*

This is the simplest type of tariff according to which the cost of energy is charged on the basis of units consumed and can be expressed in the form

y = Rs ax

where a = charges in rupees per unit, and

x = total electrical energy consumed in units or kwh.

(iii) *Flat rate tariff.*

This types of tariff differs from the former one in the sense that the different types of consumers are charged at different rates, i.e. flat rate for light and fan loads is slightly higher than that for power load. The rate for each category of consumers is arrived at by taking into account its load factor and diversity factor.

(iv) *Step rate tariff.*

The step rate tariff is a group of flat rate tariffs of decreasing unit charges for higher range of consumption.

(v) *Block rate tariff.*

In this type of tariff a given block of energy is charged at higher rate and succeeding blocks of energy are charged at progressively reduced rates.

(vi) *Hopkinson demand rate or two part tariff.*

The total energy charge to be made to the consumer is split into two components

(a) Fixed charge

(b) Running charge. This type of tariff is expressed as

$$y = \text{Rs } a \text{ kw} + \text{Rs } b \text{ kwh}$$

where Rs a = charge per kw of maximum demand assessed

Rs b = charge per kwh of energy consumed.

This tariff is mostly applicable to medium industrial consumers.

(vii) *Maximum demand tariff.*

This tariff is similar to that of two part tariff except that in this case maximum demand is actually measured by a maximum demand indicator instead of merely assessing it on the basis of rateable value.

(viii) *KVA maximum demand tariff.*

It is a modified form of two part tariff. In this case maximum demand is measured in KVa instead of in kW. This type of tariff encourages the consumers to operate their machines/equipment at improved power factor because low power factor will cause more demand charges.

(ix) *Doherty rate or three part tariff.*

In this tariff total energy charge is split into three elements

(a) fixed charg

(b) semi-fixed charge and

(c) variable charge.

Such a tariff is expressed as,

$$y = \text{Rs } a + b\text{kw} + c \text{ kwh}$$

where a = a constant charge

b = unit charge in Rs per kw of maximum demand in kw during billing period

c = unit charge for energy in Rs per kwh of energy consumed.

This type of tariff is usually applicable to bulk supplies.

(x) Off peak tariff.

The load on the power station usually has pronounced peak loads in the morning and early evening and a very low load during the night (from 10 P.M to 6 A.M). Thus during the nigh and other off-peak period which may occur, a large proportion of the generating and distribution equipment will be lying idle. In case the consumers are encouraged to use electricity during off peak hours by giving a special discount, the energy can be supplied without incurring an additional capital cost and should therefore prove very profitable. This type of tariff is very advantageous for certain processes such as water heating by thermal storage, pumping, refrigeration etc.

POWER FACTOR IMPROVEMENT

The low power factor leads to high capital cost for the alternators, switchgears, transformers, transmission lines, distributors and cables etc.

Cause of Low Power Factor.

All ac motors (except over excited synchronous motors and certain types of commutator motors), arc lamps and discharge lamps, industrial heating furnaces operate at low lagging power fact ro. The power factor at which ac motors operate falls with the decrease in load and increase in supply voltage and because of improper maintenance and repairs of motors.

Advantages of Power Factor Improvement.

(i) Reduction in load current

(ii) Increase in voltage level across the load

(iii) Reduction in energy loss in the system (generators, transformers, transmission lines and distributors) due to reduction in load current

(iv) Reduction in KVA loading of the generators and the transformers which may relieve an over loaded system or release capacity for additional growth of load

(v) Reduction in KVA demand charge for large consumers.

Methods of Power Factor Improvement.

(1) By use of static capacitors.

Power factor can be improved by connecting the capacitors in parallel with the equipment operating at lagging power factor such as induction motors, fluorescent tubes.

Advantages.

(i) small losses (less than $\frac{1}{2}$ %)

(ii) higher efficiency (say 99.6%)

(iii) low initial cost;

(iv) little maintenance

(v) easy installation

Power factor can also be improved by connecting static capacitors in series with the line. Capacitors connected in series with the line neutralize the line reactance. The capacitors, when connected in series with line, are called the series capacitors, and when connected in parallel with the equipment, are called the shunt capacitors.

(2) By use of synchronous or high power factor machines.

Synchronous machines are excited by dc, and the power factor may be controlled by controlling the field excitation.

(3) By use of synchronous condensers. An over-excited synchronous motor running on no load is called the synchronous condenser or synchronous phase advancer and behaves like a capacitor, the capacitive reactance of which depends upon the motor excitation. Power factor can be improved by using synchronous condensers like shunt capacitors connected across the supply.

EXERCISE – I

1. Coolant used in fast breeder reactor is
   (a) sodium
   (b) heavy water
   (c) air
   (d) cadmium

2. Percentage of U^{235} in naturally available uranium is about
   (a) 0.01   (b) 0.7
   (c) 0.001   (d) 10

3. Coolant used in nuclear reactors should have
   (a) high melting and boiling point
   (b) high melting and low boiling point
   (c) low melting and boiling point
   (d) low melting and high boiling point

4. In fast breeder reactors
   (a) heavy water is used as moderator
   (b) no moderator is used
   (c) graphite is used as moderator
   (d) cadmium is used as moderator

5. Moderator in a nuclear reactor
   (a) stops the chain reaction
   (b) absorbs neutrons
   (c) reduces the speed of fast moving neutrons
   (d) acts as a cooling agent

6. Function of using reflector in nuclear reactor is to
   (a) economize the reactor
   (b) send back the escaping neutrons
   (c) both (a) and (b)
   (d) none of these

7. Overall efficiency of a thermal plant is
   (a) ratio of heat equivalent of energy transferred to shaft to heat equivalent of electrical output
   (b) heat equivalent of electrical output to heat of combustion
   (c) heat equivalent of energy transferred to shaft to heat to combustion
   (d) none of these

8. Feedwater in the economizer is in the form of
   (a) steam at high pressure
   (b) water at low temperature
   (c) water at high temperature
   (d) super saturated water

9. Which of the following plant has maximum efficiency?
   (a) Tidal power station
   (b) Hydro power station
   (c) Thermal power station
   (d) Nuclear power station

10. Condenser used in steam power plant is to
    (a) reduce the back pressure at the turbine exhaust
    (b) increase the back pressure at the turbine exhaust
    (c) to make the back pressure zero
    (d) none of these

11. Overall efficiency of thermal plant is reduced due to low value of
    (a) generator efficiency
    (b) boiler efficiency
    (c) efficiency of steam turbine and condenser
    (d) none of these

12. Turbo alternators are used in thermal plants is
    (a) stationary field type
    (b) cylindrical rotor type
    (c) salient pole type
    (d) none of these

13. Gross head of a hydroelectric power plant is
    (a) height of water level in river where tail race is located
    (b) height of water level in reservoir behind the dam
    (c) difference of two
    (d) water level in penstock

14. Frequency of the generated voltage is maintained constant by adjusting
    (a) speed of prime mover
    (b) excitation
    (c) load
    (d) number of poles

15. Fluctuations of speed in the diesel plant can be smoothened by fly wheel with
    (a) high moment of inertia
    (b) low moment of inertia
    (c) both (a) and (b)
    (d) none of these

16. Peak load plants supply power at
    (a) low capital cost and low running cost
    (b) high capital cost and high running cost
    (c) low capital cost and high running cost
    (d) low capital cost and low running cost

17. Base load plants supply power at
    (a) low capital cost and low running cost
    (b) low capital cost and high running cost
    (c) high capital cost and high running cost
    (d) high capital cost and low running cost

18. Hydro electric generators are
    (a) stationary field type
    (b) cylindrical rotor type
    (c) double cage rotor type
    (d) salient pole type

19. Pilot exciter is needed if
    (a) induction motor is used
    (b) main exciter is self excited
    (c) main exciter is separately excited
    (d) main exciter is not working

20. For separately exciter, complication of additional rotating machine is
    (a) not there   (b) less
    (c) more   (d) none of these

21. For centralised excitation system, number of exciters used are
    (a) more than generatng units
    (b) less than generating units
    (c) equal to generating units
    (d) uncertain

22. For greater power system stability, speed of the exciter response should always
    (a) increase   (b) decrease
    (c) remain same   (d) zero

23. Centralised excitable system is
    (a) more reliable than unit system
    (b) less reliable than unit system
    (c) same as unit system
    (d) none of these

24. Response of separately excited exciter is
    (a) equal to that of self excited generator
    (b) slower than that of self excited generator
    (c) faster than that of self excited generator
    (d) none of these

25. Division of reactive and active powers in two generators operating in parallel depend upon
    (a) voltage load curve
    (b) speed load curve
    (c) speed load and voltage load curves respectively
    (d) voltage load and speed load curves respectively

26. Connected load is sum of
    (a) maximum load consumed per year
    (b) maximum load consumed any particular time
    (c) continuous ratings of load-consuming apparatus connected
    (d) none of these

27. Cold reserve is that reserve which is
    (a) available for use but is not in service
    (b) available for service but is not in use
    (c) always available
    (d) connected to the bus and ready to take load

28. Spinning reserve is that generating capacity, which is
    (a) connected to the bus bar and is ready to take load
    (b) always available
    (c) available for service but not in use
    (d) available for use but not in service

29. Amortization of a plant is
    (a) more than the plant life
    (b) less than the plant life
    (c) equal to the plant life
    (d) none of these

30. Diversity factor reduces
    (a) simultaneous maximum demand on station for same individual demands
    (b) capital cost for the station
    (c) overall rate for generation of electricity
    (d) all of these

31. Station maximum demand is mostly dependent upon
    (a) line losses
    (b) domestic consumers
    (c) industrial consumers
    (d) all of these

32. Load factor is defined as
    (a) Maximum demand/average demand
    (b) Average demand/Maximum demand
    (c) Maximum demand/Peak load
    (d) Maximum demand/Minimum load

33. In flat rate tariffs, rate is fixed by taking into account their
   (a) diversity factor   (b) load factor
   (c) plant use factor   (d) a and b

34. Consumers pay less fixed charges in
   (a) two part tariff
   (b) flat rate tariff
   (c) block rate tariff
   (d) maximum demand tariff

35. Generators kept for spinning reserve are
   (a) not in operation
   (b) kept running on light loads
   (c) kept running on heavy loads
   (d) none of these

36. Maximum demand for a bulk consumer is measured in
   (a) KV   (b) KVA
   (c) KVAR   (d) KW

37. Operating plant factor is
   (a) ratio of average load to maximum load
   (b) ratio of maximum load to peak load
   (c) ratio of average load to the plant capacity
   (d) average load on the machine

38. If load factor is varied; in two part tariff
   (a) running cost is affected
   (b) fixed cost is affected
   (c) both (a) and (b)
   (d) depreciation is affected

39. By interconnection of stations, the cost is
   (a) increased   (b) reduced
   (c) same as before   (d) uncertain

40. Frequency of the system
   (a) should be constant
   (b) need not be constant
   (c) can be tolerated upto ±10%
   (d) should be unity

41. Energy accumulations are balanced by deliveries of power
   (a) during off-peak periods
   (b) on weak ends
   (c) during the corresponding period of accumulation
   (d) none of these

42. Synchronous impendance of an alternator is defined as the ratio of open circuit voltage to the short circuit current for same
   (a) speed   (b) excitation
   (c) both (a) and (b) (d) none of these

43. Speed drop of governor means
   (a) reduction in speed as load changes from no load to full load
   (b) increase in speed as load changes from no load to full load
   (c) degree of speed change needed to cause a change in the power output of turbine
   (d) none of these

44. While determining the regulation of an alternator by actual test, constant parameters are
   (a) speed and current
   (b) voltage and current
   (c) speed and excitation
   (d) short circuit current and excitation

45. Incremental rate is defined as
   (a) rate of change of given input
   (b) ratio of change in input to change in output
   (c) ratio of rate of change of output to input
   (d) ratio of rate of change of input to rate of change of output

46. For maximum power transfer to take place between two interconnected stations, angle between voltages of the two should be
   (a) 0°   (b) 45°
   (c) 60°   (d) 90°

47. Economical loading based on incremental rate gives
   (a) turbine efficiency
   (b) overall efficiency
   (c) brake thermal efficiency
   (d) best thermal efficiency

48. Different methods of prices charging is called
   (a) tariff
   (b) KVAR method
   (c) KW method
   (d) KVA method

49. For stable operation of interconnected stations, the element used is
   (a) resistor   (b) capacitor
   (c) reactor   (d) none of these

50. Quadrature boost employed in the interconnected system is used to transfer
    - (a) real power
    - (b) reactive power
    - (c) apparant power
    - (d) all of these

51. Power loss is important for the design of
    - (a) generator
    - (b) motor
    - (c) feeder
    - (d) transmission line

52. Voltage regulation is important for the design of
    - (a) generator
    - (b) motor
    - (c) feeder
    - (d) transmission line

53. Capital cost of the thermal plant depend on
    - (a) fuel cost
    - (b) size of the plant
    - (c) both (a) and (b)
    - (d) labour charges

54. For an alternator delivering a balanced load at unity power factor, phase angle between line voltage and line current is
    - (a) 0°
    - (b) 180°
    - (c) 30°
    - (d) 90°

55. Coincidence factor is always obtained as increase of the
    - (a) load factor
    - (b) plant use factor
    - (c) plant capacity factor
    - (d) deversity factor

56. Which of the following has highest capital cost?
    - (a) Thermal plant
    - (b) Hydro plant
    - (c) Diesel plant
    - (d) Nuclear plant

57. For conventional power plants, running cost is minimum for
    - (a) thermal plant
    - (b) nuclear plant
    - (c) hydro plant
    - (d) diesel plant

58. Disadvantage of flat rate tariff is that it is difficult to
    - (a) arrive at a load factor and diversity factor to decide the tariff
    - (b) estimate the cost of generation
    - (c) control the desired power factor
    - (d) all of these

59. Difference between load factor and capacity factor is the indication of
    - (a) hot reserve
    - (b) cold reserve
    - (c) reserve capacity
    - (d) spinning reserve

60. In the two part tariff, running charges increases as
    - (a) maximum energy consumed increases
    - (b) maximum energy consumed decreases
    - (c) average energy consumed decreases
    - (d) average energy consumed increases

61. When power factor of the load increases, losses in the transmission and distribution lines
    - (a) increases
    - (b) decreases
    - (c) remains same
    - (d) uncertain

62. Advantages of d.c. over a.c. is
    - (a) no skin effect
    - (b) charging currents are eliminated
    - (c) line regulation is improved
    - (d) all of these

63. Alternative source of energy should be utilised such that
    - (a) production cost is minimised
    - (b) efficient plant should be loaded to maximum
    - (c) generation is maximum
    - (d) fuel used is maximum

64. To improve the overall efficiency of thermal plant
    - (a) boiler pressure is decreased
    - (b) load on the units is decreased
    - (c) initial pressure and temperature and exhaust pressure and temperature are at maximum
    - (d) additional fuel is used

65. Transfer of power between two power systems take place with power flowing from the system with the
    - (a) leading power factor
    - (b) lagging power factor
    - (c) higher voltage level
    - (d) none of these

66. Load division between two parallel operating alternators are affected by
    - (a) more lagging power angle
    - (b) change in generated voltage
    - (c) change in input to prime mover
    - (d) increasing the system frequency

67. If fuel input increases, the load on thermal unit
    - (a) decreases
    - (b) increases
    - (c) remain same
    - (d) bears no relation

68. If load on the isolated generator is decreased without decreasing the power input to the prime mover speed of the generator
   (a) remain unaltered
   (b) decrease
   (c) increase
   (d) uncertain

69. Advantage of computer control of generating unit is that
   (a) all the units will be equally loaded
   (b) feedback is easy
   (c) VAR output of units is decreased
   (d) loading of the units are adjusted at equal incremental fuel costs

70. Phase shift between sending and receiving ends is determined by
   (a) operating voltage
   (b) reactance of the lines
   (c) cross-section of conductor
   (d) none of these

71. If field current is increased by 25% above rated value and load is kept constant on an alternator,
   (a) it may go out of synchronism
   (b) speed will cross the rated speed
   (c) it will burn
   (d) it will stop instantaneously

72. In interconnection of hydro and thermal plant, hydro-generation is increased by
   (a) increasing load on the plant
   (b) decreasing load on the plant
   (c) keeping load on the plant constant
   (d) none of these

73. Accumulated time error in power system can be corrected by
   (a) increasing generation
   (b) decreasing generation
   (c) coordinating with other interconnected systems
   (d) none of these

74. Speed control by governors of electric generating units normally have a/an
   (a) increase of speed with increasing load
   (b) decrease of speed with increasing load
   (c) decrease of speed with decreasing load
   (d) flat load characteristic

75. Time error for system operating at less than 50 Hz is
   (a) slow
   (b) fast
   (c) zero
   (d) none of these

76. In interconnected systems, each system
   (a) should operate with flat frequency response
   (b) can provide its own reserve capacity
   (c) should depend on other for reserve capacity
   (d) should be feeded with frequency changes

77. Equal area criterion is used to find
   (a) solution of swing equation
   (b) critical reclosure time
   (c) change in frequency errors
   (d) change in velocity errors

78. Equal area criterion is applicable for only
   (a) single machine and infinite bus
   (b) two machines and infinite bus
   (c) three machines and infinite bus
   (d) four machines and infinite bus

79. Steady state stability mean
   (a) a constant power is flowing
   (b) frequency is exactly 50 Hz
   (c) there is synchronism between machines and external tie lines
   (d) all of these

80. If torque angle increases infinitely, the system will show
   (a) stability
   (b) instability
   (c) steady state stability
   (d) none of these

81. Transient stability depends on
   (a) fault clearing time
   (b) strength of transmitting network
   (c) short circuit ratio of generating unit
   (d) all of these

82. Transiently stable power system
   (a) may be dynamically unstable
   (b) is always dynamically unstable
   (c) will oscillate beyond the first swing
   (d) none of these

83. Steady state stability limit refers to maximum flow of power through a point
    (a) with stability loss when the power is increased gradually
    (b) without stability loss when the power is increased gradually
    (c) both (a) and (b)
    (d) none of these

84. Factors affecting the power system reliability is
    (a) nominal transmission voltage levels
    (b) available reserve capacity margin
    (c) increased ambient air temperature
    (d) flow of power from open tie

85. Disadvantage of low power factor is
    (a) Cost of station and distribution equipment is more for a given load
    (b) Low power factor makes voltage regulation poor
    (c) Bigger sized conductors are required for same energy transmission at low power factor
    (d) All of these

86. Cause of low power factor is
    (a) transformer drawing more magnetising current
    (b) extensive use of induction motors
    (c) use of arc lamps
    (d) all of these

87. Low power factor be avoided by
    (a) using synchronous motors instead of induction motors
    (b) using high speed induction motors to low speed machines
    (c) not operating induction motors at less than rated output
    (d) all of these

88. Power factor is improved by the use of
    (a) static capacitors
    (b) synchronous compensators or phase modifiers
    (c) phase advancer
    (d) all of these

89. Best location for power factor improvement apparatus is
    (a) where the apparatus responsible for low power factor is installed
    (b) at the receiving end
    (c) both (a) and (b)
    (d) none of these

90. As the frequency of the supply increases, capacity of the static condenser required for phase advancement
    (a) decreases   (b) increases
    (c) remains same   (d) uncertain

91. Stepless control of power factor is achieved by using
    (a) static condenser
    (b) series capacitor
    (c) synchronous condenser
    (d) none of these

92. In KWH and KV Arh tariff, the KV Arh rate is
    (a) higher than KWH rate
    (b) lower than KWH rate
    (c) equal to KWH rate
    (d) none of these

93. Static condensers to be connected to improve the power factor should be in
    (a) delta
    (b) star
    (c) parallel with the supply
    (d) series with the supply

94. Maximum power transferred through the interconnected is called
    (a) maximum capacity
    (b) percentage regulation
    (c) synchronous capacity
    (d) none of these

95. The overall efficiency of thermal plant is low due to low efficiency of
    (a) boiler
    (b) alternator
    (c) steam turbine and condenser
    (d) non-salient pole rotor

96. Heat balance in a boiler furnace is improved by sending air to the furnace
    (a) at low temperature
    (b) at high temperature
    (c) mixed with CO_2
    (d) both (b) and (c) above

97. Induced draught fan in steam power plant is used to create draught
    (a) in the boiler
    (b) in the chimney
    (c) at the inlet of air preheater
    (d) in the alternator

98. Speed fluctuation in diesel electric plant occurs in engine employing which of the following number of strokes ?
  (a) 2   (b) 4
  (c) 6   (d) 8

99. Fluctuating speed of dielectric electric plants may be reduced by the use of flywheel having moment of inertia which is
  (a) zero   (b) low
  (c) medium   (d) high

100. Main features of a typical hydro-electric station are
  (a) dam, reservoir, catchment area
  (b) tunnels, surge tanks, pipelines and tailrace
  (c) hydraulic turbines and coupled alternators
  (d) all of these

101. Prime movers for water turbines are
  (a) reaction turbines for low and medium heads
  (b) impulse turbines for medium and high heads
  (c) both (a) and (b) above
  (d) Pelton turbines for low heads

102. As compared to steam-station, hydro-electric stations have
  (a) more cost of installation
  (b) less maintenance and fuel cost
  (c) both (a) and (b) above
  (d) low depreciation charges

103. The rotor used in alternators of hydro-electric station is
  (a) cylindrical rotor
  (b) salient pole rotor
  (c) nonsalient pole rotor
  (d) round rotor with ac excitation

104. The cross-sectional area of the penstock will be smaller if the velocity of water is to be
  (a) high
  (b) low
  (c) under pressure
  (d) both (b) and (c) above

105. Water hammer is developed in
  (a) penstock   (b) dam
  (c) surge tank   (d) turbine

106. Effect of water hammer is reduced by using
  (a) surge tank   (b) an anvil
  (c) spillway   (d) overhead tank

107. Spillways are used to
  (a) discharge excess water in the reservoir
  (b) reduce loss of head due to friction in penstock
  (c) get more head for hydel plant
  (d) both (b) and (c) above

108. A positive pressure is developed in the penstock when the alternator load is suddenly
  (a) increased   (b) decreased
  (c) removed   (d) short-circuited

109. Surge tank is located
  (a) close to the power house
  (b) at an elevated place
  (c) both (a) and (b) above
  (d) at a lower place

110. Vacuum is created in penstock when the turbine gates are suddenly
  (a) opened
  (b) closed
  (c) loaded
  (d) both (b) and (c) above

111. The curve between discharge in m³/s and time is called
  (a) discharge duration curve
  (b) hydrograph
  (c) load curve
  (d) flow histogram

112. Energy produced by fission reaction uranium having mass of atom m and velocity of light c is
  (a) mc   (b) $\frac{1}{2}m^2c$
  (c) mc^2 (d) $\frac{1}{2}mc^2$

113. Percentage of U-235 in natural uranium is
  (a) 0.235   (b) 235
  (c) 2.35   (d) 0.7

114. In a nuclear power station, moderator is used to
  (a) absorb neutrons
  (b) reduce the speed of neutrons
  (c) accelerate the speed of neutrons
  (d) stop the chain reaction

115. Commonly used atomic fuels are
  (a) Uranium, U-235
  (b) Plutonium, Pu-239
  (c) Thorium, Th-232
  (d) all of these

116. The heat produced by 1 kg of atomic fuel is equal to that produced by coal of weight
    (a) 1 ton
    (b) 100 tons
    (c) 1000 tons
    (d) 4237 tons

117. Coolents used in reactors are
    (a) air, hydrogen, helium
    (b) water, graphite
    (c) liquid metals, lead bismuth alloys
    (d) all of these

118. Reactor used in nuclear reactor serves to
    (a) reflect back the escaping neutrons
    (b) improve its economy
    (c) both (a) and (b) above
    (d) none of these

119. Cooling system used in boiler water reactor is
    (a) direct cooling
    (b) single circuit
    (c) double circuit
    (d) reflector type radiator

120. Single circuit coolant system is preferred in
    (a) fast breeder reactor
    (b) boiler water reactor
    (c) pressurized water reactor
    (d) none of these

121. Coolant used is fast breeder reactor is
    (a) heavy water
    (b) graphite
    (c) sodium
    (d) none of these

122. Moderator used in fast breeder reacor is
    (a) heavy water
    (b) graphite
    (c) both (a) and (b) above
    (d) none of these

123. In fast breeder reactors, neutron shielding is provided by
    (a) graphite
    (b) copper
    (c) tinalloy
    (d) boron

124. Location of nuclear plant is
    (a) dependent upon the geographical factors
    (b) independent of the geographical factors
    (c) requires large quantity of water
    (d) both (b) and (c) above

125. Steam produced by geothermal field is
    (a) dry
    (b) wet
    (c) both (a) and (b) above
    (d) none of these

126. Water steam mixture in geothermal field is separated by the use of
    (a) filters
    (b) evaporators
    (c) bypass valve
    (d) centrifugal action

127. Geothermal steam contains
    (a) CO_2
    (b) H_2S
    (c) NH_3
    (d) all of these

128. Constructional material used in geothermal plant is
    (a) steel
    (b) brass
    (c) stainless steel
    (d) any of these

129. The source of geoenergy is
    (a) radioactivity within crystal rocks
    (b) boiling of water in the ground due to oil burning
    (c) use of jet type of condenser
    (d) both (a) and (b) above

130. Photo-voltaic cell produces electric energy from
    (a) electromagnetic energy
    (b) electrostatic energy
    (c) geothermal energy
    (d) both (a) and (b) above

131. Collectros used for collecting solar energy are
    (a) paraboloid
    (b) solar radiators
    (c) flat plate and focussing solar collectors
    (d) none of these

132. Photo-chemical electric generation is possible if the reverse reaction involves
    (a) reduction
    (b) oxidation
    (c) either (a) or (b) above
    (d) none of these

133. Cell having hydrogen and lithium electrodes produce electricity at an operating temperature of
    (a) –150°C
    (b) 0°C
    (c) + 150°C
    (d) 350°C

134. In MHD generation, emf induced is
 (a) motionally induced emf
 (b) static emf
 (c) Hall emf
 (d) both (a) and (c) above

135. The essential parts of MHD generators are
 (a) gas   (b) field poles
 (c) duct   (d) all of these

136. The current developed in MHD generator is
 (a) ac
 (b) dc
 (c) pulsating
 (d) either (a) or (b) above

137. The conduction used in MHD generator is
 (a) copper   (b) aluminum
 (c) liquid   (d) gas

138. The rating of MHD generator per unit volume is proportional to
 (a) square of magnetic flux density
 (b) square of the flow velocity of the fluid
 (c) the electrical conductivity of the fluid
 (d) all of these

139. Wind energy
 (a) is clean, almost free and domestically produced
 (b) has higher cost comparatively
 (c) develops power proportional to the power of the wind
 (d) all of these

140. The magnitude of power constant in wind mill depends on
 (a) shape of rotor blades
 (b) wind velocity
 (c) orientation of rotor blades
 (d) both (a) and (b) above

141. The principal type of failure in wind power generation is in
 (a) aerodynamic system
 (b) electrical system
 (c) mechanical system
 (d) both (b) and (c) above

142. The EHV system is one operating beyond
 (a) 11 kV
 (b) 132 kV
 (c) 200 kV
 (d) 400 kV

143. The advantage of dc systems over ac systems is
 (a) improved line regulation
 (b) no skin effect
 (c) no charging currents
 (d) all of these

144. Pilot exciter is used when main exciter is
 (a) self excited
 (b) separately excited
 (c) induction motor driven
 (d) none of these

145. Static voltage regulators use
 (a) saturable reactor
 (b) integrated circuit
 (c) microprocessors
 (d) any of these

146. Current reactors are used
 (a) to improve voltage regulation
 (b) to reduce the fault level
 (c) to improve efficiency
 (d) to improve power factor

147. Regulating transformers are used in power system to control
 (a) load flow   (b) power factor
 (c) voltage   (d) all of these

148. Series reactors usually have
 (a) low resistance   (b) high resistance
 (c) low impedance   (d) high impedance

149. As per Indian Standard, the permissible range of power supply frequency is
 (a) 49.5 to 50.5 Hz
 (b) 49 to 51 Hz
 (c) 48 to 52 Hz
 (d) 47.5 to 52.5 Hz

150. Which of the following generating station has minimum running cost ?
 (a) thermal power station
 (b) hydro-electric power station
 (c) nuclear power station
 (d) none of these

151. Which of the following method of generating electric power from sea water is more advantageous ?
 (a) ocean currents   (b) tidal power
 (c) wave power   (d) none of these

152. Which of the following hydraulic turbine is used for water heads exceeding 400 metres ?
(a) kaplan turbine (b) Francis turbine
(c) Pelton wheel (d) none of these

153. Nuclear reactors generally employ
(a) fission
(b) fusion
(c) both fission and fusion
(d) none of these

154. Heavy water implies
(a) H_2O (b) W_2O
(c) B_2O (d) D_2O

155. Running cost of a power plant is based on the cost of
(a) energy or fuel
(b) consumable items
(c) maintenance and operation
(d) all of these

156. In straight line method of depreciation, the money to be reserved for depreciation is
(a) directly proportional to time
(b) inversely proportional to time
(c) directly proportional to square of time
(d) inversely proportional to square of time

157. In straight line method of depreciation, the money deposited carries
(a) fixed interest
(b) compound interest
(c) no interest
(d) a straight line interest

158. In diminishing value method of depreciation
(a) a fixed rate is set aside each year
(b) depreciation charges are heavy in early years and maintenance charges are low
(c) in later years, maintenance charges are heavy and depreciation charges are low
(d) all of these

159. In reducing balance method of depreciation, the calculation of depreciaiton in any year is a fixed proportion of the cost at the
(a) beginning of that particular year
(b) beginning of the project
(c) average of that particular year
(d) maximum of that particular year

160. In sinking fund method of depreciation
(a) a fixed amount is deposited annually
(b) the rate of interest is compounded yearly
(c) it requires smaller amount as compared to straight line method
(d) all of these

161. The book value of plant is
(a) cost of plant
(b) accrued depreciation
(c) difference of (a) and (b) above
(d) sum of (a) and (b) above

162. The main objective of tariff is to distribute equatabily the cost of
(a) installation and fuel
(b) power transmission and distribution
(c) supplying energy among the various classification of users
(d) energy production among all its consumers

163. All types of tariffs must recover the cost of
(a) capital investment in generating equipment
(b) operation, supplies and maintenance of equipment
(c) metering equipment, billing, collection costs, profit and wages
(d) all of these

164. Factors involved in fixing tariffs are
(a) secured return from each consumer
(b) simplicity, cheapness and easy explainability
(c) incentive to consumers and charge according to use
(d) all of these

165. Depreciation rate is less in the case of
(a) diesel engine plant
(b) nuclear plant
(c) hydro-electric plant
(d) steam power plant

166. Economical loading based on the incremental rate gives
(a) maximum conversion efficiency
(b) good energy conversion efficiency
(c) best system efficiency
(d) economical demand factor

167. Causes of low power factor are
    (a) induction motors and arc lamp loads
    (b) generating equipment during low loads
    (c) industrial heating furnaces and arc furnaces
    (d) both (a) and (c) above

168. Drawbacks of low power factor are
    (a) high ratings of generating, transmitting and distributing equipment
    (b) large voltage drop and poor voltage regulation
    (c) large copper losses and high capital costs
    (d) all of these

169. Power factor of a power system can be improved by
    (a) using phase advances, static capacitors, capacitance boosters
    (b) unexcited synchronous motors on load
    (c) over excited synchronous motors on no load
    (d) both (a) and (b) above

170. Diversity factor of a power system is the
    (a) ratio of sum of consumer's maximum demands to maximum load on the station
    (b) ratio of average demand to maximum demand
    (c) reciprocal of (a) above
    (d) reciprocal of (b) above

EXERCISE – II

1. Which one of the following statements correctly represents the post acceleration in a Cathode-Ray Tube? **(RRB 2012)**
    (a) It provides deflection of the beam
    (b) It increases the brightness of the trace if the signal frequency is higher than 10 MHz
    (c) It accelerates the beam before deflection
    (d) It increases the brightness of the trace of low frequency signal

2. Which one of the following transducers can be used for measurement of pressures as high as 100,000 atmosphere? **(RRB 2012)**
    (a) Mcleod gauge   (b) Pirani gauge
    (c) Bridgman gauge   (d) Knudsen gauge

3. An energy-meter having a meter constant of 1200 rev per kWH is found to make 5 revolutions in 75s. The load power is **(RRB 2012)**
    (a) 500 W   (b) 100 W
    (c) 200 W   (d) 1000 W

4. A power station's plant load factor is defined as the ratio of **(RRB 2012)**
    (a) the energy generated to that of maximum energy that could have been generated
    (b) average load to peak load
    (c) minimum load to peak load
    (d) minimum load to average load

5. In pumped storage power plants **(RRB 2012)**
    (a) water is recirculated through water turbines
    (b) reversible turbines are used which operate as turbines for power generation during peak load hours and as pumps for pumping water during peak-off hours
    (c) plain Francis turbines are used
    (d) both (a) and (c) above are employed

6. Taking the density of water to be 1000 kg/m³, how much power would be developed by a hydroelectric generator unit, assuming 100% efficiency, with 1.0 m head and 1.0 m³/s discharge? **(RRB 2012)**
    (a) 2.90 kW   (b) 4.45 kW
    (c) 9.80 kW   (d) 19.60 kW

7. For elimination of 5th harmonics from the output of an inverter, what will be the position of pulse in a PWM inverter ? **(RRB 2012)**
    (a) 70°   (b) 36°
    (c) 60°   (d) 90°

8. For a 3-element feed water control in a coal fixed thermal power station, measurements of level of water in the boiler drums is made so that the water level does not **(RRB 2012)**
    (a) Exceed a specified upper limit
    (b) Fall below a specified lower limit
    (c) Violate specified upper and lower limits
    (d) Restrict to a specified limit

9. What will happen if a short circuit fault occurs in a switched capacitor controlled reactor?
    (a) Oscillation
    (b) Capacitor discharge
    (c) Over voltage
    (d) Noise   **(RRB 2012)**

10. Which of the following power stations is mainly used to cover peak load on the system?
    (a) Coal based thermal power plant **(RRB 2012)**
    (b) Nuclear power plant
    (c) Gas based thermal power plant
    (d) Pumped storage hydro power plant

11. Complete combustion of pulverized coal in a steam raising thermal power plant is ensured by what type of an analysis of flue gas going out by the chimney ?

    (a) O_2 content for given air intake

    (b) CO_2 content for given fuel rate feed

    (c) CO content

    (d) All of these   **(RRB 2012)**

12. The time period of periodic time T of an alternating quantity is the time taken in seconds to complete

    (a) one cycle

    (b) one alternation

    (c) any of these

    (d) none of these   **(RRB)**

13. In fast breeder reactors

    (a) heavy water is used as moderator

    (b) no moderator is used

    (c) graphite is used as moderator

    (d) cadmium is used as moderator   **(RRB)**

14. Condenser used in steam power plant is to

    (a) reduce the back pressure at the turbine exhaust

    (b) increase the back pressure at the turbine exhaust

    (c) to make the back pressure zero

    (d) none of these   **(RRB)**

15. Diversity factor reduces

    (a) simultaneous maximum demand on station for same individual demands

    (b) capital cost for the station

    (c) overall rate for generation of electricity

    (d) all of these   **(RRB)**

16. Stepless control of power factor is achieved by using

    (a) static condenser

    (b) series capacitor

    (c) synchronous condenser

    (d) none of these   **(RRB)**

17. Heat balance in a boiler furnace is improved by sending air to the furnace

    (a) at low temperature

    (b) at high temperature

    (c) mixed with CO_2

    (d) both (b) and (c) above   **(RRB)**

18. In MHD generation, emf induced is

    (a) motionally induced emf

    (b) static emf

    (c) Hall emf

    (d) both (a) and (c) above   **(RRB)**

19. Coolant used in fast breeder reactor is

    (a) sodium   (b) heavy water

    (c) air   (d) cadmium   **(RRB)**

20. Fluctuations of speed in the diesel plant can be smoothened by fly wheel with   **(RRB)**

    (a) high moment of inertia

    (b) low moment of inertia

    (c) both (a) and (b)

    (d) none of these

21. A single-phase SCR based ac regulator is feeding power to a load consisting of 5 Ω resistance and 16 mH inductance. The input supply is 230 V, 50 Hz ac. The maximum firing angle at which the voltage across the device becomes zero all throughout and the rms value of current through SCR, under this operating condition, are **(RRB)**

    (a) 30° and 46 A   (b) 30° and 23 A

    (c) 45° and 23 A   (d) 45° and 32 A

22. A voltage $\overline{V}$ is applied to an ac circuit resulting in the delivery of a current $\overline{I}$. Which of the following expressions would yield the true power delivered by the source ?   **(DMRC 2014)**

    1. Real part of $\overline{VI}^*$

    2. Real part of $\overline{VI}$

    3. F times the real part of $\dfrac{\overline{V}}{\overline{I}}$

    Select the correct answer using the codes given below:

    (a) 1 alone   (b) 1 and 3

    (c) 2 and 3   (d) 3 alone

23. The current 'I' through a resistance R is measured with the following uncertainties

    $$I = 4A \pm 0.5 \%$$
    $$R = 100\Omega \pm 0.2\%$$

    If power is computed from these two measured quantities, the uncertainty in the power computed will be   **(DMRC 2014)**

    (a) $\pm 0.01\%$ (b) $\pm 0.29\,\%$

    (c) $\pm 0.07\,\%$ (d) $\pm 1.2\,\%$

24. An indicating instrument is more sensitive if its torque to weight ratio is **(DMRC 2014)**

(a) much larger than unity

(b) of the order of unity

(c) much less than unity

(d) made deflection-dependent

25. In a flux meter, the controlling torque is **(DMRC 2014)**

(a) produced by weights attached to the moving coil

(b) produced by springs

(c) not provided at all

(d) provided by crossed coil mechanism

26. Dummy strain gauge is used in conjunction with the main strain gauge to **(DMRC 2014)**

(a) calibrate the system

(b) compensate temperature effects.

(c) improve sensitivity

(d) reduce strain on the main gauge

27. In a two-wattmeter method of measuring power, one of the watt- meters is reading zero watts. The power factor of the circuit is

(a) Zero **(DMRC 2014)**

(b) 1

(c) 0.5

(d) 0.8

28. Hall effect device can be used to **(DMRC 2014)**

(a) multiply two signals

(b) divide one signal by another on an instantaneous basis

(c) add two signals

(d) subtract one signal from another

29. Piezoelectric effect is generally observed in

(a) insulators **(DMRC)**

(b) insulators and semiconductors

(c) conductors and superconductors

(d) conductors and semiconductors

30. The measurement junction of a thermocouple is taken from an environment of 300°C to 600°C. If time constant of the thermocouple is 1 s, temperature indicated by it after 1 s will be nearly **(DMRC)**

(a) 300°C   (b) 400° C

(c) 500° C   (d) 600° C

31. In a single phase induction type energy meter, the Lag adjustment is done to ensure that **(DMRC)**

(a) current coil flux lags the applied voltage by 90°

(b) pressure coil flux lags the applied voltage by 90°

(c) pressure coil flux is in phase with the applied voltage

(d) current coil lags the pressure coil flux by 90°

32. LCD displays are preferred over LED displays because they **(DMRC)**

(a) are more reliable   (b) consume less power

(c) respond quickly   (d) are cheaper

33. Compression ratio for diesel engine may have a range of **(SSC, CPWD 2008)**

(a) 8 to 10   (b) 16 to 20

(c) 10 to 15   (d) None of these

34. The two stroke cycle engine has **(SSC, CPWD 2008)**

(a) one suction valve and one exhaust valve operated by one cam

(b) one suction valve and one exhaust valve operated by two cams

(c) only ports covered and uncovered by piston to effect charging and exhausting

(d) None of the above

35. Morse test is used for multi-cylinder spark ignition engine to determine **(SSC, CPWD 2008)**

(a) Thermal efficiency

(b) Mechanical efficiency

(c) Volumetric efficiency

(d) Relative efficiency

36. Characteristic equation of gas is given by (V = specific volume; m = mass of gas) **(SSC, CPWD 2008)**

(a) $pV = RT$ (b) $pV = mRT$

(c) $pV^n = C$ (d) $pV^\gamma = C$

37. Dryness fraction of steam is defined as:

(a) $\dfrac{\text{Mass of dry steam}}{\text{Mass of water vapour in suspension}}$

(b) $\dfrac{\text{Mass of water vapour in suspension}}{\text{Mass of dry steam}}$

(c) $\dfrac{\text{Mass of dry steam}}{\text{Mass of dry} + \text{Mass of water vapour in suspension}}$

(d) $\dfrac{\text{Mass of water vapour in suspension}}{\text{Mass of water vapour in suspension} + \text{Mass of dry steam}}$

38. Lancashire Boiler is a **(SSC, CPWD 2008)**
   (a) Water tube boiler (b) Fire tube boiler
   (c) Locomotive boiler (d) High pressure boiler

39. Rankine's theory is valid to **(SSC, CPWD 2008)**
   (a) long column   (b) short column
   (c) both   (d) None of the above

40. Poisson's ratio is used in **(SSC, CPWD 2008)**
   (a) one-dimensional body
   (b) two dimensional body
   (c) three dimensional body
   (d) both two and three dimensional body

41. Which is the correct expression?
   (SSC, CPWD 2008)
   (a) $E = 2C\left(1 - \dfrac{1}{m}\right)$ (b) $E = 3C\left(1 - \dfrac{1}{2m}\right)$
   (c) $E = 3C\left(2 - \dfrac{1}{m}\right)$ (d) $E = 3C\left(1 - \dfrac{1}{3m}\right)$

42. Constant efficiency curves of turbines are drawn between (on both axes) **(SSC, CPWD 2008)**
   (a) power and speed
   (b) efficiency and speed
   (c) efficiency and power
   (d) efficiency and head

43. Specific speed of a centrifugal pump is defined as the speed at which the pump would deliver
   (a) 1 HP   **(SSC, CPWD 2008)**
   (b) 1 kW
   (c) 1 m³/sec
   (d) 1000 kg/sec under 1 meter of head

44. The cripling load for both ends fixed long column is given by **(SSC, CPWD 2008)**
   (a) $\dfrac{\pi^2 EI}{l^2}$ (b) $\dfrac{\pi^2 EI}{4l^2}$
   (c) $\dfrac{4\pi^2 EI}{l^2}$ (d) $\dfrac{2\pi^2 EI}{l^2}$

45. Uniform sand hardness is obtained throughout the mould by which of the following moulding machines?
   (a) Diaphragm moulding   **(SSC, CPWD 2008)**
   (b) Stripper plate
   (c) Sand slinger
   (d) Squeezing

46. The main advantage of shell moulding is that
   (SSC, CPWD 2008)
   (a) a metallic pattern is used
   (b) the moulds are stronger
   (c) thin sections can be easily obtained
   (d) high production rate is possible

47. Reaming is the operation of **(SSC, CPWD 2008)**
   (a) enlarging the end of a hole cylindrically
   (b) cone shaped enlargement of the end of a hole
   (c) smoothing and squaring the surface around a hole
   (d) sizing and finishing a hole

48. Zeroth law of thermodynamics defines
   (SSC, CPWD 2008)
   (a) internal energy   (b) enthalpy
   (c) temperature   (d) pressure

49. Which of the following welding processes uses non-consumable electrode? **(SSC, CPWD 2008)**
   (a) Laser welding   (b) MIG welding
   (c) TIG welding   (d) Ion beam welding

50. In sand moulding, the bottommost part of the flask is called **(SSC, CPWD 2008)**
   (a) cope   (b) cheek
   (c) drag   (d) flask bottom

51. In order to ram the sand softer on the pattern face and harder at the back of the mould, which of the following types of moulding machines is used? **(SSC, CPWD 2008)**
   (a) Jolt   (b) Sand slinger
   (c) Squeezing   (d) Stripper plate

52. As per Law of fluid friction for steady streamline flow, the frictional resistance **(SSC, CPWD 2008)**
   (a) varies proportionally to pressure
   (b) varies in inverse proportion to pressure
   (c) does not depend on pressure
   (d) first increase then decreases

53. Which one of the following assumptions of Bernoulli's theorem is not correct?
   (SSC, CPWD 2008)
   (a) Flow should not be unsteady
   (b) Flow should be continuous
   (c) The fluid should be compressible
   (d) Flow should be frictionless

54. What will be the maximum hydraulic efficiency in case of direct impact of a jet on a series of flat vanes mounted on the periphery of a large wheel?
   (SSC, CPWD 2008)
   (a) 33%   (b) 50%
   (c) 66%   (d) Cannot be a fixed value

55. For diesel enging, the method of governing employed is **(SSC, CPWD 2008)**
   (a) Quality governing
   (b) Quantity governing
   (c) Hit and miss governing
   (d) None of the above

56. Francis Turbine is a **(SSC, CPWD 2008)**
    (a) Axial flow turbine (b) Radial flow turbine
    (c) Impulse turbine (d) Outward flow turbine

57. In laminar, incompressible flow in a circular pipe, the ratio between average velocity and maximum velocity would be **(SSC, CPWD 2008)**
    (a) $-\dfrac{1}{2}$ (b) $\dfrac{1}{3}$
    (c) $\dfrac{2}{3}$ (d) $\dfrac{1}{\sqrt{2}}$

58. The product of module and diametral pitch is equal to **(SSC, CPWD 2008)**
    (a) 1.0 (b) $\dfrac{\pi}{2}$
    (c) π (d) 2π

59. The path of contact in cycloidal gear is **(SSC, CPWD 2008)**
    (a) straight line (b) curved line
    (c) circle (d) none of the above

60. Which one of the following is a gravity controlled type governor? **(SSC, CPWD 2008)**
    (a) Hartnell governor (b) Hartung governor
    (c) Watt governor (d) Pickering governor

61. The friction torque, transmitted in case of flat pivot bearing for uniform ratio of wear is equal to **(SSC, CPWD 2008)**
    (a) μWR (b) $\dfrac{2}{3}\mu WR$
    (c) $\dfrac{1}{3}\mu WR$ (d) $\dfrac{1}{2}\mu WR$

62. At the point of contraflexure **(SSC, CPWD 2008)**
    (a) shear force changes its behaviour
    (b) bending moment changes its behaviour
    (c) shear force is maximum
    (d) shear force is minimum

63. Proof resilience in a member is stored strain energy **(SSC, CPWD 2008)**
    (a) per unit volume (b) in whole volume
    (c) per unit area (d) per unit length

64. In double slider crank chain, the number of revolute pairs is/are **(SSC, CPWD 2008)**
    (a) 1 (b) 2
    (c) 3 (d) 4

65. Oldham's coupling is inversion of
    (a) 4-bar chain **(SSC, CPWD 2008)**
    (b) 6-bar chain
    (c) single slider crank chain
    (d) double slider crank chain

66. The power factor of industrial loads is generally **(SSC, CPWD 2008)**
    (a) unity (b) lagging
    (c) leading (d) zero

67. The value of demand factor is **(SSC, CPWD 2008)**
    (a) less than one (b) greater than one
    (c) equal to one (d) zero

68. Equation of continuity of flow is based on the principle of conservation of **(SSC, CPWD 2009)**
    (a) mass (b) force
    (c) momentum (d) energy

69. Pitot tube is used for the measurement of **(SSC, CPWD 2009)**
    (a) pressure (b) flow
    (c) velocity (d) discharge

70. In a centrifugal pump, the liquid enters the pump **(SSC, CPWD 2009)**
    (a) at the top
    (b) at the bottom
    (c) at the centre
    (d) None of the above

71. In reaction turbine **(SSC, CPWD 2009)**
    (a) kinetic energy is appreciable as the fluid leaves the runner and enters the draft tube
    (b) the vanes are partly filled
    (c) total energy of fluid is converted to kinetic energy in the runner
    (d) it is exposed to the atmosphere

72. For the same compression ratio **(SSC, CPWD 2009)**
    (a) Otto cycle is more efficient than the Diesel cycle
    (b) Diesel cycle is more efficient than the Otto cycle
    (c) both Otto and Diesel cycles are equally efficient
    (d) compression ratio has nothing to do with efficiency

73. Water tube boilers are those in which **(SSC, CPWD 2009)**
    (a) flue gases pass through tubes and water around it
    (b) water passes through the tubes
    (c) work is done during adiabatic expansion
    (d) there is change in enthalpy

74. An ideal flow of any fluid must satisfy
(SSC, CPWD 2009)
   (a) Pascal's law
   (b) Newton's law of viscosity
   (c) Boundary layer theory
   (d) Continuity equation

75. The flow which neglects changes in a transverse direction is known as **(SSC, CPWD 2009)**
   (a) one-dimensional flow
   (b) uniform flow
   (c) steady flow
   (d) turbulent flow

76. Cam size depends upon **(SSC, CPWD 2009)**
   (a) base circle   (b) pitch circle
   (c) prime circle   (d) outer circle

77. Hartnell governor could be classified under the head of **(SSC, CPWD 2009)**
   (a) inertia type governors
   (b) pendulum type governors
   (c) centrifugal type governors
   (d) dead weight type-governors

78. Which of the following clutches is positive type?
(SSC, CPWD 2009)
   (a) Cone   (b) Disc
   (c) Jaw   (d) Centrifugal

79. Creep in belt is due to **(SSC, CPWD 2009)**
   (a) material of the pulley
   (b) material of the belt
   (c) larger size of driver pulley
   (d) uneven extensions and contractions due to varying tension

80. For simple supported beam having load at the centre the bending moment will be
(SSC, CPWD 2009)
   (a) minimum at the support
   (b) minimum at the centre
   (c) maximum at the support
   (d) None of the above

81. The effective length of the column with one end fixed and the other end free is
(SSC, CPWD 2009)
   (a) its own length
   (b) twice its length
   (c) half its length
   (d) None of the above

82. Kinetic pairs are those which have two elements that **(SSC, CPWD 2009)**
   (a) have line contact
   (b) have surface contact
   (c) permit relative motion
   (d) are held together

83. Governor is used in automobile to
(SSC, CPWD 2009)
   (a) decrease the variation of speed
   (b) control $\delta N/\delta t$
   (c) control δN
   (d) All the above

84. For coding of large size generators hydrogen is used because **(SSC, CPWD 2009)**
   (a) it offers reduced fire risk
   (b) it is light in weight
   (c) it is of high thermal conductivity
   (d) All the above

85. The connected load of a consumer is 2 kW and his maximum demand is 1.5 kW. The demand factor of the consumer is **(SSC, CPWD 2009)**
   (a) 0.75   (b) 0.375
   (c) 1.33   (d) 1

86. To meet the reactive power requirements at load centres usually **(SSC, CPWD 2009)**
   (a) shunt capacitors are used
   (b) series capacitors are used
   (c) shunt reactors are used
   (d) tap changing transformers are used

87. The power factor will be leading in case of
(SSC, CPWD 2009)
   (a) Dielectric heating
   (b) Resistance heating
   (c) Induction heating
   (d) All the above

88. First law of thermodynamics furnishes the relationship between **(SSC, CPWD 2009)**
   (a) heat and work
   (b) heat, work and properties of the system
   (c) various properties of the system
   (d) various thermodynamic processes

89. Triple point of a pure substance is a point at which
(SSC, CPWD 2009)
   (a) liquid and vapour exist together
   (b) solid and liquid exist together
   (c) solid and vapour exist together
   (d) solid, liquid and vapour phase exist together

90. Which of the following is not an internal combustion engine? **(SSC, CPWD 2009)**
(a) 2-stroke petrol engine
(b) 4-stroke petrol engine
(c) Diesel engine
(d) Steam engine

91. Change of entropy depends upon **(SSC, CPWD 2009)**
(a) change of mass
(b) change of temperature
(c) change of specific heat
(d) change of heat

92. Thermal plant works on **(SSC, CPWD 2009)**
(a) Carnot cycle
(b) Joule cycle
(c) Rankine cycle
(d) All the above

93. Hooke's law holds good upto **(SSC, CPWD 2009)**
(a) yield point
(b) limit of proportionality
(c) breaking point
(d) elastic limit

94. The percentage reduction in area in case of cast iron when it is subjected to tensile test is of the order of **(SSC, CPWD 2009)**
(a) 0%
(b) 10%
(c) 20%
(d) 25%

95. A cantilever beam is deflected by d due to load P. If load is doubled, then deflection compared to earlier case will be changed by a factor of: **(SSC, CPWD 2009)**
(a) 2
(b) $\frac{1}{2}$
(c) $\frac{1}{8}$
(d) 8

96. Principle plane is one which carries **(SSC, CPWD 2009)**
(a) no shear stress
(b) maximum shear stress
(c) no normal stress
(d) maximum resultant of stresses

97. A universal dividing head is used to perform a milling operation by **(SSC, CPWD 2009)**
(a) plain indexing
(b) direct indexing
(c) differential indexing
(d) compound indexing

98. In grinding operation, for grinding harder material **(SSC, CPWD 2009)**
(a) coarse grain size is used
(b) fine grain size is used
(c) medium grain size is used
(d) any grain size may be used

99. When turning long shaft on a lathe, its bending can be prevented by **(SSC, CPWD 2009)**
(a) running the shaft at low speed
(b) using high speed
(c) using sturdy machine
(d) using steady rest

100. The operation of sharpening a grinding wheel is called **(SSC, CPWD 2009)**
(a) trueing
(b) dressing
(c) aligning
(d) balancing

101. In which of the following operations on lathe, will the spindle speed be minimum? **(SSC, CPWD 2009)**
(a) Knurling
(b) Fine finishing
(c) Taper turning
(d) Thread cutting

102. For drilling operation, the cylindrical job should always be clamped on a **(SSC, CPWD 2009)**
(a) collect
(b) socket
(c) jaw
(d) V-block

103. Which of the following machines does not require quick return mechanism? **(SSC, CPWD 2009)**
(a) Slotter
(b) Planer
(c) Shaper
(d) Broaching

104. Milling machine is classified as horizontal or vertical type, depending on the position of **(SSC, CPWD 2009)**
(a) spindle
(b) work piece
(c) milling cutter
(d) work table or bed

105. The taper provided on pattern for its easy and clean withdrawal from the mould is called **(SSC, CPWD 2009)**
(a) taper allowance
(b) draft allowance
(c) distortion allowance
(d) pattern allowance

106. Which of the following is not a casting process? **(SSC, CPWD 2009)**
(a) Carthias process
(b) Extrusion
(c) Semi-centrifuge method
(d) Slush process

107. In arc welding, arc is created between the electrode and work by   **(SSC, CPWD 2009)**

(a) flow of current

(b) voltage

(c) material characteristics

(d) contact resistance

108. Oxygen to acetylene ratio in case of neutral flame is   **(SSC, CPWD 2009)**

(a) 0.8 : 1.0   (b) 1 : 1

(c) 1.2 : 1   (d) 2 : 1

109. The principle of dynamically induced emf is utilised is :   **(SSC, CPWD 2009)**

(a) Choke   (b) Transformer

(c) Thermocouple   (d) Generator

110. The moderator used in fast breeder reactor is   **(SSC, CPWD 2010)**

(a) Heavy water   (b) Graphite

(c) Ordinary water   (d) Any of the above

111. The earth's potential is taken as   **(SSC, CPWD 2010)**

(a) infinite   (b) supply voltage

(c) 1 volt   (d) zero

112. The value of diversity factor is   **(SSC, CPWD 2010)**

(a) less than one   (b) greater than one

(c) equal to one   (d) any one of the above

113. The resistance welding process requires a   **(SSC, CPWD 2010)**

(a) high value of ac current at low voltage

(b) low value of ac current at high voltage

(c) high value of dc current at low voltage

(d) low value of dc current at high voltage

114. The tarrif most suitable for large industrial consumers is   **(SSC, CPWD 2010)**

(a) Flat demand rate   (b) Block meter rate

(c) Two part tarrif   (d) All the above

115. Dielectric heating is also called   **(SSC, CPWD 2010)**

(a) volume heating   (b) infrared heating

(c) surface heating   (d) eddy current heating

116. Laboratory wattmeters are   **(SSC, CPWD 2010)**

(a) Induction type

(b) Moving iron type

(c) Electrostatic type

(d) Electro-dynamometer type

117. An electric motor may give noise due to   **(SSC, CPWD 2010)**

(a) magnetic effect

(b) defective bearing

(c) cooling air

(d) all the above

118. Which of the following motor is used in household refrigerator?   **(SSC, CPWD 2010)**

(a) Synchronous motor

(b) D.C. shunt motor

(c) 3-phase induction motor

(d) 1-phase induction motor

119. The knowledge of diversity factor helps in computing   **(SSC, CPWD 2010)**

(a) plant capacity   (b) average load

(c) units generated   (d) peak demand

120. The controlling torque in gravity controlled meter is proportional to   **(SSC, CPWD 2010)**

(a) $\cos \theta$ (b) $\sin \theta$

(c) $\tan \theta$ (d) θ

121. In an induction type energy meter, everything else remaining game, if the radial distance of the brake magnet poles from the spindle is decreased by 10%, the rotational speed of the dise will approximately   **(SSC, CPWD 2011)**

(a) increase by 23.5%

(b) decrease by 10.6%

(c) decrease by 19.4%

(d) increase by 11%

122. The capacity factor of a plant is given by   **(SSC, CPWD 2011)**

(a) maximum load / average load

(b) average load / maximum load

(c) average load / plant capacity

(d) maximum load / plant capacity

123. In a power supply system, "demand factor" is defined as   **(SSC, CPWD 2011)**

(a) $\dfrac{\text{Average demand}}{\text{Maximum demand}}$

(b) $\dfrac{\text{Maximum demand}}{\text{Installed capacity}}$

(c) $\dfrac{\text{Average demand}}{\text{Installed capacity}}$

(d) $\dfrac{\text{Maximum demand}}{\text{Connected load}}$

124. In designing lighting scheme, utilization factor is used. It is defined as **(SSC, CPWD 2011)**

(a) utilization factor =

$$\frac{\text{total lumens utilized on working plane}}{\text{total lumens radiated by lamp}}$$

(b) utilization factor =

$$\frac{\text{total lumens utilized on working plane}}{\text{illumination when everything is clean}}$$

(c) utilization factor =

$$\frac{\text{illumination under normal working condition}}{\text{illumination when everything is clean}}$$

(d) utilization factor =

$$\frac{\text{total lumens radiated by lamp}}{\text{total lumens utilized on working plane}}$$

125. Which of the following equipments has the lowest power factor ? **(SSC, CPWD 2011)**

(a) Fully loaded induction motor

(b) Immersion heater

(c) Incandescent lamp

(d) Arc lamp

126. Low head plants generally use

(SSC, CPWD 2011)

(a) Pelton turbines   (b) Francis turbines

(c) Kaplan turbines   (d) both (a) and (b)

127. In a system, if the base load is the same as the maximum demand, the load factor will be

(SSC, CPWD 2011)

(a) 1.0   (b) 0.5

(c) zero   (d) infinity

128. Which of the following surfaces has the lowest reflection factor for white light ?

(SSC, CPWD 2011)

(a) Aluminium sheets

(b) White plaster work

(c) Blue curtains

(d) White oil paint

129. Form factor of an alternating wave is

(SSC, CPWD 2012)

(a) Form factor = $\dfrac{\text{averge value}}{\text{rms value}}$

(b) Form factor = $\dfrac{(\text{rms value})^2}{\text{average value}}$

(c) Form factor = $\dfrac{\text{rms value}}{\text{average value}}$

(d) Form factor = rms value × average value

130. Which of the following method is suitable for heating of conducting medium ?

(SSC, CPWD 2012)

(a) Induction heating

(b) Both (a) and (d)

(c) Radiant heating

(d) Eddy current heating

131. Furnaces used for cremation use

(SSC, CPWD 2012)

(a) Dielectric heating   (b) Arc heating

(c) Resistance heating   (d) Induction heating

132. The household energy meter is

(SSC, CPWD 2012)

(a) Recording instrument

(b) None of these

(c) Indicating instrument

(d) Integrating instrument

133. Resistance temperature coefficient of copper at 20°C is **(SSC, CPWD 2013)**

(a) 0.0045/°C   (b) 0.0017/°C

(c) 0.00393/°C   (d) 0.0038/°C

134. Silicon content in iron lamination is kept within 5% as it **(SSC, CPWD 2013)**

(a) makes the material brittle

(b) reduces the curie point

(c) increases hysteresis loss

(d) increases cost

135. Which of the following is correct?

(SSC, CPWD 2013)

(a) Load factor

         = capacity factor × utilisation factor

(b) Utilisation factor

         = capacity factor × load factor

(c) Capacity factor

         = load factor × utilisation factor

(d) Load factor has no relation with capacity factor and utilisation factor

136. One B.O.T. unit is **(SSC, CPWD 2013)**

(a) 1000 kWh   (b) 10 kWh

(c) 1 kWh   (d) 0.1 kWh

137. An electric heater draws 1000 watts from a 250 V source. The power drawn from a 200 V source is

(SSC, CPWD 2013)

(a) 800 W   (b) 640 W

(c) 1000 W   (d) 1562.5 W

138. Two single-phase ac motors A and B operate from a 1000 V supply. A consumes 2 kW at a power factor of 0.8 (lagging) and B consumes 1 kW at a power factor of 0.5 (lagging). The total current drawn from the supply is approximately

(SSC, CPWD 2013)

(a) 4.5 A (b) 2.1A
(c) 4.41A (d) 9A

139. Which of the following motor will give relatively high starting torque? **(SSC, CPWD 2014)**

(a) Shaded pole motor
(b) Capacitor start motor
(c) Capacitor run motor
(d) Split phase motor

140. In a power plant if the maximum demand on the plant is equal to the plant capacity, then :

(SSC, CPWD 2014)

(a) load factor will be nearly 60%
(b) plant reserve capacity will be zero
(c) diversity factor will be unity
(d) load factor will be unity

141. The least expensive fractional horse power motor is _____ motor : **(SSC, CPWD 2014)**

(a) A.C. series (b) shaded pole
(c) capacitor start (d) split phase

142. Diversity factor has direct effect on the :

(SSC, CPWD 2014)

(a) Operating cost of unit
(b) Fixed cost of the unit generated
(c) Variable cost of the unit generated
(d) Both variable and fixed cost of unit generated

143. Regulation of an alternator supplying resistive or inductive load is : **(SSC, CPWD 2014)**

(a) infinity (b) always negative
(c) always positive (d) zero

144. A consumer has annual consumption of 7,00,800 units. If his maximum demand is 200 kW. The load factor will be :

(SSC, CPWD 2014)

(a) 70% (b) 20%
(c) 40% (d) 50%

145. The rated voltage of a 3-phase power system is given as : **(SSC, CPWD 2014)**

(a) peak line to line voltage
(b) rms phase voltage
(c) peak phase voltage
(d) rms line to line voltage

146. For a half wave rectified sine wave the ripple factor is : **(SSC, CPWD 2014)**

(a) 1.00 (b) 1.65
(c) 1.45 (d) 1.21

147. The efficiency normally obtained in a circuit under the conditions of maximum power transfer is :

(SSC, CPWD 2014)

(a) 100% (b) 25%
(c) 50% (d) 75%

148. A magnet is kept in the medium of air surrounded by an iron ring. The magnetic lines of force from the magnet will be : **(SSC, CPWD 2014)**

(a) Very small in the ring
(b) Crowded in the ring
(c) Passing out of the ring
(d) Evenly distributed within the ring

149. A generating station supplies the following loads 15000 kW, 12000 kW, 8500 kW, 6000 kW and 450 kW. The station has maximum demand of 22000 kW. Calculate the diversity factor.

(SSC, CPWD 2014)

(a) 1.91 (b) 0.52
(c) 0.68 (d) 1.34

150. The maximum demand of a consumer is 2 kW and his daily energy consumption is 20 units. His load factor is : **(SSC, CPWD 2014)**

(a) 21 % (b) 10.15 %
(c) 41.6% (d) 50%

151. A stove element draws 15 A when connected to 230 V line. How long does it take to consume one unit of energy? **(SSC CPWD 2014)**

(a) 3.45 h (b) 2.16 h
(c) 1.0 h (d) 0.29 h

152. In electrodynamometer ammeter, the deflection of the pointer is proportional to

(a) mean of currents in fixed coil a moving coil
(b) square of the current in moving coil
(c) RMS value of current in fixed coil
(d) mean-square of currents in fixed coil and moving coil **(SSC CPWD 2014)**

153. Two holes are drilled in the disc on a diameter of energy-meter to **(SSC CPWD 2014)**

(a) increase ventilation
(b) reduce the weight of disc
(c) eliminate creeping on no-load
(d) increase deflecting torque

154. Which of the following instruments has the highest torque/weight ratio among the given instruments ? **(SSC CPWD 2014)**

(*a*) Attraction type MI instrument

(*b*) Repulsion type MI instrument

(*c*) Permanent magnet moving coil instrument

(*d*) Electrodynamometer instrument

155. If current through the operating coil of a moving iron instrument is doubled, the operating force becomes **(SSC CPWD 2014)**

(*a*) one and a half times

(*b*) 2 times

(*c*) 3 times

(*d*) 4 times

156. Which of the following single phase motors is available with speed as low as one revolution per minute ? **(SSC CPWD 2014)**

(*a*) Shaded pole

(*b*) Reluctance

(*c*) Hysteresis

(*d*) Universal

157. The maximum demand of a consumer is 2 kW and his daily energy consumption is 24 units. His load factor is —— %. **(SSC CPWD 2014)**

(*a*) 24

(*b*) 41.6

(*c*) 50

(*d*) 80

158. To reduce the cost of the electricity generated **(SSC CPWD 2014)**

(*a*) the load factor and diversity factor must be low

(*b*) the load factor must be low but diversity factor high

(*c*) the load factor must be high but diversity factor low

(*d*) the load factor and diversity factor must be high

159. The domestic load that has UPF is **(SSC CPWD 2014)**

(*a*) Fan

(*b*) Mixer

(*c*) Tube

(*d*) Filament lamp

160. An industrial consumer has a daily load pattern of 2000 kW, 0.8 lag for 12 hours and 1000 kW UPF for 12 hours. The load factor is

(*a*) 0.5 **(SSC CPWD 2014)**

(*b*) 0.75

(*c*) 0.6

(*d*) 2.0

161. In a Cathode Ray Tube, the focussing anode is located **(SSC CPWD 2014)**

(*a*) after accelerating anode

(*b*) between pre-accelerating and accelerating anodes

(*c*) before pre-accelerating anode

(*d*) just after electron-gun

162. How much energy is stored by a 100 mH inductance when a current of 1A is flowing through it? **(SSC CPWD 2015)**

(*a*) 0.005 J

(*b*) 0.5 J

(*c*) 5.0 J

(*d*) 0.05 J

163. Creeping in a single phase induction type energy meter may be due to? **(SSC CPWD 2015)**

(*a*) All of the given options

(*b*) Over voltage

(*c*) Vibrations

(*d*) Over compensation for friction

164. Base load of a power station stands for?

(*a*) 2 - 4 hours/day

(*b*) 12 - 24 hours/day

(*c*) 8 - 12 hours/day

(*d*) 4 - 8 hours/day **(SSC CPWD 2015)**

ANSWERS

EXERCISE – I

1. (a)	2. (b)	3. (d)	4. (b)	5. (c)	6. (c)	7. (b)	8. (c)	9. (d)	10. (a)
11. (c)	12. (b)	13. (c)	14. (a)	15. (a)	16. (c)	17. (d)	18. (d)	19. (c)	20. (c)
21. (b)	22. (a)	23. (b)	24. (c)	25. (d)	26. (c)	27. (b)	28. (a)	29. (b)	30. (d)
31. (c)	32. (b)	33. (d)	34. (d)	35. (b)	36. (b)	37. (d)	38. (a)	39. (b)	40. (a)
41. (c)	42. (c)	43. (a)	44. (c)	45. (b)	46. (d)	47. (d)	48. (a)	49. (c)	50. (a)
51. (d)	52. (c)	53. (b)	54. (c)	55. (d)	56. (d)	57. (c)	58. (a)	59. (c)	60. (d)
61. (b)	62. (d)	63. (a)	64. (c)	65. (a)	66. (c)	67. (b)	68. (c)	69. (d)	70. (b)
71. (a)	72. (a)	73. (c)	74. (b)	75. (a)	76. (b)	77. (b)	78. (a)	79. (c)	80. (b)
81. (d)	82. (a)	83. (a)	84. (b)	85. (d)	86. (d)	87. (d)	88. (d)	89. (c)	90. (b)
91. (c)	92. (b)	93. (c)	94. (c)	95. (c)	96. (b)	97. (b)	98. (b)	99. (d)	100. (d)
101. (c)	102. (c)	103. (b)	104. (a)	105. (c)	106. (a)	107. (a)	108. (b)	109. (c)	110. (a)
111. (b)	112. (b)	113. (d)	114. (b)	115. (d)	116. (d)	117. (d)	118. (a)	119. (a)	120. (c)
121. (c)	122. (d)	123. (d)	124. (d)	125. (c)	126. (d)	127. (d)	128. (c)	129. (a)	130. (a)
131. (c)	132. (c)	133. (d)	134. (d)	135. (d)	136. (b)	137. (d)	138. (d)	139. (d)	140. (b)
141. (a)	142. (d)	143. (d)	144. (b)	145. (d)	146. (b)	147. (a)	148. (a)	149. (d)	150. (b)
151. (b)	152. (c)	153. (a)	154. (d)	155. (d)	156. (b)	157. (c)	158. (d)	159. (a)	160. (d)
161. (c)	162. (c)	163. (d)	164. (d)	165. (c)	166. (c)	167. (d)	168. (d)	169. (d)	170. (a)

EXERCISE – II

1. (b)	2. (b)	3. (a)	4. (b)	5. (b)	6. (c)	7. (a)	8. (c)	9. (a)	10. (d)
11. (d)	12. (a)	13. (b)	14. (a)	15. (d)	16. (c)	17. (b)	18. (d)	19. (a)	20. (a)
21. (c)	22. (c)	23. (d)	24. (a)	25. (c)	26. (b)	27. (c)	28. (a)	29. (a)	30. (b)
31. (b)	32. (b)	33. (b)	34. (c)	35. (b)	36. (b)	37. (c)	38. (b)	39. (c)	40. (d)
41. (*)	42. (b)	43. (c)	44. (c)	45. (a)	46. (c)	47. (d)	48. (c)	49. (c)	50. (c)
51. (c)	52. (a)	53. (c)	54. (b)	55. (a)	56. (b)	57. (a)	58. (a)	59. (a)	60. (c)
61. (a)	62. (b)	63. (b)	64. (b)	65. (d)	66. (b)	67. (a)	68. (a)	69. (c)	70. (c)

71. (a) **72.** (a) **73.** (b) **74.** (d) **75.** (a) **76.** (a) **77.** (c) **78.** (c) **79.** (d) **80.** (a)

81. (b) **82.** (c) **83.** (c) **84.** (d) **85.** (a) **86.** (a) **87.** (a) **88.** (b) **89.** (d) **90.** (d)

91. (d) **92.** (c) **93.** (b) **94.** (a) **95.** (a) **96.** (a) **97.** (c,d) **98.** (b) **99.** (d) **100.** (b)

101. $(*)$ **102.** (c) **103.** (a) **104.** (a) **105.** (b) **106.** (b) **107.** (d) **108.** $(*)$ **109.** (b) **110.** $(*)$

111. (d) **112.** (b) **113.** (a) **114.** (c) **115.** (a) **116.** (d) **117.** (d) **118.** (d) **119.** (d) **120.** (b)

121. (d) **122.** (c) **123.** (d) **124.** (a) **125.** (d) **126.** (c) **127.** (a) **128.** (c) **129.** (c) **130.** (b)

131. (c) **132.** (d) **133.** (c) **134.** (a) **135.** (c) **136.** (c) **137.** (b) **138.** (a) **139.** (b) **140.** (b)

141. (b) **142.** (b) **143.** (c) **144.** (c) **145.** (d) **146.** (d) **147.** (c) **148.** (b) **149.** (a) **150.** (c)

151. (d) **152.** (d) **153.** (c) **154.** (c) **155.** (d) **156.** (a) **157.** (c) **158.** (d) **159.** (d) **160.** (c)

161. (b) **162.** (d) **163.** (a) **164.** (b)

■■

Transmission and Distribution

DISTRIBUTION SYSTEM

The part of power system which distributes electrical power for local use is called distribution system.

Distribution system is the electrical system, between the sub-station fed by the transmission system and the consumers meters. *It generally consists of*

(i) **Feeders.** A feeder is a conductor which connects the sub-station (or localised generating station) to the area where power is to be distributed. Generally, no tappings are taken from the feeder so that current in it remains the same throughout. The main consideration in the design of the feeder is the current carrying capacity.

(ii) **Distributor.** A distributor is a conductor from which tappings are taken for supply to the consumers. The current through a distributor is not constant because tappings are taken at various places along its length. While designing a distributor, voltage drop along its length is the main consideration since the statutory limit of voltage variations is ± 6% of rated value at the consumer's terminals.

(iii) **Service mains.** A service mains is generally a small cable which connects the distributor to the consumer's terminals.

Classification of distribution system

1. Nature of Current. According to nature of current, distribution system may be classified as

(i) d.c. distribution system

(ii) a.c. distribution system

Now-a-days, a.c. system is universally adopted for distribution of electric power as it is simpler and more economical than direct current method.

2. Type of Construction. According to type of construction, distribution system may be classified as

(i) **Overhead system :** It generally employed for distribution as it is 5 to 10 times cheaper than the equivalent underground system.

(ii) **Underground system :** It is used at places where overhead construction is impracticable or prohibited by the local laws.

3. Scheme of Connection. According to scheme of connection, the distribution system may be classified as

(i) radial system,

(ii) ring main system,

(iii) inter-connected system.

A.C. TRANSMISSION AND DISTRIBUTION

Alternating current is used in preference to direct current due to fact that alternating voltage can be conveniently changed in magnitude by means of a transformer. High transmission and distribution voltages have greatly reduced the current in the conductors and the resulting line losses.

Types of a.c. distribution system

(i) **Primary distribution system.** It is that part of a.c. distribution system which operates in voltage somewhat higher than general utilisation and handles large blocks of electrical energy than the average low-voltage consumer uses. The most commonly used primary distribution voltages are 11 kV, 6-6 kV and 3-3 kV. Due to economic considerations, primary distribution is carried out by 3-phase, 4-wire system.

(ii) **Secondary distribution system.** It is that part of a.c. distribution system which includes the range of voltages at which the ultimate consumer utilises the electrical energy delivered to him. The secondary distribution employees 400/230 V, 3-phase, 4-wire system.

SYSTEMS OF A.C. DISTRIBUTION

A.C. power transmission is always at high voltage and mostly by 3-phase system. The use of single-phase system is limited to single-phase electric railways. Single-phase power transmission is used only for short distances and for relatively low voltages. 3-phase power transmission requires less copper than either single-phase or 2-phase power transmission.

The distribution system begins either at the sub-stations where power is delivered by overhead transmission lines and stepped down by transformers or in some cases at the generating station itself. Where a large area is involved, primary and secondary distributions may be used.

Systems available for the distribution of a.c. power.

1. Single-phase, 2-wire system.
2. Single-phase, 3-wire system.
3. Two-phase, 3-wire system.
4. Two-phase, 4-wire system.
5. Three-phase, 3-wire system.

Single-phase, 2-wire system.

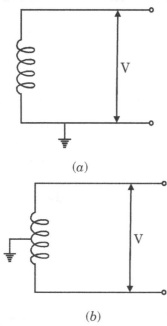

(a)

(b)

Single phase, 3-wire system. The 1-phase, 3-wire system is identical in principle with the 3-wire d.c. system. As shown below in figure, the third wire or neutral is connected to the centre of the transformers secondary and earthed for protecting personnel from electric shock should the transformer insulation break down or the secondary main contact high voltage wire.

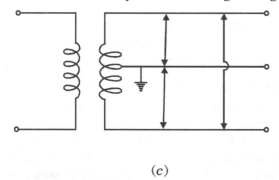

(c)

CONDUCTOR MATERIALS FOR OVERHEAD SYSTEMS

Assumptions :

1. Amount of power transmitted by each system is the same.
2. Distance of transmission is the same in each case.

3. Transmission efficiency is the same *i.e.*, the losses are the same in each case.
4. Loads are balanced in the case of 3-wire system.
5. Cross-section of the neutral wire is half that of any outer.
6. Maximum voltage to earth is the same in all cases.

Requirements of a good system

1. The voltage at the consumer's premises must be maintained within ± 4 or ± 6% of the declared voltage, the actual value depending on the type of load.
2. The loss of power in the system itself should be a small percentage (About 10%) of the power transmitted.
3. The transmission cost should not be unduly excessive.
4. The maximum current passing through the conductor should be limited to such a value as not to overheat the conductor or injure its insulation.
5. The insulation resistance of the whole system should be very high so that there is no undue leakage or danger to human life.

Reasons for producing power in the form of alternating current rather than direct current.

1. It is possible, to construct large high-speed a.c. generators of capacities up to 500 MW. Such generators are economical both in the matter of cost power kWh of electric energy produced as well as in operation. Unfortunately d.c. generators cannot be built of ratings higher than 5 MW because of commutation trouble. Moreover, since they must operate at low speeds, it necessitates large and heavy machines.
2. A.C. voltage can be efficiently and conveniently raised or lowered for economic transmission and distribution of electric power respectively.

Generation and transmission is almost exclusively three-phase. The secondary transmission is also 3-phase whereas the distribution to the ultimate customer may be 3-phase or single phase depending upon the requirements of the customers.

Primary or high voltage transmission is carried out at 132 kV. The transmission voltage is, to a very large extent, determined by economic consideration. High voltage transmission requires conductors of smaller cross-section which results in economy of copper or aluminium. But at the same time cost of insulating the line and other expenses are increased. *Economical voltage of transmission is that for which the saving in copper or aluminium is not offset by the increased.*

(*i*) cost of insulating the line

(*ii*) size of transmission-line structures

(*iii*) size of generating stations and sub-stations.

3-phase, 3-wire overhead high-voltage transmission line next terminates in step-down transformers in a sub-station known as Receiving Station which usually lies at the outskirts of a city because it is not safe to bring high-voltage overhead transmission lines into thickly-populated areas. Here, the voltage is stepped down to 33 kV. It may be noted here that for ensuring continuity of service transmission is always by duplicate lines.

From Receiving Sation, power is next transmitted at 33 kV by underground cables (and occasionally by overhead lines) to various sub-stations located at various strategic points in the city. This is known as secondary or low-voltage transmission.

At the sub-station (SS) voltage is reduced from 33 kV to 3.3 kV 3-wire for primary distribution. Consumers whose demands exceeds 50 kVA are usually supplied from SS by special 3.3 kV feeders.

Secondary distribution is done at 400/230 V for which purpose voltage is reduced from 3.3 kV to 400 V at the distribution sub-station. Feeders radiating from distribution sub-station supply power to distribution networks in their respective areas. If distribution network happens to be at a great distance from sub-station, then they are supplied from the secondaries of distribution transformers which are either pole-mounted at else housed in kiosks at suitable points of the distribution networks. The most common system for secondary distribution is 400/230-V, 3-phase 4-wire system. The single-phase residential lighting load is connected between any one line and the neutral whereas 3-phase, 400-V motor load is connected across 3-phase lines directly.

HVDC TRANSMISSION

In a combined AC and DC system, generated ac voltage is converted into dc voltage at the sending end, then the dc voltage is inverted back to AC voltage at the receiving end for distribution purpose.

CLASSIFICATION.

HVDC can be classified into two scheme.

1. Mono polar link.

A mono polar link has a single conductor, usually of negative polarity and uses earth or sea for return path of current. Some timer metallic return is also used.

Bipolar link has two conductor one positive and the other negative with respect to earth. The midpoints of converters at each terminal station are earthed via electrode lines and earth electrode.

2. Bipolar link.

A bipolar system is advantageous in the sense that when one pole goes out of operation, the system may be changed to monopolar mode with ground returns.

Advantages of HVDC transmission over AC transmission.

(*i*) In dc, number of conductors are lesser and therefore reduced conductor and insulator cost.

(*ii*) Lesser phase to phase clearance and lesser phase to ground clearance.

(*iii*) Lighter and cheaper towers.

(*iv*) Lesser right of way requirements.

(*v*) Lesser corona loss and reduced television and radio interference.

(*vi*) Power losses is reduced.

(*vii*) There is flexibility of operation, bipolar and unipolar operation.

(*viii*)No stability problem with dc line.

(*xii*) Power flow can be controlled more rapidly and accurately.

GROUND RETURN LINES

H.V.D.C. transmission lines use ground or sea water as the return conductor either continuously (monopolar) or for short time of emergency (bipolar). These return paths are called *ground return* even if sea water is used as a return path. For the same length of transmission resistance offered by the ground in case of d.c. is much less as compared to a.c. transmission because d.c. spreads over a very large cross sectional area in both depth and width as compared to a.c. or transient currents. In fact the earth resistance in case of d.c. is independent of the length (for long lines) and equals sum of the electrode resistances. Since resistance in case of d.c. is low as compared to a.c. there is low power loss in comparison with a metallic line conductor of economical size and equal length if ground electrodes are properly designed.

Advantages

(*i*) A line with ground return (monopolar) is more economical than a bipolar line because ground return saves most of the cost of one metallic conductor and the losses in it.

(*ii*) A d.c. line can be built in two stages if initial load requirement demands. Initially it will operate as a monopolar line with ground as return and later on in the second stage it can be built as a bipolar line. Thus a considerable part of the total investment can be deferred until the second stage.

(iii) Reliability of the system *i.e.,* in the event of an outage of one conductor of the bipolar line, it can be operated temporarily at almost half of its rated power by the use of the healthy line and the ground. For this reason the reliability of a bipolar line is equal to that of a double circuit 3-phase line although it has only two conductors instead of six for 3-phase line.

Disadvantages

(i) The ground currents cause electrolytic corrosion of buried or immersed metallic structures.

(ii) It is difficult to design ground electrodes for low resistance and low cost of installation and maintenance.

(iii) Ground currents cause dangerous step and touch voltages.

(iv) The ground currents interfere with the operation of other services such as a.c. power transmission, ships' compasses and reilway signals.

CIRCUIT BREAKING

It is easy to interrupt a.c. currents because of their natural zeros. Since d.c. is a steady unidirectional current it does not have a natural zero and therefore it is difficult to interrupt large d.c. currents at high voltages.

The d.c. transmission projects till this date are two terminal projects and it is not difficult to interrupt the fault currents. The faults on the d.c. line or in the converters are cleared by using control grids of the converter valves to stop the direct current temporarily.

The lack of d.c. breakers has inhibited the networking of d.c lines. The transient faults can be cleared using grid control, but permanent faults can be cleared using a combination of grid control, fault locators and isolating switches. Reasonable proposals have been made for clearing faults on such lines by running the whole system to zero using grid control, opening switches to isolate the faulty section and then reising the voltage back to normal. The time taken for this sequence of operation is approximately equal to the rapid reclosure of a.c. circuit breakers.

The requirement for d.c. circuit breaking is not to break the actual short circuit currents but to interrupt load currents in circuits at high potential with respect to ground because the short circuit currents can be limited to normal load currents using the gird control. If such switches could be developed, lines could be switched into or out of an unfaulted network without running the voltage down. Some such switches have been suggested wherein an artificial zero of current is created through the contacts of the switch by

the oscillatory discharge of a capacitor. The crest value of the oscillatory currents should be greater than the direct current to be interrupted.

D.C. TRANSMISSION

Advantages

1. d.c. power vary much more with the voltages than in the case of a.c. transmission, where the power is proportional to the product of line end voltages.

2. **Line circuit.** The line construction is simpler as compared to a.c. transmission. A single conductor line with ground as return can be compared with a 3-phase single circuit line. Hence the line is relatively cheaper and has the same reliability as that of a 3-phase single circuit line because 3-phase lines cannot operate, except for a short time when there is a single line to ground fault or a L-L fault as this creates unbalancing in the voltages and hence interfere with the communication lines and other sensitive apparatus on the system. Bipolar d.c. lines has same reliability index as a two-circuit 3-phase line having six line conductors.

3. **Power per conductor.** For transmitting power both on a.c. and d.c circuits, assume that two lines have same number of conductors and insulators. Assuming that the current is limited by temperature rise, direct current equals rms alternating current. Since crest voltage in both cases is same for the insulators, the direct voltage is $\sqrt{2}$ times the rms alternating voltage.

4. **Power per circuit.** The d.c. line is cheaper and simpler as it requires two conductors instead of three and hence $\frac{2}{3}$ as many insulators, and the towers are cheaper and narrower and hence a narrow right of way could be used.

5. **No charging current.** In case of a.c. charging current flows in the cable conductor; a severe decrease in the value of load current transmittable occurs if thermal rating is not to be exceeded; in the higher voltage range lengths of the order of 32 km create a need for drastic derating. A further current loading reduction is caused by the appreciable magnitude of dielectric losses at high voltages. Since in case of d.c. charging current is totally absent, length of transmission is not limited and the cable need not be derated.

6. **No skin effect.** a.c resistance of a conductor is somewhat higher than its d.c. resistance because in case of a.c. current is not uniformly distributed over the section of the conductor. The current density is higher on the outer section of the

conductor as compared to the inner section. This is called *skin effect*. As a result of this, conductor section is not utilized fully. This effect is absent in case of d.c.

7. **No compensation required.** Long distance a.c. power transmission is feasible only with the use of series and shunt compensation, applied at intervals along the line. For such lines shunt compensation (shunt reactors) is required to absorb the line charging kVAs during light load conditions and series compensation (use of series capacitors) forstability reasons. Since d.c. line operate at unity power factor and charging currents are absent no compensation is required.

8. **Less corona loss and radio interference.** In case of d.c., the corona losses are less as compared to a.c. Corona loss and radio interference are directly related and hence radio interference in case of d.c. is less as compared to a.c. Also corona and radio interference slightly decrease by foul weather conditions (snow, rain or fog) in cas of d.c. whereas they increase appreciably in case of a.c. supply.

9. **Higher operating voltages possible.** The modern high voltage transmission lines are designed based on the expected switching surges rather than the lightning voltages because former are more severe as compared to the latter. The level of switching surges due to d.c. is lower as compared to a.c. and hence, same size of conductors and string insulators can be used for higher voltages in case of d.c. as compared to a.c. In cables, where limiting factor is usually the normaly working voltage the insulation will withstand a direct voltage higher than that of alternating voltage, which is already 1.4 times the rms value of the alternating voltage.

10. **No stability problem.** Longer the length of the line, higher is the value of X and hence lower will be the capability of the system to transmit power from one end to the other. With this the steady state stability limit of the system is reduced. The transient state stability limit is normally lower than the steady state; therefore with longer lines used for transmission the transient stability also becomes very low. A d.c. transmission line does not have any stability proble in itself because d.c. operation is an asynchronous operation of the machines. In fact two separate a.c. systems interconnected only by a d.c. link do not operate in synchronism even if their nominal frequencies are equal and they can operate at different nominal frequencies *e.g.*, one operating at 60 Hz and the other at 50 Hz.

11. **Low short circuit currents.** The interconnection of a.c. system through an a.c. system increases the fault level to the extent that sometimes existing switchgear has to be replaced. However, interconnection of a.c. system with d.c. links does not increase the level so much and is limited automatically by the grid control to twice its rated current. As a result of this fault, d.c. links do not draw large currents from the a.c. system.

Disadvantages

1. **Expensive converters.** The converters required at both ends of the line have proved to be reliable but they are much more expensive than the conventional a.c. equipments. The converters have very little overload capacity and they absorb reactive power which must be supplied locally. The converters produce lot of harmonics both on d.c. and a.c. sides which may cause interference with the audio-frequency communication lines. Filters are required on the a.c. side of each converter for diminishing the magnitude of hamonics in the a.c. networks. These also increase the cost of the converters.

2. **Voltage transformation.** The power transmitted can be used at lower voltage only. Voltage transformation is not easier in case of d.c. and hence it has to be done on the a.c. side of the system.

3. Circuit breaking for multi-terminal lines is difficult.

CABLES

The a.c. transmission through cables is limited in distance due to the charging current.

The charging kVA of 3-phase single circuit cables per km are 1250 kVA at 132 kV; 3125 kVA at 220 kV; 9375 kVA at 400 kV

Enormous amount of charging kVA are required; therefore, if a.c. transmission by cables is required, charging current has to be absorbed at intermediate stations if distances exceed the following:

64 km at 132 kV; 40 km at 220 kV; 24 km at 400 kV

Since in case of d.c. charging current is absent, there is no distance limitation on transmission by underground or undersea cables.

LINE INSULATORS AND SUPPORT

In the design of insulator following considerations are made.

(*i*) The insulator should have high permittivity so that it can withstand high electrical stress i.e. dielectric strength of the insulator should be high.

(ii) Insulator should have high mechanical strength to bear the conductor load.

(iii) High resistance to temperature changes to reduce damage from power flashover.

(iv) Leakage current to earth should be minimum to reduce the corona loss and radio interference.

(v) Insulator material should not be porous.

Insulation Failure.

It may take place by two processes:

(i) **By puncture.** If puncture takes place then the insulator will be permanently damaged. Hence flashover should take place before puncture. In puncture arc passes through the body of insulator.

(ii) **By flash-over.** In flash over. arc discharge between conductor and earth through air surrounding the insulator.

For satisfactory operation flashover should take place before puncture. Ratio of puncture voltage to flashover is called *factor of safety* and is kept high. For satisfactory operation, the rain sheds should have the shape like those of equipotential surfaces and the insulator body should be constructed along the line of electrostatic field around the pin.

INSULATOR MATERIALS

Insulators (EHV lines) are made from toughened glass or high quality wet process procelain.

Proclain insulator are glazed over all exposed surface.

Toughened glass insulators have their surface layers in state of high compression due to which their resistance to with-stand mechanical and thermal stress is greater.

Advantages of Toughened glass over porcelain insulators

(i) Toughened glass insulators have greater puncture strength.

(ii) Possess greater mechanical strength.

(iii) High thermal shock resistance hence flash over is limited.

CORONA AND RADIO INTERFERENCE

For EHV lines when electric field in the air due to high voltage in the lines reaches upto (3×10^6 V/m or 3000 kV/m), then air in the immediate vicinity of conductors no more remains a dielectric but it is ionised and become conducting.

Electric break-down.

It results in following phenomenas.

(i) A giant glow around conductors.

(ii) There is an accoustical noise.

(iii) There is a tendency in the conductor to vibrate.

(iv) Ozone and oxides of nitrogens are produced.

(v) There is a loss of power.

(vi) There is radio interference.

If voltage gradient is increased further, then size of brightness of luminous envelope increases and finally a spark or arc is established between conductor because of complete breakdown of the insulating property of air between them.

Factors affecting corana.

(i) Conductor surface gradient.

(ii) Condition of conductor surface.

(iii) Atmospheric conditions.

(iv) Frequency and waveform of supply voltage.

(v) Air density factor.

Disruptive critical voltage.

Minimum voltage at which breakdown of the insulating property of air occurs and corona starts is called *disruptive critical voltage.*

Visual critical voltage.

Visual flow of corona occurs at a voltage higher than the disruptive critical voltage. The voltage at which the visual corona begins is called *visual critical voltage.*

Bundled conductors.

Bundled conductors are used mainly to minimize corona. The bundled acts as far as the electric field is concerned like a conductor of diameter much larger than that of the component conductors. This reduces the voltage gradient. In other words, a higher voltage can be used for permissible levels of radio interference. The GMR of a bundle is high and therefore the conductive reactance of the line is low. The bundle conductors have higher capacitance and therefore lower surge impedance as compared to single conductor of equivalent diameter. The lower value of inductive reactance helps in reducing the cost of series capacitor which are used to increase the transient stability limit of very long lines. Due to higher capacitance of bundled conductor; generated reactive power capacity is also reduced.

EXERCISE – I

1. The topmost conductor in hv transmission line is
   (a) R-phase conductor (b) Y-phase conductor
   (c) B-phase conductor (d) earth conductor

2. Insulators used on EHT transmission lines are made of
   (a) PVC   (b) porcelain
   (c) glass   (d) stealite

3. HV transmission line uses
   (a) pin type insulators
   (b) suspension insulators
   (c) both(a) and (b)
   (d) none of these

4. The insulators used on 220 kv transmission lines are of
   (a) suspension type   (b) pin type
   (c) shackle type   (d) none of these

5. Corona occurs between two transmission conductors when they
   (a) have high potential difference
   (b) are closely spaced
   (c) carry d c power
   (d) both (a) and (b)

6. Which of the following affects the corona least ?
   (a) Mean free length
   (b) Atmospheric temperature
   (c) Number of ions
   (d) Size and charge per ion

7. The effect of corona is
   (a) increased inductance
   (b) increased reactance
   (c) increased power loss
   (d) all of these

8. Corona is affected by
   (a) size of conductor
   (b) shape and surface condition of the conductor
   (c) operating voltage
   (d) all of these

9. The only advantage of corona is that is
   (a) produces a pleasing luminous glow
   (b) makes line current sinusoidal
   (c) works as a safety valve for surges
   (d) ozone gas is produced

10. Corona has the disadvantage(s) of
    (a) power loss
    (b) interference with neighbouring communication circuits
    (c) introducing the harmonics, predominately third harmonics, into the transmission lines
    (d) all of these

11. The dielectric strength of air under normal conditions is around
    (a) 30 kv/cm.   (b) 100 kv/cm.
    (c) 150 kv/cm.   (d) 200 kv/cm

12. Power loss due to corona is directly proportional to
    (a) spacing between conductors.
    (b) radius of conductor
    (c) supply frequency
    (d) none of these

13. Critical voltage limit of a transmission line is increased by
    (a) increasing the radius of the conductors
    (b) increasing the spacing between conductors
    (c) reducing the spacing between conductors
    (d) reducing the radius of the conductors

14. Transmission line constants are
    (a) resistance   (b) inductance
    (c) capacitance   (d) all of these

15. The inductance of line is minimum when
    (a) G M D is high
    (b) G M R is high
    (c) both G M D and G M R are high
    (d) G M D is low but G M R is high

16. The inductance of single phase two wire power transmission line per km gets doubled when the
    (a) distance between the wires is doubled
    (b) distance between the wires is doubled
    (c) distance between the wires is increased as square of the original distance
    (d) radius of the wore is doubled

17. Capacitance of a transmission line
    (a) increases
    (b) decreases
    (c) remains same with increase in its length
    (d) none of these

18. Capacitance in equivalent circuit of a transmission line is due to
    (a) current in the line
    (b) difference in potential of line
    (c) leakage of current
    (d) presence of magnetic flux

19. In a transmission line the distributed constants are
    (a) resistance and shunt conductance only
    (b) resistance and inductance only
    (c) resistance, inductance and capacitance only
    (d) resistance, inductance, capacitance and shunt conductance.

20. Skin effect in transmission line is due to
    (a) supply frequency
    (b) self inductance of conductor
    (c) high sensitivity of material in the centre
    (d) both (a) and (b)

21. The conductor carries more current on the surface in comparison to its core. This phenomenon is called the
    (a) skin effect
    (b) corona
    (c) Ferranti effect
    (d) Lenz's effect

22. Increase in frequency of transmission line causes
    (a) no change in line resistance
    (b) increase in line resistance
    (c) decrease in line resistance
    (d) decrease in line series reactance

23. Skin effect
    (a) increases the effective resistance and effective internal reactance
    (b) reduces the effective resistance and effective internal reactance
    (c) increases the effective resistance but reduces the effective internal reactance
    (d) reduces the effective resistance but increases the effective internal reactance.

24. The skin effect of a conductor reduces with the increase in
    (a) supply frequency
    (b) resistivity of the conductor material
    (c) x-section of conductor
    (d) permeability of conductor material

25. Skin effect in conductor is proportional to
    (a) (diameter of conductor).$^{1/2}$
    (b) diameter of conductor.
    (c) (diameter of conductor).^{2}
    (d) (diameter of conductor).^{4}

26. The presence of earth in case of overhead lines
    (a) increases the capacitance
    (b) increases the inductance
    (c) decreases the capacitance
    (d) decreases the inductance

27. If the effect of earth is taken into account, then the capacitance of line to ground
    (a) decreases   (b) increases
    (c) remains unaltered (d) becomes infinite

28. The presence of earth in case of overhead lines
    (a) increases the capacitance
    (b) increases the inductance
    (c) decreases the capacitance and increases the inductance
    (d) does not effect any of the line constants

29. Transposition of transmission line is done to reduce the
    (a) line losses
    (b) capacitive effect
    (c) disturbances to nearby communication circuits
    (d) effect of surge voltages induced on the line

30. Transposition of transmission line is done to
    (a) reduce line loss
    (b) reduce skin effect
    (c) balance line voltage drop
    (d) reduce corona

31. High voltage transmission lines are transposed because then
    (a) corona losses can be minimized
    (b) computation of inductance becomes easier
    (c) voltage drop in the lines can be minimized
    (d) phase voltage imbalances can be minimized

32. Compared with solid conductor of the same radius, corona appears on a stranded conductor at a lower voltage, because stranding
    (a) assists ionisation
    (b) makes the current flow spirally about the axis of the conductor
    (c) produces oblique sections to a plane perpendicular to the axis of the conductor
    (d) produces surfaces of smaller radius.

33. Proximity effect
   (a) is more pronounced for large conductors, high frequencies and close proximity
   (b) increases the resistance of the conductors and reduces the self reactance
   (c) is substantially eliminated with stranded conductors
   (d) all of these

34. The transmission lines are said to be long if the length of the line exceeds
   (a) 50 km.
   (b) 150 km.
   (c) 250 km.
   (d) 500 km.

35. Shunt capacitance is neglected in case of
   (a) short transmission lines
   (b) medium transmission lines
   (c) long transmission lines
   (d) medium and long transmission lines

36. The effect of capacitance can be neglected when the length of overhead transmission line does not exceed
   (a) 20 km.
   (b) 60 km.
   (c) 120 km.
   (d) 300 km.

37. 120 km ling transmission line is considered as a
   (a) short line
   (b) medium line
   (c) long line
   (d) either (a) or (b)

38. A 25 km 33 kv transmission line is considered to be
   (a) short transmission line
   (b) medium transmission line
   (c) long transmission line
   (d) high power line

39. A 160 km, 110 kv transmission line falls under the category of
   (a) short transmission line
   (b) medium transmission line
   (c) long transmission line
   (d) ultra high voltage line

40. Which of the following is neglected while analysing a short transmission line?
   (a) Shunt admittances.
   (b) Power losses.
   (c) Series impedance.
   (d) None of these.

41. For 11 kV transmission line the inductance per km will be about
   (a) 1 H.
   (b) 0.1 H.
   (c) 1 mH.
   (d) 0.1 mH.

42. For 11 kV transmission line the cpacitance per km will be about
   (a) 0.01 F.
   (b) 0.1 F.
   (c) 0.1μF.
   (d) 0.1μF.

43. Percentage regulation of transmission line is given by the expression
   (a) $\dfrac{V_R - V_S}{V_R} \times 100$
   (b) $\dfrac{V_R - V_S}{V_S} \times 100$
   (c) $\dfrac{V_S - V_R}{V_R} \times 100$
   (d) $\dfrac{V_S - V_R}{V_S} \times 100$

44. Which of the following regulations is considered best ?
   (a) $\dfrac{21}{2}\%$
   (b) 15%
   (c) 25%
   (d) 40%

45. For a short line if the receiving end voltage is equal to sending end voltage under loaded conditions
   (a) the sending end power factor is unity
   (b) the receiving end power factor is unity
   (c) the sending end power factor is leading
   (d) the receiving end power factor is leading

46. Transmission efficiency of a transmission line increases with the
   (a) decrease in power factor and voltage
   (b) increase in power factor and voltage
   (c) increase in power factor but decrease in voltage
   (d) increase in voltage but decrease in power factor

47. Constant power locus of a transmission line at a particular sending end and receiving end voltage is
   (a) a straight line
   (b) a circle
   (c) a parabola
   (d) an ellipse

48. Constant voltage transmission have the advantage(s) of
   (a) increase of short-circuit current of the system
   (b) large reserve of lines in case of line trouble
   (c) improvement of power factor at the times of moderate and heavy loads
   (d) all of these

49. A synchronous phase modifier as compared to synchronous motor of the same rating has
    (a) larger shaft diameter and higher speed
    (b) smaller shaft diameter and higher speed
    (c) larger shaft diameter and smaller speed
    (d) smaller shaft diameter and smaller speed

50. Phase modifier is normally installed in case of
    (a) short transmission lines
    (b) medium length lines
    (c) long lines
    (d) for any length of lines

51. Series capacitors on transmission lines are of little use when the required reactive voltamperes are
    (a) small   (b) large
    (c) fluctuating   (d) any of the these

52. The function of guard ring transmission lines is
    (a) to reduce the transmission losses
    (b) to reduce the earth capacitance of the lowest unit
    (c) to increase the earth capacitance of the lowest unit
    (d) none of these

53. Use of bundle conductors causes the critical voltage for corona formation
    (a) to decrease
    (b) to increase
    (c) to remain unlatered
    (d) does not existent

54. For maximum efficiency in transmission of bulk ac power, the power factor of the load should be
    (a) unity
    (b) slightly less than unity lagging
    (c) slightly less than unity leading
    (d) considerably less than unity

55. The surge impedance of a long power transmission line is of the order of
    (a) 50 Ω   (b) 75 Ω
    (c) 400 Ω   (d) 800 Ω

56. As the height of the transmission tower is increased, the line capacitance and line inductance respectively
    (a) decreases, decreases
    (b) increases, decreases
    (c) decreases, remains unlatered
    (d) increases, increases

57. The corona discharge on transmission lines may be avoided by
    (a) increasing effective conductor radius
    (b) increasing the operating voltage
    (c) decreasing the spacing between the conductors
    (d) none of these

58. Voltage gradient on a transmission line conductor is highest
    (a) at the surface of the conductor
    (b) at the centre of the conductor
    (c) at the distance equal to one radius from the surface
    (d) none of these

59. Booster transformer is located at
    (a) sending end of transmission line
    (b) receiving end of transmission line
    (c) intermediate point on a transmission line
    (d) none of these

60. The transmission line between tower assumes the shape of a
    (a) parabola   (b) hyperbola
    (c) catanary   (d) arc of a circle

61. Voltage control in a power transmission line is achieved by
    (a) booster transformer
    (b) tap-changing transformer
    (c) injection of reactive power
    (d) all of these

62. In a power transmission line, the sag depends on
    (a) conductor material alone
    (b) tension in conductors alone
    (c) span of transmission line
    (d) all of these

63. If the span of a transmission line is increased by 10%, the sag of line increases by about
    (a) 7%   (b) 14%
    (c) 21%   (d) 28%

64. String efficiency is defined as
    (a) V_{Fn}/V_{F1}
    (b) $n\,V_{F1}/V_{Fn}$
    (c) $VF_n/(n\,V_{F1})$
    (d) V_{F1}/V_{Fn}
    where V_{F1} is the flash over voltage of one unit V_{Fn} is the flash over voltage of string of n-units.

65. The string efficiency of an insulator can be increased by
(a) reducing the number of strings in the insulator
(b) increasing the number of strings in the insulator
(c) correct grading of insulators of various capacities
(d) none of these

66. The topmost wire in a distribution line is
(a) neutral wire (b) earth wire
(c) phase wire (d) any of these

67. Sheaths are used in power cables to
(a) provide adequate insulation
(b) increase the strength of the cable
(c) prevent moisture from entering the cable
(d) none of these

68. For high voltage applications, the insulators used are of
(a) suspension type
(b) pin type
(c) strain type
(d) none of these

69. On a transmission line, whenever the conductors are dead ended or there is change in the direction of transmission line, the insulators used are
(a) strain type (b) suspension type
(c) pin type (d) none of these

70. Pin insulators are normally used for voltages upto
(a) 30 kV (b) 50 kV
(c) 70 kV (d) 100 kV

71. Conductors used in high voltage transmission lines are stranded to
(a) make it easy to handle
(b) reduce the cost
(c) increase its conductivity
(d) increase its tensile strength

72. Due to skin effect at high frequencies, the effective value of conductor resistance
(a) decreases
(b) increases
(c) remains unaltered
(d) may increase or decrease

73. Surge conductance in power transmission lines is due to leakage over
(a) insulators (b) conductors
(c) poles (d) jumpers

74. Charging current in a transmission line
(a) increases the line losses
(b) decreases the line losses
(c) does not effect the line losses
(d) none of these

75. Ground wire is used in transmission system
(a) to avoid overloading
(b) to give good insulation
(c) to connect a circuit conductor or other device to an earth plate
(d) none of these

76. The current by alternate charging and discharging of transmission line due to ac voltage is called
(a) oscillating voltage
(b) charging current
(c) line current
(d) discharging current

77. Transposition of conductors in transmission line system is done when
(a) the conductors are not spaced equilaterally
(b) the conductors are spaced equilaterally
(c) a telephone line runs parallel to power line
(d) none of these

78. Relative to fair weather, in humid weather corona occurs at
(a) lower voltage
(b) higher voltage
(c) almost the same voltage
(d) none of these

79. In a power transmission line, grounding is generally done at
(a) the supply end
(b) the receiving end
(c) middle of the line
(d) none of these

80. Earthing of power transmission line is necessary to provide protection against
(a) overload
(b) voltage fluctuation
(c) electric shock
(d) temperature rise of conductors

81. As the height of a transmission tower is altered, the parameter which changes is
(a) inductance (b) capacitance
(c) conductance (d) none of these

82. In conductor of power transmission line, the voltage gradient is maximum at its
    (a) centre
    (b) surface
    (c) circle with half the radius
    (d) somewhere between (b) and (c) above

83. EHV cables are filled with thin oil under pressure to
    (a) prevent formation of voids
    (b) prevent entry of moisture
    (c) to strengthen the cable conductor
    (d) to provide insulation

84. Cables in power transmission line are provided with intersheaths to
    (a) minimize stress
    (b) minimize high voltage
    (c) provide uniform stress distribution
    (d) minimize charging current

85. Impedance and capacitance of a transmission line depend upon
    (a) current in the line alone
    (b) voltage in the line alone
    (c) both (a) and (b)
    (d) physical configuration of conductors in space

86. Transmission lines are classified as short, medium and long depending on the
    (a) length of line
    (b) charging current or no load current
    (c) capacitance of line
    (d) both (a) and (b) above

87. A series compensated transmission line has better
    (a) transient stability
    (b) steady state stability
    (c) short circuit capacity
    (d) reactive capacity

88. Reactive power can be injected into a transmission line by using
    (a) series capacitors
    (b) shunt capacitors and reactors
    (c) synchronous capacitors
    (d) any of these

89. The earthing switch is generally installed on
    (a) main board
    (b) isolator frame
    (c) circuit breaker frame
    (d) none of these

90. Corona is observed on
    (a) a.c. transmission lines only
    (b) d.c. transmission lines only
    (c) both a.c and d.c. transmission lines
    (d) none of these

91. An advantage of corona on transmission lines is that
    (a) it minimizes power loss
    (b) it reflects electrical surges
    (c) it works as a surge modifier during overloads
    (d) none of these

92. Temperature increase produces which of the following effect on a transmission line?
    (a) tension of the conductor and its sag increase
    (b) tension of the conductor and its sag decrease
    (c) tension of the conductor decreases and its sag increases
    (d) tension of the conductor increases and its sag decreases

93. Transformer connection at the sending end of a transmission line is usually
    (a) star-delta   (b) delta-delta
    (c) delta-star   (d) star-star

94. High tension cables can be used for power transmission for voltages not exceeding
    (a) 11 kV   (b) 22 kV
    (c) 33 kV   (d) 110 kV

95. As the moisture content in the air increases, the disruptive critical voltage
    (a) increases
    (b) decreases
    (c) remains constant
    (d) may increase or decrease

96. The critical voltage of a transmission line may be increased by
    (a) increasing the conductor diameter
    (b) increasing the air spacing between the conductors
    (c) both (a) and (b) above
    (d) none of these

97. Void formation in the dielectric material of an underground cable may be controlled by
    (a) using a high permitivity solid dielectric
    (b) providing a strong metallic sheath outside the cable
    (c) filling oil at high pressure as dielectric
    (d) none of these

98. Bundle conductors are used to reduce the effect of
    (a) inductance of the circuit
    (b) capacitance of the circuit
    (c) corona and power loss due to corona
    (d) both (a) and (b) above

99. When the conductors of a 3-phase transmission line are not spaced equilaterally, transmission is done to
    (a) decrease the line inductance per phase
    (b) balance the 3 phases of the circuit
    (c) minimize the effect of adjoining communication circuit
    (d) none of these

100. Size of the earth wire is determined by
    (a) the ampere capacity of the service
    (b) the atmospheric conditions
    (c) the voltage of the service wires
    (d) none of these

101. In short overhead transmission line (upto 80 km), we may neglect
    (a) series resistance
    (b) shunt conductance
    (c) shunt capacitance
    (d) both shunt coductance and capacitance

102. If the voltage as well as reactance of a transmission line is doubled, the maximum steady state power limit of the line
    (a) remains unaltered (b) doubles
    (c) becomes 4 times (d) becomes 8 times

103. Rise of temperature of transmission line
    (a) increases the stress and decreases the length
    (b) increases the stress and increases the length
    (c) decreases the stress and increases the length
    (d) decreases the stress and decreases the length

104. A short transmission line has equivalent circuit consisting of
    (a) series resistance R and series inductance L
    (b) series resistance R and shunt capacitance C
    (c) series resistance R and shunt capacitance G
    (d) series inductance L and shunt capacitance G

105. Proximity effect is due to current flowing in the
    (a) earth
    (b) sheath
    (c) neighbouring conductor
    (d) all of these

106. Insulation resistance of a cable decreases with
    (a) decrease in he length of the insulation of cable
    (b) increase in the length of the insulation of cable
    (c) increase in electric stress
    (d) increase in temperature

107. The amount of active power transmitted over a transmission line is proportional to
    (a) sending end voltage V_s
    (b) receiving end voltage V_R
    (c) torque angle δ between V_S and V_R
    (d) difference voltage $(V_S - V_R)$

108. The characteristic impedance of a lossless cable is typically
    (a) 40 to 60 Ω (b) 100 to 120 Ω
    (c) 400 to 600 Ω (d) 1000 to 1500 Ω

109. The power loss in a long transmission line at no load equals
    (a) 0 (b) $\frac{1}{4}I_0^2 R$
    (c) $\frac{1}{3}I_0^2 R$ (d) $\frac{1}{2}I_0^2 R$

110. For a power system, to be stable, the phase constant β of its transmission line should be
    (a) $\frac{R_L R_O}{R_O + R_L}$ (b) $\frac{R_L - R_O}{R_L + R_O}$
    (c) $\frac{R_L + R_O}{R_L - R_O}$ (d) $\frac{R_L R_O}{R_O R_L}$

111. For the same voltage boost, the reactive power capacity is more for a
    (a) Shunt capacitor.
    (b) Series capacitor.
    (c) It is same for both series and shunt.
    (d) None of the above.

112. To increase the power transmitting capacity of a transmission line we
    (a) increase its line capacitance
    (b) increase its line inductance
    (c) decrease its line capacitance
    (d) none of these

113. Guy is attached to a transmission line pole to
    (a) reduce the sag
    (b) hold the telephone lines
    (c) strengthen the pole
    (d) none of these

114. During rains, the direct capacitance of suspension type insulator
    (a) decreases
    (b) increases
    (c) remain unchanged
    (d) may increase or decrease

115. While calculating the fault current, the reactances of the machines connected to the power system are taken to be
    (a) zero
    (b) constant
    (c) increasing with load
    (d) decreasing with load

116. Compared to the normal impedance, the fault impedance of a circuit is
    (a) the same
    (b) higher
    (c) lower
    (d) may be lower or higher

117. Visual corona takes place in parallel wires at a voltage
    (a) higher than disruptive critical voltage
    (b) higher than Curie voltage
    (c) equal to disruptive voltage
    (d) none of these

118. Corona loss is maximum when using
    (a) ACSR   (b) stranded wire
    (c) unstranded wire (d) transposed wire

119. Corona always causes
    (a) system faults   (b) radio interference
    (c) insulation failure (d) none of these

120. If fault occurs near an impedance relay, the V I ratio is
    (a) constant for all the locations of fault
    (b) lower than the value if fault occurs away from the relay
    (c) higher than the value if fault occurs away from the relay
    (d) may be lower or higher than the value if fault occurs away from the relay

121. The fault MVA is given by
    (a) $\dfrac{\text{Base MVA}}{\text{P.U. Xeq}}$ (b) Base MVA × P.U. Xeq
    (c) $\dfrac{\text{Base MVA}}{(\text{P.U. Xeq})^2}$ (d) none of these

    where Xeq is the fault impedance at the point where fault has occurred

122. The peak short circuit current equals
    (a) $\sqrt{2}$ ac component
    (b) $1.8 \times \sqrt{2}$ ac component
    (c) $\sqrt{3} \times \sqrt{2}$ ac component
    (d) $2 \times \sqrt{2}$ ac component

123. For most reliable distribution supply, the configuration used is
    (a) radial main
    (b) ring main
    (c) parabolic main
    (d) balancing main

124. Breakdown of insulation of a cable can be avoided economically by the use of
    (a) insulating material with different dielectric
    (b) intersheath
    (c) both (a) and (b) above
    (d) none of these

125. Which of the following system is preferred for good efficiency and high economy in distribution system ?
    (a) single phase system
    (b) 2 phase 3 wire system
    (c) 3 phase 3 wire system
    (d) 3 phase 4 wire system

126. If the neutral of 3-phase star assembly is grounded, then for line currents Ia, Ib and Ic the current in the neutral wire is
    (a) 0
    (b) $I_a + I_b + I_c$
    (c) $\dfrac{I_a + I_b + I_c}{2}$
    (d) $\sqrt{2(I_a + I_b + I_c)}$

127. Any voltage surge travelling on the transmission line first enters
    (a) step down transformer
    (b) lightning arrestor
    (c) switch gear
    (d) over voltage relay

128. ACSR is used for transmission of power in preference to copper conductors because
    (a) it is lighter
    (b) it is more economical
    (c) it has higher current carrying capacity
    (d) it can stand higher surge voltages

129. Two transmission lines each having surge impedance of 75Ω are separated by cable link. For zero reflection, the surge impedance of the cable should be
(a) 0Ω
(b) 75Ω
(c) 150Ω
(d) 300Ω

130. For a 400 kV transmission line, the switching over voltage crest in kV is
(a) 400
(b) $400\sqrt{2}$
(c) 825
(d) 1155

131. For a 400 kV transmission line, the number of standard disc used in practice are
(a) 8
(b) 12
(c) 16
(d) 24

132. Compared to the insulation level of the station equipment, the line insulation is
(a) the same
(b) greater
(c) less
(d) not directly related

133. The sag of a transmission line is affected by
(a) its own weight and weight of the ice formed
(b) temperature and wind condition
(c) both (a) and (b) above
(d) none of these

134. In a transmission line, the shunt conductance results due to
(a) axial current in the conductor
(b) radial current in the conductor
(c) leakage over the insulator
(d) short circuiting of line by the load

135. Due to skin effect, resistance of the conductor
(a) decreases
(b) increases
(c) remains same
(d) uncertain

136. Considerable power is taken up for charging
(a) D.C. transmission
(b) A.C. transmission
(c) electron transmission
(d) none of these

137. As the transmission voltage increases, percentage resistance drop
(a) increases
(b) decreases
(c) remain same
(d) increase in random manner

138. The primary parameters of transmission line are
(a) series inductance
(b) shunt capacitance
(c) series and shunt resistance
(d) all of these

139. If a long transmission line is very lightly loaded or left open then the receiving end voltage rises. This effect is called
(a) Joules effect
(b) Einstein's effect
(c) Raman effect
(d) Ferranti effect

140. Transposition of power lines is done to
(a) reduce copper losses
(b) prevent short circuit between two lines
(c) prevent interference with telephone lines
(d) all of these

141. Capacitance current of a transmission system is usually reckoned in the case of
(a) short line
(b) medium line
(c) long line
(d) none of these

142. For a short line, receiving end voltage is more than sending end for
(a) lagging power factor
(b) leading power factor
(c) unity power factor
(d) zero power factor

143. Bundled conductors are used to
(a) reduce radio interference
(b) reduce reactance
(c) both (a) and (b)
(d) none of these

144. In a short line
(a) shunting effects are neglected
(b) shunting effects are included
(c) may include or neglect
(d) none of these

145. Charging current of a line is more at
(a) mid point
(b) one third of line
(c) receiving end
(d) sending end

146. For bulk power transmission over a long distance, economical method is transmission of
(a) lower voltage
(b) higher current
(c) higher voltage
(d) none of these

147. Angle between sending and receiving end voltage is called
(a) load angle
(b) power angle
(c) torque angle
(d) all of these

148. Two terminal network representing a 3 phase line is called
    (a) active network   (b) passive network
    (c) either (a) or (b)   (d) none of these

149. Real part of propagation constant of a transmission line is called
    (a) phase constant
    (b) gain constant
    (c) attenuation constant
    (d) none of these

150. In short lines, regulation and pressure drop are
    (a) vectorially equal
    (b) equal in phase
    (c) numerically equal
    (d) none of these

151. Secondary transmission and distribution system are of
    (a) radial structure   (b) ring structure
    (c) mesh structure   (d) none of these

152. Typical load always consumes
    (a) active power   (b) reactive power
    (c) inverse power   (d) none of these

153. Unit for energy transmission under steady state condition is called
    (a) static transmission capacity
    (b) static distribution
    (c) either (a) or (b)
    (d) none of these

154. In power systems, regulating transformers are used to control
    (a) current flow   (b) load flow
    (c) electrons flow   (d) none of these

155. Synchronous machines can be controlled by
    (a) terminal voltage and rotor current
    (b) terminal voltage and phase angle
    (c) rotor current and reactance
    (d) terminal voltage and reactance

156. Low voltage a.c. distribution is
    (a) 220 V between phases
    (b) 400 V between phases
    (c) 3.3 kV between phases
    (d) none of these

157. Light points available in the houses are
    (a) power source   (b) current source
    (c) voltage source   (d) all of these

158. Systems getting supply from one end only are
    (a) ring type
    (b) mesh type
    (c) radial type
    (d) all of these

159. System which suffers from maximum voltage fluctuations is
    (a) ring type
    (b) radial type
    (c) mesh type
    (d) none of these

160. In d.c. transmission, voltage between feeder and distributor is changed by using
    (a) transformers
    (b) generator
    (c) rotating machines
    (d) mercury arc rectifiers

161. Bus coupler is needed in
    (a) main and transfer bus arrangement
    (b) double bus breaker arrangement
    (c) single bus arrangement
    (d) all of these

162. Outdoor sub-stations are preferred for voltages above
    (a) 3.3 kV   (b) 11 kV
    (c) 33 kV   (d) 66 kV

163. Synchronous motors installed at sub-stations give
    (a) unity power factor
    (b) lagging power factor
    (c) leading power factor
    (d) none of these

164. Outdoor busbars are of
    (a) strain type
    (b) rigid type
    (c) strain or rigid type
    (d) none of these

165. Under groung cables are generally not used for more than a distance of
    (a) 50 km   (b) 75 km
    (c) 90 km   (d) 100 km

166. For greater flexibility, degree of stranding for a cable when compared with overhead lines should be
    (a) lesser   (b) higher
    (c) same   (d) none of these

167. In underground cables, maximum stress is at the
(a) surface of the conductor
(b) sheath surface of the cable
(c) centre of the conductor
(d) between sheath and the conductor

168. Cables are sheathed to
(a) protect the insulation
(b) increase the rate of heat dissipation
(c) increase the cable capacity
(d) protect the cable from mechanical stresses

169. Cables are pulled into a conduit and spliced in a
(a) pole
(b) manhole
(c) feeder pillar
(d) all of these

170. Capacitance grading of a cable mean that the cable
(a) uses different dielectrics
(b) uses different intersheaths
(c) is classified according to its capacitance
(d) none of these

171. In H.S.L. type cables
(a) each case has its own lead sheath
(b) screen is perforated and each core has separate lead sheath
(c) each core is surrounded by a metallised and perforated paper which is kept at earth potential
(d) none of these

172. Cable with varnished cambric insulation has
(a) high dielectric strength
(b) high insulation resistance
(c) high mechanical stresses bearing capacity
(d) all of these

173. Induced currents in the sheaths are
(a) sheath eddy current
(b) sheath circuit eddy current
(c) induction current
(d) none of these

174. Grading of cables is done to
(a) increase its conduction efficiency
(b) increase its strength
(c) achieve a uniform stress distribution
(d) all of these

175. Pressure cables are filled with
(a) oil
(b) air
(c) nitrogen
(d) helium

176. Pressure in pressure cables is approximately
(a) 5 to 7 atm
(b) 7 to 9 atm
(c) 9 to 12 atm
(d) 12 to 15 atm

177. If inductance calculating method for overhead lines is applied to the underground cables also, then result will involve an error because of the
(a) sheath effects
(b) skin and proximity effects
(c) both (a) and (b)
(d) none of these

178. Formation of voids in the dielectric of a cable is due to effect of
(a) loading cycles in service
(b) increased pressure
(c) extra potential difference
(d) all of these

179. Sheath loss is a function of
(a) $(\text{frequency})^2$
(b) maximum voltage
(c) power factor
(d) corona loss

180. Cables should not be operated too hot because
(a) sheath may burst due to oil expansion
(b) decreased viscosity at high temperature cause oil to drain off from the higher levels
(c) due to unequal expansion the voids may be created
(d) all of these

181. For oil impregnated cables, maximum operating temperature is
(a) 10 C
(b) 25 C
(c) 45 C
(d) 65 C

182. Transformers and network pretectors used in underground cable system may be
(a) submersible type
(b) non-submersible type
(c) combined (a) and (b)
(d) none of these

183. Safe value of current carrying capacity of cables is determined by
(a) maximum voltage
(b) maximum temperature
(c) power factor
(d) maximum pressure

184. Test for conductor failure in cables can be done by comparing
   (a) resistances of the conductors
   (b) capacitance of the insulated conductors
   (c) maximum pressure on conductors
   (d) none of these

185. Dielectric losses in the insulation in case of cable is negligible in
   (a) d.c. transmission   (b) a.c. transmission
   (c) both (a) and (b)   (d) none of these

186. Underground cables have large charging current which
   (a) lags the voltage by 90°
   (b) leads the voltage by 90°
   (c) is in phase with voltage
   (d) is out of phase by 180° with voltage

187. All high voltage cables usually operate at a power factor
   (a) small but lagging
   (b) close to unity
   (c) small but leading
   (d) large and lagging

188. For high voltage applications, the insulator used is
   (a) pin type   (b) suspension type
   (c) strain type   (d) all of these

189. Insulators are used on overhead line to insulate the wire from
   (a) the pole   (b) each other
   (c) both (a) and (b)   (d) none of these

190. Insulators are required to withstand
   (a) electrical stresses
   (b) mechanical stresses
   (c) both (a) and (b)
   (d) none of these

191. Lines above 50 kV uses
   (a) pin type insulator
   (b) suspension type insulator
   (c) strain type insulator
   (d) any of them

192. Insulator disc subjected to maximum stress is
   (a) near the conductor
   (b) near the cross arm
   (c) in the middle of string
   (d) are exprinces equal stress

193. In case of wet suspension type insulator
   (a) string efficiency is increased
   (b) string efficiency is decreased
   (c) capacitance between units is decreased
   (d) capacitance between units is increased

194. For improving string efficiency, ratio of capacity to earth to capacity per insulator should
   (a) decrease   (b) increase
   (c) remain same   (d) uncertain

195. Number of insulators used for a 230 kV line is
   (a) 13   (b) 14
   (c) 15   (d) 16

196. A guard ring is used to
   (a) decrease potential across each units
   (b) increase potential across each units
   (c) make potential across each unit equal
   (d) none of these

197. In string type insulator, if number of discs are increased the string efficiency
   (a) decreases   (b) increases
   (c) remains same   (d) uncertain]

198. By increasing potential of a conductor
   (a) potential between conductor and ground decreases
   (b) corona loss is reduced
   (c) insulation required is less
   (d) its potential gradient increases

199. Rectification at the ends of E.H.V. d.c. transmission is done by using
   (a) shunt generators
   (b) power capacitors
   (c) SCR
   (d) motor-generator set

200. EHV system is beyond
   (a) 11 kV   (b) 33 kV
   (c) 132 kV   (d) 200 kV

201. Series reactors have
   (a) low reactance   (b) low resistance
   (c) low impedance   (d) high resistance

202. E.H.V. cables are filled with oil under pressure of gas because
   (a) pressure provides the necessary strength
   (b) pressure provides the necessary voltage bearing capacity
   (c) pressure will avoid the formation of voids
   (d) all of these

203. For E.H.V. transmission bundled conductors are preferred because
(a) of less cost, line inductance & corona loss
(b) they are easy to fabricate
(c) only bundled conductors can withstand high voltages
(d) all of these

204. On a lightly loaded transmission line
(a) receiving end voltage can exceed sending end voltage
(b) receiving end voltage can't exceed sending end voltage
(c) capacitive charging current is reduced
(d) none of these

205. Characteristic impedance of a telephone line is of the order of
(a) 50 Ω
(b) 60 Ω
(c) 75 Ω
(d) 100 Ω

206. Difference between surge impedance and characteristic impedence is that in surge impendance
(a) line resistance is considered
(b) line resistance is assumed to be zero
(c) line capacitance is assumed to be zero
(d) line impedance is assumed to be zero

207. Increase of temperature in transmission line
(a) increases stress & decreases length
(b) increases stress & length
(c) decreases stress & length
(d) decreases stress & increases length

208. Now-a-days copper is replaced by aluminium in lines because of
(a) heavy weight of copper
(b) high cost of copper
(c) less conductivity of copper
(d) scarcity of copper

209. If height of transmission tower is increased, line inductance
(a) increases
(b) decreases
(c) remains same
(d) uncertain

210. Voltage gradient is highest at the
(a) centre of the conductor
(b) surface of the conductor
(c) 1/3 of the conductor
(d) none of these

211. With impurities in copper, conductivity
(a) increases
(b) decreases
(c) does not affect
(d) uncertain

212. Shunt conductance in power transmission is due to leakage over
(a) insulator
(b) conductors
(c) poles
(d) ground

213. Entire line performance can be determined by
(a) sending end power circle diagram
(b) receiving end power circle diagram
(c) universal power circle diagram
(d) none of these

214. Booster transformer is located at
(a) sending end
(b) receiving end
(c) mid point of line
(d) anywhere on the line

215. Concrete poles are used because of their
(a) longer life
(b) less maintenance cost
(c) both (a) and (b)
(d) none of these

216. Voltage control method used in transmission system is by
(a) tap changing transformers
(b) injection of reactive power
(c) booster transformer
(d) all of these

217. Vertical loading in pole results on account of
(a) dead weight of the equipment
(b) conductor tension at angles in lines
(c) interference in transmission lines
(d) vibration of conductors

218. Transformer at sending end of a line is usually
(a) Star-star
(b) Star-delta
(c) Delta-star
(d) Delta-delta

219. In a d.c. 3 wire transmission system, cross-section of the neutral is generally
(a) 1/2 of the outer conductor
(b) 1/3 of the outer couductor
(c) 1/4 of the outer conductor
(d) none of these

220. Guy is fastened to a pole to
    (a) strengthen the pole
    (b) hold telephone cables
    (c) keep the wires from sagging
    (d) none of these

221. As transmission voltage increases, volume of the conductor
    (a) increases
    (b) decreases
    (c) remain same
    (d) increases proportionately

222. With 10% increase in span of the line, sag increases by
    (a) 18%   (b) 19%
    (c) 20%   (d) 21%

223. Spacing of the conductors is determined by
    (a) machanical considerations
    (b) electrical considerations
    (c) both (a) and (b)
    (d) none of these

224. Power transmission capacity of the transmission line is
    (a) proportional to voltage
    (b) proportional to square of operating voltage
    (c) inversely proportional to voltage
    (d) inversely proportional to square of voltage

225. Topmost wire in a transmission line carrying distribution line is
    (a) phase wire   (b) neutral wire
    (c) earth wire   (d) all of these

226. Corona loss occurs in
    (a) transmission lines
    (b) distribution transformer
    (c) generator
    (d) cables

227. Capacitance of a transmission line is a result of
    (a) potential difference between the conductors
    (b) current in the conductors
    (c) both (a) and (b)
    (d) none of these

228. Corona always results in
    (a) insulation failure
    (b) faults in line
    (c) radio interference
    (d) all of these

229. Inductance due to conductor's own current is called
    (a) self inductance
    (b) mutual inductance
    (c) internal inductance
    (d) none of these

230. Inductance and capacitance of a transmission line depend upon
    (a) current in the line
    (b) voltage of the line
    (c) volume of the line
    (d) physical configuration

231. Transfer reactance of a line is reduced by
    (a) series compensation
    (b) shunt compensation
    (c) mixed series & shunt compensation
    (d) it can not be compensated

232. Corona loss is more in
    (a) stranded wire   (b) unstranded wire
    (c) naked wire   (d) equal in all wires

233. Corona
    (a) minimizes the power losses
    (b) reflects electrical surges
    (c) works as surge modifier during over voltages
    (d) all of these

234. Corona introduces
    (a) lagging current
    (b) leading current
    (c) high current
    (d) harmonic current

235. Power loss due to corona in winter is
    (a) same as in summer
    (b) less than in summer
    (c) more than in summer
    (d) none of these

236. By corona, surge voltage
    (a) attenuates   (b) amplifies
    (c) has no effect   (d) none of these

237. Ground wire is provided in an overhead line to
    (a) provide more mechanical strength to the line
    (b) provide a return path for all zero sequence currents
    (c) work as lightening conductor
    (d) all of these

238. Corona power loss can be reduced by
(a) increasing the wire diameter
(b) decreasing the wire diameter
(c) using insulated wire
(d) none of these

239. An infinite bus bar has a surge impedance equal to
(a) zero
(b) infinite
(c) surge impedance of the transmission line connected to it
(d) all of these

240. Critical voltage of the line can be increased by increasing
(a) spacing
(b) diameter
(c) both (a) and (b)
(d) none of these

241. Cross-sectional area of the neutral wire in a 3 phase, 4 wire system is equal to
(a) that of phase conductor
(b) 1/2 times that of phase conductor
(c) 1/4 times that of phase conductor
(d) 2 times that of phase conductor

EXERCISE – II

1. A synchro transmitter consists of a
(a) salient pole rotor winding excited by an ac supply and a three-phase balanced stator winding
(b) three-phase balance stator winding excited by a three- phase balanced ac signal and rotor connected to a dc voltage source
(c) salient pole rotor winding excited by a dc signal
(d) cylindrical rotor winding and a stepped stator excited by pulses **(RRB 2012)**

2. A travelling wave due to lightning with an incident voltage V travels through the overhead line of surge impedance of 400 Ω and enters a cable of surge impedance of 40 Ω. What is the voltage entering the cable at the junction?
(a) V/11
(b) 4V/11
(c) 2V/11
(d) V **(RRB 2012)**

3. Which is the main relay for protecting up to 90% of the transmission line-length in the forward direction?
(a) Directional over-current relay
(b) Mho relay
(c) Carrier-current protective relay
(d) Impedance relay **(RRB 2012)**

4. When is the Ferranti effect on long overhead lines experienced?
(a) The line is lightly loaded
(b) The line is heavily loaded
(c) The line is fully loaded
(d) The power factor is unity **(RRB 2012)**

5. Which of the following statements is NOT correct for a storage type oscilloscope? **(RRB 2012)**
(a) The storage target is a conductive mesh covered with magnesium fluoride.

(b) Secondary emission electrons etch a positively charged pattern
(c) The flood guns used for display, emit high velocity electrons
(d) The flood guns are placed between the deflection plates and storage target

6. A standard resistance is made 'Bifilar' type of eliminate **(RRB 2012)**
(a) stray capacitance
(b) temperature effect
(c) inductive effect
(d) skin effect

7. Which one of the following truly represents the output on the screen of spectrum analyzer when an amplitude modulated wave is connected to it?
(a) Single vertical line on the screen
(b) Two vertical lines on the screen
(c) Three vertical lines with amplitude
(d) Three vertical lines out of which two have equal magnitude **(RRB 2012)**

8. The diagram given below shows the connection of a four–wire delta bank for obtaining a 3–phase 4–wire distribution system. The secondary voltages between the terminals are as indicated,

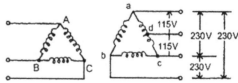

What is the voltage between the terminals b and d in the above system when the primary side is energized from an appropriate symmetrical 3–phase system? **(RRB 2012)**

(a) $\dfrac{230}{\sqrt{2}\,\text{V}}$
(b) $\dfrac{230}{\sqrt{3}\,\text{V}}$
(c) $115 \times \sqrt{3}\,\text{V}$
(d) $115 \times \sqrt{2}\,\text{V}$

9. A handshake signal in a data transfer is transmitted **(RRB 2012)**
   (a) along with the data bits
   (b) before the data transfer
   (c) after the data transfer
   (d) either along with the bits or after the data transfer

10. HV transmission line uses **(RRB)**
    (a) pin type insulators
    (b) suspension insulators
    (c) both(a) and (b)
    (d) none of these

11. The skin effect of a conductor reduces with the increase in **(RRB)**
    (a) supply frequency
    (b) resistivity of the conductor material
    (c) x-section of conductor
    (d) permeability of conductor material

12. The current by alternate charging and discharging of transmission line due to ac voltage is called
    (a) oscillating voltage
    (b) charging current
    (c) line current
    (d) discharging current **(RRB)**

13. Insulation resistance of a cable decreases with
    (a) decrease in he length of the insulation of cable
    (b) increase in the length of the insulation of cable
    (c) increase in electric stress
    (d) increase in temperature **(RRB)**

14. Corona loss is maximum when using **(RRB)**
    (a) ACSR
    (b) stranded wire
    (c) unstranded wire
    (d) transposed wire

15. Voltage control method used in transmission system is by **(RRB)**
    (a) tap changing transformers
    (b) injection of reactive power
    (c) booster transformer
    (d) all of these

16. Thyrite is used in lightning arrestors because of its **(RRB)**
    (a) straight line characteristic
    (b) non-linear characteristic
    (c) none of these
    (d) all of these

17. Main advantage of distributing the winding in slots is to **(RRB)**
    (a) add mechanical strength to the winding
    (b) reduce the amount of copper required
    (c) reduce the harmonics in the generated e.m.f.
    (d) reduce the size of the machine.

18. Transposition of transmission line is done to
    (a) reduce line loss
    (b) reduce skin effect
    (c) balance line voltage drop
    (d) reduce corona **(RRB)**

19. Proximity effect
    (a) is more pronounced for large conductors, high frequencies and close proximity
    (b) increases the resistance of the conductors and reduces the self reactance
    (c) is substantially eliminated with stranded conductors
    (d) all of these **(RRB)**

20. In short overhead transmission line (upto 80 km), we may neglect **(RRB)**
    (a) series resistance
    (b) shunt conductance
    (c) shunt capacitance
    (d) both shunt coductance and capacitance

21. Secondary transmission and distribution system are of **(RRB)**
    (a) radial structure (b) ring structure
    (c) mesh structure (d) none of these

22. Shunt reactors are sometimes used in high voltage transmission systems to **(RRB)**
    (a) limit the short circuit current through the line
    (b) compensate for the series reactance of the line under heavily loaded condition
    (c) limit over-voltages at the load side under lightly loaded condition
    (d) compensate for the voltage drop in the line under heavily loaded condition

23. The directivity of an isotropic antenna is **(DMRC 2014)**
    (a) zero   (b) less than unity
    (c) unity   (d) infinity

24. Consider the following statements:
    For a uniform plane electromagnetic wave
    1. the direction of energy flow is the same as the direction of propagation of the wave.
    2. electric and magnetic fields in time quadrature.
    3. electric and magnetic fields are in space quadrature.

Of these statements   (DMRC 2014)

(a) 2 alone is correct   (b) 1 and 3 are correct

(c) 1 and 2 are correct (d) 3 alone is correct

25. For an air dielectric transmission line. It is found that as the frequency is varied from 50 MHz upward, the current reaches a minimum at 50-01 MHz and then a maximum at 50.04 MHz the distance of the location of the short-circuit from the generator will then be **(DMRC 2014)**

(a) 10 km

(b) 2.5V km

(c) 1 km

(d) not determinable from the given data

26. Which one of the following classes of materials can be categorised as ferrites?   **(DMRC 2014)**

(a) Plastics   (b) Metals

(c) Alloys   (d) Ceramics

27. The correct sequence of increasing order of electrical resistivity of the given materials is

(a) Diamond, doped germanium, silicon, gold

(b) Gold, silicon, doped germanium, diamond

(c) Gold, doped germanium, silicon, diamond

(d) Gold, diamond, silicon, doped germanium

(DMRC 2014)

28. Which one of the following statements is correct?

(a) The absence of a hysteresis loop in plot of polarization against field is proof of the absence of spontaneous polarization

(b) The Curie temperature of a ferroelectric is the temperature above which its spontaneous polarization disappears

(c) The curie temperature of a ferroelectric is the temperature below which its spontaneous. polarization disappears

(d) Barium titanate is a ferroelectric because its lattice strains spontaneously above the Curie temperature   **(DMRC 2014)**

29. The first critical condition a which free electrons are diffracted in an FCC crystal would occur at which one of the following values of the wave number 'K'/('a' is lattice parameter)

(a) $\dfrac{2}{a}$ (b) $\dfrac{\pi\alpha}{\sqrt{3}}$

(c) $\dfrac{\pi}{\alpha}$ (d) $\sqrt{\dfrac{3\pi}{\alpha}}$ **(DMRC 2014)**

30. A ferromagnetic material exhibits different characteristics above and below the

(a) Joule's temperature

(b) Faraday temperature

(c) Curie temperature

(d) Neel temperature   **(DMRC 2014)**

31. The spins in a ferrimagnetic material are

(a) all aligned parallel   **(DMRC 2014)**

(b) partially aligned antiparallel without exactly canceling out sub-lattice magnetism

(c) randomly oriented

(d) all aligned antiparallel such that the sub-lattice magnetism cancels out exactly

32. Lithium Niobate is used in   **(DMRC 2014)**

(a) SAW devices

(b) LED's

(c) the manufacture of optical fibres

(d) laser diodes

33. A 3-phase, 3 wire supply feeds a load consisting of three equal resistors connected in star. If one of the resistors in open circuited, then the percentage reduction in the load will be

(a) 75   (b) 66.66

(c) 50   (d) 33.33 **(DMRC 2014)**

34. Which one of the following has the highest accuracy?

(a) Standard resistance

(b) Standard inductance

(c) Standard capacitance

(d) Standard mutual inductance **(DMRC 2014)**

35. The X-and Y - inputs of a CRO are respectively Vsin.t and -Vsin ωt. The resulting Lissajous pattern will be   **(DMRC 2014)**

(a) a straight line

(b) a circle

(c) an ellipse

(d) a figure of eight

36. A current $i = (10 + 10 \sin t)$ amperes is passed through an ideal moving iron type ammeter. Its reading will be   **(DMRC 2014)**

(a) zero   (b) 10 A

(c) $\sqrt{150A}$ (d) $\sqrt{2A}$

37. Doppler shift principle is used in the measurement of

(a) temperature   (b) frequency

(c) speed   (d) pressure   **(DMRC)**

38. The bandwidth requirement of an FM telemetry channel is **(DMRC)**

(a) equal to that of an AM telemetry channel

(b) smaller than that of an Am telemetry channel

(c) about 100 times that of an AM telemetry channel

(d) about ten time that of an AM telemetry channel

39. The recording head in a magnetic tape responds to **(DMRC)**

(a) electrical signal and creates a magnetic signal

(b) thermal signal and creates a magnetic signal

(c) magnetic signal and creates an electrical signal

(d) thermal signal and creates an electrical signal

40. Which one of the following materials does not have a covalent bond? **(DMRC)**

(a) Metal   (b) Silicon

(c) Organic polymers (d) Diamond

41. The conductivity of material 'A' is half that of material 'B'. The ratio of relaxation time of 'A' to that of 'B' is **(DMRC)**

(a) 0.5   (b) 1

(c) 2   (d) 4.1

42. In the optical fibre used for communication, the core and cladding material used are respectively

(a) pure silica and Ge-doped silica

(b) P-doped silica and Ge-doped silica

(c) Ge-doped silica and P-doped silica

(d) Ge-doped silica and pure silica **(DMRC)**

43. If supply frequency increases, the skin effect is **(SSC, CPWD 2008)**

(a) decreased   (b) increased

(c) remains same   (d) None of these

44. The ratio of line-to-line capacitance and line-to-neutral capacitance is **(SSC, CPWD 2009)**

(a) $\frac{1}{2}$ (b) $\frac{1}{4}$

(c) 2   (d) 4

45. The material commonly used for sheaths of underground cable is **(SSC, CPWD 2009)**

(a) lead   (b) steel

(c) rubber   (d) copper

46. Advantage of transmitting power at high voltage is **(SSC, CPWD 2010)**

(a) magnitude of current will be small

(b) power loss will be less

(c) it will reduce the voltage drop in the line impedance

(d) All the above

47. Skin effect exists only in **(SSC, CPWD 2010)**

(a) Low voltage dc overhead transmission

(b) High voltage dc overhead transmission

(c) cable carrying dc current

(d) AC transmission

48. Distribution transformers are designed to have maximum efficiency nearly at **(SSC, CPWD 2010)**

(a) 100% of full load (b) 50% of full load

(c) 25% of full load   (d) 10% of full load

49. Two generators each of capacity 10 MVA and reactance 5% are feeding a common bus bar. A transmission line of reactance 2.5% is connected with the bus bar to transmit power to the consumer end. The contribution of each generator to a three phase fault at the consumer end is **(SSC, CPWD 2011)**

(a) 200 MVA   (b) 80 MVA

(c) 100 MVA   (d) 40 MVA

50. The mmf produced by interpole is proportional to **(SSC, CPWD 2011)**

(a) field current   (b) armature current

(c) armature voltage (d) 1 / field current

51. During arcing ground conditions, the phase voltage of the system rises to **(SSC, CPWD 2011)**

(a) 15 times its normal value

(b) 10 times its normal value

(c) 5 to 6 times its normal value

(d) $\sqrt{3}$ times its normal value

52. The sag of the conductors of a transmission line is 2.5 m when the span is 250m. Now if the height of the supporting towers is increased by 25%, the sag will **(SSC, CPWD 2011)**

(a) reduce by 25%   (b) increase by 25%

(c) reduce by 12.5%   (d) remain unchanged

53. If t is the thickness of the sheet, the tip diameter for spot welding is usually **(SSC, CPWD 2011)**

(a) 2t   (b) $\sqrt{t}$

(c) t   (d) $\frac{1}{t}$

54. Which of the following materials possesses the least resistivity ? **(SSC, CPWD 2012)**

(a) Iron   (b) Manganin

(c) Aluminum   (d) Copper

55. The resistance of insulations, in general, _____ with temperature rise. **(SSC, CPWD 2012)**

(a) Decreases   (b) Increases rapidly

(c) Increases slowly (d) Does not change

56. In suburban services as compared with urban service : **(SSC, CPWD 2014)**

(a) the coasting period is smaller but free running period is longer

(b) the coasting period is smaller

(c) the coasting period is longer

(d) the coasting period and free running periods are same

57. Quadrilateral speed time curve is used for : **(SSC, CPWD 2014)**

(a) goods line service   (b) sub urban service

(c) urban service   (d) main line service

58. Bundled conductors in EHV transmission system provide : **(SSC, CPWD 2014)**

(a) increased corona loss

(b) increased line reactance

(c) reduced line capacitance

(d) reduced voltage gradient

59. To increase the range of an a.c. ammeter you would use : **(SSC, CPWD 2014)**

(a) A condenser across the meter

(b) Current transformer

(c) A potential transformer

(d) An inductance across the meter

60. The highest transmission a.c. voltage in India is : **(SSC, CPWD 2014)**

(a) 1750 kV   (b) 132 kV

(c) 220 kV   (d) 400 kV

61. The distribution losses that the utility suffers while transferring power from generating station to the consumer is accounted under :

(a) Maintenance cost   **(SSC, CPWD 2014)**

(b) Fixed charges

(c) Running charges

(d) Cost of fuel

62. Power distribution by cable is generally adopted for line length **(SSC CPWD 2014)**

(a) less than 10 km   (b) above 10 km

(c) less than 50 km   (d) above 50 km

63. A wire placed on the top of a transmission line acts as

(a) a phase wire

(b) neutral

(c) a transmission wire

(d) ground wire   **(SSC CPWD 2014)**

64. The conductor, by means of which the metal body of an equipment or an application is connected to the earth, is known as **(SSC CPWD 2014)**

(a) Neutral continuity conductor

(b) Earth discontinuity conductor

(c) Earth continuity conductor

(d) Neutral discontinuity conductor

65. Which insulation is most widely used for covering wires/cables used in internal wiring ? **(SSC CPWD 2014)**

(a) Paper   (b) Wood

(c) Glass   (d) PVC

66. Which of the following types of wiring preferred for workshop lighting ? **(SSC CPWD 2014)**

(a) Casing Capping wiring

(b) Batten wiring

(c) Concealed conduit wiring

(d) Surface conduit wiring

67. The earthing electrodes should be placed within what distance in meters from the building whose installation system is being earthed ? **(SSC CPWD 2014)**

(a) 4   (b) 2.5

(c) 1.5   (d) 0.5

68. The aluminium conductor of size ____ is used for a subcircuit in domestic wiring. **(SSC CPWD 2015)**

(a) $\dfrac{1}{1.8}$ mm   (b) $\dfrac{1}{1.2}$ mm

(c) $\dfrac{1}{2.24}$ mm   (d) $\dfrac{1}{1.4}$ mm

69. The minimum area of cross section of a three and half core cable should be? **(SSC CPWD 2015)**

(a) 50 cm^2 (b) 40 cm^2

(c) 30 cm^3 (d) 60 cm^2

70. For cleat wiring and 250 volts supply, the cables will be placed____ a part centre to centre for single core cables. **(SSC CPWD 2015)**

(a) 4 cm   (b) 3 cm

(c) 4.5 cm   (d) 2.5 cm

71. In batton wiring the cables are carried on seasoned teak wood perfectly straight and well varnished teak wood batton of thickness not less than? **(SSC CPWD 2015)**

(a) 2 cm   (b) 1 cm

(c) 3 cm   (d) 4 cm

ANSWERS

EXERCISE – I

1. (d)	**2.** (b)	**3.** (c)	**4.** (a)	**5.** (d)	**6.** (b)	**7.** (c)	**8.** (d)	**9.** (c)	**10.** (d)
11. (a)	**12.** (c)	**13.** (a)	**14.** (d)	**15.** (d)	**16.** (c)	**17.** (a)	**18.** (b)	**19.** (d)	**20.** (d)
21. (a)	**22.** (b)	**23.** (c)	**24.** (b)	**25.** (c)	**26.** (a)	**27.** (b)	**28.** (a)	**29.** (c)	**30.** (c)
31. (d)	**32.** (d)	**33.** (d)	**34.** (b)	**35.** (a)	**36.** (b)	**37.** (b)	**38.** (a)	**39.** (c)	**40.** (a)
41. (c)	**42.** (a)	**43.** (c)	**44.** (a)	**45.** (d)	**46.** (b)	**47.** (b)	**48.** (c)	**49.** (d)	**50.** (c)
51. (a)	**52.** (a)	**53.** (b)	**54.** (b)	**55.** (c)	**56.** (c)	**57.** (a)	**58.** (a)	**59.** (c)	**60.** (c)
61. (d)	**62.** (d)	**63.** (c)	**64.** (c)	**65.** (c)	**66.** (b)	**67.** (c)	**68.** (a)	**69.** (a)	**70.** (a)
71. (d)	**72.** (b)	**73.** (b)	**74.** (a)	**75.** (c)	**76.** (b)	**77.** (a)	**78.** (a)	**79.** (a)	**80.** (c)
81. (b)	**82.** (b)	**83.** (a)	**84.** (c)	**85.** (d)	**86.** (d)	**87.** (a)	**88.** (d)	**89.** (b)	**90.** (c)
91. (c)	**92.** (c)	**93.** (a)	**94.** (c)	**95.** (b)	**96.** (c)	**97.** (c)	**98.** (c)	**99.** (b)	**100.** (a)
101. (d)	**102.** (b)	**103.** (c)	**104.** (a)	**105.** (c)	**106.** (b)	**107.** (c)	**108.** (a)	**109.** (c)	**110.** (b)
111. (a)	**112.** (a)	**113.** (c)	**114.** (a)	**115.** (b)	**116.** (c)	**117.** (a)	**118.** (c)	**119.** (b)	**120.** (b)
121. (a)	**122.** (b)	**123.** (b)	**124.** (c)	**125.** (c)	**126.** (b)	**127.** (b)	**128.** (b)	**129.** (b)	**130.** (d)
131. (d)	**132.** (d)	**133.** (c)	**134.** (c)	**135.** (b)	**136.** (b)	**137.** (b)	**138.** (d)	**139.** (d)	**140.** (c)
141. (c)	**142.** (b)	**143.** (b)	**144.** (a)	**145.** (d)	**146.** (c)	**147.** (d)	**148.** (b)	**149.** (c)	**150.** (c)
151. (a)	**152.** (b)	**153.** (a)	**154.** (b)	**155.** (c)	**156.** (b)	**157.** (c)	**158.** (c)	**159.** (b)	**160.** (c)
161. (a)	**162.** (c)	**163.** (c)	**164.** (c)	**165.** (d)	**166.** (b)	**167.** (a)	**168.** (a)	**169.** (b)	**170.** (a)
171. (c)	**172.** (b)	**173.** (a)	**174.** (c)	**175.** (c)	**176.** (d)	**177.** (c)	**178.** (a)	**179.** (a)	**180.** (d)
181. (d)	**182.** (c)	**183.** (b)	**184.** (b)	**185.** (a)	**186.** (b)	**187.** (c)	**188.** (b)	**189.** (c)	**190.** (c)
191. (b)	**192.** (a)	**193.** (d)	**194.** (a)	**195.** (d)	**196.** (c)	**197.** (a)	**198.** (d)	**199.** (c)	**200.** (d)
201. (b)	**202.** (c)	**203.** (a)	**204.** (a)	**205.** (c)	**206.** (a)	**207.** (d)	**208.** (d)	**209.** (c)	**210.** (b)
211. (b)	**212.** (a)	**213.** (c)	**214.** (c)	**215.** (c)	**216.** (d)	**217.** (a)	**218.** (b)	**219.** (a)	**220.** (a)
221. (b)	**222.** (d)	**223.** (a)	**224.** (b)	**225.** (c)	**226.** (b)	**227.** (a)	**228.** (c)	**229.** (c)	**230.** (d)
231. (a)	**232.** (b)	**233.** (c)	**234.** (d)	**235.** (c)	**236.** (a)	**237.** (d)	**238.** (b)	**239.** (a)	**240.** (c)
241. (c)									

EXERCISE – II

1. (a)	**2.** (c)	**3.** (c)	**4.** (a)	**5.** (c)	**6.** (b)	**7.** (d)	**8.** (b)	**9.** (b)	**10.** (c)
11. (b)	**12.** (b)	**13.** (b)	**14.** (c)	**15.** (d)	**16.** (b)	**17.** (c)	**18.** (c)	**19.** (d)	**20.** (d)
21. (a)	**22.** (c)	**23.** (c)	**24.** (a)	**25.** (d)	**26.** (d)	**27.** (c)	**28.** (b)	**29.** (d)	**30.** (c)
31. (b)	**32.** (c)	**33.** (c)	**34.** (a)	**35.** (a)	**36.** (c)	**37.** (c)	**38.** (a)	**39.** (a)	**40.** (a)
41. (c)	**42.** (d)	**43.** (b)	**44.** (a)	**45.** (a)	**46.** (d)	**47.** (d)	**48.** (b)	**49.** (b)	**50.** (b)
51. (d)	**52.** (d)	**53.** (a)	**54.** (d)	**55.** (a)	**56.** (c)	**57.** (c)	**58.** (d)	**59.** (d)	**60.** (d)
61. (c)	**62.** (a)	**63.** (d)	**64.** (c)	**65.** (d)	**66.** (c)	**67.** (c)	**68.** (b)	**69.** (c)	**70.** (d)
71. (b)									

Power System Protection

SWITCHES

A switch is used in an electric circuit as a device for making or breaking the electric circuit. switches may be classified as.

(*i*) *Oil switches* : These are usually used in very high voltage heavy current circuits.

(*ii*) *Air switches* : These are further classified into

    (*a*) Air-break switches

    (*b*) Isolators

    (*c*) Disconnected switches

BUS- BAR ARRANGEMENTS

Bus-bars are arranged to achieve

(*i*)   adequate operating flexibility

(*ii*) sufficient reliability

(*iii*) minimum cost.

The cost can be minimised by reducing the number of circuit breakers to a minimum but complication of the protective gear are increased.

Some bus-bar arrangements.

(1) *Single bus-bar arrangement.* In this arrangement a set of bus-bars is used for complete power station and to this bus-bar are connected all generators, transformers and feeders through circuit breakers and isolating switches. Such a bus-bar arrangement is cheaper in initial as well as in maintenance cost and simple in operation and relaying.

(2) *Single bus- bar system with sectionalization.* With increased number of generators and outgoing feeders connected to the bus-bars, it becomes essential to provide arrangement for sectionalizing the bus-bars so that a fault on any one section of the bus-bars may not cause a complete shutdown. This is achieved by providing a circuit breaker and isolating switches between the sections.

(3) *Ring bus-bar system.* In this arrangement each feeder is supplied from two paths, so that in case of failure of a section, supply is not interrupted.

(4) *Duplicate bus-bars system.* Duplicate bus-bar system with sectionalization is usually adopted in order to maintain continuity of supply. Such a system consists of two-bus-bar couplers and sectionalizing breaker converts the duplicate bus-bars into a ring system having greater flexibility.

(5) *Double main and transfer bus-bar arrangement.* This arrangement incorporates all advantages of the double bus as well as transfer bus-scheme. The scheme needs a bus-coupler for the on load transfer of circuits from one main bus to the other and a transfer coupler for taking out circuit breaker of various circuits for maintenance.

FUSES

Fuse is a wire of short length or thin strip of material having low melting point and is inserted in an electric circuit as a protective device to the flow of excessive current through the circuit. The time for blowing out of fuse depends upon the magnitude of excessive current- larger the current, the more rapidly the fuse will blow.

Advantages.

(*i*)   Provides cheapest type of protection

(*ii*) Needs no maintenance

(*iii*) Affords current limiting effect under short-circuit conditions

(*iv*) Interrupts enormous short-circuit currents without noise, flame, gas or smoke.

Disadvantages.

(*i*)   Time is lost in rewiring or replacing of fuse after operation

(*ii*) Discrimination between fuses in series cannot be obtained unless there is considerable difference in the relative sizes of the fuses concerned.

Functions of fuse wire.

(*i*)   To carry the normal working current safely without heating

(*ii*) To break the circuit when the current exceeds the limited current.

The materials used for fuse wires must be of low melting points, low ohmic loss, high conductivity and free from deterioration. An alloy of lead and tin (lead 37% and tin 63%) is used for small current rating fuses and beyond 20 A rating circuits copper wire fuses are used.

Types of Fuses.

A fuse unit essentially consists of a metal fuse element, a set of contacts between which it is fixed and a body to support and isolate them. Many types of fuses also have some means for extinguishing the arc which appears when the fuse element melts.

Commonly used fuses are

(i) *Round type fuse* : It is not in common use.

(ii) *Rewirable or kitkat fuse* : It is used in domestic installations of voltage rating upto 400 V and of current rating upto 300A.

(iii) *Low voltage HRC fuses* : It is used on l t distribution against overload and short-circuit condition.

(iv) *High voltage HRC fuses* : It is used for the back up protection to circuit breakers whose short-circuit capacity has been increased owing to extension of generating plant or interconnection to a value beyond their rated MVA

(v) *Time delay fuses (or slow acting fuses)* : It is used as a backup protection for motors having long starting operations.

Selection of Fuse.

In order to ensure that the fuses will correctly and reliably protect any given section or element of any electrical circuit, their characteristics and ratings must be selected in accordance with the requirements of rated voltage, maximum current rupturing capacity and rated current.

PROTECTIVE RELAY

Protective relays and relaying systems detect abnormal condition like fault in electrical circuits and operate automatic switch gear to isolate faulty equipments from the system as quickly as possible.

Protective relay functions in association with the switch gear to avert the consequences of faults. The switch gear must be capable of interrupting both normal currents as well as fault currents.

The protective relay on the other hand must be able to recognize an abnormal condition in the power system and take suitable steps to ensure its removal with least possible disturbance to normal operation.

Fault Statistics.

Frequency of fault occurrence in different links of a power system :

Equipments	% total
OH lines	50
Cables	10
Switch gear	15
Transformer	12
CTs and PTs	2
Control equipments	3
Miscellaneous	8

Frequency of different kinds of fault occurring in overhead lines :

Types of fault	% occurrence
(i) L – G	85%
(ii) L – L	8%
(iii) L–L–G	5%
(iv) L–L–L	2 or less

L – L – L fault occur due to the carelessness of operating personnel.

Zone of protection.

Various zones in the power system are arranged to overlap so that no part of the system remains unprotected.

Essential Qualities of protection.

Every protection system which isolates a purely element is required to satisfy four basic requirements

(i) *Reliability* : circuit breaker should be reliable.

(ii) *Selectivity* : faulty selection is selected and other sections must be left intact.

(iii) Fastness of operation.

(iv) *Discrimination* : between fault and overload.

Primary or Back up protection.

If a fault in given zone is not cleared by the main or the primary protection scheme some form of backup protection is provided to do the next best thing.

e.g. over current or distant protection.

Energizing quantity.

The electrical quantity i.e. current or voltage either alone or in conjunction with other electrical quantities required for functioning of relay.

Characteristic quantity.

The quantity to which the relay is designed to respond e.g. current in over-current relay, impedance etc.

Setting.

The actual value of the energizing or characteristic quantity which the relay is designed to operate under given conditions.

Pick up.

A relay is said to pick up when it moves from the off position to the ON position. The value of the characteristic quantity above which this change occurs is known as pick up value.

Drop out or reset.

Drop out means relay moves from the on-position to the off-position. The value of the characteristic quantity below which this change occurs is known as drop out or reset value.

Operating time.

Time during which stored operating energy is dissipated after the characteristic quantity has been suddenly restored from a specified value to the value which it had at the initial position of the relay.

Over shoot time.

The time during which stored operating energy is dessipated after the characteristic quantity has been suddenly restored from a specified value to the value which it had at the initial position of the relay.

Characteristic angle.

The phase angle at which the performance of the relay is declared.

Characteristics of a relay.

This is the locus of the pick up or reset when drawn on a graph.

Reinforcing relay.

Relay which is energised by the contacts of the main relay and with its contact in parallel with those of the main relay and with its contact in parallel with those of the main relay relieves them to their current carrying duty. The seal in contacts are usually of higher current rating than those of main relay.

Auxiliary relay.

Relays which operate in response to the opening or closing of its operating circuit to assist another relay in the performance of its function.

Reach.

Remote limit of the zone of protection provided by the relay used mostly in connection with distant relays to indicate how far along a line the tripping zone of the relay extends.

Over reach or Under reach.

Errors in relay measurements resulting in wrong operation or failure to operate respectively.

METHODS OF DISCRIMINATION.

These methods are basically of two types

(1) location of fault.

(2) the type of fault.

(1) Methods Discriminative to Fault Location.

   (i) Discrimination by time : Provide time lag feature. It is possible to trip the breaker nearest to the fault prior to those farther off the point of fault.

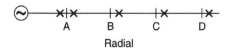

Radial

D – no added time lag

C – 0.4 sec. added time lag

B – 0.8 sec. added time lag

A – 1.2 sec. added time lag.

(ii) Discrimination by current magnitude : This depends on the current magnitudes as the magnitude of the fault current vary with the location of fault.

(iii) Discrimination by time and direction: In ring main which forms a closed loop it is not possible to isolate the faulty section with the help of time alone, hence in this case directional feature is also included.

(iv) Discrimination by distance measurement : The fault nearer the source which are more severe take longer time to clear in the case of time discrimination systems. The measurement of distance is achieved in various way by what is known as distance relay.

(v) Current balance discrimination : This is used for protection of individual elements in the power system.

This form of protection is based on one of the following two principles :

   (a) Circulating current principles :

   Circulating current principles compares the currents at the two ends of the protected section.

   (b) Opposed voltage principles :

   For external fault balance of current is not disturbed.

(2) Method discriminative to the type of fault.

   (a) Zero phase sequence networks : Zero sequence current flow only when earth faults take place.

   No zero sequence currents for load current or phase-phase fault.

   Hence zero sequence relay can be used for detection of earth fault.

   (b) Negative phase sequence network : The presence of negative phase sequence current represents some form of unbalanced condition such as phase to phase faults other the symmetrical three phase faults, broken conductor faults etc.

RELAY CLASSIFICATION

(1) According to the function in the protective scheme

(i) *Main :* Main relays are the protective elements which respond to any change in the actuating quantity e.g. current, voltage etc.

(ii) *Auxiliary relays :* These are controlled by the other relays to perform some auxiliary function such that introduction of time delay.

(iii) Signal relays

(2) According to the nature of actuating quantity to which the relay responds

(i) current realy

(ii) voltage

(iii) power

(iv) impedance

(3) According to the connection of sensing elements

(i) primary relays

(ii) secondary relays (connected through CT or PT).

(4) According to method by which the relays act upon the circuit breaker

(a) Electromagnetic relay

(b) Static relays.

Principle types of electromagnetic relays.

(i) Attracted armature relay

(ii) Induction type relay.

(i) Attracted armature type.

An electromagnetic force is produced by the magnetic flux which in turn is produced by the operating quantity.

(ii) Induction Relay.

Torque is produced in these relay when one alternating flux reacts with the current induced in the rotor by another alternating flux displaced in time and space but having the same frequency.

OVER CURRENT RELAY

The induction cup relay is employed to achieve this type of relay. Operating time of all over current relays tend to become asympotic to a definite minimum value with increase in the value of current.

In induction type of relay the distance of the armature carrying the bridge contacts to the relay contacts can be adjusted with the help of the time multiplier setting.

Taps are provided on the input of the operating quantity which can be adjusted with the help of inserting the plug. This is known as the *plug multiplier setting.*

Instantaneous Over-current Relays.

In this type of relay it operates instantly without any international time delay.

e.g. non-polarized attracted armature type. This relay is used when fault is very close to source.

Directional Relay.

Directional feature is introduced with silent pole magnet, having in addition a directional unit consisting of capacitance or resistance-capacitance circuit. Directional control unit controls the angle between two fluxes by varying R-X parameter of the lower electromagnet.

Distance Relay.

Distance relay response is some function of ratio between volts and amperes and for any given value of the ratio there may exist an infinite number of values of volts and amperes.

In other words, it is easy to think of impedance, reactance or resistance or combination of three of which the relay responds.

Principal types of distance relays.

(i) *Impedance relay :* for medium lines

(ii) *Reactance relay :* for very short lines

(iii) *Admittance relay (mho) :* for phase fault of longer line

(iv) Ohm relay

(v) Offset mho relay.

FEEDER (TRANSMISSION LINE) PROTECTION

Types of protection and their selection

(1) Over-current protection

(i) Non-directional

(ii) Directional

(2) Distance protection

(3) Pilot protection

(i) Wire pilot protection

(ii) Carrier pilot protection

(iii) Microwave pilot protection

For various type of protections to be achieved types of relay used are

• *For back up protection* – time graded over-current relays.

• *For very short lines* – Reactance relay.

- *For medium lines* – Impedance relay.
- *For phase fault of longer line* – Mho relay.

Pilot protection is used for fault occurring within individual zones of equipments. Microwave pilot protections are used for long inter-connected lines.

Over current protection.

Over-current protection of feeder may be divided into two categories

(*i*) Non directional time/current grading.

(*ii*) Directional time/current grading.

Time grading system.

Time grading is achieved by the help of definite-time relays.

Current-Graded Scheme.

This system is based on the fact that the short circuit current along the length of the protected circuit decreases as the distance from the source to the fault location increases. In current grading each relay would be set to pick up at a progressively higher current towards the source. But the problem is that the relay cannot differentiate between the faults which are very close to or either side of relay, since difference in current is very small. Hence we use IDMT relays with combination of instantaneous over current relays.

Current/Time Graded System

Current/time grading is possible with inverse time over-current relays. Most widely used relay is IDMT relay. In IDMT relay current limit and time limit can be set within the design limit.

There are two adjustable basic setting on all inverse time relays, one is time multiplier setting (TMS) and other is current setting known as plug setting Multiplier (PSM).

Earth-Fault Protection.

Earth fault current is less than the phase to phase fault current. Earth fault protection can be provided with normal over-current relay, if the minimum earth fault current is sufficient in magnitude.

The relay used for earth-fault protection is different from the once provided for phase fault. It has the peculiarity that it is set independent of load current and thus setting below normal load current can be achieved.

Over-current earth fault protection can be provided with only one over-current relay. A current will flow through the relay winding only when a fault involving earth occurs.

Reach of a distance relay.

A distance relay is set to operate to a particular value of impedance, for an impedance greater than this set value the relay should not operate. This impedance or the corresponding distance is known as the reach of the relay. The tendency of a distance relay to operate at impedance larger than its setting value is known as over reach. Similarly the tendency of the relay to restrain at the set value of impedance or impedances lower than the set value is known as under reach.

- A distance relay may be under-reach because of the introduction of fault resistance.
- A distance relay may be over-reach due to the offset current present in the fault current.

TRANSFORMER PROTECTION

Faults in the transformer is of following three

(*i*)   Fault in auxiliary equipments

(*ii*) Fault in transformer winding and connection

(*iii*) Over load and external short circuits.

(*i*) **Faults in auxiliary equipments.**

  Auxiliary equipments of the transformer are

  (*a*) Transformer oil

  (*b*) Gas cushion

  (*c*) Oil pumps and forced air fans

  (*d*) Core and winding insulation.

(*ii*) **Winding Faults.**

  There may be faults between adjacent turns or parts of coils such as phase to phase faults. Another fault may be fault to ground or across complete winding such as phase to earth-faults on the HV and LV external terminals.

(*iii*)**Over-loads and external short circuits.**

  Over-loads may be sustained for long periods, being limited only by the permitted temperature rise in the winding and the cooling medium. Excessive overloading will result in deterioration of insulation and subsequent failure.

DIFFERENTIAL PROTECTION OF TRANSFORMER.

Differential protection is the most important type of protection used for internal phase to phase and phase to earth faults and is generally applied to transformer having rating of 5 MVA and above.

The differential protection of transformer is also known as Merz-price protection for the transformer.

Drawbacks of the differential scheme.

(i) *Unmatched CT characteristics* : Difference in CTs characteristics due to different ratios may cause appropriate difference in the respective secondary currents, whenever through fault occur.

(ii) *Ratio change as a result of tapping* : Tap changing is common in the transformer. Compensating for this effect by varying the tapping on differential protection, CTs is impractical. To overcome false operation biased differential relay are used.

(iii) *Magnetizing inrush current* : When transformer is energised, the transient inrush of magnetic current flowing into the transformer may be as great as ten times full load current and it decays relatively slowly. Hence magnetic inrush current may cause false operation. To overcome this the relay may be given a setting higher inrush current.

Gas Actuated Relay-Buchholz Relay.

The heat produced by internal fault or overloading of transformer causes the transformer oil to decompose and produce a gas which can be made to detect the winding fault. Buchholz relay is the simplest form which is commonly used in all transformers produced with conservator.

CIRCUIT BREAKER

Circuit Breaker rating.

The rating of a circuit breaker refer to the characteristic values that defines the working condition for which the circuit breaker is designed and built. Circuit breaker must be capable of carrying continuously the full load current without excessive temperature rise and should be capable of withstanding the electrodynamic forces. The circuit breaker should also be in position to interrupt fault current safely.

Rated voltage.

The rated maximum voltage of a circuit breaker is the highest rms voltage above nominal system voltage for which the circuit breaker is designed and this is the upper limit for operation.

Rated current.

The rated current of a circuit breaker is the designated limit of current in rms amperes which it shall be capable of carrying continuously without exceeding the limit of observable temperature rise.

Rated frequency.

The frequency at which the circuit breaker is designed to operate standard frequency is 50 Hz.

Rated breaking capacity, symmetrical and asymmetrical.

After the fault the current starts decaying from a high initial value to a sustained value.

In addition owing to relaying time the circuit breaker starts to open its arcing contacts only some time later, after initiation of short circuit current. The actual current interrupted by circuit breaker is less than the initial value of short circuit current because of arcing.

Breaking current of a pole of a circuit breaker is the current in that pole at the instant of contact-separation. It an be expressed by two values.

(i) **Symmetrical breaking current :** This is the rms value of ac component of the circuit in the pole at the instant of contact-separation.

(ii) **Asymmetrical breaking current :** This is the rms value of the total current comprising the ac and dc components of the current in that pole at the instant of contact separation.

Breaking capacity symmetrical or asymmetrical is the value of respective breaking current which the circuit breaker is capable of breaking at a stated recovery voltage and a stated reference restriking voltage under prescribing condition.

EXERCISE – I

1. Arc voltage produced in ac circuit breaker is always
   (a) in phase opposition to the arc current
   (b) in phase with the arc current
   (c) leading the arc current by 90°
   (d) lagging the arc current by 45°

2. The dielectric strength of air at 25°C and 76 cm of mercury is
   (a) 2.11 kV rms/cm   (b) 21.1 kV rms/m
   (c) 211 kV rms/cm   (d) 2110 kV rms/m

3. Which of thermal protection switch is provided in power line system to protect against ?
   (a) overload   (b) temperature rise
   (c) short circuit   (d) over voltage

4. The following circuit breaker does not use pneumatic operating mechanism
   (a) air break circuit breaker
   (b) air blast circuit breaker
   (c) bulk oil circuit breaker
   (d) SF_6 circuit breaker

5. Fault diverters are basically
   (a) circuit breakers   (b) fast switches
   (c) relays   (d) fuses

6. In a power system, the rate of rise of restriking voltage depends upon
   (a) switching condition only
   (b) circuit power factor only
   (c) both (a) and (b) above
   (d) none of these

7. The voltage across the circuit breaker pole after final current zero is
   (a) restriking voltage   (b) recovery voltage
   (c) supply voltage   (d) none of these

8. Bulk oil circuit breaker is suitable for voltages upto
   (a) 4 kV   (b) 10 kV
   (c) 25 kV   (d) 36 kV

9. For remote operation, circuit breaker must be equipped with
   (a) shunt trip
   (b) inverse shunt trip
   (c) time delay trip
   (d) both (b) and (c) above

10. Lightining arrestor should be located
    (a) away from the circuit breaker
    (b) near the circuit breaker
    (c) away from the transformer
    (d) near the transformer

11. Which of the following circuit breaker is generally used in applications in railways?
    (a) bulk oil circuit breakers
    (b) mimumum oil circuit breakers
    (c) air break circuit breakers
    (d) none of these

12. The following medium is employed for extinction of arc in air break circuit breakers ?
    (a) oil   (b) air
    (c) water   (d) none of these

13. In a circuit breaker, the arcing contents are made of
    (a) aluminium   (b) copper tungsten alloy
    (c) electrolytic copper (d) tungsten

14. Which of the following circuit breakers takes minimum time for installation ?
    (a) bulk oil circuit breaker
    (b) minimum oil circuit breaker
    (c) air blast circuit breaker
    (d) SF_6 circuit breaker

15. Circuit breakers are essentially
    (a) current carrying contacts called electrodes
    (b) arc extinguishers
    (c) circuits to break the system
    (d) transformers to isolate two systems

16. In a circuit breaker, arc is initiated by the process of
    (a) thermal emission   (b) field emission
    (c) alternators   (d) transmission lines

17. Buchholz relay is used for the protection of
    (a) switch yard
    (b) transformers
    (c) alternators
    (d) transmission lines

18. The basic problem in a circuit breaker is to
    (a) maintain the arc
    (b) extinguish the arc
    (c) emit ionization electrons
    (d) none of these

19. In oil and air blast circuit breakers, the current zero interruption is attained by
    (a) lengthening of arc
    (b) cooling and blast effect
    (c) deionizing the oil with forced air
    (d) both (a) and (b) above

20. Air blasty circuit breaker is operated at a pressure of
    (a) 5 to 10 kg/cm²   (b) 10 to 15 kg/cm²
    (c) 15 to 20 kg/cm²   (d) 20 to 30 kg/cm²

21. The voltage appearing across the contacts after the opening of the circuit breaker is called
    (a) surge voltage   (b) recovery voltage
    (c) arc voltage   (d) break open voltage

22. Buchholz relays are used for transformers of ratings above
    (a) 100 kV   (b) 200 kV
    (c) 500 kV   (d) 1000 kV

23. Air blast circuit breakers are preferred for
    (a) short duty   (b) intermittent duty
    (c) repeated duty   (d) none of these

24. The power factor of the arc in a circuit breaker is
    (a) zero leading
    (b) zero lagging
    (c) unity
    (d) any value from zero to unity

25. For a 400 kV system, the capacity of lightning arrester should be
    (a) 1 kA   (b) 5 kA
    (c) 10 kA   (d) 50 kA

26. A high speed circuit breaker can complete its operation in
    (a) 2 to 3 cycles   (b) 3 to 8 cycles
    (c) 6 to 12 cycles   (d) 10 to 20 cycles

27. Which of following are the desirable qualities of protective relays ?
    (a) speed sensitivity
    (b) stability, reliability
    (c) selectivity, adequacy
    (d) none of these

28. Basic quantity measured in a distance relay is
    (a) impedance
    (b) voltage difference
    (c) current difference
    (d) none of these

29. Drop out to cutoff ratio for most relays is of the order of
    (a) 0.2 to 0.3   (b) 0.3 to 0.4
    (c) 0.4 to 0.6   (d) 0.6 to 1.0

30. If the operation of a relay does not involve any change in air gap, then the ratio of rest to pick up is usually
    (a) low
    (b) medium
    (c) high
    (d) independent of the change in air gap

31. Plug setting of a relay can be altered by varying
    (a) number of ampere-turns
    (b) air gap of magnetic path
    (c) adjustable back up stop
    (d) none of these

32. Directional relays respond to the
    (a) flow of current   (b) voltage polarities
    (c) flow of power   (d) all of these

33. Which of the following is not an instanta-neous relay ?
    (a) induction disc type
    (b) hinged armature type
    (c) balanced beam type
    (d) polarized type

34. Which of the following is an instantaneous relay?
    (a) thermocouple type
    (b) induction type
    (c) permanent magnet moving coil type
    (d) shaded pole type

35. Which of the following is a directional relay?
    (a) mho relay   (b) reactance relay
    (c) impedance relay   (d) both (a) and (b)

36. Protective relays are devices which detect abnormal conditions in electrical circuits by measuring
    (a) current during abnormal condition
    (b) voltage during abnormal condition
    (c) both (a) and (b) simultaneously
    (d) constantly the electrical quantities which differ during normal and abnormal conditions

37. A distance relay measures
    (a) current difference
    (b) voltage difference
    (c) impedance difference
    (d) distance between two CT's

38. Various power system faults in increasing order of severity are

    (a) LG, LL, LLG, LLLG
    (b) LLLG, LLG, LG, LL
    (c) LLG, LLLG, LL, LG
    (d) LL, LG, LLLG, LLG

39. Which of the following type of reactors are popularly used in power systems ?

    (a) compensation reactors
    (b) current limiting reactors
    (c) suppression or Peterson reactors
    (d) all of these

40. Shunt reactors are connected with transmission lines for

    (a) limiting fault current
    (b) limiting fault voltage
    (c) absorbing reactive power
    (d) absorbing high voltage surges

41. Minimum faults occur in which of the following power system equipment ?

    (a) transformer   (b) switch gear
    (c) CT, PT   (d) alternator

42. Interruption due to fault and maintenance is minimum in

    (a) main and transfer bus arrangement
    (b) single bus arrangement
    (c) sectionalized single bus arrangement
    (d) double bus, double breaker arrangement

43. When a line-to-line fault occurs, the short circuit current of an alternator depends upon its

    (a) short circuit reactance
    (b) synchronous reactance
    (c) transient reactance
    (d) subtransient reactance

44. Resistance offered by series reactor is usually

    (a) low   (b) medium
    (c) high   (d) very high

45. Time interval from instant of contact separation to time of arc extinction is called

    (a) closing time   (b) opening time
    (c) arcing time   (d) none of these

46. Maximum short circuit current occurs due to

    (a) line-to-line fault
    (b) line-to-line circuit
    (c) dead short circuit
    (d) both (a) and (b) occurring simultaneously

47. Which of following are used to reduce short circuit fault currents

    (a) reactors
    (b) resistors
    (c) capacitors
    (d) parallel combination of all these

48. Oil immersed type reactor has the advantage of

    (a) smaller size with large thermal capacity
    (b) higher safety against flashover
    (c) limiting the fault voltage
    (d) both (a) and (b) above

49. Which of the following method of protection is used to achieve earth fault operation ?

    (a) core balance method
    (b) frame leakage method
    (c) relay connected with neutral to ground
    (d) none of these

50. Large internal faults below oil level are protected by

    (a) earth fault and positive sequence relay
    (b) Merz Price percentage differential relay
    (c) horn gap and temperature relay
    (d) mho and ohm relays

51. For an arc length of l metres carrying fault current of I amperes, the arc resistance in ohms is

    (a) $\dfrac{2.9 \times 10^3 l}{I^{1.4}}$ (b) $\dfrac{2.9 \times 10^4 l}{I^{1.4}}$

    (c) $\dfrac{3.1 \times 10^4 l}{I^2}$ (d) $\dfrac{3.1 \times 10^4 l}{I}$

52. Generator internal fault protection is usually based on the principle of

    (a) differential protection
    (b) cross-differential protection
    (c) negative sequence protection
    (d) all of these

53. The phase comparison relay has the merit that

    (a) its operation does not depend upon the direction of power flow
    (b) correct relay action can be obtained by using series capacitors on the line
    (c) it can operate even for low value of fault current
    (d) none of these

54. The advantage of grounding a power system is that
 (a) earth fault current can be used to operate relays
 (b) "arcing ground" phenomenon is avoided
 (c) it provides symmetry to the line impedances
 (d) both (a) and (b) above

55. Pilot wire protection is basically used for the protection of
 (a) transmission lines
 (b) alternators
 (c) switch gears
 (d) transformers

56. Which of the following carrier frequency is used in a carrier current protection scheme?
 (a) 500 kHz to 5 kHz
 (b) 5 kHz to 50 kHz
 (c) 50 kHz to 500 kHz
 (d) 500 kHz to 5 MHz

57. Power system insulation problem involves
 (a) selection of "basic insulation level" insulation levels of system equipment and lightning arrestor
 (b) determination of line insulation
 (c) capacitance to earth and subsequent grounding
 (d) both (a) and (b) above

58. Typical gap length of rod type surge diverter used for 132 kV line is
 (a) 10 cm (b) 20 cm
 (c) 35 cm (d) 65 cm

59. A relay is said to be a high speed relay if it operation time is
 (a) 1 to 2 cycles (b) 2 to 3 cycles
 (c) 3 to 5 cycles (d) 5 to 7 cycles

60. Maximum demand of a consumer is 2kW and his daily energy consumption is 20 units. His load factor will be
 (a) 10% (b) 52%
 (c) 41.6% (d) None of above

61. Advantage of hydro-electric power station is
 (a) low operating cost
 (b) free from pollution problems
 (c) no fuel transportation problems
 (d) all of the above.

62. A sodium graphite reactor uses
 (a) sodium as moderator and graphite as coolant
 (b) sodium as coolant and graphite as moderator
 (c) a mixture of sodium and graphite as coolant
 (d) a mixture of sodium and graphite as moderator.

63. No moving parts are required in
 (a) MHD generator
 (b) Tidal power plant
 (c) Thermioic conversion
 (d) OTEC power plant.

64. A fast breeder reactor
 (a) operates with fast neutrons and produces less fissionable material than it consumes
 (b) operates with fast neutrons and produces more fissionable material than it consumes
 (c) operates with slow neutrons and produces more fissionable material than it consumes.
 (d) operates with slow neutrons and produces more fissonable material than it consumes.

65. Gas turbines can be brought to the bus bar from cold in about
 (a) 2 minutes (b) 30 minutes
 (c) 1 Hour (d) 2 Hours

66. Efficiency of a plant is secondary consideration for
 (a) base load power plants
 (b) peak load power plants
 (c) both peak load as well as base load power plants
 (d) neither peak load nor base load power plants

67. In hydrothermal source of geothermal energy
 (a) hot water or steam is available
 (b) hot gases are available
 (c) molten lava is available
 (d) none of the above.

68. A module is a
 (a) newly installed solar cell
 (b) series parallel arrangement of solar cells
 (c) a series of solar cells when not used for power generation
 (d) none of the above.

69. Connected load of a consumer is 2 kW and his maximum demand is 1.5 kW. The load factor of the consumer will be
 (a) 0.75 (b) 0.375
 (c) 1.33 (d) none of the above

70. Pumped storage plant in India
    (a) does not exist
    (b) exists in Kadamparai (Tamil Nadu)
    (c) exists in Gandhi Sagar dam (Kota)
    (d) is being installed in Haryana.

71. Tidal energy mainly makes use of
    (a) kinetic energy of water
    (b) potential energy of water
    (c) both kinetic as well as potential energy of water
    (d) none of the above.

72. In a super-heater
    (a) pressure rises, temperature drops
    (b) pressure rises, temperature remains constant
    (c) pressure remains constant and temperature rises
    (d) both pressure and temperature remains constant.

73. Equipment used for pulverising the coal is known as
    (a) Ball mill   (b) Hopper
    (c) Burner   (d) Stoker

74. A gas turbine works on
    (a) Carnot cycle   (b) Brayton cycle
    (c) Dual cycle   (d) Rankine cycle

75. Out of the following which one is not a unconventional source of energy ?
    (a) Tidal power
    (b) Geothermal energy
    (c) Nuclear energy
    (d) Wind power

76. Maximum efficiency of an open cycle gas turbine is nearly
    (a) 30%   (b) 40%
    (c) 50%   (d) 60%

77. A 100 MW thermal power plant will consume nearly how many tonnes of coal in one hour ?
    (a) 50 tonnes   (b) 150 tonnes
    (c) 1500 tonnes   (d) 15,000 tonnes

78. Most of the generators in thermal power plants run at
    (a) 3000 rpm   (b) 1500 rpm
    (c) 1000 rpm   (d) 750 rpm

79. A cooling tower can be seen in
    (a) gas turbine plant
    (b) nuclear power plant
    (c) hydroelectric power plant
    (d) thermal power plant.

80. Which of the following is considered as superior quality of coal ?
    (a) Bituminous coal
    (b) Peat
    (c) Lignite
    (d) Coke

81. In order to have lower cost of electrical energy generation :
    (a) The load factor and diversity factor should be low.
    (b) The load factor should be low but diversity factor should be high.
    (c) The load factor should be high but diversity factor low.
    (d) The load factor and diversity factors should be high.

82. The cost of generation is theoretically minimum if :
    (a) The system constraints are considered.
    (b) The operational constraints are considered.
    (c) both (a) and (b)
    (d) The constraints are not considered.

83. If the penalty factor of a plant is unity, its incremental transmission loss is
    (a) 1.0
    (b) – 1.0
    (c) Zero
    (d) None of the above

84. The loss coefficients for a two-bus system are
    (a) $B_{11} = 0.02$, $B_{22} = 0.05$, $B_{12} = 0.01$, $B_{21} = 0.015$
    (b) $B_{11} = 0.02$, $B_{22} = 0.04$, $B_{12} = -0.01$, $B_{21} = 0.01$
    (c) $B_{11} = 0.03$, $B_{22} = 0.005$, $B_{12} = 0.001$, $B_{21} = -0.001$
    (d) $B_{11} = 0.03$, $B_{22} = 0.05$, $B_{12} = 0.001$, $B_{21} = -0.001$.

85. For economic operation, the generator with highet positive incremental transmission loss will operate at
    (a) The lowest positive incremental cost of production.
    (b) The lowest negative incremental cost of production.
    (c) The highest positive incremental cost of production.
    (d) None of the above.

86. The incremental transmission loss of a plant is
    (a) Positive always.
    (b) Negative always.
    (c) Can be positive or negative.
    (d) None of the above.

87. If the loading of the line corresponds to the surge impedance loading the voltage at the receiving end is
    (a) Greater than sending end
    (b) Less than sending end
    (c) Equal to the sending end
    (d) None of the above is necessary.

88. If r is the radius of the conductor and R the radius of the sheath of the cable, the cable operates stably from the view point of dielectric strength if
    (a) $\frac{r}{R} > 1.0$
    (b) $\frac{r}{R} < 1.0$
    (c) $\frac{r}{R} < 0.632$
    (d) $\frac{r}{R} < 0.368$

89. Shunt compensation in a EHV line is resorted to
    (a) Improve the stability.
    (b) Reduce the fault level.
    (c) Improve the voltage profile.
    (d) none of the above

90. Most economic load on an overhead line is
    (a) Greater than the natural load.
    (b) Less than the natural load.
    (c) Equal to the natural load.
    (d) None of the above is necessary.

91. Insulation of the modern EHV lines is designed based on
    (a) lighting voltage
    (b) switching voltage
    (c) Corona
    (d) RI

92. Impulse ratio of a gap of given geometry and dimension is
    (a) Greater with solid than with air dielectric.
    (b) Greater with air than with solid dielectric.
    (c) Same for both solid and air dielectric.

93. The impulse ratio of a rod gap is
    (a) Unity.
    (b) Between 1.2 and 1.5.
    (c) Between 1.6 and 1.8.
    (d) Between 2 and 2.2.

94. Effect of bonding the cable is
    (a) To increase the effective resistance and inductance.
    (b) To increase the effective resistance but reduce inductance.
    (c) To decrease the effective resistance and inductance.
    (d) To decrease the effective resistance but increase the inductance.

95. For effective application of counterpoise it should be buried into the ground to a depth of
    (a) 1 metre.
    (b) 2 metres.
    (c) Just enough to avoid theft.
    (d) None of the above.

96. Corona loss is less when the shape of the conductor is
    (a) Circular.
    (b) Flat.
    (c) Oval.
    (d) Independent of shape.

97. A system is said to be effectively grounded if its
    (a) Neutral is grounded directly.
    (b) Ratio of $\frac{X_0}{X_1} > 3.0$.
    (c) Ratio of $\frac{X_0}{X_1} > 2.0$.
    (d) Ratio of $\frac{X_0}{X_1} < 3.0$.

98. Velocity of travelling wave through a cable of relative per mittivity 9 is
    (a) 9×10^8 metres/sec.
    (b) 3×10^8 metres/sec.
    (c) 10^8 metres/sec.
    (d) 2×10^8 metres/sec.

99. Voltage at the two ends of a line are 132 kV and its reactance is 40 ohms. The capacity of the line is
    (a) 435.6 MW.
    (b) 217.8 MW.
    (c) 251.5 MW.
    (d) 500 MW.

100. For a lumped inductive load, with increase in supply frequency
    (a) P and Q increase.
    (b) P increases, Q decreases.
    (c) P decreases, Q increases.
    (d) P and Q decrease.

101. Most economic load on an underground cable will be
(a) Greater than its surge loading.
(b) Less than the surge loading.
(c) Equal to the surge loading.
(d) None of the above is necessary.

102. Self GMD method is used to evaluate
(a) Inductance.
(b) Capacitance.
(c) Inductance and capacitance both
(d) None of the above

103. Surge impedance of 50 miles long underground cable is 50 ohms. For a 25 miles length it will be
(a) 25 ohms
(b) 50 ohms
(c) 100 ohms
(d) None of the above

104. Capacitance and inductance per unit length of a line operating at 110 kV are 0.01 mF and 2 mH. The surge impedance loading of the line will be
(a) 40 MVA
(b) 30 MVA
(c) 27 MVA
(d) None of the above

105. Sending end voltage of a feeder with reactance 0.2 p.u. is 1.2 p.u. If the reactive power supplied at the receiving end of the feeder is 0.3 p.u., the approximate drop of volts in the feeder will be
(a) 0.2 p.u.
(b) 0.06 p.u.
(c) 0.05 p.u.
(d) 0.072 p.u.

106. Presence of earth in case of overhead lines
(a) Increases the capacitance.
(b) Increases the inductance.
(c) Decreases the capacitance.
(d) Decreases the inductance.

107. Effect of increase in temperature in overhead transmission lines is to
(a) increase the stress and length.
(b) Decrease the stress and length.
(c) Decrease the stress but increase the length.
(d) None of the above.

108. Ferranti effect on long overhead lines is experienced when it is
(a) Lightly loaded.
(b) On full load at unity p.f.
(c) On full load at 0.8 p.f. lag.
(d) In all these cases.

109. In-rush current of a transformer at no load is maximum if the supply voltage is switched on
(a) At zero voltage value.
(b) At peak voltage value.
(c) At V / 2 value.
(d) At $\sqrt{3}/2$ V value.

110. If the inductance and capacitance of a system are 1.0 H and 0.01 μF respectively and the instantaneous value of current interrupted is 10 amp, voltage across the breaker contacts will be
(a) 50 kV
(b) 100 kV
(c) 60 kV
(d) 57 kV

111. In case of a 3-phase short circuit in a system, the power fed into the system is
(a) Mostly reactive.
(b) Mostly active.
(c) Active and reactive both equal.
(d) Reactive only.

112. Standard impulse testing of a power transformer requires
(a) Two applications of chopped wave followed by one application of a full wave.
(b) One aplication of chopped wave followed by one application of a full wave.
(c) One application of chopped wave followed by two applications of a full wave.
(d) None of the above.

113. Phase modifier is normally installed in the case of
(a) Short transmission lines.
(b) Medium length lines.
(c) Long length lines.
(d) For all length lines.

114. In order to eliminate sheath losses, a successful method is
(a) To transpose the cable along with cross bonding.
(b) Transpose the cables only.
(c) Cross bonding the cables is enough.
(d) None of the above is effective.

115. Stringing chart is useful for
(a) Finding the sag in the conductor.
(b) In the design of tower.
(c) In the design of insulator string.
(d) Finding the distance between the tower.

116. For an existing a.c. transmission line the string efficiency is 80. Now of d.c. voltage is supplied for the same set up, the string efficiency will be
    (a) 80%
    (b) More than 80%
    (c) Less than 80%
    (d) 100%

117. Coefficient of reflection for current for an open ended line is
    (a) 1.0
    (b) 0.5
    (c) – 1.0
    (d) Zero.

118. Leakage resistance of a 50 km long cable is 1 MΩ. For a 100 km long cable it will be
    (a) 1 MΩ
    (b) 2 MΩ
    (c) 0.66 MΩ
    (d) None of the above

119. A voltmeter gives 120 oscillations per minute when connected to the rotor. The stator frequency is 50 Hz. The slip of the motor is
    (a) 2%
    (b) 4%
    (c) 5%
    (d) 2.5%

120. Solution of coodination equations takes into account
    (a) All the system constraints.
    (b) All the operational constraints.
    (c) All the system and operation constraints.
    (d) None of the above.

121. Charging reactance of 50 km length of line is 1500 Ω. The charging reactance for 100 km length of line will be
    (a) 1500 Ω
    (b) 3000 Ω
    (c) 750 Ω
    (d) 600 Ω

122. In a two plant system, the load is connected at plant no 2. The loss coefficients
    (a) B_{11}, B_{12}, B_{22} are nonzero.
    (b) B_{11} and B_{22} are nonzero but B_{12} is zero.
    (c) B_{11} and B_{12} are nonzero but B_{22} is zero.
    (d) B_{11} is nonzero but B_{12} and B_{22} are zero.

123. Capacitance of a 3-core cable between any two conductors with sheath earthed is 2 μF. The capacitance per phase will be
    (a) 1 μF
    (b) 4 μF
    (c) 0.667 μF
    (d) 1.414 μF

124. For a synchronous phase modifier the load angle is
    (a) 0°
    (b) 25°
    (c) 30°
    (d) None of the above

125. The insulation resistance of a cable of length 10 km is 1 MΩ, its resistance for 50 km length will be
    (a) 1 MΩ
    (b) 5 MΩ
    (c) 0.2 MΩ
    (d) None of the above

126. Three insulating materials with same maximum working stress and permittivities 2.5, 3.0, 4.0 are used in a single core cable. The location of the materials with respect to the core of the cable will be
    (a) 2.5, 3.0, 4.0
    (b) 3.0, 2.5, 4.0
    (c) 4.0, 3.0, 2.5
    (d) 4.0, 2.5, 3.0

127. For the system shown in diagram below, a line-to-ground fault on the line side of the transformer is equivalent to

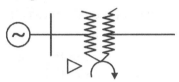

    (a) A line-to-ground fault on the generator side of the transformer.
    (b) A line-to-line fault on the generator side of the transformer.
    (c) A double line-to-ground on the generator side of the transformer.
    (d) A 3-phase fault on the generator side of the transformer.

128. Size of conductor on modern EHV lines is obtained based on
    (a) Voltage drop
    (b) Current density
    (c) Corona
    (d) above (a) and (b)

129. At a particular unbalanced node, the real powers specified are
    Leaving the node 20 MW, 25 MW
    Entering the node 60 MW, 30 MW
    Balancing power will be
    (a) 30 MW leaving the node.
    (b) 45 MW leaving the node.
    (c) 45 MW entering the node.
    (d) 22.5 MW entering the node and 22.5 MW leaving the node.

130. Positive sequence component of voltage at the point of fault is zero when it is a
    (a) 3-phase fault
    (b) L-L fault
    (c) L-L-G fault
    (d) L-G fault

131. If I_{a1} is the positive sequence current of an alternator and Z_1, Z_2 and Z_0 are the sequence impedances of the alternator. The drop produced by the current Ia_1 will be
    (a) $I_{a1} Z_1$
    (b) $I_{a1} (Z_1 + Z_2)$
    (c) $I_{a1} (Z_1 + Z_2 + Z_0)$
    (d) $I_{a1} (Z_2 + Z_0)$

132. An overhead line with surge impedance 400 ohms is terminated through a resistance R. A surge travelling over the line does not suffer any reflection at the junction if the value of R is

(a) 20 ohms   (b) 200 ohms

(c) 800 ohms   (d) None of the above

133. In case of a large size alternator the voltage control becomes serious if

(a) SCR is high.

(b) SCR is low.

(c) Voltage control is independent of SCR.

(d) none of the above.

134. Current chopping tendency is minimised by using the F6 gas at relatively

(a) High pressure and low velocity.

(b) High pressure and high velocity.

(c) Low pressure and low velocity.

(d) Low pressure and high velocity.

135. Order of the lightning discharge current is

(a) 10,000 amp   (b) 100 amp

(c) 1 amp   (d) 1 microampere

136. For the same rupturing capacity, the actual current to be inter-rupted by an HRC fuse is

(a) Much less than any CB.

(b) Much more than any CB.

(c) Equal to the CB.

(d) None of the above is necessary.

137. Arcing on transmission lines is prevented by connecting a suitable

(a) Circuit breaker.

(b) Protective relay.

(c) Inductor in the neutral.

(d) Capacitor in the neutral.

138. For rural electrification in a country like India with complex network it is preferable to use

(a) Air break C.B.   (b) Oil C.B.

(c) Vacuum C.B.   (d) M.O. C.B.

139. Chances of arc interruption in subsequent current zeros

(a) Increases in case of ABCD but decreases in OCB.

(b) Decreases in case of ABCB but increases in OCB.

(c) Decreass in both the cases.

(d) Increases in both the cases.

140. Stability of arc in vacuum depends upon

(a) The contact material only.

(b) The contact material and its vapour pressure.

(c) The circuit parameters only.

(d) The combination of (b) and (c).

141. Resistance switching is normally resorted in case of

(a) Bulk oil circuit breakers.

(b) Minimum oil circuit breakers.

(c) Air blast circuit breakers.

(d) All types of breakers.

142. Mho relay is normally used for the protection of

(a) Long transmission lines.

(b) Medium length lines.

(c) Short length lines.

(d) No length criterion.

143. Number of pilot wires required for protecting 3-phase transmission lines using translay system of protection is

(a) 6   (b) 4

(c) 3   (d) 2

144. A Mho relay is a

(a) Voltage restrained directional relay.

(b) Voltage controlled over current relay.

(c) Directional restrained over current relay.

(d) Directional restrained over voltage relay.

145. Shape of the disc of an induction disc relay is

(a) Circular   (b) Spiral

(c) Elliptic   (d) Elliptic

146. A 3-phase braker is rated at 2000 MVA, 33 kV, its making current will be

(a) 35 kA   (b) 49 kA

(c) 70 kA   (d) 89 kA.

147. An overhead line with series compensation is protected using

(a) Impedance relay

(b) Reactance relay

(c) Mho relay

(d) None of the above

148. Shunt fault is characterized by

(a) Increase in current, frequency and p.f.

(b) Increase in current reduction in frequency and p.f.

(c) Increase in current and frequency but reduction in p.f.

(d) None of the above.

149. Where voltages are high and current to be interrupted is low the breaker preferred is
    (a) Air blast C.B.
    (b) Oil C.B.
    (c) Vacuum C.B.
    (d) Any one of the above.

150. If the time of operation of a relay for unity TMS is 10 secs., the time of operation for 0.5 TMS will be
    (a) 20 secs.   (b) 5 secs.
    (c) 10 secs.   (d) None of the above

151. If the phase angle of the voltage coil of a directional relay is 50° the maximum torque angle of the relay is
    (a) 130°   (b) 100°
    (c) 25°   (d) None of the above

152. A reactance relay is
    (a) Voltage restrained directional relay.
    (b) Directional restrained over-current relay.
    (c) Voltage restrained over-current relay.
    (d) None of the above.

153. For measuring positive, negative and zero sequence voltages in a system, the reference is taken as
    (a) Neutral of the system only.
    (b) Ground only.
    (c) For zero sequence neutral and for positive and negative the ground.
    (d) None of the above.

154. Per cent bias for a generator protection lies between
    (a) 5 to 40   (b) 40 to 45
    (c) 45 to 20   (d) None of the above

155. Minimum oil circuit breaker has less volume of oil because
    (a) There is insulation between contacts.
    (b) The oil between the breaker contacts has greater strength.
    (c) Solid insulation is provided for insulating the contacts from earth.
    (d) None of the above

156. Carrier current protection scheme is normally used for
    (a) HV transmission lines only.
    (b) HV cables only.
    (c) HV transmission and cables.
    (d) None of the above.

157. To limit current chopping in vacuum circuit breakers, the contact material used has
    (a) High vapour pressure and low conductivity properties.
    (b) High vapour pressure and high conductivity properties.
    (c) Low vapour pressure and high conductivity properties.
    (d) Low vapour pressure and low conductivity properties.

158. A fault is more severe from the view point of RRRV if it is a
    (a) Short line fault.
    (b) Medium length line fault.
    (c) Long line fault.
    (d) None of the above.

159. Positive, negative and zero sequence impedances of a solidly grounded system under steady state condition always follow the relations
    (a) $Z_1 > Z_2 > Z_0$
    (b) $Z_1 < Z_2 < Z_0$
    (c) $Z_0 < Z_1 < Z_2$
    (d) None of the above

160. Phase comparators in case of static relays and electro-mechanical relays normally are
    (a) Sine and cosine comparators respectively.
    (b) Cosine and sine comparators respectively.
    (c) Both are cosine comparators.
    (d) Both are sine comparators.

161. For reducing tower footing resistance it is better to use
    (a) Chemical and ground rods only.
    (b) Chemical and counterpoise only.
    (c) Ground rod and counterpoise only.
    (d) Chemical, ground rods and counterpoise.

162. Rate of rise of restriking voltage depends
    (a) type of circuit breaker.
    (b) inductance of the system only.
    (c) capacitance of the system only.
    (d) inductance and capacitance of the system.

163. Breakdown strength of air at STP is 24 kV/cm. Its breakdown strength at 30°C and 72 cm of Hg will be
    (a) 24.25 kV/cm.   (b) 20.2 kV/cm.
    (c) 23 kV.   (d) 49.5 kV/cm.

164. Capacitor switching is easily done with
(a) Air blast circuit breaker.
(b) Oil C.B.
(c) Vacuum C.B.
(d) Any one of the above.

165. The normal practice to specify the making current of a circuit breaker is in terms of
(a) r.m.s. value
(b) Peak value
(c) Average value
(d) Both r.m.s. and peak value.

166. Chances of arc interruption in subsequent current zero
(a) Increases in case of OCB.
(b) Decreases in case of OCB
(c) Interruption is always at first current zero (in OCB)
(d) None of the above.

167. If the inductance and capacitance of a system are 4 H and 0.04 μF respectively and the instantaneous value of current interrupted is 40 amps, the value of shunt resistance across the breaker for critical damping is
(a) 400 kΩ (b) 40 kΩ
(c) 5 kΩ (d) 4 kΩ

168. For effective use of a counterpoise wire
(a) Its leakage resistance should be greater than the surge impedance.
(b) Three-phase and two-earth fault relays are required.
(c) Two-phase and two-earth fault relays are required.
(d) Two-phase and one-earth fault relays are required.

169. If the fault current is 2000 amps, the relay setting 50% and the C.T. ratio is 400/5, then the plug setting multiplier will be
(a) 25 amps   (b) 45 amps
(c) 50 amps   (d) None of the above

170. For protection of parallel feeders fed from one end the relays required are
(a) Non-directional relays at the source end and directional relays at the load end.
(b) Non-directional relays at both the ends.
(c) Directional relays at the source end and non-directional at the load end.
(d) Directional relays at both the ends.

171. High voltage d.c. testing for HV machines is resorted because
(a) Certain conclusions regarding the continuous ageing of an insulation can be drawn.
(b) The stress distribution is a representation of the service condition.
(c) Standardization on the magnitude of voltage to be applied is available.
(d) The stresses do not damage the coil end insulation.

172. If a combination of HRC fuse and circuit breaker is used, the C.B. operates for
(a) Low overload currents.
(b) Short circuit current.
(c) Under all abnormal current.
(d) The combination is never used in practice.

173. Most suitable C.B. for short line fault without switching resistor is
(a) Air blast C.B.
(b) M.O.C.B.
(c) SF$_6$ Breaker
(d) None of the above

174. A large-size alternator is protected against overloads by providing
(a) Overcurrent relays.
(b) Temperature sensitive relays.
(c) Thermal relays.
(d) A combination of (a) and (b).
(e) A combination of (b) and (c).

175. Impedance relays can be used for
(a) phase faults only
(b) earth faults only
(c) both phase and earth faults
(d) none of these

176. System frequency and system voltage respectively control
(a) active power, reactive power
(b) active power, active power
(c) reactive power, reactive power
(d) reactive power, active power

177. Surge impedance of 400W implies
(a) open circuit impedance of 400 Ω
(b) line can be theoretically loaded upto 400Ω
(c) line can be practically loaded upto 400Ω
(d) short circuit impedance of 400Ω

178. Power system uses
(a) suppression coils
(b) current limiting resistors
(c) compensation reactors
(d) all of these

179. Reactance used in case of generator is
(a) synchronous reactance
(b) transient reactance
(c) sub-tranisent reactance
(d) all of these

180. In a generator, 3φ, short circuit current is limited by
(a) transient reactance
(b) synchronous reactance
(c) sub-tranisent reactance
(d) all of these

181. 3φ, short circuit current will be
(a) infinite at infinite time
(b) maximum at infinite time
(c) zero at infinite time
(d) 10 mA at infinite time

182. Negative sequence component of a voltage is equal to
(a) zero sequence component
(b) positive sequence component
(c) complex conjugate of the positive sequence component
(d) complex conjugate of the zero sequence component

183. For L — G fault, all networks are in
(a) series
(b) parallel
(c) star
(d) delta

184. Series reactor should have
(a) high resistance
(b) low resistance
(c) high impedance
(d) low impedance

185. For L — L fault, network consists of
(a) positive sequence
(b) negative sequence
(c) zero sequence
(d) both (a) and (b)

186. Fusing factor should be
(a) equal to zero
(b) equal to one
(c) less than now
(d) more than one

187. Fuse wire should possess
(a) high specfic resistance and high melting point
(b) high specific resistance and low melting point
(c) low specific resistance and low melting point
(d) low specific resistance and high melting point

188. If strands are twisted, then fusing current will
(a) increase
(b) reduce
(c) remain same
(d) may increase or decrease

189. Fusing factor is defined as the ratio between
(a) maximum fusing current and rated voltage
(b) maximum fusing current and rated current
(c) minimum fusing current and rated current
(d) minimum fusing current and rated voltage

190. Fuses can serve upto a current of
(a) 25 A
(b) 50 A
(c) 75 A
(d) 100 A

191. Cut-off current in a fuse is the
(a) maximum value actually reached
(b) r.m.s value actually reached
(c) average value actually reached
(d) none of these

192. Best practicable material for a fuse wires is
(a) Aluminium
(b) Copper
(c) Iron
(d) Tin

193. H.R.C. fuses has
(a) high rating of current
(b) high rupturing capacity
(c) high resistance capacity
(d) none of these

194. Cartridge type fuse can be used upto a voltage of
(a) 400 V
(b) 11 kV
(c) 20 kV
(d) 33 kV

195. Liquid type H.R.C. fuses are used upto a voltage of
(a) 33 kV
(b) 66 kV
(c) 132 kV
(d) 200 kV

196. Selection of fuse is based on
(a) steady load
(b) fluctuating load
(c) a & b
(d) none of these

197. A single phasing relay can be used with
(a) 1φ motor
(b) 2^r φ motor
(c) 3 φ motor
(d) all of these

198. A relay is used to
(a) break the fault current
(b) sense the fault
(c) sense the fault and direct to trip the circuit breaker
(d) all of these

199. In impedance relay, current element torque should be
(a) equal to voltage element torque
(b) greater than voltage element torque
(c) less than voltage element torque
(d) none of these

200. Over current fault is most likely in
(a) tranformer
(b) overhead line equipment
(c) alternator
(d) motors

201. Good relay should possess
(a) speed & reliability
(b) speed & sensitivity
(c) adequateness & selectivity
(d) all of these

202. Relay gets its operating energy from
(a) transformer (b) alternator
(c) overhead lines (d) C.T., P.T.

203. An impedance relay is used for
(a) earth faults (b) interphase faults
(c) both (a) and (b) (d) none of these

204. Earthing transformer is used to
(a) improve neutral wire's current capacity
(b) avoid overheating of transformer
(c) provide artificial earthing
(d) avoid harmonics

205. Basic relay connection requirement is that the relay must operate for
(a) load (b) internal faults
(c) both (a) and (b) (d) none of these

206. MHO relay is inherently a
(a) directional type
(b) non-directional type
(c) unidirectional type
(d) none of these

207. Instantaneous relay should operate within
(a) 0.0001 sec (b) 0.001 sec
(c) 0.01 sec (d) 0.1 sec

208. Buchholz relay is used to protect against
(a) inter-turn fault
(b) external faults
(c) rotor faults
(d) every internal faults

209. Distance relays re generally
(a) impedance type
(b) MHO type
(c) reactance type
(d) all of these

210. Plug setting of a relay can be changed by changing
(a) air gap
(b) back up stop
(c) number of ampere turns
(d) all of these

211. Percentage differential protection is used to prevent against
(a) inter-turn faults (b) external faults
(c) heavy loads (d) magnetizing current

212. Relays for transmission line protection are
(a) in three zones
(b) in two zones
(c) independent of zone
(d) none of these

213. Induction cup relays responds to
(a) current (b) voltage
(c) power (d) impedance

214. Split-phase relay responds to
(a) over load faults (b) over voltage
(c) inter turn faults (d) all of these

215. Directional relays responds to
(a) power (b) current
(c) voltage (d) reactance

216. In carrier current protection, wave trap is used is for trapping
(a) high frequency waves entering in generating units
(b) power frequency waves
(c) both (a) and (b)
(d) none of these

217. For phase fault on long line, which relay is used?
(a) MHO relays (b) reactance relays
(c) impedance relays (d) all of these

218. For protection against synchronising power surges, which relay is used?
(a) split-phase relays (b) impedance relays
(c) reactance relays (d) MHO relays

219. Under voltage relays are used for
(a) motors (b) alternators
(c) bus bars (d) all of these

220. More faults occur in
    (a) generators   (b) under ground cables
    (c) transformers   (d) over head lines

221. Instantaneous relay is
    (a) hinged armature type
    (b) polarized type
    (c) balanced beam type
    (d) all of these

222. Back up protection is needed for
    (a) over voltage   (b) over current
    (c) short circuits   (d) all of these

223. An instantaneous relay is
    (a) permanent moving magnet
    (b) induction cup
    (c) shaded pole
    (d) moving coil

224. Relays which act directly on C.B. are called
    (a) auxiliary relays
    (b) main relays
    (c) both (a) and (b)
    (d) none of these

225. Time classification of relays includes
    (a) instantaneous relays
    (b) definite time lag
    (c) inverse time lag
    (d) all of these

226. Single phase preventers are used for
    (a) transformers
    (b) transmission lines
    (c) motors
    (d) underground cables

227. Operating current in relay is
    (a) a.c. only
    (b) d.c. only
    (c) both (a) and (b)
    (d) none of these

228. For motor protection, which relay is used?
    (a) Thermocouple type relays
    (b) Bimetallic relays
    (c) Electronic relays
    (d) All of these

229. Pilot wire protection is for
    (a) overhead lines   (b) transformer
    (c) motors   (d) cables

230. In an impedance relay, fault current is maximum if fault occurs near the
    (a) relay   (b) centre of the line
    (c) transformer   (d) none of these

231. Actual tripping of a static relay is obtained by
    (a) SCR   (b) thyristors
    (c) UJT   (d) none of these

232. It is possible to work on ungrounded systems of 11 kV for a length of
    (a) 10 Kms   (b) 50 Kms
    (c) 90 Kms   (d) 110 Kms

233. Advantage of grounded neutral is
    (a) persistent arcing grounds are eliminated
    (b) earth faults are utilized to disconnect the fault
    (c) both (a) and (b)
    (d) none of these

234. Neutral can be grounded by
    (a) solid grounding
    (b) resistance grounding
    (c) reactance grounding
    (d) all of these

235. Lightning arrestors are
    (a) surge reflectors   (b) surge divertors
    (c) surge absorbers   (d) surge attenuators

236. Location of lightning arrestor is
    (a) after the transformer
    (b) after the distributor
    (c) before the transformer
    (d) none of these

237. Thyrite is used in lightning arrestors because of its
    (a) straight line characteristic
    (b) non-linear characteristic
    (c) none of these
    (d) all of these

238. Ionization in circuit breakers is facilitated by
    (a) increase of field stregth
    (b) increase of mean free path
    (c) high temperature
    (d) all of these

239. Arc interruption is done by
    (a) high resistance interruption
    (b) low resistance interruption
    (c) both (a) and (b)
    (d) none of these

240. Part of circuit breaker helpful in breaking the current is
(a) Trip coil   (b) Contacts
(c) Handle   (d) Medium

241. Desired tripping of a circuit breaker is
(a) manually
(b) automatically
(c) that it should give warning
(d) none of these

242. For single frequency transients, ratio of peak restriking voltage to time between voltage zero and peak voltage is called
(a) restriking voltage
(b) recovery voltage
(c) rate of rise restriking voltage
(d) active recovery voltage

243. In a circuit breaker, to facilitate arc quenching, dielectric strength can be increased by
(a) lengthening of the gap
(b) cooling
(c) blast effect
(d) all of these

244. An ideal circuit breaker should offer
(a) zero & infinite impedance before & after interruption respectively
(b) infinite & zero impedance before & after interruption respectively
(c) equal impedance before & after interruption
(d) none of these

245. Instantaneous voltage in a circuit breaker depends upon
(a) restriking voltage
(b) rate of rise restriking voltage
(c) power factor
(d) frequency

246. Recovery voltage is the value of the r.m.s. voltage that re-appears across the poles of a circuit breaker before
(a) restriking voltage
(b) final arc distinction
(c) rise of voltage
(d) all of these

247. Which of the following is not a protective gear?
(a) Fuse
(b) Circuit breaker
(c) Relay
(d) None of these

248. Arcing time is the time between
(a) separation of circuit breaker and extinction of arc
(b) separation of circuit breaker and rise of recovery voltage
(c) normal current interrpution and arc extinction
(d) none of these

249. Time between energisation of trip coil and separation of contacts is called
(a) closing time
(b) opening time
(c) both (a) and (b)
(d) none of these

250. Rate of rise restriking voltage depends upon
(a) active recovery voltage
(b) natural frequency of oscillations
(c) both (a) and (b)
(d) rating of circuit breaker

251. Interrupting a low inductive current may lead to
(a) very high restriking voltage
(b) very high current
(c) rupture of circuit breaker
(d) current chopping

252. Current chopping can be avoided by
(a) resistance switching
(b) inductive switching
(c) capacitive switching
(d) diode switching

253. Time between separation of contacts and energisation of trip coil is called
(a) opening time   (b) closing time
(c) arching time   (d) decaying time

254. Difficulty of performing the circuit breaking operation is a function of
(a) circuit voltage
(b) magnitude of the current
(c) electrical constants of the circuit
(d) none of these

255. When contacts of circuit breaker opens
(a) arc is produced
(b) voltage rises
(c) breaker fails
(d) arc chamber is broken

256. A.C. air break circuit breakers are used for
  (a) very high voltage
  (b) very low voltage
  (c) medium voltage
  (d) medium and low voltage

257. Air blast circuit breakers are preferred for
  (a) short duty   (b) intermittant duty
  (c) repeated duty   (d) all of these

258. Phenomenon of arc interrpution takes place at
  (a) zero voltage   (b) zero current
  (c) high current   (d) high voltage

259. Over voltage may be due to
  (a) lightning impulse waveform
  (b) 50 Hz a.c.
  (c) peak value of 50 Hz a.c.
  (d) all of these

260. In oil circuit breakers, dielectric strength of oil should be
  (a) high   (b) low
  (c) medium   (d) none of these

261. Main disadvantage (s) of oil circuit breaker is that it
  (a) is easily inflammable
  (b) may form an explosive mixture with air
  (c) requires maintenance
  (d) all of these

262. Breaker should adjust itself to
  (a) fault magnitude and time
  (b) increased arc and time of quenching
  (c) R R R V
  (d) none of these

263. At higher currents, the switchgear exhibit
  (a) corona effect
  (b) skin effect
  (c) mechanical stresses
  (d) poor regulation

264. Plain circuit breakers can't be used for voltage above
  (a) 400 V   (b) 3.3 kV
  (c) 11 kV   (d) 33 kV

265. Quantity of oil in bulk oil circuit breakers increases with
  (a) decrease in voltage
  (b) increase in voltage
  (c) pressure of arc
  (d) mechanical stresses

266. Rating of circuit breaker depends upon
  (a) breaking capacity
  (b) making capacity
  (c) short time capacity
  (d) all of these

267. Symmetrical breaking current is
  (a) peak value of a.c. component
  (b) average value of a. c. component
  (c) r.m.s. value of a.c. component
  (d) all of these

268. In vacuum breakers, current wave
  (a) reaches its maximum value
  (b) attains its r.m.s value
  (c) is chopped
  (d) attains its average value

EXERCISE – II

1. A Buchholz relay is used for
  (a) Protection of a transformer against all internal faults
  (b) Protection of a transformer against external faults
  (c) Protection of a transformer against both internal and external faults
  (d) Protection of induction motors   **(RRB 2012)**

2. The elements of each row of a Y_{BUS} matrix for load flow studies in power system add up to zero   **(RRB 2012)**
  (a) always
  (b) if the shunt admittances at the buses are ignored
  (c) if mutual couplings between trans-mission lines are absent
  (d) if both (b) and (c) are satisfied

3. An SCR is rated for 650 V PIV. What is the voltage for which the device can be operated if the voltage safety factor is 2 ?   **(RRB 2012)**
  (a) 325 V rms
  (b) 230 V rms
  (c) 459 V rms
  (d) 650 V rms

4. A 50 Hz, 3-phase synchronous generator has inductance per phase of 15 mH. The capacitance of generator and circuit breaker is 0.002 µF. What is its natural frequency of oscillation?
  (a) 29 kHz
  (b) 2.9 kHz
  (c) 290 kHz
  (d) 29 MHz   **(RRB 2012)**

5. The making and breaking currents of 3 phase ac circuit breakers in power system are respectively in what form ? **(RRB 2012)**

   (a) r.m.s. value, r.m.s. value

   (b) instantaneous value, r.m.s. value

   (c) r.m.s. value

   (d) instantaneous value, instantaneous value

6. Transient stability of a 3-phase power systems having more than one synchronous generator is not affected by which one of the following specifications? **(RRB 2012)**

   (a) Initial operating conditions of generators

   (b) Quantum of large power disturbance

   (c) Fast fault clearance and redo sure

   (d) Small changes in system frequency

7. In straight line method of depreciation, the money to be reserved for depreciation is **(RRB)**

   (a) directly proportional to time

   (b) inversely proportional to time

   (c) directly proportional to square of time

   (d) inversely proportional to square of time

8. Diversity factor of a power system is the

   (a) ratio of sum of consumer's maximum demands to maximum load on the station

   (b) ratio of average demand to maximum demand

   (c) reciprocal of (a) above

   (d) reciprocal of (b) above **(RRB)**

9. Formation of voids in the dielectric of a cable is due to effect of **(RRB)**

   (a) loading cycles in service

   (b) increased pressure

   (c) extra potential difference

   (d) all of these

10. By increasing potential of a conductor

    (a) potential between conductor and ground decreases

    (b) corona loss is reduced

    (c) insulation required is less

    (d) its potential gradient increases **(RRB)**

11. Arc voltage produced in ac circuit breaker is always **(RRB)**

    (a) in phase opposition to the arc current

    (b) in phase with the arc current

    (c) leading the arc current by 90°

    (d) lagging the arc current by 45°

12. Part of circuit breaker helpful in breaking the current is **(RRB)**

    (a) Trip coil   (b) Contacts

    (c) Handle   (d) Medium

13. Instantaneous voltage in a circuit breaker depends upon **(RRB)**

    (a) restriking voltage

    (b) rate of rise restriking voltage

    (c) power factor

    (d) frequency

14. Buchholz relay is used to protect against

    (a) inter-turn fault

    (b) external faults

    (c) rotor faults

    (d) every internal faults **(RRB)**

15. Settling time is inversely proportional to product of the damping ratio and **(RRB)**

    (a) time constant

    (b) maximum overshoot

    (c) peak time

    (d) undamped natural frequency of the system

16. The insulation on a current carrying conductor is provided to prevent **(RRB)**

    (a) current leakage   (b) shock

    (c) both (a) and (b)   (d) none of these

17. The following circuit breaker does not use pneumatic operating mechanism **(RRB)**

    (a) air break circuit breaker

    (b) air blast circuit breaker

    (c) bulk oil circuit breaker

    (d) SF_6 circuit breaker

18. If the inductance and capacitance of a system are 4 H and 0.04 μF respectively and the instantaneous value of current interrupted is 40 amps, the value of shunt resistance across the breaker for critical damping is **(RRB)**

    (a) 400 kΩ   (b) 40 kΩ

    (c) 5 kΩ   (d) 4 kΩ

19. If the fault current is 2000 amps, the relay setting 50% and the C.T. ratio is 400/5, then the plug setting multiplier will be **(RRB)**

    (a) 25 amps

    (b) 45 amps

    (c) 50 amps

    (d) None of these

20. For protection of parallel feeders fed from one end the relays required are **(RRB)**
    (a) Non-directional relays at the source end and directional relays at the load end.
    (b) Non-directional relays at both the ends.
    (c) Directional relays at the source end and non-directional at the load end.
    (d) Directional relays at both the ends.

21. Arc interruption is done by **(RRB)**
    (a) high resistance interruption
    (b) low resistance interruption
    (c) both (a) and (b)
    (d) none of these

22. The horizontally placed conductors of a single phase line operating at 50 Hz are having outside diameter of 1.6 cm, and the spacing between centers of the conductors is 6 m. The permittivity of free space is 8.854×10^{-12} F/m. The capacitance to ground per kilometer of each line is
    (a) 4.2×10^{-9} F
    (b) 8.4×10^{-9} F
    (c) 4.2×10^{-12} F
    (d) 8.4×10^{-12} F   **(RRB)**

23. If the electric field $\overline{E} = 0.1\, te^{-t}\, a_x$ and $\epsilon = 4\,\epsilon_0$, then the displacement current crossing an area of 0.1 m^2 at $t = 0$ will be **(DMRC 2014)**
    (a) zero
    (b) $0.04\,\epsilon_0$
    (c) $0.4\,\epsilon_0$
    (d) $4\,\epsilon_0$

24. When the time period, of the applied voltage is much shorter than the relaxation time of a polarization process, the loss angle is
    (a) zero
    (b) between 0° and 90°.
    (c) 90°
    (d) greater than 90°   **(DMRC 2014)**

25. The Thevenin equivalent of a network is as shown in the given figure. For maximum power transfer of the variable and purely resistive load R_1, its resistance should be **(DMRC 2014)**

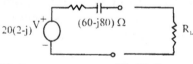

    (a) 60 Ω
    (b) 80 Ω
    (c) 100 Ω
    (d) infinity

26. The time-constant to the network shown in the figure is **(DMRC 2014)**

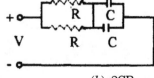

    (a) CR
    (b) 2CR
    (c) CR/4
    (d) CR/2

27. For a two-port network to be reciprocal, it is necessary that **(DMRC 2014)**
    (a) $Z_{11} = Z_{22}$ and $y_{21} = y_{12}$
    (b) $Z_{11} = Z_{22}$ and $AD - BC = 0$
    (c) $h_{21} = -h_{12}$ and $AD - BC = 0$
    (d) $y_{21} = y_{12}$ and $h_{21} = -h_{12}$

28. An initially relaxed RC-series network with R = 2MΩ and C = 1μF is switched on to a 10 V step input. The voltage across the capacitor after 2 seconds will be **(DMRC 2014)**
    (a) zero
    (b) 3.68 V
    (c) 6.32 V
    (d) 10 V

29. An initially relaxed 100 mH inductor is switched 'ON' at $t = 1$ sec. to an ideal 2 A dc current source. The voltage across the inductor would be
    (a) zero   **(DMRC 2014)**
    (b) $0.2\,\delta\,(t-1)$ V
    (c) $0.2\,\delta(t-1)$ V
    (d) 0.2 tu $(t-1)$ V

30. The current through the current coil, of a wattmeter is given by $i = (1 + 2 \sin \omega t)$ A and the voltage across the pressure coil is $v = (2 + 3 \sin 2\,\omega t)$ V
    The wattmeter will read **(DMRC 2014)**
    (a) 8.00 W
    (b) 5.05 W
    (c) 2.0 W
    (d) 1.0 W

31. An RLC resonant circuit has a resonance frequency of 1.5 HMz and a bandwidth of 10 kHz. If C = 150 pF, then the effective resistance of the circuit will be **(DMRC 2014)**
    (a) 29.5 Ω
    (b) 14.75 Ω
    (c) 9.4 Ω
    (d) 4.7 Ω

32. Two identical coils of negligible resistance, when connected in series across a 50 Hz fixed voltage source, draw a current of 10A. When the terminals of one of the coils are reversed, the current drawn is 8 A. The coefficient of coupling between the two coils is
    (a) 1/100
    (b) 1/9
    (c) 4/10
    (d) 8/10   **(DMRC 2014)**

33. Swamping resistance is a resistance which is added to the moving coil of meter to
    (a) reduce the full-scale current
    (b) reduce the temperature error
    (c) increase the sensitivity
    (d) increase the field strength   **(DMRC 2014)**

34. A high frequency ac signal is applied to a PMMC instrument. If the rms value of the ac signal is 2 V, then the reading of the instrument will be

(DMRC 2014)

(a) zero

(b) 2V

(c) $\sqrt{2}$V

(d) 4 $\sqrt{2}$V

35. When the input to a system was withdrawn at $t = 0$, its output was found to decrease exponentially from 100 units to 500 units. in 1.386 seconds..The time constant of the system is **(DMRC)**

(a) 0.500

(b) 0.693

(c) 1.386

(d) 2.000

36. The hot resistance of the filament of a bulb is higher than the cold resistance because. The temperature coefficient of the filament is

(a) negative

(b) infinite

(c) zero

(d) positive   **(DMRC)**

37. The voltage across the 1 kΩ resistor between the nodes A and B of the network shown in the given figure is

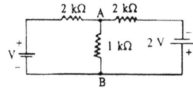

(a) 2 V

(b) 3 V

(c) 4 V

(d) 8 V   **(DMRC)**

38. Initially, the circuit shown in the given figure was relaxed. If the switch is closed

at $t = 0$, the values of $i(0^+)$, $\dfrac{di}{dt}(0^+)$ and $\dfrac{d^2i}{dt^2}(0^+)$ will respectively be

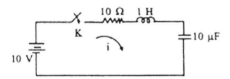

(a) 0, 10 and –100

(b) 0, 10 and 100

(c) 10, 100 and 0

(d) 100, 0 and 10   **(DMRC)**

39. For a two-port symmetrical bilateral network, if A = 3 and B = 1 Ω, the value of parameter C will be   **(DMRC)**

(a) 4s

(b) 6s

(c) 8s

(d) 16s

40. The ac bridge shown in the given figure will remain balanced if impedance Z consists of

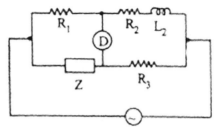

(a) resistance and inductance in series

(b) resistance and capacitance in parallel

(c) capacitance only

(d) inductance only   **(DMRC)**

41. In the potentiometer circuit shown in the given figure, the value of unknown voltage 'E' under balanced condition will be

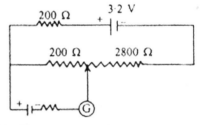

(a) 200mV

(b) 2.8V

(c) 3V

(d) 3.2 V   **(DMRC)**

42. A wattmeter has a range of 1000 W with an error of ±1% of full scale deflection. If the true power passed through it is 100 W, then the relative error would be

(a) ± 10%

(b) ± 5%

(c) ± 1%

(d) ± 0.5%   **(DMRC)**

43. In a permanent magnet moving coil instrument, if the control spring is replaced by another one having a higher spring constant, then the natural frequency and damping ratio will

(a) decrease

(b) increase and decrease respectively

(c) decrease and increase respectively

(d) increase   **(DMRC)**

44. High resistance are provided with a guard terminal in order to

(a) protect the resistance against stray electrostatic field

(b) bypass the leakage current

(c) protect the resistance against overloads

(d) protect the resistance against stray electromagnetic field   **(DMRC)**

45. The capacitance and loss angle of a capacitor can be accurately measured by **(DMRC)**

(a) Kelvin's bridge

(b) Anderson's bridge

(c) Schering bridge

(d) Carey-Foster's bridge

46. A resistance strain gauge is fastened to a beam subjected to a strain of 1×10^{-6}, yielding a resistance change of 240 μΩ. If the original resistance of the strain gauge is 120Ω, the gauge factor would be

(a) 5   (b) 2

(c) 1   (d) 0.2   **(DMRC)**

47. A voltage of {200 $\sqrt{2}$ sin 314t + 6 2 sin $(942t + 30°) + 8 \sqrt{2}$ cost $(1570t + 30°)$} V is given to a harmonic distortion meter. The meter will indicate a total harmonic distortion of approximately **(DMRC)**

(a) 4.5%   (b) 6.5%

(c) 7.5%   (d) 8.5%

48. To eliminate 50 Hz pick-up in a dual slope DVM, the minimum period of integration of the input signal is **(DMRC)**

(a) 1 ms   (b) 20 ms

(c) 1 s   (d) 100 s

49. Which one of the following sets of building block mainly decides the accuracy of a frequency counter? **(DMRC)**

(a) Crystal and ADC

(b) ADC and DAC

(c) DAC and gate width generator

(d) Gate width generator and crystal

50. A filamentary current of 10 π A flows in the negative z - direction. The magnetic field at $(0, 5, 0)$ is **(DMRC)**

(a) $\bar{a}_x$ A/m   (b) $\bar{a}_y$ A/m

(c) $\bar{a}_z$ A/m   (d) $\left(\bar{a}_x + \bar{a}_y\right)$ A/m

51. A relay performs the function of **(SSC, CPWD 2008)**

(a) fault isolation   (b) fault detection

(c) fault prevention   (d) All the above

52. HRC fuse provides best protection against **(SSC, CPWD 2008)**

(a) open circuit   (b) overload

(c) reverse current   (d) short circuit

53. A dynamometer type wattmeter responds to the **(SSC, CPWD 2008)**

(a) average value of active power

(b) average value of reactive power

(c) peak value of active power

(d) peak value of reactive power

54. Mho relay is used to protect? **(SSC, CPWD 2008)**

(a) long transmission line

(b) medium length line

(c) short length line

(d) All the above

55. For arc heating, the electrodes are made of **(SSC, CPWD 2008)**

(a) copper   (b) aluminium

(c) graphite   (d) ACSR conductor

56. The most common type of three phase in unsymmetrical fault is **(SSC, CPWD 2008)**

(a) single line to ground

(b) line to line

(c) double line to ground

(d) three phase

57. Megger is an instrument to measure **(SSC, CPWD 2008)**

(a) a very low resistance

(b) insulation resistance

(c) Q of coil

(d) inductance of coil

58. Arc lamp operates at **(SSC, CPWD 2008)**

(a) low lagging power factor

(b) high leading power factor

(c) unity power factor

(d) zero power factor

59. Two heaters rated a 1000W, 250V each are connected in series across a 250V, 50 Hz AC mains. The total power drawn from the supply would be **(SSC, CPWD 2008)**

(a) 1000 watt   (b) 500 watt

(c) 250 watt   (d) 2000 watt

60. Earth fault relays are **(SSC, CPWD 2009)**

(a) directional relays

(b) non-directional relays

(c) short operate time relays

(d) long operate time relays

61. The rating of fuse is expressed in terms of
(SSC, CPWD 2009)

(a) amperes   (b) volts

(c) VAR   (d) KVA

62. By burden of the relay we mean
(SSC, CPWD 2009)

(a) volt- ampere rating of relay

(b) current rating of relay

(c) voltage rating of relay

(d) watt rating of relay

63. Reactance relays are employed for phase fault in **(SSC, CPWD 2009)**

(a) long time   (b) medium line

(c) short line   (d) any of these

64. The recovery voltage will be maximum for power factor of **(SSC, CPWD 2009)**

(a) zero   (b) 0.5

(c) 0.707   (d) unity

65. An air blast circuit breaker is usually employed for **(SSC, CPWD 2009)**

(a) instantaneous voltage

(b) intermittent duty

(c) repeated duty

(d) short duty

66. The permissible variation of frequency in power system P_s is **(SSC, CPWD 2009)**

(a) ±1%   (b) ±3%

(c) ±5%   (d) ±10%

67. A 4-pole generator with 16 coils has a two layer lap winding. The pole pitch is
(SSC, CPWD 2009)

(a) 32   (b) 16

(c) 8   (d) 4

68. The ratio of resistances of a 100 W, 220 V lamp to that of a 100 W, 110 V lamp will be at respective voltages **(SSC, CPWD 2010)**

(a) 4   (b) 2

(c) 1/2   (d) 1/4

69. The ratio of the puncture voltage to the flashover voltage of an insulator is **(SSC, CPWD 2010)**

(a) equal to one   (b) lower than one

(c) zero   (d) greater than one

70. Bucholtz relay cannot be used on

(a) 500 kV transformer   **(SSC, CPWD 2010)**

(b) 1000 kV transformer

(c) Three phase transformer

(d) Air-cooled transformer

71. An ammeter is obtained by shunting a 30 Ω Galvanometer with 30 Ω resistance. What additional shunt should be connected across it to double the range? **(SSC, CPWD 2010)**

(a) 15 Ω   (b) 10 Ω

(c) 5 Ω   (d) 30 Ω

72. Swamping resistance is used to compensate error due to **(SSC, CPWD 2010)**

(a) Stray magnetic field

(b) Large supply voltage

(c) Large supply frequency

(d) Temperature variations

73. Which of the following is of high importance in case of induction heating? **(SSC, CPWD 2010)**

(a) voltage   (b) frequency

(c) current   (d) all the above

74. A FET is essentially a **(SSC, CPWD 2010)**

(a) Current driven device

(b) Voltage driven device

(c) Power driven source

(d) Solar device

75. Differential relays are used to protect the equipment against **(SSC, CPWD 2010)**

(a) internal faults   (b) reverse current

(c) overvoltage   (d) overcurrent

76. The making current of 3-phase breaker with rating 2000 MVA, 33 kV will be

(SSC, CPWD 2010)

(a) 35 kA   (b) 50 kA

(c) 70 kA   (d) 89 kA

77. The lighting arrester is conducted

(SSC, CPWD 2010)

(a) in series with the line

(b) between line and earth

(c) to a pole near the line

(d) to circuit breaker

78. If R_g in the circuit shown in figure 1 is variable between 20 Ω and 80 Ω then maximum power transferred to the load R_L will be

(SSC, CPWD 2010)

Figure 1

(a) 15 W   (b) 13.33 W

(c) 6.67 W   (d) 2.4 W

79. Electronic switching are becoming more and more popular because of **(SSC, CPWD 2010)**

(a) noiseless operation

(b) long life

(c) smaller size and weight

(d) all the above

80. Time constant of the network shown in figure is **(SSC, CPWD 2010)**

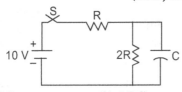

(a) 2 RC

(b) 3 RC

(c) $\dfrac{RC}{2}$

(d) $\dfrac{2RC}{3}$

81. Permeance is analogous to **(SSC, CPWD 2010)**

(a) Conductance

(b) Reluctance

(c) Inductance

(d) Resistance

82. A wire has a resistance 10Ω. It is stretched by one-tenth of its original length. Then its resistance will be **(SSC, CPWD 2010)**

(a) 10 Ω

(b) 12.1 Ω

(c) 9 Ω

(d) 11 Ω

83. Potential transformers are used **(SSC, CPWD 2010)**

(a) to measure high a.c. voltage

(b) to measure high d.c. voltage

(c) both (a) and (b)

(d) as protective device in high voltage circuits

84. To increase the range of a voltmeter **(SSC, CPWD 2010)**

(a) a low resistance is connected in series

(b) a low resistance is connected in parallel

(c) a high resistance is connected in series

(d) a high resistance is connected in parallel

85. A three phase power transformer is provided with star-delta connections. In order to protect against fault, the connection for current transformer should be in **(SSC, CPWD 2010)**

(a) Star-star

(b) Delta-star

(c) Delta-delta

(d) Star-delta

86. The advantage of electric breaking is **(SSC, CPWD 2010)**

(a) It is instantaneous

(b) More heat is generated during breaking

(c) It avoids wear of track

(d) Motor continue to remain loaded during breaking

87. A single phase motor is made self-starting by the addition of a/an **(SSC, CPWD 2010)**

(a) Running winding

(b) Starting winding

(c) Electric starter

(d) Autotransformer

88. A voltage divider circuit and its Thevenin's equivalent are shown below. The values of V_{th} and R_{th} will be **(SSC, CPWD 2011)**

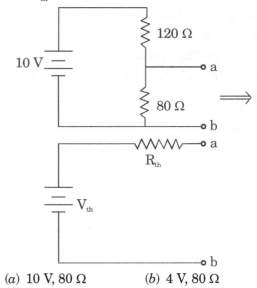

(a) 10 V, 80 Ω

(b) 4 V, 80 Ω

(c) 4 V, 48 Ω

(d) 5 V, 50 Ω

89. Two coils with self-inductances 1 H and 2 H having a mutual inductance of 1 H between them carry currents of 2 A and $\sqrt{2}$ A respectively. The total energy stored in the field, in joules, is **(SSC, CPWD 2011)**

(a) $2(1+\sqrt{2})$

(b) $2(2+\sqrt{2})$

(c) $3(1+\sqrt{2})$

(d) $3(2+\sqrt{2})$

90. In dynamometer wattmeter compen-sating coil **(SSC, CPWD 2011)**

(a) has equal number of turns of voltage coil and is connected in series with current coil

(b) has equal number of turns of current coil and is connected in series with voltage coil

(c) has equal number of turns of current coil and is connected in series with current coil

(d) has equal number of turns of voltage coil and is connected in series with voltage coil

91. Megger is an instrument by which we can measure **(SSC, CPWD 2011)**

(a) high resistance

(b) low resistance

(c) high current

(d) high voltage

92. With the decrease in the strength of the permanent magnet in an insulation Megger due to ageing, the Megger reading will
(SSC, CPWD 2011)

(a) be lower than actual

(b) be higher than actual

(c) remain unaffected

(d) fluctuate rapidly

93. In the circuit shown in the figure given below, instantaneous current i(t) under steady state is given by **(SSC, CPWD 2011)**

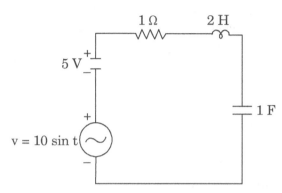

(a) zero   (b) 5

(c) 7.07 sin t   (d) 7.07 sin (t – 45°)

94. The V – 1 relation for the networks shown in the given box is V = 41 = 9. If now a resistor R = 2 Ω is connected across it, then the value of I will be.
(SSC, CPWD 2011)

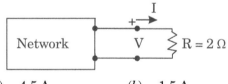

(a) – 4.5 A   (b) – 1.5 A

(c) 1.5 A   (d) 4.5 A

95. A wattmeter is being losted under phantom loading condition. If the wattmeter reading is 60 W, the actual power consumed from the supply, is **(SSC, CPWD 2011)**

(a) much higher than 60 W

(b) 60 W

(c) much less than 60 W

(d) 30 W

96. Guard electrodes are used in capacitance measurement to minimize **(SSC, CPWD 2011)**

(a) fringing of electric field

(b) thermo emf

(c) dielectric loss

(d) eddy current

97. A static combination of control coil and compensating coil is used in Megger to minimize the effect of **(SSC, CPWD 2011)**

(a) stray capacitance

(b) surface leakage

(c) stray magnetic field

(d) aging of magnet

98. Megger is an instrument used for measurement of **(SSC, CPWD 2011)**

(a) high resistance   (b) medium resistance

(c) low resistance   (d) leakage current

99. A fault involving all the three phases of a power system is known as **(SSC, CPWD 2011)**

(a) line to line to ground fault

(b) symmetrical fault

(c) unsymmetrical fault

(d) unbalanced fault

100. A single phase radial distributor is fed at one end at 220 V and is loaded with unity power factor loads as under : **(SSC, CPWD 2011)**

Distance from feeding point in metres	Load current in amperes
100	22
220	17
260	20
300	25

If the total resistance for go and return of the distributor is 0.1 Ω, the voltage at the far end is

(a) 213.79 V   (b) 216.89 V

(c) 207.57 V   (d) 215.8 V

101. In the Merz Price system of protection of alternator, if i_1 and i_2 are the CT secondary currents, and n_r and n_o are the number of restraining coils and operating coils respectively, then the torque-balance equation is
(SSC, CPWD 2011)

(a) $\dfrac{i_1 + i_2}{(i_1 - i_2)/2} = \dfrac{n_r}{n_o}$ (b) $\dfrac{i_1 + i_2}{(i_1 - i_2)/2} = \dfrac{n_o}{n_r}$

(c) $\dfrac{i_1 - i_2}{(i_1 + i_2)/2} = \dfrac{n_r}{n_o}$ (d) $\dfrac{i_1 - i_2}{(i_1 + i_2)/2} = \dfrac{n_o}{n_r}$

102. The presence of earth in case of overhead lines
(SSC, CPWD 2011)

(a) increases the capacitance of the line

(b) increases the inductance of the line

(c) decreases the capacitance of the line

(d) decreases the inductance of the line

103. In arc welding, the voltage required to maintain the arc is in the range of   **(SSC, CPWD 2011)**

(a) 200 – 250 volts

(b) 1000 – 1200 volts

(c) 2 – 5 volts

(d) 20 – 30 volts

104. Isolators are capable of breaking

(SSC, CPWD 2011)

(a) fault current   (b) no current

(c) load current   (d) charging current

105. An equipment has an impedance of 0.9 p.u. to a base of 20 MVA, 33 kV. To the base of 50 MVA, 11 kV, the p.u. impedance will be

(SSC, CPWD 2011)

(a) 4.7   (b) 20.25

(c) 0.9   (d) 6.75

106. The recovery voltage that appears across the circuit breaker contacts will be maximum for power factor of   **(SSC, CPWD 2011)**

(a) zero   (b) 0.5

(c) 0.707   (d) unity

107. The colour of light emitted by sodium vapour discharge lamp when glowing, steadily, is

(SSC, CPWD 2011)

(a) pink   (b) yellow

(c) bluish green   (d) blue

108. The inner surface of a fluorescent tube is coated with a fluorescent material which

(SSC, CPWD 2011)

(a) absorbs ultraviolet rays and radiates visible rays

(b) reduces glare

(c) improves life

(d) absorbs infra-red rays and radiates visible rays

109. A transistor has a current gain of 0.99 in common base mode. Its current gain in common emitter mode is   **(SSC, CPWD 2011)**

(a) 0.99   (b) 99

(c) 10.1   (d) 100

110. In arc welding, once the arc is struck, the voltage required to maintain it will be

(SSC, CPWD 2011)

(a) (20 – 30) V   (b) (100 – 120) V

(c) (200 – 220) V   (d) (500 – 1000) V

111. The emf induced per phase in a three-phase star connected synchronous generator having the following data :   **(SSC, CPWD 2012)**

Distribution factor = 0.955;

Coil – span factor = 0.966 ;

Frequency = 50 Hz;

Flux per pole = 25 mwb ;

Turns per phase = 240, emf per phase is

(a) 2128.36 Volts   (b) 1228.81 Volts

(c) 869.46 Volts   (d) 1737.80 Volts

112. A resistance and another circuit element are connected in series across a dc voltage V. The voltage and zero after time. The other element is pure

(SSC, CPWD 2012)

(a) Capacitance   (b) Both (a) and (c)

(c) Resistance   (d) Inductance

113. For RLC ac series circuits at resonance the current is   **(SSC, CPWD 2012)**

(a) Minimum at leading p.f.

(b) Minimum at lagging p.f.

(c) Maximum at unity p.f.

(d) Maximum at leading p.f.

114. A series R-L-C circuit resonates at 1 MHz. At frequency 1.1 MHz the circuit impedance will be

(SSC, CPWD 2012)

(a) Resistive

(b) Will depend on the relative amplitude of R, L and C.

(c) Capacitive

(d) Inductive

115. The equivalent resistance between terminals X and Y of the network shown is   **(SSC, CPWD 2012)**

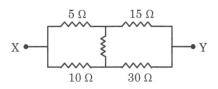

(a) 8 Ω   (b) $\dfrac{100}{3}\Omega$

(c) $\dfrac{40}{3}\Omega$ (d) $\dfrac{20}{9}\Omega$

116. Application of Thevenin's Theorem in a circuit result in   **(SSC, CPWD 2012)**

(a) An ideal voltage source

(b) An ideal current source

(c) A current source and an impedance in parallel.

(d) A voltage source and an impedance in series.

117. A current of i = 6 + 10 sin (100 πt) + 20 sin (200 πt) is flowing through a series combination of a PMMC and moving iron instrument. Ratio of the two currents as registered by the m.i. and PMMC meter is **(SSC, CPWD 2012)**
(a) 1.81
(b) 3.11
(c) 2.82
(d) 2.63

118. Three resistance 5 Ω each are connected in star. Values of equivalent delta resistances are
(SSC, CPWD 2012)
(a) 1.5 Ω each
(b) 2.5 Ω each
(c) 5/3 Ω each
(d) 15 Ω each

119. A 120 V, 60 W incandescent lamp has to be operated from 220 V, 50 c/s, 1 phase ac supply. In order to do, this a circuit element has to be connected in series with the lamp. Which one of the following series element is preferable ?
(a) Pure capacitance **(SSC, CPWD 2012)**
(b) Pure inductance or capacitance
(c) Resistance
(d) Pure inductance

120. The bandwidth of an ac series circit consisting of R, L and C is **(SSC, CPWD 2012)**
(a) $\dfrac{L}{R}$
(b) $\dfrac{R}{L}$
(c) $\dfrac{L}{RC}$
(d) $\dfrac{RC}{L}$

121. For balanced 3-phase supply system, the phasor sum of the line currents is NOT zero if the load is **(SSC, CPWD 2012)**
(a) Balanced delta connected
(b) Unbalanced delta connected
(c) Balanced star connected
(d) Unbalanced star connected

122. At series resonance of an ac R-L-C circuit the impressed voltage is **(SSC, CPWD 2012)**
(a) Equal to the resistive drop
(b) Equal to the capacity drop
(c) Greater than the resistive drop
(d) Equal to the inductive drop

123. In a series RLC circuit R = 20 Ω X_L = 30 Ω and X_C = 30 Ω. If the supply voltage across the combination is v = 100 sin (100 πt + 30°) Volts, the instantaneous current and the power factor of the circuit are respectively **(SSC, CPWD 2012)**
(a) I = 3.536 sin (100 πt + 30°) Amps, p.f. = 0.866
(b) I = 5 sin (100 πt + 30°) Amps, p.f. = unity
(c) I = 3.536 sin (100 πt + 30°) Amps, p.f. = unity
(d) I = 5 sin (100 πt + 30°) Amps, p.f. = 0.866

124. The rms value of the alternating current given by the equation **(SSC, CPWD 2012)**
i = 50 sin (314 t − 10°) + 30 sin (314 t − 20°)
(a) 41.23 A
(b) 58.31 A
(c) 38.73 A
(d) 77.43 A

125. A series R-L-C circuit will have unity power factor if operated at a frequency of **(SSC, CPWD 2012)**
(a) $1/(2\pi\sqrt{LC})$
(b) LC
(c) 1/(LC)
(d) $1/\sqrt{(LC)}$

126. In a balanced 3-phase system, the current coil of a wattmeter is inserted in line 1 and the potential coil across 2 and 3. If the wattmeter reads 100 W, the reactive power drawn by the 3-phase load is
(SSC, CPWD 2012)
(a) 173.2 VAR
(b) 50 VAR
(c) 100 VAR
(d) 141.4 VAR

127. An electric iron is rated at 230 V, 400 W, 50 Hz. The voltage rating 230 V refers to
(SSC, CPWD 2012)
(a) Rms value
(b) Peak-to-peak value
(c) Average value
(d) Peak value

128. A non-sinsusoidal periodic waveform is free from DC component, cosine components and even harmonics. The waveform has
(SSC, CPWD 2012)
(a) Half wave and odd function symmetry.
(b) Half wave and even function symmetry.
(c) Only odd function symmetry
(d) Only half wave symmetry

129. A periodic train of rectangular pulses x(t) with a time period of 25 seconds, has a pulse width of 9 second as shown in Figure. The RMS value of the waveform is **(SSC, CPWD 2012)**

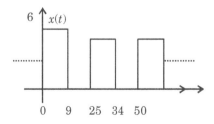

(a) 10 V
(b) $\sqrt{6}$V
(c) 3.6 V
(d) 2.16 V

130. The time constant of the network shown in the figure is **(SSC, CPWD 2012)**

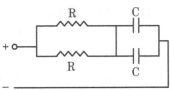

(a) CR/4
(b) CR/2

(c) CR
(d) 2 CR

131. In the series RC circuit, the voltage across C stars increasing, the moment the circuit is switched to V Volts dc. The rate of increase of voltage across C at the instant just after the switch is closed (i.e. at $t = 0^+$) is **(SSC, CPWD 2012)**

(a) RV/C
(b) CV/R

(c) V/RC
(d) R/CV

132. The phase difference between the following voltage and current waves, **(SSC, CPWD 2012)**

$v = 311 \sin (100 \pi t + 30°)$ Volts

$i = 17 \sin (100 \pi t - 20°)$ Amps

(a) 20°
(b) 50°

(c) 10°
(d) 30°

133. A 10 µF and a 20 µF capacitor are in series. The combination is supplied at 150 V from a sinusoidal voltage source. The voltage across the 20 µF capacitor is then. **(SSC, CPWD 2012)**

(a) 75 V
(b) 125 V

(c) 100 V
(d) 50 V

134. The conditions at which the following potential divider is independent of frequency, may be **(SSC, CPWD 2012)**

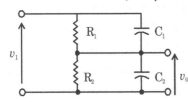

(i) $\dfrac{R_1}{R_2} = \dfrac{C_1}{C_2}$

(ii) $\dfrac{R_1}{R_2} = \dfrac{C_2}{C_1}$

(iii) $R_1 C_1 \ll 1, R_2 C_2 \ll 1$

(iv) $R_1 + R_2 + \dfrac{1}{C_1} + \dfrac{1}{C_2}$

(a) (ii) and (iv) are true

(b) (i) and (iii) are true

(c) (i) is true only

(d) (ii) is true only

135. A 20 micro farad capacitor is connected across an ideal voltage source. The current in the capacitor **(SSC, CPWD 2012)**

(a) Will be very high at first, then exponentially decay and at steady state will become zero.

(b) None of these are true.

(c) Will be zero at first, then exponentially rise

(d) Will be very high at first, then exponentially decay

136. Magnetic blowout coils are generally used in **(SSC, CPWD 2012)**

(a) Vacuum circuit breaker

(b) Air break circuit breaker

(c) Air blast circuit breaker

(d) Oil circuit breaker

137. A load is connected to supply. A current transformer (CT) and a potential transformer (PT) is used in between load and supply. A power factor of 0.5 is measured at the secondary side of CT and PT. **(SSC, CPWD 2012)**

If phase angle error of CT and PT are 0.4° and 0.7°, power factor of the load is

(a) Cos 60.3°
(b) Cos 58.9°

(c) Cos 59.7°
(d) Cos 61.1°

138. Three lamps are in circuit as shown in Figure. At what condition 100 W lamp will have the maximum brightness ? **(SSC, CPWD 2012)**

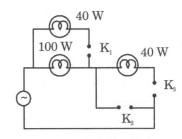

(a) K_1 is closed, K_2 is open and K_3 is also open

(b) Both (c) and (d)

(c) Key K_1 is closed, K_2 is open and K_3 is closed

(d) Key K_1 is open, K_2 is closed and K_3 is open

139. If the length of a bar of magnetic material is increased by 20% and the cross-sectional area is decreased by 20%, then the reluctance is **(SSC, CPWD 2012)**

(a) Increased by 50%

(b) Remaining same

(c) Decreased by 33%

(d) Increased by 67%

140. Two coupled inductors $L_1 = 0.2$ H and $L_2 = 0.8$ H, have coefficient of coupling K = 0.8. The mutual inductance M is **(SSC, CPWD 2012)**

(a) 0.16 H   (b) 0.02 H

(c) 0.32 H   (d) 0.24 H

141. Two inductors have self inductances of 9 mH and 25 mH. The mutual inductance between the two is 12 mH. The coefficient of inductive coupling between the two inductors is
(SSC, CPWD 2012)

(a) 18.75   (b) 0.25

(c) 0.8   (d) 1.25

142. When a multiplier is added to an existing voltmeter for extending its range, its electromagnetic damping **(SSC, CPWD 2013)**

(a) remains unaffected

(b) increases

(c) decreases

(d) changes by an amount depending on the controlling torque

143. Phasor diagram of load voltage (V), current in pressure coil (I_P) and current in current coil (I_C) is shown in the figure when an electrodynamic wattmeter is used to measure power. The reading of the wattmeter will be proportinal to

(SSC, CPWD 2013)

(a) $\cos(\beta + \psi)$

(b) $\cos \psi$

(c) $\cos \beta \cos \psi$

(d) $\cos \beta \cos(\beta + \psi)$

144. A balanced 3-phase, 3-wire supply feeds balanced star connected resistors. If one of the resistors is disconnected, then the percentage reduction in load will be **(SSC, CPWD 2013)**

(a) 33.33   (b) 50

(c) 66.67   (d) 75

145. The switching transistor as shown, carries in the collector side an rms current of 8 mA. If the frequency of rectangular pulse train v_i is 50 Hz, then on-time of the transistor is

(SSC, CPWD 2013)

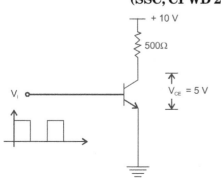

(a) 20 ms   (b) 6.4 ms

(c) 12.8 ms   (d) 16 ms

146. An ammeter of resistance R_m is placed in an arrangement as shown in the figure. Material of R_m, R_{sh} is copper whereas that of R_s, R_x is manganin. The condition for which the meter performance is compensated against temperature, is **(SSC, CPWD 2013)**

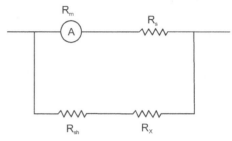

(a) $\dfrac{1}{R_m} + \dfrac{1}{R_{sh}} = \dfrac{1}{R_s} + \dfrac{1}{R_x}$

(b) $R_m R_s = R_{sh} R_x$

(c) $R_m + R_s = R_{sh} + R_x$

(d) $\dfrac{R_m}{R_s} = \dfrac{R_{sh}}{R_x}$

147. If a 110 V, 50 Hz is applied across a PMMC voltmeter of full-scale range 0 – 220 V and internal resistance of 10 kΩ, reading of the voltmeter will be **(SSC, CPWD 2013)**

(a) 0 V   (b) $110\sqrt{2}$ V

(c) 78 V   (d) 55 V

148. To maximize the driving torque in an induction type instrument, flux produced by shunt coil and series coil should be **(SSC, CPWD 2013)**

(a) in phase with each other

(b) in quadrature with each other

(c) displaced by 45° with respect to each other

(d) out of phase with respect to each other

149. To minimize the errors due to lead and contact resistances, low resistances used in electrical measurement work are provided with

(SSC, CPWD 2013)

(a) guard rings   (b) four terminals

(c) thick insulation   (d) metal shields

150. The small pockets of air in the high voltage cable provide _____ relative permittivity, _____ electric field and at these sites breakdown is likely to be initiated. **(SSC, CPWD 2013)**

(a) high, high   (b) low, low

(c) low, high   (d) high, low

151. The capacitance measured between any two cores of a 3-core cable with the sheath earthed is 3 μF. The capacitance per phase will be

(SSC, CPWD 2013)

(a) 1.5 μF

(b) 6 μF

(c) 1 μF

(d) None of the above

152. In an insulated cable having core diameter d and overall diameter D, the ratio of maximum to minimum dielectric stress is given by

(SSC, CPWD 2013)

(a) $(D/d)^{1/2}$ (b) $(D/d)^2$

(c) D/d   (d) d/D

153. Compared to the breaking capacity of a circuit breaker, its making capacity should be

(SSC, CPWD 2013)

(a) more

(b) less

(c) equal

(d) the two are unrelated to each other

154. In electronic circuits, for blocking the DC component of a voltage signal, a/an _____ is connected is series with the voltage source.

(SSC, CPWD 2013)

(a) capacitor   (b) diode

(c) resistor   (d) inductor

155. Resistance switching is normally employed in

(SSC, CPWD 2013)

(a) bulk oil breakers

(b) minimum oil breakers

(c) air blast circuit breakers

(d) all of A, B and C

156. In a balanced 3-phase circuit, the line current is 12 A. When the power is measured by two wattmeter method, one meter reads 11 kW while the other reads zero. Power factor of the load is

(SSC, CPWD 2013)

(a) 0   (b) 0.5

(c) 0.866   (d) 1.0

157. In case of frosted GLS lamps, frosting is done by

(SSC, CPWD 2013)

(a) acid etching

(b) ammonia

(c) ozone

(d) salt water

158. In a motor starter, the electromechanical contactor provides inherent protection against

(SSC, CPWD 2013)

(a) over-current   (b) short-circuit

(c) single-phasing   (d) under-voltage

159. Two lossy capacitors with equal capacitance values and power factors of 0.01 and 0.02 are in parallel, and the combination is supplied from a sinusoidal voltage source. The power factor of the combination is **(SSC, CPWD 2013)**

(a) 0.03   (b) 0.015

(c) 0.01   (d) 0.0002

160. A voltmeter when connected across a dc supply, reads 124 V. When a series combination of the voltmeter and an unknown resistance X is connected across the supply, the meter reads 4 V. If the resistance of the voltmeter is 50 kΩ, the value of X is **(SSC, CPWD 2013)**

(a) 1550 kΩ   (b) 1600 kΩ

(c) 1.6 kΩ   (d) 1.5 MΩ

161. The purpose of providing a choke in the tube-light is **(SSC, CPWD 2013)**

(a) to eliminate the corona effects

(b) to avoid radio interference

(c) to improve power factor

(d) to limit current to appropriate value

162. In a 3-phase 400 V, 4-wire system, two incandescent lamps, one having 230 V, 100 W specification and the other 230 V, 200 W are connected between R phase-neutral and Y phase-neutral respectively. If the neutral wire breaks

(SSC, CPWD 2013)

(a) 100 W lamp will fuse first

(b) 200 W lamp will fuse first

(c) Both the lamps will fuse together

(d) Both the lamps will glow

163. A lamp having mean spherical candle power of 800 is suspended at a height of 10 m. Calculate the illumination just below the lamp.

(SSC, CPWD 2014)

(a) 8000 lux   (b) 8 lux

(c) 80 lux   (d) 800 lux

164. Two wires A and B have the same cross-section and are made of the same material. R_A = 800 Ω and R_B = 100 Ω. The number of times A is longer than B is : **(SSC, CPWD 2014)**

(a) 5   (b) 6

(c) 2   (d) 4

165. In the circuit shown in figure, find the transient current $i(t)$ when the switch is closed at $t = 0$. Assume zero initial condition.

(SSC, CPWD 2014)

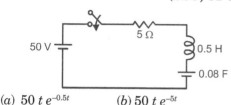

(a) $50\,t\,e^{-0.5t}$ (b) $50\,t\,e^{-5t}$

(c) $100\,t\,e^{-5t}$ (d) $100\,t\,e^{-0.5t}$

166. Speed of the megger is kept at:

(SSC, CPWD 2014)

(a) 160 rpm   (b) 100 rpm

(c) 120 rpm   (d) 140 rpm

167. Two 100 W, 200 V lamps are connected in series across a 200 V supply. The total power consumed by each lamp will be watts : **(SSC, CPWD 2014)**

(a) 200   (b) 25

(c) 50   (d) 100

168. The active and reactive powers of an inductive circuit are 60 W and 80 VAR respectively. The power factor of the circuit is :

(SSC, CPWD 2014)

(a) 0.8 lag   (b) 0.5 lag

(c) 0.6 lag   (d) 0.75 lag

169. For which of the following the excitation control method is satisfactory ?   **(SSC, CPWD 2014)**

(a) Long lines

(b) Low voltage lines

(c) High voltage lines

(d) Short lines

170. The type of protection that does not respond to faults occurring beyond its zone even though the fault current may pass thro' the zone is :

(SSC, CPWD 2014)

(a) Back-up protection

(b) Busbar protection

(c) Unit protection

(d) Generator protection

171. In a $3\dfrac{1}{2}$ digit voltmeter, the largest number that can be read is :   **(SSC, CPWD 2014)**

(a) 9999   (b) 0999

(c) 1999   (d) 5999

172. After closing the switch 's' at $t = 0$, the current $i(t)$ at any instant 't' in the network shown in the figure :   **(SSC, CPWD 2014)**

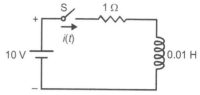

(a) $10 - 10\,e^{-100t}$ (b) $10 + 10\,e^{100t}$

(c) $10 - 10\,e^{100t}$ (d) $10 + 10\,e^{-100t}$

173. The voltage across $5 - H$ inductor is

$$V(t) = \begin{cases} 30t^2, & t > 0 \\ 0, & t < 0 \end{cases}$$

Find the energy stored at $t = 5\ s$.

(SSC, CPWD 2014)

Assume zero initial current.

(a) 312.5 kJ

(b) 0.625 kJ

(c) 3.125 kJ

(d) 156.25 kJ

174. An isolator is used in series with Air blast Circuit Breaker employed at UHV lines because :

(SSC, CPWD 2014)

(a) CB life is enhanced with the use of isolator

(b) current to be interrupted will be large

(c) gap between CB contacts is small so an isolator is used to switch off voltage

(d) gap between CB poles is small

175. Which one of the following bridges is generally used for measurement of frequency and also capacitance ?   **(SSC, CPWD 2014)**

(a) Wien bridge

(b) Hay's bridge

(c) Owen's bridge

(d) Schering bridge

176. Two voltmeters of $(0 - 300\ V)$ range are connected in parallel to a A.C. circuit One voltmeter is moving iron type reads 200 V. If the other is PMMC instrument, its reading will be :

(SSC, CPWD 2014)

(a) 127.4V

(b) slightly less 200 V

(c) zero

(d) 222 V

177. The least number of 1-φ wattmeters required to measure total power consumed by an unbalanced load fed from a 3φ, 4 wire system is :

(SSC, CPWD 2014)

(a) 4   (b) 1

(c) 2   (d) 3

178. If resistance is 20 Ω and inductance is 2 H in a RL series circuit, then time constant of this circuit will be :   **(SSC, CPWD 2014)**

(a) 100 s   (b) 0.001s

(c) 0.1 s   (d) 10 s

179. Transient current in RLC circuit is oscillatory when the value of R is :   **(SSC, CPWD 2014)**

(a) more than $2\sqrt{\dfrac{C}{L}}$

(b) less than $2\sqrt{\dfrac{L}{C}}$

(c) less than $2\sqrt{\dfrac{C}{L}}$

(d) more than $2\sqrt{\dfrac{L}{C}}$

180. For average values of load current, current chopping occurs more frequently in :

(SSC, CPWD 2014)

(a) VCB's   (b) OCB's

(c) ACB's   (d) SF$_6$CB's

181. Determine the voltage at point C shown below with respect to ground :   **(SSC, CPWD 2014)**

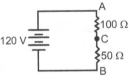

(a) 80 V   (b) 120 V

(c) 40 V   (d) 70 V

182. Which semiconductor device behaves like two SCR's ?   **(SSC, CPWD 2014)**

(a) Triac   (b) MOSFET

(c) JFET   (d) UJT

183. Moving coil (PMMC) and moving iron instruments can be distinguished by observing its :

(SSC, CPWD 2014)

(a) size of terminals

(b) pointer

(c) range

(d) scale

184. In a fluorescent tube circuit, the function of choke is primarily to :   **(SSC, CPWD 2014)**

(a) improve the brightness of the tube

(b) initiate the discharge

(c) reduce the flicker

(d) reduce the starting current

185. The magnetic field energy in an inductor changes from maximum value to minimum value in 5 m sec when connected to an a.c. source. The frequency of the source is : **(SSC, CPWD 2014)**

(a) 500 Hz   (b) 20 Hz

(c) 50 Hz   (d) 200 Hz

186. Two electric bulbs have tungsten filament of same thickness. If one of them gives 60 W and the other gives 100 W, then :   **(SSC, CPWD 2014)**

(a) 60 W and 100 W lamp filaments have equal length

(b) 60 W lamp filament has shorter length

(c) 100 W lamp filament has longer length

(d) 60 W lamp filament has longer length

187. A capacitor with no initial charge at $t = \infty$ acts :

(SSC, CPWD 2014)

(a) Open-Circuit   (b) Voltage Source

(c) Current Source (d) Short-Circuits

188. "Danger 440 V" plates are   **(SSC, CPWD 2014)**

(a) informal notices

(b) danger notices

(c) caution notices

(d) advisory notices

189. The purpose of choke in a fluorescent tube is to :

(SSC, CPWD 2014)

(a) increase voltage momentarily

(b) decrease current

(c) increase current

(d) decrease voltage momentarily

190. As per IE rules the permissible variation of voltage at the consumer end is :

(SSC, CPWD 2014)

(a) ± 6%   (b) ± 10%

(c) ± 12%   (d) ± 2%

191. What is the order of minimum displacement that can be measured with capacitive transducers ?

(SSC, CPWD 2014)

(a) 1×10^{-12} m   (b) 1 cm

(c) 1mm   (d) 1 μm

192. A piece of oil soaked paper has been inserted between the plates of a parallel plate capacitor. Then the potential difference between the plates will   **(SSC CPWD 2014)**

(a) increase   (b) decrease

(c) remain unaltered   (d) become zero

193. The current drawn by a tungsten filament lamp is measured by an ammeter. The ammeter reading under steady state condition will be——— the ammeter reading when the supply is switched on.   **(SSC CPWD 2014)**

(a) same as   (b) less than

(c) greater than   (d) double

194. Power consumed in the given circuit is

(SSC CPWD 2014)

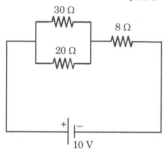

(a) 100 watts   (b) 5 watts

(c) 20 watts   (d) 40 watts

195. A 200 W, 200 V bulb and a 100 W, 200 V bulb are connected in series and the voltage of 400 V is applied across the series connected bulbs, Under this condition   **(SSC CPWD 2014)**

(a) 100 W bulb will be brighter than 200 W bulb

(b) 200 W bulb will be brighter than 100 W bulb

(c) Both the bulbsz will have equal brightness

(d) Both the bulbs will be darker than when they are connected across rated voltage

196. In the network shown, if one of the 4Ω resistances is disconnected, when the circuit is active, the current flowing now will   **(SSC CPWD 2014)**

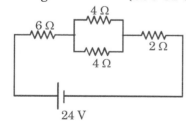

(a) increase very much

(b) decrease

(c) be zero

(d) increase very slightly

197. In the network shown in the figure, the value of R_L such that maximum possible power will be transferred to R_L is   **(SSC CPWD 2014)**

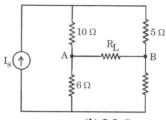

(a) 5.76 Ω   (b) 6.0 Ω

(c) 10.0 Ω   (d) 15.0 Ω

198. A current of 5 mA flows in a resistanceless choke from a 200 V alternating source. The energy consumed in the choke is   **(SSC CPWD 2014)**

(a) 0 J   (b) 4.4 J

(c) 500 J   (d) 1000 J

199. A series circuit has R = 4 Ω, X_L = 12 Ω and X_C = 9 Ω and is supplied with 200 V, 50 Hz Calculate the power.   **(SSC CPWD 2014)**

(a) 6400 W   (b) 8000 W

(c) 14,400 W   (d) 19,200 W

200. The reactance of 1 farad capacitance when connected to a DC circuit is **(SSC CPWD 2014)**

(a) infinite   (b) 1 Ω

(c) 0.5 Ω   (d) zero ohms

201. The AC bridge used for measurement of dielectric loss of capacitor is   **(SSC CPWD 2014)**

(a) Anderson bridge   (b) Schering bridge

(c) Wien bridge   (d) Hay's bridge

202. A moving coil instrument has a resistance of 10 Ω and gives full scale deflection at 0.5 V potential difference across it. How can it be adapted to measure a current upto 100 A ?

(a) By connecting shunt resistance of 0.005 Ω across the meter

(b) By connecting shunt resistance of 0.05 Ω across the meter

(c) By connecting shunt resistance of 5 Ω across the meter

(d) By connecting shunt resistance of 10 Ω across the meter   **(SSC CPWD 2014)**

203. The multiplying power of the shunt of a milliammeter is 8. If the circuit current is 200 mA, then current through the meter is

(SSC CPWD 2014)

(a) 25 mA   (b) 200 mA

(c) 1600 mA   (d) 3200 mA

204. The leakage resistance of a 50 km long cable is 1 MΩ. For a 100 km long cable it will be
(SSC CPWD 2014)

(a) 0.5 MΩ   (b) 2 MΩ

(c) 0.66 MΩ   (d) None of these

205. If voltage is increased by 'n' times, the size of the conductor would

(a) increase by 'n' times

(b) reduce by '1/n' times

(c) increase by 'n^2' times

(d) reduce by '$1/n^2$' times   **(SSC CPWD 2014)**

206. Supplier's fuse, which is provided in domestic wiring system is

(a) after the energy meter

(b) before the energy meter

(c) before distribution board

(d) after main switch   **(SSC CPWD 2014)**

207. As per recommendation of ISI, the maximum number of points of lights, fans and socket outlets that can be connected in one sub-circuit is

(a) 8   **(SSC CPWD 2014)**

(b) 10

(c) 15

(d) 20

208. In a 3-pin plug   **(SSC CPWD 2014)**

(a) all the three pins are of the same size

(b) two pins are of the same size but third one is thicker

(c) two pins are of the same size but third one is thicker and longer

(d) all the three pins are of different sizes

209. The acceptable value of grounding resistance to domestic application is   **(SSC CPWD 2014)**

(a) 0.1 Ω   (b) 1 Ω

(c) 10 Ω   (d) 100 Ω

210. Inside the earth pit, the earthing electrode should be placed   **(SSC CPWD 2014)**

(a) vertical

(b) horizontal

(c) inclined at 45°

(d) inclined at any angle other than 45°

211. The colour of the light given out by a sodium vapour discharge lamp is   **(SSC CPWD 2014)**

(a) pink   (b) bluish green

(c) yellow   (d) blue

212. The technique of adding a precise amount time between the trigger point and beginning of the scope sweep in a CRO is known as

(a) Free running sweep

(b) Delayed sweep

(c) Triggered sweep

(d) Non-sawtooth sweep   **(SSC CPWD 2014)**

213. In a CRO, a sinusoidal waveform of a certain frequency is displayed. The value of the quantity that can be made out by observation is
(SSC CPWD 2014)

(a) RMS value of the sine wave

(b) average value of the sine wave

(c) form factor of the sine wave

(d) peak-peak value of the sine wave

214. The internal resistance of a voltage source is 10 Ω and has 10 volts at its terminals. Find the maximum power that can be transferred to the load.   **(SSC CPWD 2015)**

(a) 25 W   (b) 5 W

(c) 0.25 W   (d) 2.5 W

215. A 150 V moving iron voltmeter of accuracy class 1.0 reads 75 V when used in a circuit under standard conditions. The maximum possible percentage error in the reading is:
(SSC CPWD 2015)

(a) 2.0   (b) 0.5

(c) 4.0   (d) 1.0

216. The magnitude of AT required to establish a given value of flux in the air gap will be much greater than that required for Iron part of a magnetic circuit, because: **(SSC CPWD 2015)**

(a) air is a gas

(b) air is a good conductor of magnetic flux

(c) air has the lowest relative permeability

(d) iron has the lowest permeability

217. The unit of luminous flux is **(SSC CPWD 2015)**

(a) candela   (b) lumen

(c) lux   (d) steradian

218. For painful shock, what is the range of electric shock current at 50 Hz?

(a) 0 - 1 mA   (b) 3 - 5 mA

(c) 0 - 3 mA   (d) 5 - 10 mA

219. What is the power consumed by the resistor of 20 Ω connected across 100 V source?

(a) 300 W   (b) 100 W

(c) 500 W   (d) 50 W

220. Two lamps, Green (G) and Red (R) are connected in a motor circuit as shown in the figure. The conditions under which the lamps will burn are? (Supply is available at terminals A & B)

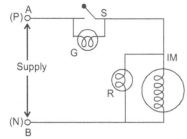

(a) Green lamp burns only when 'S' is open and red lamp burns only when "S" is closed.

(b) Green lamp will not burn always, red lamp burns only when switch 'S' is closed.

(c) Green and red lamp burns when switch 'S' is closed.

(d) Green lamp burns always, red lamp burns only when switch 'S' is closed. **(SSC CPWD 2015)**

221. There are 3 lamps 40 W, 100 W and 60 W. To realise the full rated power of the lamps they are to be connected in: **(SSC CPWD 2015)**

(a) Parallel only   (b) Series or parallel

(c) Series only   (d) Series-parallel

222. In a three phase system, the volt ampere rating is given by? **(SSC CPWD 2015)**

(a) $3 V_L I_L$ (b) $V_{ph} I_{ph}$

(c) $V_L I_L$ (d) $\sqrt{3} V_L I_L$

223. With the positive probe on an NPN base, an ohmmeter reading between the other transistor terminals should be? **(SSC CPWD 2015)**

(a) Infinite   (b) Open

(c) Low resistance   (d) High resistance

224. If a dynamometer type wattmeter is connected in an ac circuit, the power indicated by the wattmeter will be: **(SSC CPWD 2015)**

(a) Instantaneous power

(b) Peak power

(c) Volt ampere product

(d) Average power

225. A lissajous pattern on an oscilloscope has 5 horizontal tangencies and 2 vertical tangencies. The frequency of the horizontal input is 100 Hz. **(SSC CPWD 2015)**

The frequency of the vertical input will be:

(a) 400 Hz   (b) 2500 Hz

(c) 4000 Hz   (d) 5000 Hz

226. Three wattmeter method of power measurement can be used to measure power in

(a) None of the options

(b) Balanced Circuits

(c) Both balanced and unbalanced Circuits

(d) Unbalanced Circuits   **(SSC CPWD 2015)**

227. A short shunt compound generator supplies a loud current of 100 A at 250 V. The generator has the following winding resistances : shunt field = 130Ω, Armature = 0.1Ω and series field = 0. 1Ω. Find the Emf generated if the brush drop is IV per brush.   **(SSC CPWD 2015)**

(a) 272.2 volt   (b) 262.2 volt

(c) 272.0 volt   (d) 262.0 volt

228. Modern electronic multimeters measure resistance by?   **(SSC CPWD 2015)**

(a) Using a bridge circuit

(b) Using a electrical bridge circuit

(c) Forcing a constant current and measuring the voltage across the unknown resistance

(d) Using an electronic bridge compensator for melling

229. If span length is doubled with no change in other factors, the sag of the line will become?

(SSC CPWD 2015)

(a) 0.5 time   (b) 4 times

(c) 8 times   (d) 2 times

230. A 200 V lamp takes a current of 1 A, it produces a total flux of 2860 lumens. The efficiency of the lamp is?   **(SSC CPWD 2015)**

(a) 10.9 lumens/W   (b) 9.9 lumens/W

(c) 8.9 lumens/W   (d) 14.3 lumens/W

231. Leakage flux in a transformer occurs because:

(SSC CPWD 2015)

(a) applied voltage is sinusoidal

(b) air is not a good magnetic insulator

(c) transformer is not an efficient device

(d) iron core has high permeability

232. Each of the following statements regarding a shaded pole motor is true except

(SSC CPWD 2015)

(a) it has high starting torque

(b) its direction of rotation is from unshaded to shaded portion of poles.

(c) it has very poor power factor

(d) it has very poor efficiency

233. Which of the following fault is coming under symmetrical fault? **(SSC CPWD 2015)**
    (a) LLLG fault   (b) LG fault
    (c) LL fault   (d) LLG fault

234. The no load input power to a transformer is practically equal to ____ loss in the transformer.
    (a) Windage   (b) Eddy current
    (c) Copper   (d) Iron
                            (SSC CPWD 2015)

235. Which of the following braking is not suitable for motors? **(SSC CPWD 2015)**
    (a) Plugging   (b) Regenerative braking
    (c) Dynamic braking   (d) Friction braking

236. An arc blow is a welding defect that is countered with the help of carrying? **(SSC CPWD 2015)**
    (a) The resistance welding
    (b) The arc welding using DC supply
    (c) The thermit welding
    (d) The arc welding using AC supply

237. The per phase D.C. armature resistance of an alternator is 0.5 Ω. The effective a.c. armature resistance would be about? **(SSC CPWD 2015)**
    (a) 0.25 Ω   (b) 0.5 Ω
    (c) 1 Ω   (d) 0.75 Ω

238. One sine wave has a period of 2 ms, another has a period of 5 ms, and other has a period of 10 ms. Which sine wave is changing at a faster rate?
                            (SSC CPWD 2015)
    (a) all are at the same rate
    (b) sine wave with period 2 ms
    (c) sine wave with period of 10 msec
    (d) sine wave with period 5 ms

239. Humans are more vulnerable to electric shock current at? **(SSC CPWD 2015)**
    (a) 50 Hz   (b) 48 Hz
    (c) 45 Hz   (d) 40 Hz

240. An active element in a circuit is one which:
                            (SSC CPWD 2015)
    (a) dissipates energy
    (b) receives energy
    (c) both receives and supplies
    (d) supplies energy

241. The permissible voltage drop from supply terminal to any point on the wiring system should not exceed? **(SSC CPWD 2015)**
    (a) 2% + 1 volt   (b) 1% + 1 volt
    (c) 4% + 1 volt   (d) 3 % + 1 volt

242. If in an R-L-C series circuit, the frequency is below the resonant frequency, then **(SSC CPWD 2015)**
    (a) $X_C < X_L$ (b) $X_C > X_L$
    (c) $X_C = X_L$ (d) None of the options

243. If the power factor is high, then the consumer maximum KVA demand: **(SSC CPWD 2015)**
    (a) increases   (b) remains constant
    (c) becomes Zero   (d) decreases

244. A CRO Screen has ten divisions on the horizontal scale. If a voltage signal 5 sin (314t + 45º) is examined with a line base setting of 5 msec/div, the number of cycle of signal displayed on the screen will be? **(SSC CPWD 2015)**
    (a) 0.5 cycle   (b) 2.5 cycle
    (c) 5 cycles   (d) 10 cycles

245. During the resistance welding, the heat produced at the joint is proportional to?
    (a) Current   (b) Volt-Ampere
    (c) I^2R (d) Voltage
                            (SSC CPWD 2015)

246. An RLC series circuit has R = 10Ω, L = 2H. What value of capacitance will make the circuit critically damped? **(SSC CPWD 2015)**
    (a) 0.02 F   (b) 0.2 F
    (c) 0.4 F   (d) 0.08 F

247. The errors in Current, Transformers can be reduced by designing them with
    (a) All of the given options **(SSC CPWD 2015)**
    (b) using primary and secondary winding as close to each other as possible
    (c) high permeability and low loss core materials, avoiding any joints in the core and also keeping the flux density to a low value.
    (d) using large cross section for both primary and secondary winding conductors.

248. A primary cell has an emf of 1.5 V. When short circuited, it gives a current of 3 A. The internal resistance of cell is? **(SSC CPWD 2015)**
    (a) 0.5 Ω   (b) 0.2 Ω
    (c) 2 Ω   (d) 4.5 Ω

249. What is the maximum number of point of light, fan and socket-outlets that can be connected in one sub-circuit? **(SSC CPWD 2015)**
    (a) Four   (b) Twelve
    (c) Six   (d) Ten

250. A current of 2A passes through a coil of 350 kms wound on a ring of mean diameter 12 cm. The flux density established in the ring is 1-4 wb/m². Find the value of relative permeability of Iron.
                            (SSC CPWD 2015)
    (a) 191   (b) 1200
    (c) 600   (d) 210×10^3

251. Electrical Resistivity ρ is: **(SSC CPWD 2015)**
 (a) High for copper as well as for alloy
 (b) Low for copper and high for alloy
 (c) High for copper and low for alloy
 (d) Low for copper as well as for alloy

252. Silicon has a preference in IC technology because?
 (a) it is an indirect semiconductor
 (b) it is an elemental semiconductor
 (c) it is a covalent semiconductor
 (d) of the availability of nature oxide SiO
 (SSC CPWD 2015)

253. In dc operation of flouroscent tube, the life of the tube
 (a) Ramain same
 (b) Decreases by about 80% as that with ac operation
 (c) May increase or decrease
 (d) Increases by about 80% as that with ac operation **(SSC CPWD 2015)**

254. Which instrument is used to measure the high resistance?
 (a) Kelvin's Double bridge
 (b) Meggar
 (c) Carey-Foster bridge
 (d) Wheat stone bridge **(SSC CPWD 2015)**

255. A resistor is connected across a 50 V source. The current in the resistor if the colour code is red, orange, orange, silver is? **(SSC CPWD 2015)**
 (a) 21.4 mA   (b) 2 mA
 (c) 2.2 mA   (d) 214 mA

256. The electric driver posses the following drawback:
 (a) requires a continuous power supply
 (b) requires hazardous fuel requirement

 (c) not available with various rating
 (d) not adoptable to various environments
 (SSC CPWD 2015)

257. A circuit breaker is rated as follows: 1500 A, 33 KV, 3 sec, 3-phase oil circuit breaker. Determine the making current?
 (a) 35 KA   (b) 1.5 KA
 (c) 110 KA   (d) 89 KA
 (SSC CPWD 2015)

258. An electric heater draws 3.5 A from a 110 V source. The resistance of the heating element is approximately? **(SSC CPWD 2015)**
 (a) $31\ \Omega$ (b) $3.1\ \Omega$
 (c) $385\ \Omega$ (d) $38.5\ \Omega$

259. The acceptable value of grounding resistance for domestic applications is? **(SSC CPWD 2015)**
 (a) $2\ \Omega$ (b) $0.5\ \Omega$
 (c) $1.5\ \Omega$ (d) $1\ \Omega$

260. In a Parallel RLC circuit if the lower cut-off frequency is 2400 Hz and the upper cut off frequency is 2800 Hz, What is the band width?
 (a) 2800 Hz
 (b) 2400 Hz
 (c) 400 Hz
 (d) 5200 Hz **(SSC CPWD 2015)**

261. If 750 μA is flowing through 11 kΩ of resistance, what is the voltage drop across the resistor?
 (a) 14.6 V
 (b) 146 V
 (c) 82.5 V
 (d) 8.25 V **(SSC CPWD 2015)**

ANSWERS

EXERCISE – I

1. (b)	**2.** (b)	**3.** (a)	**4.** (c)	**5.** (b)	**6.** (c)	**7.** (b)	**8.** (d)	**9.** (a)	**10.** (d)
11. (c)	**12.** (b)	**13.** (b)	**14.** (d)	**15.** (a)	**16.** (d)	**17.** (b)	**18.** (b)	**19.** (d)	**20.** (d)
21. (b)	**22.** (c)	**23.** (c)	**24.** (c)	**25.** (c)	**26.** (b)	**27.** (d)	**28.** (a)	**29.** (d)	**30.** (c)
31. (a)	**32.** (c)	**33.** (a)	**34.** (c)	**35.** (d)	**36.** (d)	**37.** (c)	**38.** (a)	**39.** (d)	**40.** (c)
41. (d)	**42.** (d)	**43.** (b)	**44.** (a)	**45.** (b)	**46.** (d)	**47.** (a)	**48.** (b)	**49.** (a)	**50.** (c)
51. (a)	**52.** (a)	**53.** (c)	**54.** (c)	**55.** (d)	**56.** (a)	**57.** (a)	**58.** (c)	**59.** (a)	**60.** (c)
61. (d)	**62.** (b)	**63.** (c)	**64.** (b)	**65.** (a)	**66.** (b)	**67.** (a)	**68.** (b)	**69.** (d)	**70.** (b)
71. (b)	**72.** (c)	**73.** (a)	**74.** (b)	**75.** (c)	**76.** (a)	**77.** (a)	**78.** (a)	**79.** (d)	**80.** (a)
81. (d)	**82.** (d)	**83.** (c)	**84.** (c)	**85.** (a)	**86.** (c)	**87.** (c)	**88.** (d)	**89.** (c)	**90.** (a)
91. (b)	**92.** (a)	**93.** (b)	**94.** (b)	**95.** (c)	**96.** (a)	**97.** (d)	**98.** (c)	**99.** (a)	**100.** (c)
101. (b)	**102.** (a)	**103.** (b)	**104.** (c)	**105.** (c)	**106.** (a)	**107.** (c)	**108.** (a)	**109.** (a)	**110.** (b)

111.(a)	112.(a)	113.(c)	114.(a)	115.(a)	116.(d)	117.(c)	118.(d)	119.(b)	120.(d)
121.(c)	122.(d)	123.(b)	124.(a)	125.(c)	126.(c)	127.(b)	128.(c)	129.(b)	130.(a)
131.(a)	132.(d)	133.(b)	134.(c)	135.(a)	136.(a)	137.(c)	138.(c)	139.(b)	140.(d)
141.(c)	142.(a)	143.(d)	144.(a)	145.(b)	146.(d)	147.(d)	148.(b)	149.(c)	150.(b)
151.(d)	152.(b)	153.(d)	154.(a)	155.(c)	156.(a)	157.(a)	158.(a)	159.(a)	160.(b)
161.(c)	162.(d)	163.(d)	164.(c)	165.(b)	166.(a)	167.(c)	168.(b)	169.(d)	170.(a)
171.(a)	172.(a)	173.(c)	174.(b)	175.(c)	176.(a)	177.(b)	178.(d)	179.(d)	180.(b)
181.(c)	182.(c)	183.(a)	184.(b)	185.(d)	186.(d)	187.(d)	188.(b)	189.(c)	190.(d)
191.(a)	192.(b)	193.(b)	194.(d)	195.(c)	196.(c)	197.(c)	198.(c)	199.(a)	200.(b)
201.(d)	202.(d)	203.(c)	204.(c)	205.(b)	206.(a)	207.(c)	208.(d)	209.(b)	210.(c)
211.(d)	212.(a)	213.(d)	214.(c)	215.(a)	216.(a)	217.(c)	218.(d)	219.(d)	220.(d)
221.(a)	222.(c)	223.(a)	224.(b)	225.(d)	226.(c)	227.(c)	228.(d)	229.(a)	230.(a)
231.(d)	232.(d)	233.(c)	234.(d)	235.(b)	236.(c)	237.(b)	238.(d)	239.(c)	240.(b)
241.(b)	242.(c)	243.(d)	244.(a)	245.(c)	246.(b)	247.(d)	248.(a)	249.(d)	250.(c)
251.(d)	252.(a)	253.(a)	254.(c)	255.(a)	256.(d)	257.(c)	258.(b)	259.(d)	260.(a)
261.(d)	262.(a)	263.(b)	264.(c)	265.(b)	266.(d)	267.(c)	268.(c)		

EXERCISE – II

1.(a)	2.(d)	3.(b)	4.(d)	5.(d)	6.(d)	7.(b)	8.(a)	9.(a)	10.(b)
11.(c)	12.(b)	13.(c)	14.(d)	15.(b)	16.(b)	17.(c)	18.(c)	19.(d)	20.(a)
21.(c)	22.(b)	23.(b)	24.(a)	25.(c)	26.(a)	27.(d)	28.(c)	29.(c)	30.(c)
31.(d)	32.(b)	33.(b)	34.(a)	35.(d)	36.(d)	37.(a)	38.(a)	39.(c)	40.(b)
41.(a)	42.(a)	43.(b)	44.(b)	45.(c)	46.(b)	47.(a)	48.(c)	49.(d)	50.(d)
51.(b)	52.(d)	53.(a)	54.(a)	55.(c)	56.(a)	57.(b)	58.(a)	59.(b)	60.(b)
61.(a)	62.(a)	63.(c)	64.(a)	65.(c)	66.(b)	67.(d)	68.(a)	69.(d)	70.(d)
71.(a)	72.(d)	73.(b)	74.(b)	75.(d)	76.(d)	77.(b)	78.(a)	79.(d)	80.(d)
81.(a)	82.(b)	83.(a)	84.(c)	85.(b)	86.(d)	87.(b)	88.(c)	89.(b)	90.(b)
91.(a)	92.(a)	93.(a)	94.(c)	95.(c)	96.(c)	97.(c)	98.(a)	99.(b)	100.(b)
101.(c)	102.(a)	103.(d)	104.(d)	105.(b)	106.(a)	107.(b)	108.(a)	109.(b)	110.(a)
111.(b)	112.(d)	113.(c)	114.(b)	115.(c)	116.(d)	117.(c)	118.(d)	119.(a)	120.(b)
121.(d)	122.(a)	123.(b)	124.(a)	125.(a)	126.(a)	127.(a)	128.(a)	129.(c)	130.(c)
131.(c)	132.(b)	133.(d)	134.(d)	135.(a)	136.(b)	137.(d)	138.(d)	139.(a)	140.(c)
141.(c)	142.(c)	143.(c)	144.(b)	145.(c)	146.(d)	147.(a)	148.(b)	149.(b)	150.(c)
151.(b)	152.(c)	153.(a)	154.(a)	155.(c)	156.(b)	157.(b)	158.(d)	159.(b)	160.(d)
161.(d)	162.(a)	163.(b)	164.(b)	165.(c)	166.(a)	167.(b)	168.(c)	169.(d)	170.(c)
171.(c)	172.(a)	173.(d)	174.(c)	175.(a)	176.(c)	177.(d)	178.(c)	179.(b)	180.(a)
181.(c)	182.(a)	183.(d)	184.(b)	185.(c)	186.(d)	187.(a)	188.(c)	189.(a)	190.(a)
191.(d)	192.(b)	193.(b)	194.(b)	195.(a)	196.(b)	197.(b)	198.(a)	199.(a)	200.(a)
201.(b)	202.(a)	203.(a)	204.(a)	205.(d)	206.(a)	207.(b)	208.(c)	209.(b)	210.(a)
211.(c)	212.(b)	213.(d)	214.(d)	215.(b)	216.(c)	217.(b)	218.(b)	219.(c)	220.(a)
221.(a)	222.(d)	223.(c)	224.(d)	225.(*)	226.(c)	227.(b)	228.(c)	229.(d)	230.(d)
231.(b)	232.(a)	233.(a)	234.(d)	235.(d)	236.(b)	237.(d)	238.(b)	239.(d)	240.(d)
241.(d)	242.(b)	243.(d)	244.(b)	245.(c)	246.(d)	247.(c)	248.(a)	249.(b)	250.(c)
251.(c)	252.(d)	253.(b)	254.(b)	255.(b)	256.(a)	257.(*)	258.(a)	259.(d)	260.(c)
261.(d)									

■■

Control Systems

Servomechanism : It is a feedback control system in which the output is mechanical position, velocity or acceleration.

Open loop control system : In these output has no effect upon the control action.

Closed loop control system : In these output signal has direct effect upon the control action.

Mason's gain formula is $P = \dfrac{1}{\Delta} \displaystyle\sum_k P_k \Delta_k$

(a) If all the roots of the characteristic equation have negative real parts, the system is stable.

(b) If any root of the characteristic equation has a positive real parts or if there is a repeated root on the jω - axis, the system is unstable.

(c) If the condition (a) is satisfied except for the presence of one or more nonrepeated roots on the jω-axis, the system is marginally stable.

The positiveness of the co-efficients of the characteristic equation is necessary as well as sufficient condition for stability of the system of first and second order.

Routh and Hurwitz's criterion are equivalent of each other.

Root locus method : In this roots of the characteristic equation are plotted for all values of a system parameter.

For frequency response, there are three commonly used representations of sinusoidal transfer functions.

(a) Bode plot or logarithmic plot

(b) Polar plot

(c) Phase plot or log-magnitude plot

Relation between location of roots of the characteristic equation and open loop frequency response can be studied by Nyquist stability criterion.

The relation between constant M and N circles to log-magnitude and phase angle is called *Nicholas chart*.

EXERCISE – I

1. Effect of feedback on the plant is to
   (a) control system transient response
   (b) reduce the sensitivity to plant parameter variations
   (c) both (a) and (b)
   (d) none of these

2. In an open loop system
   (a) output control the input signal
   (b) output has no control over input signal
   (c) some other variables control the input signal
   (d) neither output nor any other variable has any effect on input

3. Electrical resistance is analogous to
   (a) intertia   (b) dampers
   (c) spring   (d) fluid capacity

4. Output of the feedback control system should be a function of
   (a) input   (b) reference and output
   (c) feedback signal   (d) none of these

5. Transient response in the system is basically due to
   (a) stored energy   (b) forces
   (c) friction   (d) coupling

6. Transfer function of a system is defined as the ratio of output to input in
   (a) Z-transform   (b) Fourier transform
   (c) Laplace transform (d) All of these

7. Transfer function of a system can be used to study its
   (a) steady state behaviour
   (b) transient behaviour
   (c) both (a) and (b)
   (d) none of these

8. Automatic control system in which output is a variable is called
   (a) closed loop system
   (b) servomechanism
   (c) automatic regulating system
   (d) process control system

9. With feedback system sensitivity to parameter
   (a) decreases   (b) increases
   (c) becomes zero   (d) becomes infinite

10. With feedback system, tranient response
    (a) decays constantly (b) decays slowly
    (c) decays quickly   (d) rises fast

11. In control system non-linearity caused by gear trains is
    (a) Backlash   (b) Dead space
    (c) Coulomb friction   (d) Saturation

12. Time sharing of an expansive control system can be achieved by using a/an
    (a) a.c. control system
    (b) analog control system
    (c) sampled data control system
    (d) none of these

13. Laplace transform is not applicable to non-linear system because
    (a) non-linear systems are time varying
    (b) time domain analysis is easier than frequency domain analysis
    (c) initial conditions are not zero in non linear systems
    (d) superposition law is not applicable to non-linear system

14. Linear differential transformer is an
    (a) electromechanical device
    (b) electric device
    (c) electromagnetic device
    (d) electrostatic device

15. Which of the following is not a desirable feature of a modern control system ?
    (a) no oscillation
    (b) accuracy
    (c) quick response
    (d) correct power level

16. Device used for conversion of coordinates is
    (a) Syschros
    (b) Microsyn
    (c) Synchro resolver
    (d) Synchro transformer

17. Most common use of the synchros is as
    (a) error detector
    (b) transmission of angular data
    (c) transmission of arithmetic data
    (d) for synchronisation

18. In a closed loop system, source power is modulated with
    (a) error signal
    (b) reference signal
    (c) actuating signal
    (d) feed back signal

19. Non-linearity in the servo system due to saturation is caused by
    (a) servo motor   (b) gear trains
    (c) relays   (d) none of these

20. Microsyn is the name given to
    (a) potentiometer
    (b) magnetic amplifier
    (c) resolver
    (d) rotary differential transformer

21. Differential is used in synchro differential unit for generators only
    (a) indicating difference of rotation angle of two synchro generators only
    (b) indicating sum of rotation angle of the synchor genes rators only
    (c) both (a) and (b)
    (d) none of these

22. Value of $i(0^+)$ for the system whose transfer function is given by the equation
    $$I(s) = \frac{2s+3}{(s+1)(s+3)} \text{ is}$$
    (a) 0   (b) 1
    (c) 2   (d) 3

23. If transfer function of the system is $\frac{1}{TS+1}$, then steady state error to the unit step input is
    (a) 1   (b) zero
    (c) T   (d) infinite

24. Power amplification in a magnetic amplifier can be increased
    (a) by negative feed back
    (b) by positive feed back
    (c) with higher inductane of a.c. coil
    (d) none of these

25. Friction coefficient is usually kept low to
    (a) minimize velocity-lag error
    (b) maximize velocity-lag error
    (c) minimize time constant
    (d) maximize speed of response

26. If for second order system damping factor is less than one, then system response will be
   (a) Under damped   (b) Over damped
   (c) Critically damped (d) None of these

27. In the derivative error compensation
   (a) damping decreases and settling time increases
   (b) damping increases and settling time increases
   (c) damping decreases and settling time decreases
   (d) damping increases and settling time decreases

28. Second-derivative input signal adjust
   (a) time constant of the system
   (b) time constant and supress the oscillations
   (c) damping of the system
   (d) gain of the system

29. For unity damping factor, the system will be
   (a) under damped   (b) critically damped
   (c) over damped   (d) oscillatory

30. System generally preferred is
   (a) under damped   (b) critically damped
   (c) over damped   (d) oscillatory

31. For second order linear system, settling time is
   (a) $\dfrac{1}{4}$ of the time constant
   (b) $\dfrac{1}{2}$ of the time constant
   (c) 4 times the time constant
   (d) 2 times the time constant

32. For a desirable transient response of a second order system damping ratio must be between
   (a) 0.4 and 0.8   (b) 0.8 and 1.0
   (c) 1.0 and 1.2   (d) 1.2 and 1.4

33. If overshoot is excessive, then damping ratio is
   (a) equal to 0.4
   (b) less than 0.4
   (c) more than 0.4
   (d) infinity

34. Physical meaning of zero initial condition is that the
   (a) system is at rest and stores no energy
   (b) system is at rest but stores energy
   (c) reference input to working system is zero
   (d) system is working but stores no energy

35. A low value of friction coefficient
   (a) minimize the velocity lag error
   (b) maximize the velocity lag error
   (c) minimize the time constant of the system
   (d) maximize the time constant of the system

36. If gain of the system is increased, then
   (a) roots move away from the zeros
   (b) roots move towards the origin of the S-plot
   (c) roots move away from the poles
   (d) none of these

37. If gain of the critically damped system is increased, the system will behave as
   (a) under damped   (b) over damped
   (c) critically damped (d) oscillatory

38. Settling time is inversely proportional to product of the damping ratio and
   (a) time constant
   (b) maximum overshoot
   (c) peak time
   (d) undamped natural frequency of the system

39. If gain of the system is zero, then the roots
   (a) coincide with the poles
   (b) move away from the zeros
   (c) move away from the poles
   (d) none of these

40. 0 type system has
   (a) zero steady state error
   (b) small steady state error
   (c) high gain constant
   (d) high error with high K

41. At resonance peak, ratio of output to input is
   (a) zero   (b) lowest
   (c) highest   (d) none of these

42. Relation between Fourier integral and Laplace transform is through
   (a) time domain
   (b) frequency domain
   (c) both (a) and (b)
   (d) none of these

43. Steady state error is always zero in response to the displacement input for
   (a) type 0 system
   (b) type 1 system
   (c) type 2 system
   (d) type (N > 1) system for N = 0, 1, 2....N

44. If steady state state error for type 1 system for unit ramp input is kept constant, then constant output is

    (*a*) distance   (*b*) velocity

    (*c*) acceleration   (*d*) power

45. For type 2 system, position error arises at steady state when input is

    (*a*) ramp

    (*b*) step displacement

    (*c*) constant acceleration

    (*d*) none of these

46. To decrease the type number of system

    (*a*) first integrator and then diffrentiator is inserted

    (*b*) first diffentiator and then integrator is inserted

    (*c*) only diffrentiator is inserted in the forward path

    (*d*) only integrator is inserted in the forward path

47. If feeback is introduced in the system the transient response

    (*a*) does not very   (*b*) decays very fast

    (*c*) decays slowly   (*d*) dies off

48. The frequency range over which response of the system is within acceptable units is called the system

    (*a*) band width

    (*b*) modulation frequency

    (*c*) demodulation frequency

    (*d*) carrier frequency

49. Lead compensation in the system add

    (*a*) zeros   (*b*) poles

    (*c*) both (*a*) and (*b*)   (*d*) none of these

50. In type 1 system steady state accleration error is

    (*a*) 0   (*b*) 1

    (*c*) infinity   (*d*) none of these

51. Lead lag compensation improve

    (*a*) transient response of the system

    (*b*) steady state response of the system

    (*c*) both (*a*) and (*b*)

    (*d*) none of these

52. If open loop transfer function of a system is

$$G(s)H(s) = \frac{K}{S(1+T_1S)(1+T_2S)}$$

then system will be

    (*a*) unstable   (*b*) conditionally stable

    (*c*) stable   (*d*) marginally stable

53. To decrease time constant of the servomechanism

    (*a*) decrease torque of servomotor

    (*b*) increase damping of the system

    (*c*) increase intertia of the system

    (*d*) decrease inertia of the system

54. Servomechanism is called a proportional error device when output of the system is function of

    (*a*) error

    (*b*) error and its first derivative

    (*c*) first derivative of erro

    (*d*) none of these

55. Which of the following motor is suitable for servomechanism ?

    (*a*) a.c. series motor

    (*b*) 1 ϕ induction motor

    (*c*) 2 ϕ induction motor

    (*d*) 3 ϕ induction motor

56. Servomechanism with step-displacement input is

    (*a*) Type 0 system   (*b*) Type 1 system

    (*c*) Type 2 system   (*d*) Type 3 system

57. Main difference between servomotor and standard motor is that

    (*a*) servomotor has low inertia and higher starting torque

    (*b*) servomotor has low inertia and low starting torque

    (*c*) servomotor has high inertia and high starting torque

    (*d*) none of these

58. Self balancing instrument uses

    (*a*) D.C. servomotor

    (*b*) A.C. servomotor

    (*c*) tachometer

    (*d*) magnetic amplifier

59. If poles of the system are lying on the imaginary axis in s-plane, then system will be

    (*a*) stable

    (*b*) marginally stable

    (*c*) conditionally stable

    (*d*) unstable

60. According to Hurwitz criterion the characteristic equation

$$s^4 + 8 s^3 + 18 s^2 + 16 s + 5 = 0 \text{ is}$$

    (*a*) unstable

    (*b*) marginally stable

    (*c*) conditionally stable

    (*d*) unstable

61. A system is called absolutely stable is any oscillations set up in the system are
    (a) damped out
    (b) self-sustaining and tend to last indefinitely
    (c) negative peaked only
    (d) none of these

62. Best method to determine stability and transient response of the system is
    (a) Bode plot   (b) Signal flow graph
    (c) Nyquist plot   (d) Root locus

63. If poles of system are lying on the imaginary axis in s-plane, the system will be
    (a) unstable
    (b) marginally stable
    (c) conditionally stable
    (d) unstable

64. The number of pure integrations in the system transfer function determine
    (a) degree of stability
    (b) stability of the system
    (c) transient performance of the system
    (d) steady state performance

65. Which system conveniently see the impact of poles and zeros on phase and gain margin ?
    (a) Root locus
    (b) Nyquist plot
    (c) Routh-Hurwitz criterion
    (d) Bode plot

66. Factor which cannot be can cancelled from numerator and denominator of $G(s) E(s)$ in
    (a) Bode plot   (b) Nyquist plot
    (c) higher frequencies (d) none of these

67. If value of gain is increased, then roots of the system will move to
    (a) origin
    (b) lower frequencies
    (c) higher frequencies
    (d) none of these

68. Intersection of root locus branches with the imaginary axis can be determined by the use of
    (a) polar plot   (b) routh's criterion
    (c) nyquist criterion   (d) none of these

69. If gain is zero, then
    (a) roots move away from zeros
    (b) roots coincide with poles
    (c) roots move away from poles
    (d) none of these

70. To increase damping of a pair of complex roots compensator used is
    (a) phase lag
    (b) phase lead
    (c) phase lag lead
    (d) one with 60° lead circuit

71. For type 3 system, lowest frequency asymptote will have the slope of
    (a) 15 db/octave   (b) – 16 db/octave
    (c) 17 db/octave   (d) – 18 db/octave

72. If a pole is added to a system it causes
    (a) lag compensation
    (b) lead compensation
    (c) lead-lag compensation
    (d) none of these

73. For steady state transient inprovement, compensator used is
    (a) lead copensator
    (b) lag compensator
    (c) lead lag compensator
    (d) none of these

74. Which gives the information between number of poles and zeros of the closed loop transfer function ?
    (a) Routh Hurwitz criterion
    (b) Bode diagram
    (c) Root locus method
    (d) Nyquist plot

75. To study time delay of the system which of the following is used ?
    (a) Nyquist plot
    (b) Bode plot
    (c) Routh Hurwitz method
    (d) Nicholas chart

76. Closed loop ples are
    (a) zeros of $1 + G(S). H(s)$
    (b) zeros of $G(s) H(s)$
    (c) poles of $G(s) H(s)$
    (d) poles of $1 + G(s) H(s)$

77. Maximum over shoot is the function of
    (a) damping ratio
    (b) natural frequency of ocillation
    (c) both (a) and (b)
    (d) damped frequency of ocillation

78. Feed back control systems are basically
 (a) low pass filter
 (b) high pass filter
 (c) band pass filter
 (d) band stop filter

79. A linear system obeys the principle of
 (a) homogenity
 (b) reciprocity
 (c) superposition and homogenity
 (d) none of these

80. If poles are more than zeros in G(S) F(S), then number of root locus segment is equal to
 (a) number of poles
 (b) number of zeros
 (c) sum of poles and zeros
 (d) difference of poles and zeros

81. For G(S) F(S) = $\dfrac{k(S+z)}{S+p}$, $(z < p)$ the plot is
 (a) one pole on the imaginary axis
 (b) one zero on the right hand side of the plane
 (c) one pole and one zero on the left hand side of plane
 (d) 2 poles and 2 zeros on the left hand side of plane

82. Number of root-locus segments which do not terminate on the zeros is equal to
 (a) number of poles
 (b) number of zeros
 (c) sum of poles and zeros
 (d) difference of poles and zeros

83. In a root locus plot, the increase in k will
 (a) increase damping ratio
 (b) decrease damping ratio
 (c) not change damping ratio
 (d) none of these

84. In a root locus plot, increase in k will
 (a) increase overshoot of the response
 (b) derease overshoot of the response
 (c) not change overshoot of the response
 (d) none of these

85. In a root locus plot, increase in k will
 (a) result in decrease in the damped and undamped natural frequencies
 (b) result in increase in the damped and undamped natural frequencies
 (c) not change the damped and undamped natural frequencies
 (d) none of these

86. In root plot if k is greater than critical value, then increasing k will
 (a) increase valuve of the real part of closed loop
 (b) decrease value of the real part of closed loop
 (c) not change value of the real part of closed loop
 (d) none of these

87. Plot of the constant gain loci of the system is
 (a) asymptote
 (b) circle with centre at the origin
 (c) parabola
 (d) ellipse

88. In root locus technique, angle between adjacent asymptote is
 (a) $180°/(m+n)$
 (b) $360°/(m+n)$
 (c) $360°/(m-n)$
 (d) $180°/(m-n)$

89. Frequency response mean
 (a) transient response of a system to a sinusoidal input
 (b) steady state response of a system to a sinusoidal input
 (c) oscillatory response of a system to a sinusoidal input
 (d) none of these

90. Bode plot approach is applied to
 (a) minimum phase network
 (b) non minimum phase network
 (c) any network
 (d) none of these

91. The type of transfer function used in Bode plot is
 (a) G(s)
 (b) G(j)
 (c) G(jw)
 (d) G(js)

92. Bode analysis method can be applied
 (a) if transfer function has no poles and zeros on R.H. of s-plane
 (b) if transfer function has no poles on R.H. of s-plane
 (c) if tranfer function has no zero on R.H. of s-plane
 (d) to all transfer functions

93. A complex-conjugate pair of poles near the jw axis will produce a
   (a) high oscillatory mode of transient response
   (b) steady state mode of response
   (c) sinusoidal mode of response
   (d) none of these

94. Frequency range over which response of the system is within acceptable limits is called system
   (a) modulation frequency
   (b) demodulation frequency
   (c) carrier frequency
   (d) band width

95. Polar plots for +ve and –ve frequencies
   (a) are always symmetrical
   (b) can never be symmetrical
   (c) may be symmetrical
   (d) none of these

96. Slope in Bode plot is expressed as
   (a) $-6\,db$/decade   (b) $-6\,db$/octave
   (c) $-8\,db$/octave   (d) $-7\,db$/octave

97. Transfer founction, when the Bode diagram is plotted should be of the form
   (a) $(1 + T)$ (b) $(1 + S)$
   (c) (Ts) (d) $(1 + Ts)$

98. In Nyquist criterion roots of the characteristic equation are given by
   (a) zeros of open loop transfer function
   (b) zeros of closed loop transfer function
   (c) poles of closed loop transfer function
   (d) poles of open loop tsansfer function

99. Nyquist stability criterion requires polar plot of
   (a) characteristic equation
   (b) closed loop transfer function
   (c) open loop transfer function
   (d) none of these

100. Gain margin expressed in decibels is
   (a) positive if Kg greater than 1 and negative for Kg less than 1
   (b) negative if Kg is greater than 1 and positive for Kg less than 1
   (c) always zero
   (d) infinity for Kg equal to 1

101. By adding a pole at $s = 0$, Nyquist plot of the system will
   (a) shift 90° clockwise
   (b) shift 90° anticlockwise
   (c) shift 180°
   (d) not change at all

102. Gain margin of a first or second order system is
   (a) zero
   (b) 1
   (c) 100
   (d) infinite

103. For relative stability of the system which of the following is sufficient ?
   (a) Gain margin
   (b) Phase margin
   (c) Both (a) and (b)
   (d) None of these

104. For all frequencies, a unit circle in the Nyquist plot trans forms into
   (a) db line of amplitude plot in Bode diagram
   (b) 1 db line of amplitude plot in Bode diagram
   (c) either (a) and (b)
   (d) none of these

105. Cut off frequency is the frequency at which magnitude of closed loop frequency response is
   (a) 1 db below its zero frequency
   (b) 2 db below its zero frequency
   (c) 3 db below its zero frequency
   (d) 4 db below its zero frequency

106. Bandwidth gives an indication of
   (a) characteristic equation of the system
   (b) speed of response of a control system
   (c) transfer function of the control system
   (d) transients in the system

107. Cut off rate is the slope of log-magnitude curve
   (a) at the start of curve
   (b) at the end of of curve
   (c) near the cut off frequency
   (d) none of these

EXERCISE – II

1. The system function, $H(s) = \dfrac{1}{s+1}$.

   For an signal $\cos t$, the steady state response is

   (a) $\dfrac{1}{\sqrt{2}}\cos\left(t-\dfrac{\pi}{4}\right)$

   (b) $\cos t$

   (c) $\cos\left(t-\dfrac{\pi}{4}\right)$

   (d) $\dfrac{1}{2}\cos t$ **(RRB 2012)**

2. In the system shown in the given figure, $r(t) = 1 + 2t$ $(t \geq 0)$. The steady-state value of the error $e(t)$ is equal to

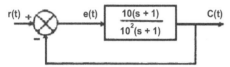

   (a) Zero

   (b) 2/10

   (c) 10/2

   (d) Infinity **(RRB 2012)**

3. If the Nyquist plot cuts the negative real axis at a distance of 0.4, then the gain margin of the system is

   (a) 0.4

   (b) – 0.4

   (c) 4%

   (d) 2.5   **(RRB 2012)**

4. In order to use Routh Hurwitz Criterion for determining the stability of sampled data system, the characteristic equation $1 + G(z) H(z) = 0$ should be modified by using bilinear transform of

   (RRB 2012)

   (a) $z = r + 1$

   (b) $z = r - 1$

   (c) $z = \dfrac{r-1}{r+1}$

   (d) $z = \dfrac{r+1}{r-1}$

5. Indicate which one of the following transfer functions represents phase lead compensator?

   (RRB 2012)

   (a) $\dfrac{s+1}{s+2}$

   (b) $\dfrac{6s+3}{6s+2}$

   (c) $\dfrac{s+5}{3s+2}$

   (d) $\dfrac{s+8}{s+5s+6}$

6. For an AM signal, the bandwidth is 10 kHz and the highest frequency component present is 705 kHz. What is the carrier frequency used for this AM signal?   **(RRB 2012)**

   (a) 695 kHz

   (b) 700 kHz

   (c) 705 kHz

   (d) 710 kHz

7. An angle modulated signal is described by the equation   **(RRB 2012)**

   $x_c(t) = 10 \cos [2\pi f_c t + 10 \sin (4000\pi t)$
   $+ 5 \sin 2000\ \pi t]$

   What is the bandwidth of this modulated signal ?

   (a) 6 kHz

   (b) 15.6 kHz

   (c) 54 kHz

   (d) 63 kHz

8. For a driving point impedance function

   $$Z(s) = \dfrac{s+\alpha}{s+\beta}$$

   the voltage will lead the current for sinusoidal input, is   **(RRB 2012)**

   (a) α and β are real positive and $\alpha > \beta$

   (b) α is real positive and β is real negative and $\alpha > \beta$

   (c) α and β are real positive and $\beta > \alpha$

   (d) α and β are real negative and $\beta > \alpha$

9. Backlash in a stable control system may cause

   (a) underdamping

   (b) overdamping

   (c) high level oscillations

   (d) low level oscillations   **(RRB 2012)**

10. Given the transfer function   **(RRB 2012)**

    $G(s) = \dfrac{121}{s+13.2s+121}$ of a system. Which of the following characteristics does it have?

    (a) Overdamped and settling time 1.1s

    (b) Underdamped and settling time 0.6s

    (c) Critically damped and settling time 0.8s

    (d) Underdamped and settling time 0.707s

11. Which one of the following effects in the system is NOT caused by negative feedback?

    (a) Reduction in gain

    (b) Increase in bandwidth

    (c) Increase in distortion

    (d) Reduction in output impedance   **(RRB 2012)**

12. A unity feedback control system has a forward loop transfer function as $\dfrac{e^{-Ts}}{\left[s(s+1)\right]}$. Its phase value will be zero at frequency ω_1. Which one of the following equations should be satisfied by ω_1?

    (a) $\omega_1 = \cot (T\omega_1)$

    (b) $\omega_1 = \tan (T\omega_1)$

    (c) $T\omega_1 = \cot (\omega_1)$

    (d) $T\omega_1 = \tan (\omega_1)$

    (RRB 2012)

13. A minimum phase unity feedback system has a Bode plot with a constant slope of -20 db/decade for all frequencies. What is the value of the maximum phase margin for the system?

(a) 0°
(b) 90°
(c) $-90°$
(d) 180° **(RRB 2012)**

14. The number of pure integrations in the system transfer function determine **(RRB)**

(a) degree of stability
(b) stability of the system
(c) transient performance of the system
(d) steady state performance

15. Bandwidth gives an indication of **(RRB)**

(a) characteristic equation of the system
(b) speed of response of a control system
(c) transfer function of the control system
(d) transients in the system

16. The state transition matrix for the system
$$\begin{bmatrix} \dot{x}_1 \\ \dot{x}_2 \end{bmatrix} = \begin{bmatrix} 1 & 0 \\ 1 & 1 \end{bmatrix} \begin{bmatrix} x_1 \\ x_2 \end{bmatrix} + \begin{bmatrix} 1 \\ 1 \end{bmatrix} u \text{ is}$$

(a) $\begin{bmatrix} e^t & 0 \\ e^t & e^t \end{bmatrix}$

(b) $\begin{bmatrix} e^t & 0 \\ t^2 e^t & e^t \end{bmatrix}$

(c) $\begin{bmatrix} e^t & 0 \\ te^t & e^t \end{bmatrix}$

(d) $\begin{bmatrix} e^t & te^t \\ 0 & e^t \end{bmatrix}$ **(RRB)**

17. A discrete system is represented by the difference equation
$$\begin{bmatrix} X_1(k+1) \\ X_2(k+1) \end{bmatrix} = \begin{bmatrix} a & a-1 \\ a+1 & a \end{bmatrix} \begin{bmatrix} X_1(k) \\ X_2(k) \end{bmatrix}$$

It has initial conditions $X_1(0) = 1$; $X_2(0) = 0$. The pole locations of the system for $a = 1$, are

(a) $1 \pm j0$
(b) $-1 \pm j0$
(c) $\pm 1 + j0$
(d) $0 \pm j1$ **(RRB)**

18. For the transfer function
$$G(s) = \frac{5(s+4)}{s(s+0.25)(s^2+4s+25)}$$

The values of the constant gain term and the highest corner frequency of the Bode plot respectively are **(RRB)**

(a) 3.2, 5.0
(b) 16.0, 4.0
(c) 3.2, 4.0
(d) 16.0, 5.0

19. The driving-point impedance of a one-port reactive network is given by

(a) $\dfrac{(s^2+1)(s^2+2)}{s(s^2+3)(s^2+4)}$
(b) $\dfrac{(s^2+1)(s^2+3)}{s(s^2+2)(s^2+4)}$

(c) $\dfrac{s(s^2+1)}{(s^2+2)(s^2+3)}$
(d) $\dfrac{1}{s+1}$ **(DMRC 2014)**

20. On eliminating the feedback loop in the system shown in the figure, **(DMRC 2014)**

it would lead to a simplification with a single edge of gain

(a) $\dfrac{T_{12}}{1+T_{22}}$
(b) $\dfrac{T_{22}}{1-T_{12}}$

(c) T_{12}
(d) $\dfrac{T_{12}}{1-T_{22}}$

21. For $V(s) = \dfrac{s+2}{s(s+1)}$ the initial and final values of $v(t)$ will be respectively **(DMRC 2014)**

(a) 1 and 1
(b) 2 and 2
(c) 2 and 1
(d) 1 and 2

22. The network function $F(s) = \dfrac{(s+2)}{(s+1)(s+3)}$ represents an

(a) RC impedance **(DMRC 2014)**
(b) RL impedance
(c) RC impedance and an RL admittance
(d) RC admittance and an RL impedance

23. The voltage-ratio transfer function of an active filter is given by
$$\frac{V_2(s)}{V_1(s)} = \frac{(s^2+\delta)}{(s^2+\alpha s+\delta)}$$

The circuit in questions a **(DMRC 2014)**

(a) low- pass filter
(b) high-pass filter
(c) band-pass filter
(d) band-reject filter

24. In distortion factor meter, the filter is used to suppress **(DMRC)**

(a) dc component
(b) odd harmonics
(c) even harmonics
(d) fundamentals

25. When the signal flow graph is as shown in the figure, the overall transfer function of the system will be **(DMRC)**

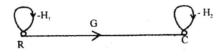

(a) $\dfrac{C}{R} = G$

(b) $\dfrac{C}{R} = \dfrac{G}{1 + H_2}$

(c) $\dfrac{C}{R} = \dfrac{G}{(1 + H_2)(1 + H_2)}$

(d) $\dfrac{C}{R} = \dfrac{G}{1 + H_2 + H_2}$

26. The block diagram shown in Fig. I is equivalent to **(DMRC)**

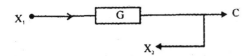

*Fig. I*Paper II

(a)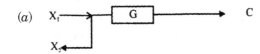

(b)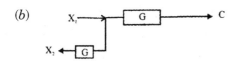

(c)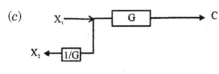

(d)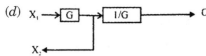

27. A liner second-order system with the transfer function **(DMRC)**

$$G(s) = \dfrac{49}{s^2 + 16s + 49}$$

is initially at rest and is subjected to a step input signal. The response of the system will exhibit a peak overshoot of

(a) 16 %   (b) 9 %

(c) 2 %   (d) zero

28. A system has the following transfer function :

$$G(s) = \dfrac{100(s+5)(s+50)}{s^4(s+10)(s^2+3s+10)}$$

The type and order of the system are respectively

(a) 4 and 9   (b) 4 and 7

(c) 5 and 7   (d) 7 and 5   **(DMRC)**

29. The open-loop transfer function of a unity feedback control system is:

$$G(s) = \dfrac{K(s+10)(s+20)}{s^2(s+2)}$$

The closed-loop system will be stable if the value of K is

(a) 2   (b) 3

(c) 4   (d) 5   **(DMRC)**

30. The loop transfer function GH of a control system is given by **(DMRC)**

$$GH = \dfrac{K}{s(s+1)(s+2)(s+3)}$$

Which of the following statements regarding the conditions of the system root loci diagram is/are correct?

1. There will be four asymptotes.
2. There will be three separate root loci.
3. Asymptotes will intersect at real axis at $s_A = -2/3$

Select the correct answer using the codes given below:

(a) 1 alone   (b) 2 alone

(c) 3 alone   (d) 1, 2 and 3

31. The value of A matrix in X = AX for the system described by the differential equation $y + 2y + 3y = 0$ is **(DMRC)**

(a) $\begin{bmatrix} 1 & 0 \\ -2 & -1 \end{bmatrix}$ (b) $\begin{bmatrix} 1 & 0 \\ -1 & -2 \end{bmatrix}$

(c) $\begin{bmatrix} 0 & 1 \\ -2 & -1 \end{bmatrix}$ (d) $\begin{bmatrix} 0 & 1 \\ -2 & -1 \end{bmatrix}$

32. Consider the following statements regarding a linear system $y = f(x_2)$: **(DMRC)**

1. $f(x_1 + x) = f(x_1) + f(x_2)$
2. $f[x(t + T)] = f[x(t)] + f[x(T)]$
3. $f(Kx) = KF(x)$

Of these statements

(a) 1, 2 and 3 are correct

(b) 1 and 2 are correct

(c) 2 alone is correct

(d) 1 and 3 are correct

33. The phase portrait of a non-linear system is shown in the figure. Here the origin is a **(DMRC)**

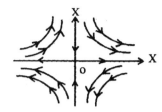

(a) stable focus   (b) vortex

(c) stable node   (d) saddle point

34. For the system $x + ax\dot{x} \pm b\dot{x} = 0$, the equation for the phase-plane isocline of slope m is

(a) $m^2 + am + b = 0$ **(DMRC)**

(b) $m = -ax - \dfrac{bx}{\dot{x}}$

(c) $m = ax + \dfrac{bx}{\dot{x}}$

(d) $m^2 + axm + b = 0$

35. A system with transfer function

$G(s) = \dfrac{1}{(1+s)}$ is subjected to a sinusoidal input

$r(t) = \sin \omega t$. In steady–state, the phase angle of the output relative to the input at $\omega = 0$ and $\omega = \infty$ will be respectively **(DMRC)**

(a) $0°$ and $-90°$

(b) $0°$ and $0°$

(c) $90°$ and $0°$

(d) $90°$ and $-90°$

36. A system has fourteen poles and two zeros. The slope of its highest frequency asymptote in its magnitude plot is **(DMRC)**

(a) −40 dB/decade

(b) −240 dB/decade

(c) −280 dB/decade

(d) −320 dB/decade

37. The open-loop transfer unction of a feedback control system is $\dfrac{K}{s(s^2 + 2s + 6)}$. The break-away point(s) of its root locus plot **(DMRC)**

(a) exist at $(-1 \pm j1)$

(b) exist at $(-\dfrac{3}{2} \pm \dfrac{15}{16})$

(c) exists at origin

(d) do not exist

38. $[-a \pm jb]$ are the complex conjugate roots of the characteristic equation of a second order system. Its damping coefficient and natural frequency will be respectively **(DMRC)**

(a) $\dfrac{b}{\sqrt{a^2 + b^2}}$ and $\sqrt{a^2 + b^2}$

(b) $\dfrac{b}{\sqrt{a^2 + b^2}}$ and $a^2 = b^2$

(c) $\dfrac{a}{\sqrt{a^2 + b^2}}$ and $\sqrt{a^2 + b^2}$

(d) $\dfrac{a}{\sqrt{a^2 + b^2}}$ and $a^2 + b^2$

39. A unity feedback control system has a forward, path transfer function **(DMRC)**

$G(s) = \dfrac{10(1 + 4s)}{s^2(1 + s)}$.

If the system is subjected to an input $r(t) = 1 + t + \dfrac{t^2}{2}$ ($t \geq 0$), the steady-state error of the system will be

(a) zero   (b) 0.1

(c) 10   (d) infinity

40. For the function $X(s) = \dfrac{1}{s(s+1)^2(s+2)}$ the residues associated with the simple poles at $s = 0$ and $s = -2$ are respectively **(DMRC)**

(a) $\dfrac{1}{2}$ and $\dfrac{1}{2}$ (b) 1 and 1

(c) −1 and −1   (d) $-\dfrac{1}{2}$ and $\dfrac{1}{2}$

41. The frequency spectrum of a signal lies within the band $f_0 \leq f \leq f_1$ Hz. To sample the signal properly, the sampling period should be

(a) $> \dfrac{1}{2f_0}$ (b) $< \dfrac{2}{f_0}$ **(DMRC)**

(c) $< \dfrac{1}{2f_1}$ (d) $> \dfrac{2}{f_1}$

42. The Laplace transform of the function $f(t)$ is $F(s)$. $u(t)$ represents the unit step function. The inverse Laplace transform of $e^{-s} F(s)$ is **(DMRC)**

(a) $f(t) u(t^{-1})$

(b) $f(t^{-1}) u(t)$

(c) $f(t_{-1}) u(t^{-1})$

(d) $f(t)/(t^{-1})$

43. If the unilateral Laplace transform X(s) of a signal $x(t)$ is $\dfrac{7s+10}{s(s+2)}$, then the initial and final values of the signal would be respectively

(a) 3.5 and 5 **(DMRC)**

(b) zero and 7

(c) 5 and zero

(d) 7 and 5

44. In an amplifier, the increase in gain is 12 dB if the frequency doubled. If the frequency is increased by 10 times, then the increase in gain will be

(a) 2.4 dB (b) 20 dB

(c) 40 dB (d) 60 dB **(DMRC)**

45. For a second order system, if both the roots of the characteristic equation are real, then value of damping ratio will be **(DMRC)**

(a) less than unity

(b) equal to unity

(c) equal to zero

(d) greater than unity

46. To achieve, the optimum transient response, the indicating instruments are so designed as to

(a) be critically damped

(b) be undamped

(c) provide damping which is slightly more than the critical value

(d) provide damping which is slightly less than the critical value **(DMRC)**

47. If the largest frequency present in the measured signal and number of bits used in the binary code, are respectively 'f_m' and 'n', then the minimum bandwidth of a pulse code modulation channel used for telemetry would be **(DMRC)**

(a) $\dfrac{f_m}{2n}$ (b) $\dfrac{f_m}{n}$

(c) nf_m (d) $2nf_m$

48. Two sinusoidal equations are given as

$$e_1 = A\sin\left(\omega t + \frac{\pi}{4}\right) \text{ and } e_2 = B\sin\left(\omega t - \frac{\pi}{6}\right)$$

The phase difference between the two quantities is **(SSC, CPWD 2010)**

(a) 75º (b) 60º

(c) 105º (d) 15º

ANSWERS

EXERCISE – I

1. (c)	**2.** (d)	**3.** (b)	**4.** (b)	**5.** (a)	**6.** (c)	**7.** (c)	**8.** (d)	**9.** (a)	**10.** (c)
11. (a)	**12.** (c)	**13.** (d)	**14.** (a)	**15.** (a)	**16.** (c)	**17.** (d)	**18.** (a)	**19.** (a)	**20.** (c)
21. (a)	**22.** (c)	**23.** (b)	**24.** (d)	**25.** (a)	**26.** (a)	**27.** (d)	**28.** (b)	**29.** (b)	**30.** (a)
31. (c)	**32.** (a)	**33.** (b)	**34.** (a)	**35.** (a)	**36.** (c)	**37.** (a)	**38.** (b)	**39.** (a)	**40.** (b)
41. (c)	**42.** (c)	**43.** (d)	**44.** (b)	**45.** (c)	**46.** (c)	**47.** (b)	**48.** (a)	**49.** (b)	**50.** (c)
51. (c)	**52.** (c)	**53.** (d)	**54.** (a)	**55.** (c)	**56.** (b)	**57.** (b)	**58.** (b)	**59.** (b)	**60.** (a)
61. (a)	**62.** (c)	**63.** (b)	**64.** (d)	**65.** (d)	**66.** (c)	**67.** (c)	**68.** (b)	**69.** (b)	**70.** (b)
71. (d)	**72.** (b)	**73.** (c)	**74.** (d)	**75.** (a)	**76.** (a)	**77.** (b)	**78.** (a)	**79.** (c)	**80.** (a)
81. (c)	**82.** (d)	**83.** (b)	**84.** (a)	**85.** (b)	**86.** (c)	**87.** (b)	**88.** (c)	**89.** (b)	**90.** (a)
91. (a)	**92.** (a)	**93.** (a)	**94.** (d)	**95.** (a)	**96.** (b)	**97.** (d)	**98.** (c)	**99.** (c)	**100.** (a)
101. (a)	**102.** (d)	**103.** (c)	**104.** (c)	**105.** (c)	**106.** (b)	**107.** (c)			

EXERCISE – II

1. (a)	**2.** (b)	**3.** (b)	**4.** (d)	**5.** (b)	**6.** (b)	**7.** (b)	**8.** (c)	**9.** (d)	**10.** (b)
11. (c)	**12.** (a)	**13.** (b)	**14.** (d)	**15.** (b)	**16.** (d)	**17.** (a)	**18.** (a)	**19.** (b)	**20.** (d)
21. (d)	**22.** (c)	**23.** (d)	**24.** (d)	**25.** (c)	**26.** (b)	**27.** (d)	**28.** (b)	**29.** (d)	**30.** (a)
31. (d)	**32.** (d)	**33.** (d)	**34.** (b)	**35.** (c)	**36.** (c)	**37.** (a)	**38.** (c)	**39.** (d)	**40.** (a)
41. (c)	**42.** (c)	**43.** (d)	**44.** (c)	**45.** (d)	**46.** (d)	**47.** (c)	**48.** (a)		

CPSIA information can be obtained
at www.ICGtesting.com
Printed in the USA
BVHW021212130723
667186BV00014B/975